Trade Unions in the Green Economy

Combating climate change will increasingly impact on production industries. Whether creating 'greener' technologies or transforming economies to become sustainable, production will change. Even policies that focus on reducing or changing consumption aim to influence production. Research to date has largely ignored the effect of climate change policies on workers and trade union policies. This book brings scholars and practitioners across the globe together: sociologists, psychologists, political scientists, historians, economists, unionists and environmentalists based in Australia, Brazil, South Africa, Taiwan, Spain, Sweden, the UK and the US. Together they will open up a new area of research: environmental labour studies.

What effect will moving to green production have on workers? How can unions influence processes of re-skilling, avoiding redundancies? Can North–South union solidarity create a 'level playing field' globally? How can unions reconcile the protection of jobs and the protection of the environment? These questions are addressed by analysing how unions and environmental movements are learning from each other through a range of different initiatives. The book explores the red–green alliances in the US, Australia, South Korea and Taiwan; the theoretical and practical implications of the unions' "just transition" policy and the problems and perspectives of "green jobs" policies in the US. More generally it looks at how food workers' rights can be used as a path to low carbon agriculture, the role workers' identities and social security play in union climate change policies and the strategies employed by unions towards environmental degradation. In introducing the topic of environmental labour studies, this book opens the climate change debate up to trade unionists, business managers and policy makers, whilst also being of interest to academics in the fields of environmental management, environmental politics and climate change policy.

Nora Räthzel is Professor of Sociology at the University of Umeå, Sweden.

David Uzzell is Professor of Environmental Psychology at the University of Surrey, UK.

'This book itself is evidence that the outmoded dialectics of a divide between labour and nature have had their day. Drawing together an impressive collection of essays from academics, trade-unionists and environmentalists, Uzzell and Räthzel set out to build a vision of transformation that integrates the urgency of ecological limits with the paramount importance of social justice.'

Tim Jackson, University of Surrey, UK and author of Prosperity Without Growth

'In this ground breaking book, Räthzel, Uzell and colleagues confront the unthinkable: our current global economy is unable to deliver a sustainable environment or employment. At a time of unprecedented global youth unemployment these authors also offer a fierce challenge to the complacent hope that green growth is an answer. Instead, using case-studies and nuanced argument, these writers explain how a more systemic transformation might be achieved. This fascinating book not only unites environment and labour studies, it renews Rosa Luxemburg's vision of 'revolutionary reformism' for a new generation.'

Bronwyn Hayward, University of Canterbury, New Zealand

'Räthzel and Uzzell present a very welcome and long overdue examination of the relations between the labour and environmental movements, one that goes far beyond the tensions they sometimes experience, toward explicating their complex and often sympathetic aspirations and relations. This is the exciting harbinger of a new field of enquiry.'

Robert Gifford, University of Victoria, Canada

'An international compilation the time for which is clearly ripe! Recognising the often hostile historical relationship between labour organisations and environmental movements, the book reveals a significant but complex greening of union organisations, as well as significant tensions amongst such requiring theoretical and political solution.'

Peter Waterman, InterfaceJournal, Netherlands

'A passionate, timely and path-breaking book! Trade Unions in the Green Economy maps the historic divide between labour and environment and examines international, national and local labour strategies that make environmental responsibility a union issue. Integrating elegant scholarship and activism, Nora Räthzel and David Uzzell bring labour back in to the struggle to slow global warming, arguing that it can transform unions, while it opens a new space for action and engaged scholarship.'

Carla Lipsig-Mummé, York University, Canada

'For too long the labour movement has been considered as being on the sidelines of the environmental discourse. This book turns this view on its head. This primer shows how the labour movements from the north to the south are reclaiming environmental degradation as a union issue.'

*Dinga Sikwebu and Woody Aroun, National Union of
Metalworkers of South Africa (NUMSA), South Africa*

'Articles in this volume bridge the conceptual divide between green economy and employment. It is good as text as well as reference material. Useful for positioning actions and directions for labour unions in new development paradigm, especially in developing countries- the emerging economic growth centres of the world.'

Joyashree Roy, Professor of Economics, Jadavpur University, India

Trade Unions in the Green Economy

Working for the environment

**Edited by Nora Räthzel
and David Uzzell**

Routledge
Taylor & Francis Group

LONDON AND NEW YORK

earthscan
from Routledge

First published 2013
by Routledge
2 Park Square, Milton Park, Abingdon, Oxon OX14 4RN

Simultaneously published in the USA and Canada
by Routledge
711 Third Avenue, New York, NY 10017

Routledge is an imprint of the Taylor & Francis Group, an informa business

British Library Cataloguing in Publication Data
A catalogue record for this book is available from the British Library

Library of Congress Cataloging in Publication Data
Trade unions in the green economy : working for the environment / edited by Nora Räthzel and David Uzzell.
p. cm.
Includes bibliographical references and index.
1. Sustainable development. 2. Labor unions--Political activity.
3. Environmental policy. I. Räthzel, Nora. II. Uzzell, David L.
HC79.E5T7318 2013
331.88--dc23
2012017350

ISBN13: 978-1-849-71464-8 (hbk)
ISBN13: 978-0-415-52984-6 (pbk)
ISBN13: 978-0-203-10967-0 (ebk)

Typeset in Times New Roman
by Taylor & Francis Books

In memory of Gabriel Moser (1944–2011) and
Fritz Wittek (1947–2011)

Contents

Contributors

John Barry is Reader in the School of Politics, International Studies and Philosophy and Associate Director of the Institute for a Sustainable World at Queen's University, Belfast. He has written extensively about normative aspects of the politics and ethics of sustainability, citizenship and sustainability, and the political economy of sustainability and the politics of renewable energy. He is a Green Party councillor and former leader of the Green Party in Northern Ireland. His publications include *Rethinking Green Politics: Nature, Virtue, Progress* (Sage, 1999 – Winner of the PSA's WJM Mackenzie Prize for best book published in political science) and *Environment and Social Theory* (Routledge, 2007). He co-edited *The State and the Global Ecological Crisis* (2005) and is co-editor of the journal *Environmental Politics*. He has just published *The Politics of Actually Existing Unsustainability: Human Flourishing in a Climate Changed, Carbon Constrained World* (2012).

Andrew Bennie completed his Master's degree in Sociology at the University of the Witwatersrand, and the research from this has contributed substantially to his chapter. He now works in developing cooperatives and solidarity economy alternatives at the Cooperative and Policy Alternative Centre (COPAC), and is soon to begin work on his PhD.

Verity Burgmann is Professor of Political Science at the University of Melbourne. She is the author of numerous publications on labour movement history and politics, protest movements, radical ideologies and environmental politics. Her books include: *'In Our Time': Socialism and the Rise of Labor* (1985); *Power and Protest* (1993); *Revolutionary Industrial Unionism* (1995); *Green Bans, Red Union* (1998); *Unions and the Environment* (2002); *Power, Profit and Protest* (2003); and *Climate Politics and the Climate Movement in Australia* (2012). Her current research interests are international labour movements' opposition to globalisation, and utopianism and autonomist Marxism.

João Paulo Cândia Veiga is Professor of Political Science and International Relations at São Paulo University in Brazil. His research interests include non-state actors and the ways in which they make rules and set standards in transnational governance, particularly in the labour and environmental arenas. He´s the author of *A Questão do Trabalho Infantil* (1997) and co-author of *The Orange and Yellow-Green Cooperation: The FNV and CUT Partnership* (2011).

Jacklyn Cock is Professor Emeritus in the Department of Sociology at the University of the Witwatersrand in Johannesburg and Honorary Research Associate of the Society, Work and Development Institute. She is involved in research and activism on labour, environmental and gender issues, and her publications include *Maids and Madams: A Study in the Politics of Exploitation* (1989); *Going Green: People, Politics and the Environment* (1991) and most recently, *The War Against Ourselves: Nature, Power and Justice* (2007).

Peter Fairbrother is the Director of the Centre for Sustainable Organisations and Work, RMIT University. His research focuses on debates about union renewal, public sector restructuring and socio-economic regeneration and transition. These interests have been drawn together to address issues surrounding the transition to a low carbon economy and the implications for workers. He is joint Series Editor of *Employment and Work Relations in Context* (Routledge), and co-editor of *Globalisation, State and Labour* (2006).

Begoña María-Tomé Gil studied Environmental Sciences, specialising in energy, at the Autonomous University of Madrid and she did a Master's degree in waste management. In 2008 she joined the Union Institute of Work, Environment and Health (ISTAS), a Foundation of the Spanish Trade Union *Comisiones Obreras* (CCOO) where she is a researcher on Energy, Climate Change and Green Economy. She participates in the sustainable development working groups in the European Trade Union Confederation and the International Trade Union Confederation. She is founder partner of Renewable Energy Foundation in Spain (*Fundación Renovables*), a non-profit organisation that promotes energy efficiency, savings and renewable energies.

Meg Gingrich studied in the *Ecosystems, Governance, and Globalization* programme at Stockholm University from 2007 to 2009, where she wrote her Master's thesis on trade union action on climate change. Upon completion of the thesis, she worked as a research assistant for the *Work in a Warming World* project, based at York University in Toronto, Canada. Currently, Meg works as a researcher for the Service Employees International Union in Toronto.

Lars Henriksson is an autoworker who has been working on the assembly line at Volvo Cars in Gothenburg Sweden since the late 1970s. He has been a trade union and political activist since then, 'with or without official union positions'. He is also a freelance writer who published the book *Slutkört* in

2011 (Ordfront Publishing House), which argues the case for the conversion and transformation of the auto industry as a union strategy for saving jobs and the climate.

Dorit Kemter is the Knowledge Management Expert of the Green Jobs Programme of the International Labour Organization (ILO). Prior to joining the ILO in 2009, Dorit Kemter worked in the area of rural local development and community participation in Latin America. She holds a Master's degree in social sciences from the University of Applied Sciences, FH Campus Wien, Austria.

Rob Lambert is Winthrop Professor of Employment Relations at the University of Western Australia Business School. He has published widely on the implications of global restructuring and is a co-author of the book, *Grounding Globalization: Labour in The Age of Insecurity* (2008), which was the winner of the 2009 Distinguished Scholarly Monograph Prize, awarded by the American Sociological Association Labor and Labor Movements section. He is also a founder and the Coordinator of SIGTUR (the Southern Initiative on Globalization and Trade Union Rights), which is a movement of democratic unions in the Global South formed in 1991 and now representing these unions in 35 countries.

Hwa-Jen Liu is Assistant Professor of Sociology at the National Taiwan University. Her areas of interest include collective action, late industrialisation, and labour and environmental movements worldwide. Her most recent research centres on the historical connections between labour, peasant and environmental movements in Taiwan and South Korea.

Scott B. Martin works as a freelance international consultant for organisations such as the Economist Intelligence Unit. Scott Martin has taught international affairs at Columbia since 1997, and has been regular, part-time faculty at the New School's Graduate Program in International Affairs since September 2005. He co-edited *Business and Industry* (2003). Current research focuses on transnational labour rights advocacy, national labour reform and unionism in Brazil and Mexico.

Laura Martín Murillo is the Executive Director of SustainLabour, the International Labour Foundation for Sustainable Development. Assisting in its creation, Laura Martín has been working in the Foundation since its inception carrying out pioneer work that involves trade unions in environmental processes. A trade union representative at the UNEP Governing Council since 2005, she has also been representing unions on an ongoing basis at the United Nations Commission for Sustainable Development (CSD) as well as at the United Nations Framework Convention on Climate Change (UNFCCC). In addition to labour and environmental issues Laura has also undertaken research and social action on gender issues.

Lene Olsen works in the International Labour Organization's (ILO) Bureau for Workers' Activities (ACTRAV) in Geneva. She is in charge of environmentally sustainable development issues and holds a Certificate of Advanced Studies in Environmental Diplomacy from the University of Geneva. She is also involved in the Global Union Research Network (GURN). From 1999 to 2001 Lene worked on the ILO/ACTRAV environment project *Trade Unions and Environmentally Sustainable Development*. Recent publications include articles on how International Labour Standards can be used to address challenges of climate change in a framework of just transition. Before joining the ILO in 1999 she worked for the Norwegian Confederation of Trade Unions' office in Brussels.

Nora Räthzel is Professor of Sociology at the University of Umeå. She has conducted research on the ways in which gender, class and ethnic relations intersect in the everyday to produce forms of resistance and subordination (*Finding the Way Home*, 2007). During the last ten years her research has predominantly been in the area of labour studies, investigating the lives of people working for the same transnational corporation in Sweden, Mexico and South Africa and, since 2006, developing a research programme with David Uzzell on trade unions and their environmental policies, nationally and internationally.

Anabella Rosemberg is Policy Officer for Environment and Occupational Health and Safety in the International Trade Union Confederation (ITUC). She has coordinated the international trade union movement's input to major environmental intergovernmental processes, notably the UNFCCC, since 2007, and coordinated the work of the trade union movement in preparation for the RIO+20 Summit. Born in Villalonga, a small town in the Argentinian Patagonia, she holds a Master's degree on Development Studies, Institut d'Etudes Politiques de Paris. Before joining the ITUC, she worked for non-governmental organisations, in the area of democracy and youth empowerment.

Peter Rossman has been the International Campaigns and Communications Director of the International Union of Food, Agricultural, Hotel, Restaurant, Catering and Tobacco Workers (IUF), an international trade union federation based in Geneva, since 1991. He has written and published on, among other themes, issues concerning food policy, trade, finance and the environment in relationship to trade union organizing.

Darryn Snell is Senior Lecturer in the School of Management at the Royal Melbourne Institute of Technology University (RMIT) in Australia. He is a member of RMIT's Centre for Sustainable Organisations and Work where he coordinates the Climate Change and Sustainable Transitions Research Cluster. His current research seeks to understand how organisations, communities and other social actors, particularly trade unions, are assessing and engaging with climate change and the transition to a low carbon economy.

Dimitris Stevis is Professor of World Politics at Colorado State University. His long-term research and teaching have been on transnational political economy and social governance with a focus on labour and the environment. In 2007 he published, with Terry Boswell, *Globalization and Labor: Democratizing Global Governance.* His current research includes global labour politics, the environmental politics of labour unions, and strategies for green and just production.

Sean Sweeney is the Director and founder of the Global Labor Institute, a programme of the Cornell School of Industrial and Labor Relations (ILR) based in New York City. Dr Sweeney has been involved in college-level trade union and worker education since 1987 with Hofstra University's pioneering programme with the United Auto Workers, District 65. He serves on the International Trade Union Confederation's climate working group. He co-authored the UN Environment Program's 2008 report, *Green Jobs: Towards Decent Work in a Sustainable, Low-Carbon World* that was sponsored by the ITUC and the ILO. Most recently, he has co-authored a report that challenged the jobs claimed by the oil industry pertaining to the Keystone XL pipeline, entitled *Pipe Dreams: Jobs Gained, Jobs Lost in the Construction of the Keystone XL Pipeline.* Sean Sweeney has written for the *Los Angeles Times* and appeared on National Public Radio and is a frequent contributor to *New Labor Forum.*

David Uzzell is Professor of Environmental Psychology at the University of Surrey. His principal research interests focus on public understandings of climate change, critical psychological approaches to changing consumption and production practices, environmental risk, and identity and the past. Since 2006, David has been working on three research projects with Nora Räthzel examining national and international trade union policies towards climate change, the opportunities and constraints on the workforce in the workplace to contribute to a low carbon economy and the role of the individuals in transforming organisations in times of crisis. He chairs the British Psychological Society Working Party on climate change and gave the 2010 British Academy/British Psychological Society Annual Lecture on 'Psychology and Climate Change'.

Acknowledgements

First, we want to thank the trade unionists who gave us their time, inspired us with their visions and supported our research by facilitating contacts and inviting us to their meetings and conferences. Despite their heavy workloads and their involvement in the preparatory work for COP 17 and Rio +20, some of them gave us even more of their time and expertise by agreeing to contribute to this volume. Special thanks go to Woody Aroun (NUMSA), Anabella Rosemberg (ITUC) and Dinga Sikwebu (NUMSA), who went out of their way to supply us with documents, contacts, but more than anything with their inspiring ideas and determination.

This book was only made possible initially through the efforts and enthusiasm of Alison Kuznets, the first commissioning editor, before Earthscan was acquired by Taylor & Francis. She approached David Uzzell with the idea of a publication as she saw it filling an important gap in the Earthscan catalogue. We want to thank her specifically for her support and professionalism. Thank you also to the new editors of the book and especially to Charlotte Russell, who helped to realise the project under the new ownership.

We are grateful to Stefan Ståhle from Stockholm's Moderna Museet and to the Visual Arts Copyright Society in Sweden for allowing us to reproduce the painting 'Green Split' by Wassily Kandinsky.

Finally, we would like to acknowledge and thank the Swedish Council for Working Life and Social Research (FAS) for supporting the publication of this volume and the research that led to it, some of which is presented in Chapters 1 and 18.

Foreword

Work is more than just the means to a livelihood. It is a vital ingredient in our connection to each other. Part of the 'glue' of society. Good work offers respect, motivation, fulfilment, involvement in community and, for some, a sense of meaning and purpose in life. For all these reasons, not to mention that work generates income, anything that threatens full employment is to be feared and avoided. No wonder that for over a century, trade unionists have fought vigorously for the rights of workers and for the conditions of good work.

Hitherto labour unions have paid far less attention to the environmental impacts of the system of production and consumption. As Uzzell and Räthzel point out in their opening chapter, nature has traditionally been seen as 'labour's other'. At times this ambivalence towards the natural world has tipped over into outright opposition towards environmentalism. Those who sought to protect the environment have been seen – and admittedly have sometimes acted – as opponents of those who sought to protect employment and the conditions of work.

To the extent that protecting the environment inevitably requires shifts in the patterns of production and consumption, this antagonism has some clear foundations. Avoiding the over-consumption of materials has impacts on the lives of miners. Protecting fish stocks from collapse has repercussions for livelihoods in the fishing industry. And weaning the world from fossil fuels will change the conditions and nature of employment in the energy industry.

Explicable though this historical antagonism between labour and nature may be, it requires only the briefest reflection to understand that it represents a thoroughly false dichotomy. An industry that demolishes its own supply chain in pursuit of profit is destined for an eventual collapse. The sector might stave off its fate for a few years or even a few decades. But the outcome is as inevitable as it is disastrous. The long-term interests of labour are inextricably aligned with the interests of nature.

Nowhere is this more evident than in the arena of climate change. Shifting the structure of the energy industry away from fossil fuels, changing the architecture of the built environment and transforming carbon-intensive transport systems towards low-carbon alternatives will inevitably have impacts on the lives and livelihoods of workers. Without clear foresight and appropriate response, the fight against climate change will have short-term losers as well as long-term winners. But a world in which climate change runs rampant holds cold comfort for anyone, least of all for the interests of either employers or employees.

This book itself is evidence that the outmoded dialectics of a divide between labour and nature have had their day. Drawing together an impressive collection of essays from academics, trade unionists and environmentalists, Uzzell and Räthzel set out to build a vision of transformation that integrates the urgency of ecological limits with the paramount importance of social justice.

It is an impressively interdisciplinary book benefitting from the perspectives of sociologists, psychologists, political scientists, historians, economists alike. Its papers are drawn from the Global South as well as the North and reveal a vitally necessary diversity of perspectives. Unlike the emphasis in many governments' policies, these essays reveal clearly that individualistic approaches towards change will not be sufficient. The book focuses on the need for collective action. In particular, it complements ideas about transformation and changing the economy by highlighting the importance of the activities of workers' representatives.

At the end of the day, the counterfactual scenario to an alliance between labour and nature is not some consumer paradise where technological ingenuity allows us all continually to evade the ecological limits of a finite planet. Rather it is a world in which the opposing interests of labour and capital continue to drive each other into counter-productive spirals of collapse: resource scarcity, ecosystem degradation, runaway climate change and – inevitably – mass unemployment.

This book offers real and meaningful alternatives to such dystopian outcomes. Its over-riding message is that transformation is possible. But this must be seen and prosecuted as part of a 'just' transition to a sustainable society: a process in which it may at last be possible to restore the value of decent work to its rightful place at the heart of society.

Tim Jackson
Professor of Sustainable Development and author of
*Prosperity without Growth – economics for a
finite planet* (Routledge, London/New York)

1 Mending the breach between labour and nature

A case for environmental labour studies

David Uzzell and Nora Räthzel

Conflicts between environmentalists and labour: nature as labour's 'Other'

Over the past 40 years the relationship between environmentalists on the one hand and labour on the other has largely vacillated between distrust and suspicion at best through to rancour and open hostility at worst. Environmental movements have accused trade unions of defending jobs at any cost to nature, while trade unions have accused environmentalists of putting nature before workers' needs for jobs, and indeed, for survival.

If we look at the two movements historically there is evidence that labour movements in industrialised countries have viewed nature predominantly in two ways: in the beginning, trade unions were more organised like we think of social movements today. They founded 'organizations to advocate and develop gender equality, consumers' interests (the cooperative movement), popular health and welfare, housing, culture in all its aspects, education, leisure activities, and human rights (including anti-colonial movements)' (Gallin 2000, 4). For instance, the International Friends of Nature were founded 1895 in Vienna by a group of socialists, coming together through an advertisement in the *Arbeiter Zeitung* ('Newspaper for Workers'). In the UK, workers and 'environmentalists' joined together on 24 April 1932 for an act of mass trespass when they walked across the grouse moors of Kinder Scout (owned by the landed gentry and wealthy industrialists) to protest at the lack of access to green spaces around the industrial cities of the North of England. The 'right to roam' was initiated by the British Workers' Sports Federation (BWSF), largely made up of members and supporters of the Communist Party, which enjoyed significant working-class support. For these groups nature was a space for recreation and leisure that needed to be preserved as well as enjoyed.

The second way in which labour organisations have dealt with nature, has been in the context of health and safety concerns for their members. They have fought against the pollution of water, air and soil when this constituted a threat to the health of workers and their families. Most of the time though, health and safety issues are dealt with within the workplace, where unions see to it that workers are protected from the hazards of the production process.

Here, one could argue, they care for nature in the form of workers' bodies, although they may not formulate it this way. They see their work as caring for the social needs of workers of which health is an important part. In the image of nature as a space of recreation or an environment that needs to be protected from pollution, nature becomes labour's 'Other'. It is constructed as a pristine place external to society and to the labour process (Smith 1996, 41). In neither case is nature seen as an integral part of the production process, as a source of wealth, or as labour's ally. This omission was already apparent in the first programme of the German Social Democratic Party, the Programme of Gotha, where the first paragraph read: 'Labor is the source of wealth and all culture, and since useful labor is possible only in society and through society, the proceeds of labor belong undiminished with equal right to all members of society' (cited in Marx 1875). In his critique, Marx argued: 'Labor is not the source of all wealth. Nature is just as much the source of use values ... as labor, which itself is only the manifestation of a force of nature, human labor power' (Marx 1875). Both dimensions – nature as a source of use value, and human labour power as a part of nature – have been neglected in the history of the labour movement.

For environmental movements nature needs to be defended against uncontrolled and thoughtless industrialisation, and the 'productivism' of capital and labour alike. Their point of departure is that there is a fundamental contradiction between production and ecology. In one of her influential publications, Carolyn Merchant formulates it in the following way: 'The particular forms of production in modern society – industrial production, both capitalist and state socialist – creates accumulating ecological stresses on air, water, soil, and biota (including human beings) and on society's ability to maintain and reproduce itself over time' (Merchant 1992, 9). There are many environmental movements (just as there are many different forms of trade unionism, although they do not cover an equally broad political spectrum), from nature conservationists, to environmental NGOs with considerable financial resources (WWF-UK income in 2011 was £57 million [WWF-UK 2011]), to environmental justice movements, socialist ecologists, ecofeminists and deep ecologists. One cannot do them justice with one definition. It is safe to say though, that when it comes to conflicts between industry and environmental protection they will put environmental protection first – after all, protecting the environment is their raison d'être. What they have in common with the labour movement is a construction of nature as labour's 'Other'. Neither labour movements nor environmental movements see labour and nature as allies, needing each other to produce the material resources necessary for human survival.

The difficulty of seeing labour and nature as inseparable elements for the production of life (since without production there is no human life), lies in their separation historically. In a process that accelerated with the industrial revolution, nature has become (and is still becoming) a private asset, just like the products of labour and nature, tools, machines and buildings (Smith 2008; Castree 2010). For workers, privatised nature stands on the other side of the capital–labour relationship; it has become capital. Workers experience the protection of nature as a threat, not only to their jobs, but also to their identities as producers. From the point of view of environmentalists, workers are seen to be on the side of capital who regard nature only as an exploitable 'natural resource', a means to an end for production. Both are caught in a contradictory structure that involves a trialectical relationship between labour, capital and nature (Soja 1996). When unions defend their jobs at the expense of nature, they are at the same time defending the relations of production (the private appropriation of nature) under which they are themselves subordinated. Sweeney (in this volume) describes the paradoxical effects this can have, when unions defend the economic activities of politicians who act in an anti-labour fashion. The same can be said for environmentalists who criticise unions for defending their jobs without suggesting any alternatives that would allow workers a living without being at the mercy of those who own nature and control labour.

What is lived as a conflict between environmental and labour movements is mirrored by academic disciplines' mutual disregard.

Where's the environment in labour studies, where's the labour in environmental studies?

The fact that labour studies and environmental studies are separate spheres of research serves to reinforce the failure of researchers to appreciate the importance of their reciprocal significance and contribution. This shortcoming has been carried through to the lecture theatre. It is extremely rare for academic courses on the environment and climate change to discuss issues of labour. Likewise, there are few courses on labour that explore the implications of climate change for working conditions and labour rights. While attention may be paid to production processes such as the impact of new technologies on labour, climate-motivated labour and production changes such as regulations, changes in markets, the migration of production, are rarely discussed. Equally, there is little discussion as to how labour is responding to these changes. For example, what impact will climate-change-motivated regulations have on the working lives of those who are employed in high-carbon and consequently high-risk industries? Work for many, as we know, is more than just bringing in a wage. It provides dignity, identity and solidarity (Collinson 1992; Räthzel and Uzzell 2011). When industries are attacked (i.e. because they are seen to be damaging to the environment), those who work in those industries may also feel attacked.

It is striking that if one attends conferences on the human dimensions of climate change, very few papers focus on the workplace. With some confidence one can say that even less address labour issues in general or the position and role of trade unions towards climate change, whether in terms of their policy response or how climate mitigation and adaptation are affecting jobs or workers' rights. Likewise, conferences in the area of labour studies are silent on these issues. In the social environmental sciences – psychology, sociology or economics – the focus of research, and what is carried across into the lecture theatre, is on changing consumer behaviour and largely comes under the heading of 'behaviour change strategies' (e.g. Darnton 2008). These draw on theories from behavioural psychology and behavioural economics that can be characterised as individualistic and reductionist because they reduce people to de-socialised monads, taking decisions on their own (cf. Institute for Government 2009). To add 'influences' from other people does not solve the problem because it only multiplies the number of monads conceived as meeting in a void. The societal relations (relations of production, relations of consumption, political and social power relations [Uzzell and Räthzel 2009]) that shape practices are neglected together with the 'hardware' of such practices, infrastructures and technologies. Such research tends to concentrate on individual action in the home, in the supermarket, on holiday and through various transport means used to move between these locations. The closest these studies come to the workplace is the car that takes the commuter to work. Sustainable behaviour strategies in the workplace mirror those advocated for the consumers in general, such that research has focused on how companies can implement, for example, 'green travel plans' or encourage their workforce to recycle waste and turn lights off (Bartlett 2011). While these are valuable measures, they do not get to the heart of the matter, namely the production process itself and its impact on the environment. Environmental social scientists in turn have almost entirely ignored the role of labour in these processes, the impact of climate change on the psychology and sociology of workers, and the potential for collective as opposed to individual action.

The separation between environmental studies, focusing on the effects of production processes on nature, and labour studies, focusing on the effects of production processes on workers, can be traced back to the separation between natural sciences and social sciences. Bruno Latour (1993) argues that this separation has its origins in the debate between Hobbes and Boyle, the latter arguing on the basis of experimentally created facts, the former on the basis of theories of the social (ibid. 29f). Latour maintains that 'things' and the 'social' co-constitute each other and thus have to be studied in relation to each other. In the same vein we suggest that production processes have to be studied as a relationship between humans and nature evolving within specific societal relations.

Some scholars have taken up the challenge to theorise this relationship. Predominantly, they come from a Marxist tradition (Vorst et al. 1993; Harvey 1996; Layfield 2008). For example, O'Connor (1998) develops a theory of the 'human interaction with nature' and Foster (2000) reconstructs what he calls 'Marx's Ecology', bringing together writings of materialists and of Marx on nature and the human–nature metabolism, while Harvey theorises the social relations of nature from the perspective of a Marxist geography. While ecologists have criticised Marx and Marxists (Goldblatt 1996, Bramwell 1989; Smith 2001) for neglecting nature or conceptualising it only as a means to an end of human reproduction, others, like Pepper (1993), Gare (1995) and Merchant (1992), have linked the ecological to Marxist theory. There is a lively debate around a Marxist or socialist ecology, especially in the journals *Capital, Nature, Socialism* and *Monthly Review*, but it has not been taken up in the fields of labour or environmental studies, with a view of providing a theoretical framework for empirical research. This volume seeks to bring these two areas of discourse together by joining the writings of academics with those who are working at the 'coalface' of these issues, the trades unions.

New movements in the trade union movements

We use the plural of movement in this title because there is no such thing as a unitary labour or trade union movement. Differences and often conflicts exist on all levels, between sectors, within and between countries, and between unions of the global North and the global South. Nevertheless, while academic research remains largely corralled in its disciplines and sub-disciplines, union movements across the world have been moving fast to incorporate a concern for nature by taking on climate change as an issue of trade union policies. This is why this book, which is the first to address the environmental policies of unions worldwide, begins with the views of trade unionists in international, national and local trade unions. They do not purport to represent majority positions in the labour movements. However, they occupy important positions and represent some of the most advanced views of unionists today and thus the possible policies that unions could develop in the future.

The authors represent international unions: Rosemberg is the policy officer of Occupational Health and Environment in the International Trade Union Confederation (ITUC), Rossman is international campaign and communications director in the International Union of Food, Farm and Hotel Workers (IUF), and Martín Murillo heads Sustainlabour, an international trade union organisation especially set up to assist unionists in the global South in their efforts to combat the 'double exposure' effects (Leichenko and O'Brien 2008) of climate change and the lack of workers' rights. Olsen and Kemter work in the Bureau for Workers' Activities (ACTRAV) of the International Labour Organisation (ILO) and are responsible for environmental sustainability. We also invited representatives of national unions to contribute their perspectives: Gil works in the Spanish research centre ISTAS, set up by the Spanish union Comisiones Obreras in 1996, and is responsible for investigating environmental issues, health and safety and working conditions, Henriksson is an assembly worker in the Volvo car producer plant owned since 2010 by the Chinese Geely Holding Group, and a member of the Swedish metal workers union (IF Metall).

From the perspective of the ILO Olsen and Kemter present a history of labour involvement with nature as one that moves from a concern for workers' health and safety and the pollution of factory environments to a broader concern for climate change and a just transition to decent green jobs. Through this period, nature moves from being seen as a condition for a healthy life, where attention focuses on local spaces (whether in the workplace or for recreation) to being redefined by unions as a global issue in terms of climate change.

As Rosemberg and Murillo argue, this process has been accelerating since the Trade Union Assembly in Nairobi in 2006, where trade unions from all over the world came together to discuss environmental issues for the first time. In the same year the ITUC was founded as a merger between the former International Confederation of Free Trade Unions and the World Confederation of Labour. This was also the time when the first programme on climate change was agreed by an international union (Murillo). Since then, there has been a growing interest among trade union officials to incorporate the environment as an issue of climate change into trade union programmes. Rosemberg analyses how this agenda has developed within the ITUC and is including an increasing number of national unions from across the world. In many national and international unions special positions have been created for unionists to take responsibility for environmental issues and to formulate union positions on climate change.

All the authors in this book argue that this implies a transformation of trade unions as organisations that are solely concerned with workers' lives within, the factory walls. Cock and Lambert promote the notion of social movement unionism, Gil envisages an eco-unionism and Henriksson suggests how workers can develop the self-confidence to use their skills and knowledge for a transformation of their industries on the way to just and low carbon societies. Henriksson's perspective is one in which workers cease reacting to the capitalist crises to defend their achievements, but attempt to meet the challenge by embarking on a struggle in which they seek to become the inventors of new forms of production.

International solidarity has been a defining characteristic of trade unions since the nineteenth century (Waterman and Timms 2004), but it has usually meant unions supporting each other in their local struggles. The rise of the internet has now made global protest possible but is usually industry/sector specific. To incorporate a global phenomenon like climate change, however, into the trade union agenda requires unions and their members to investigate the global effects of their local actions. In this respect, unions are a perfect example of 'glocality' (Meyrowitz 2005), working on the local and the global level simultaneously. Therefore, Sweeney calls on unions to realise this potential, especially the ITUC, and try to convince unions in the US that they should oppose tar sand extraction because it will not only damage the area in which tar sands are exploited, but will also add enormously to global greenhouse gas emissions.

An insight into the global effects of local production processes implies that unions broaden their self-definition from a responsibility to their members to a responsibility to society at large, as Gil and Murillo suggest. Rossman emphasises this argument by turning it around. He shows that big business agriculture is one of the most dangerous GHG emitters and polluters of the environment and this immediately affects the health and well-being of workers and small farmers in agriculture. Therefore, he concludes that the struggle for workers' rights is an indispensable part of the struggle to mitigate climate change.

Comprehensive union policies that merge the protection of workers and the protection of nature have several implications for trade union policies. They imply that unions need to (re)invent themselves as social movements, aiming not only to improve their members' lives but to transform societies and the present economic system. This implies, as all the authors in this book argue, that trade unions need to build alliances with environmental movements. Indeed, such alliances are forming in countries around the globe.

In the US, the BlueGreen Alliance started with a collaboration between the Sierra Club and the United Steelworkers union (Stevis, Sweeney and Gingrich). In South Africa, Earthlife is organising courses on environmental issues for unionists and collaborating with COSATU and NUMSA in the One Million Climate Jobs Campaign (Cock and Lambert, Uzzell and Räthzel); in Brazil, the umbrella organisations for environmental organisations (Forum Brasileiro de ONGs e Movimentos Sociais para o Meio Ambiente e o Desenvolvimento, FBOMS) includes the national trade union CUT as a leading board member. Some unions, like the STTR in the Amazonian region, have not only allied themselves with environmental movements, but are themselves a grassroots environmental movement (Cândia Veiga and Martin). Here, as in many areas of the global South, the close connection between defending work and defending nature is evident and was exemplified by the famous trade union leader Chico Mendes, who was both a unionist of the rubber tappers and an environmentalist. He paid for his commitment and engagement with his life (Revkin 2004). This tradition of trade union environmentalism is alive in the Brazilian trade union movement, predominantly among agricultural unions. In other countries an alliance between agricultural workers, unions and rural communities has yet to be developed. For example, with regards to South Africa, Bennie suggests that South African industrial and mining unions need to understand that rural communities are not necessarily keen to exchange their ways of life for an opportunity to work in what others may perceive as a modern industry, even if they are promised what is conventionally regarded as a better life. The rural communities he researched refuse to accept the label of being poor.

In South Korea and Taiwan, two of the fast industrialising countries of Asia, unions and environmental movements are coming together after they have both seen their support in society dwindle. Liu analyses labour and environmental activities, campaigns and discourses, and suggests where both need to learn from each other in order to not only be able to work together, but also to improve the success of their own political campaigns. In Australia, unions and environmentalists have been working together as early as the 1970s, forming associations like the 'Environmentalists for Employment' (Burgmann). Today, trade union environmental policies have diversified and so have their alliances with different environmental movements and political parties in Australia (Snell and Fairbrother). In none of the countries examined here are red–green alliances free of frictions and conflicts, due to a history of different discourses and political priorities of the respective movements. Sweeney gives an example of this fragility when he reports that the Laborers' International Union of North America (LiUNA) has left the alliance because two transport unions (ATU and TWU) in the alliance supported the decision of the Obama administration to reject the building of the Keystone X pipeline. Such conflicts illuminate that the 'job versus environment' dilemma is far from resolved, even though it is now considered a false dichotomy by many scholars, politicians and unionists who argue that a 'green economy' will provide much more 'green jobs' than might be lost through measures enabling a transformation into low carbon societies.

There are a number of ambiguities in the demand for 'green jobs'. First, green jobs are not necessarily well paid, safe, and secure jobs as Olsen and Kemter, and Stevis, point out. Especially in relation to Australia and the US, which have a comparatively longer tradition of green jobs and green economic policies, the authors (Stevis, Snell and Fairbrother, and Sweeney) engage with the limitations of these concepts. They argue for a need to question the relationship between 'green jobs' and 'just jobs', to examine the taken-for-granted growth perspective, to take the relationship between different production sectors within a country and globally into account, and to rethink the system of production that has led to climate change. The question is, whether a demand for green jobs leads to 'shallow reforms' or whether it transcends the present forms of production (Cock and Lambert) and envisages an economic system beyond the growth paradigm (Barry). However, a radical trade union position that sees capitalism as the source of the global environmental destruction, does not necessarily lead to the formulation of radical positions on how to combat climate change (Bennie).

Burgmann and Snell and Fairbrother argue that the perspective of green jobs can overcome the jobs vs. environment dilemma by offering unions and workers a way to embrace climate change measures without fearing unemployment. This seems only to be true on a more abstract level of formulating agendas and programmes. However, when a union is faced with the alternative of supporting environmentally damaging productions, which will create jobs immediately or to oppose such a production for the sake of green jobs in an uncertain future, most will opt for the first alternative (Räthzel and Uzzell 2011). A radical agenda, fighting for 'system change, not climate change' as demonstrators at the recent COP meetings in Copenhagen (2009) and Durban (2011) demanded, points to the root cause of climate change, namely a profit and therefore growth-oriented production system. While it can (and, as some authors argue, must) provide the perspective for a long-term formulation of trade union policies it will not suffice to convince unions at local levels, who also fight for their members' livelihood in the present. Strategies like the One Million Climate Jobs Campaign in South Africa (Cock and Lambert) are essential to develop awareness, arguments and action for trade union policies at the local level and in the public domain. However, their demands are directed towards governments and sometimes business. They involve unionists and workers as campaigners only, not as makers of their own futures. In our view, these campaigns need to be accompanied by strategies like the one Henriksson is proposing, namely to involve workers directly in designing new forms of productions.

As in the public debates, one can trace a line through the argumentation in this book among those authors (Snell and Fairbrother, Burgmann) who critically advocate the need for so-called reformist strategies by unions to develop viable perspectives out of the climate change threat. Others (Cock and Lambert, Bennie, Barry) have more doubts and see reformism as a potential threat to effective policies that can halt climate change. Stevis terms these differences as weak and strong environmental modernisation and foresees that the opposition to climate change measures now prominent in the US can only be overcome if the strong environmental modernism argument wins through. Rosa Luxemburg (1999) coined the concept of 'revolutionary reformism', meaning that labour movements have to present alternatives within the day-to-day political agendas with the aim of improving the situation for workers and the society now. But such alternatives should at the same time make a transformative agenda visible and achievable. They should sow the seeds of alternative forms of working and living in practice. It seems to us that a strategy that links the 'green jobs' campaign with a trade union programme that makes use of workers' skills and knowledge to explore and design ways in which industries (and services for that matter) can be converted, would constitute such a strategy of 'revolutionary reformism'. In this context it is noteworthy that although official union documents as well as the views of influential unionists are presented and discussed in political and occasionally scholarly work, we have limited reliable knowledge through either quantitative or qualitative research of what workers in factories and offices think about climate change. In addition to the LOCAW Study[1] which is being undertaken by the authors for the European Commission, we are only aware of the national surveys undertaken by the Labour Research Department, on behalf of the TUC in the UK, amongst union 'Green Representatives' on trade union action on environment and climate change in the workplace and the role of the trade union movement.

One of the major obstacles to the success of environmental trade union policies are the different points of departures of unions due to their different national histories, their sectoral anchoring, their strength in terms of membership and their political convictions. Gingrich analyses some of these differences and their effects on climate change policies for unions in the US and in Sweden. Whether unions are closely related to government and political actors, or more flexible in choosing their allies, makes a significant difference in terms of whether they are willing and able to create new forms of cooperation with environmental movements. There is also a difference between international and national confederations and federations. While an international union may have the vision and organisational capacity to develop a broader perspective for environmental policies, a local union will be much more tied to the immediate, everyday interests of their members, which may act as a serious constraint on them not only envisaging but also practising a broader social movement unionism. Trade union histories and traditions not only influence the ways in which unions formulate their interests within the societal context at large, they also shape their relations to the state and to labour parties in the respective countries. One of the most pertinent divisions is between the Global North and the Global South. Uzzell and Räthzel suggest that the history of colonialism continues to be reflected in North–South relations between unions. While there are multiple differences between Southern and Northern unions, these are cross-cut by what Southern unionists experience as domination by Northern unions due to the latter's superior resources and organising power. While Northern unions practise solidarity in helping Southern unions with their resources and knowledge, this often comes at a price, namely a desire of Northern unions to influence the political practices of Southern unions. These power relationships thwart the possibilities for developing national and international environmental policies against climate change. To give an example of the potential power of comprehensive international trade union policies, the International Trade Union Confederation has 308 affiliated member organisations in 153 countries and territories, with a total membership of 175 million workers. The potential influence of such a body and its constituent members is huge, and if it can be mobilised to take collective action, we might start to see some of the changes that will be necessary across the global North and South if we are to slow down and even reverse the pernicious consequences of climate change.

For a new research area: environmental labour studies

The way in which nature and labour are intrinsically linked and equally threatened by globalising capital provides the theoretical rationale, while the development of environmental trade union policies worldwide provides the empirical rationale for an area of study that we suggest calling environmental labour studies.

This book, we argue, proves that such a new field of research is emerging and that its themes, tasks and issues are multiple, urgent and unsolved. That the authors of this book work in departments of sociology, psychology, political science, economics and management demonstrate that environmental labour studies can and should be multi- and inter-disciplinary. It can also include different theoretical approaches and different methodologies, ranging from the macro studies of world system theory to the micro studies of workers' identities and everyday practices. There are many omissions in this book as can be expected in any publication especially in a new field of study, but perhaps the most striking one is that the trade union policies, which are mainly in focus here, are those of (heavy) industrial unions. In some ways this may not be surprising as these are the industries that have tended to feel vulnerable to criticisms from environmentalists, which claim that these industries are largely responsible for carbon emissions, global warming and climate change (e.g. transport, steel, chemical, cement). On the one hand this is an interesting and important counterpoint to the pre-eminence of post-industrial, service economies, as industrialised societies are characterised. On the other, it does exclude the majority of workers in the countries of the North, who work in the service sector and offices, the requirements of which also make a significant contribution to climate change, which is often overlooked.

Except for David Uzzell, who is an environmental psychologist, all of the authors in this book come from labour studies in one way or another. It is to be hoped that in future this important area will be recognised by environmental social scientists who will be encouraged to investigate labour policies, the effects of climate change and environmental degradation on workers and working conditions. A few studies exist on the effects of heat on workers' health and well being (cf. Kjellstrom 2009), but the range of issues identified in this book go beyond this type of analysis and demonstrate that the relationship between work, workers and the environment is multifaceted and complex. As a starting point, we wanted to concentrate specifically on trade union policies. In this respect we hope that this book marks just a beginning of a moment, when researchers appreciate the need to connect the areas of environmental and labour studies.

Note

1 LOCAW: Low Carbon at Work: modelling agents and organisations to achieve transition to a low carbon Europe. In a study funded by the European Union, the authors, together with researchers in Romania, Italy, Spain, the Netherlands and the UK, are investigating these questions in areas of small and heavy industry and public services: www.locaw-fp7.com/ (accessed 20 March 2012).

References

Bartlett, D. (2011) *Going Green: The Psychology of Sustainability in the Workplace.* Leicester: British Psychology Society.

Bramwell, A. (1989) *Ecology in the Twentieth Century.* New Haven, CT: Yale University Press.

Castree, N. (2010) 'Neoliberalism and the Biophysical Environment 2: Theorising the Neoliberalisation of Nature', *Geography Compass,* 4(12): 1734–46.

Collinson, D. L. (1992). *Managing the Shopfloor: Subjectivity, Masculinity and Workplace Culture.* Berlin: de Gruyter.

Darnton, A. (2008) *Practical Guide: An overview of behaviour change models and their uses.* London: Government Social Research Unit, HM Treasury.

Foster, J. B. (2000) *Marx's Ecology. Materialism and Nature.* New York: Monthly Review Press.

Gallin, D. (2000) *Trade Unions and NGOs: A Necessary Partnership for Social Development.* Civil Society and Social Movements Programme Paper Number 1, June 2000. United Nations Research Institute for Social Development.

Gare, A. E. (1995) *Postmodernism and the Environmental Crisis*. London: Routledge.

Goldblatt, D. (1996) *Social Theory and Environment*. Boulder, CO: Westview Press.

Harvey, D. (1996) *Justice, Nature and the Geography of Difference*. Malden and Oxford: Blackwell, available from www.nfi.at/index.php?option=com_content&task=view&id=3&Itemid=9 (accessed 10 March 2012).

Institute for Government (2009) *Mindspace: influencing behaviour through public policy*. London: Cabinet Office, available from www.socialsciencespace.com/2011/01/mindspace-a-simple-checklist-for-behaviour-change/ (accessed 23 March 2012).

Kjellstrom, T. (2009) 'Climate change, direct heat exposure, health and well-being in low and middle-income countries'. Global Health Action 2009. www.ncbi.nlm.nih.gov/pmc/articles/PMC2780846/ (accessed 24 July 2012).

Latour, B. (1993) *We have never been Modern*. Cambridge, CA: Harvard University Press.

Layfield, D. (2008) *Marxism and Environmental Crises*. Bury St Edmunds: Arena Books.

Leichenko, R. M. and O'Brien, K. (2008) *Environmental Change and Globalization. Double Exposures*. Oxford and New York: Oxford University Press.

Luxemburg, R. ([1900]1999) 'Reform or Revolution'. Available at: www.marxists.org/archive/luxemburg/1900/reform-revolution/index.htm (accessed 20 March 2012).

Marx, K. (1875) 'Critique of the Gotha Programme'. Available from www.marxists.org/archive/marx/works/1875/gotha/ch01.htm (accessed 20 March 2012).

Merchant, C. (1992) *Radical Ecology. The Search for a Livable World*. New York and London: Routledge.

Meyrowitz, J. (2005) 'The rise of glocality. New senses of place and identity in the global village'. In K. Nyiri (ed.) *A sense of place: The global and the local in mobile communication*. Vienna: Passagen, pp. 21–30.

O'Connor, J. (1998). *Natural Causes: Essays in ecological Marxism*. New York: The Guildford Press.

Pepper, D. (1993) *Eco-Socialism: From deep ecology to social justice*. London: Routledge.

Räthzel, N. and Uzzell, D. (2011) 'Trade Unions and Climate Change: The Jobs versus Environment Dilemma', *Global Environmental Change*, 21: 1215–23.

Revkin, A. (2004) *The Burning Season: the murder of Chico Mendes and the fight for the Amazon Rain Forest*. Washington: First Island Press, Sherewater Books Printing.

Smith, M. (2001) *An Ethics of Place: Radical ecology, postmodernity, and social theory*. Albany, NY: State University of New York Press.

Smith, N. (1996) 'The production of nature'. In G. Robertson, M. Mash, L. Tichner, J. Bird, B. Curtis and T. Putman (eds) *Future Natural*. London: Routledge.

——(2008) *Uneven Development: Nature, Capital, and the Production of Space*, Third Edition. Athens: University of Georgia Press.

Soja, E. (1996) *Thirdspace, journeys to Los Angeles and other real-and-imagined places*. London and New York: Blackwell.

Uzzell, D. and Räthzel, N. (2009) 'Transforming Environmental Psychology', *Journal of Environmental Psychology*, 29(3): 340–50.

Vorst, J., Dobson, R. and Fletcher, R. (eds) (1993) *Green on Red: Evolving Ecological Socialism*. Halifax: Society for Socialist Studies, Fernwood Publishing.

Waterman, P. and Timms, J. (2004) Trade Union Internationalism and a Global Civil Society. In H. Anheier, M. Glasius and M. Kaldor (eds) *Global Civil Society 2004/5*, London: Sage, pp. 175–202.

WWF-UK (2011) WWF-UK's Annual Report and Financial Statement. Godalming: WWF-UK.

Trade union perspectives

2 Developing global environmental union policies through the International Trade Union Confederation

Anabella Rosemberg

Introduction

In a world that is in the midst of the worst economic crisis since the 1930s and in which a majority of the world's workers are either officially unemployed or in the informal economy, with no social protection or rights, one could logically be led to think that environmental issues are low on the list of trade union priorities. The ILO has indicated that there are 27 million more unemployed workers than at the start of the crisis and today global unemployment affects 225 million people, 74.8 million of which are youth aged 15–24 (ILO 2012).

Yet, in practice, the growing recognition of the organic linkages that connect the multiple crises (food, energy, unemployment and climate) has consolidated existing trade union efforts to come up with an integrated response to the current crises in which environmental concerns play a critical role.

Substantial progress has been made by trade unions at the national and local levels. A myriad of trade union initiatives is currently underway; initiatives that explicitly link together social and environmental concerns. The fact that despite a terrible climate of violence against trade unions, the USO in Colombia has incorporated the impacts of polluting industries on communities' health – paying for this commitment with the life of their leaders – (ITUC, 2012) or the development by a trade union in Spain – Comisiones Obreras – of an authoritative source of information on chemicals' exposures or emission sources like the ISTAS – to mention just two initiatives – shows that concrete steps are being taken by trade unions at all levels. These and hundreds of other initiatives deserve our attention, as their diversity and nature are an informative expression of the substantial progress that has been made by the labour movement in the environmental field.

Having said this, we will specifically focus on the international dimension of trade unions' work on the environment, and on the ways in which this work has contributed to guiding local and national trade union actions. In particular, work at the international level has helped local unions to understand the linkages between the environmental question and the interests of workers, to forge future campaigns and, based on their own local realities, to imagine and promote an alternative economic development that is socially, economically and environmentally sustainable.

Ever since its creation in 2006, the International Trade Union Confederation (ITUC) has incorporated environmental issues into its broader mandate as global trade union representative and promoter of decent work at the international level. This decision can be linked to the evolutions in the international sustainable development agenda and the decision to discuss climate change by its predecessor, the International Confederation of Free Trade Unions (ICFTU). ITUC work on the environment has played a substantial part in firmly placing the environmental issue at the heart of the trade union movement's priorities.

The aim of this article is to look at the recent evolution of environmental policies at the International Trade Union Confederation (ITUC) (I shall also draw on historical data from the International Confederation of Free Trade Unions), the debates that have been organised within it and the emerging challenges. The article is structured in three parts. The first examines the evolution of the ITUC's environmental policies, particularly the development of policies on climate change and the promotion of the just transition framework. The second will discuss emerging debates on the role of environmental protection in alternative economic thinking, and how they have been received by the international labour movement. In a third and final section, I will introduce the challenges that lie ahead for the international labour movement when dealing with environmental issues.

The history and development of ITUC policies on the environment

From Agenda 21 to the ITUC Vienna Foundational Congress

In 1992, the United Nations Conference on Environment and Development held in Rio adopted Agenda 21 as an action plan towards sustainable development. Agenda 21 is universally recognised as a substantial step towards more ambitious policy making by national governments, the United Nations system and civil society – including organised labour (the latter being regrouped into the 'workers and trade unions' major group). By recognising trade unions as important stakeholders in the international development debate, the Rio conference indirectly contributed to firmly anchoring the environmental question within the international movement by raising trade union awareness on the sustainable development agenda. It also contributed to building a different perception of trade unions. They were now perceived as possible game-changers in the ongoing debates and considered as a possible link between the social dimension of sustainable development, where they were traditionally active, and the environmental dimension, in which labour-related policies were desperately needed.

According to Chapter 29:

> As workers' representatives, trade unions are vital actors in facilitating the achievement of sustainable development in view of their experience in

addressing industrial change, the extremely high priority they give to protection of the working environment and the related natural environment, and their promotion of socially responsible and economic development.

For this reason, according to Agenda 21, 'workers should be full participants in the implementation and evaluation of activities related to Agenda 21' (UN 1992).

Agenda 21 provided an initial list of actions that trade unions could take to foster sustainable development. These were mainly related to the linkages between occupational health and safety and the environment, and strongly focused on workplace action. When it comes to the international level, the only reference made was to the role of trade unions within the UN system. Over the last 20 years, and just at the international level, trade unions largely surpassed this restricted mandate and initiated work in many areas, including capacity building, training, advocacy, policy making and campaigning.

Progress on those areas was reflected in the outcomes of the first ever trade union Assembly on Labour and Environment, held in Nairobi, Kenya in 2006, where trade unions enumerated a series of policies and interests, as well as a series of commitments that were going to be enshrined later in the work programme of the future International Trade Union Confederation, at its Foundational Congress.

The Assembly on Labour and Environment, also called WILL (for 'Workers Initiatives for a Lasting Legacy'), adopted a resolution that covers all aspects of trade union involvement on environmental issues, but most importantly, it commits the movement to 'strengthen the link between poverty reduction, environmental protection and decent work' and it adds that 'creating decent and secure jobs is only possible if environmental sustainability is attained' (UNEP 2006).

The Assembly was organised only a few months before the creation of the International Trade Union Confederation, and had an important impact on the way environmental concerns were going to be integrated into the ITUC mandate. It is to be noted that before then, there were no mentions of environmental issues as such in the mandate of the ICFTU.

When national trade union confederations met in Vienna, Austria, the Congress called on the ITUC to 'change globalisation fundamentally'. It acknowledged that this change

> … is essential to the achievement of the permanent aims of the Confederation that the policies of free market neo-liberalism, and the manifest failings and incoherence of the international community in respect of the current process of globalisation, give way to governance of the global economy which combines the three pillars of sustainable development – economic, social and environmental … .

(ITUC 2006, 1)

It also

> ... underlines the need for the international community to implement an overarching strategy for sustainable development. It calls on the ITUC to integrate the link between health and the environment fully into its work ... . It further calls for an end to unsustainable consumption practices, and cooperation for implementation of the Kyoto Protocol to the UN Framework Convention on Climate Change.
>
> (ITUC 2006, 3)

Progress at the policy level

The incorporation of environmental issues in the ITUC's mandate was instrumental in creating momentum to discuss environmentally related policy issues within the newly created organisation.

It is to be noted that prior to this decision the ICFTU made a number of public remarks on sustainable development and particularly sustainable management of chemicals. It closely monitored and participated in various United Nations processes and conferences, such as the World Summit on Sustainable Development (WSSD), the Commission on Sustainable Development (CSD) and the UN Strategic Approach on International Chemicals Management (SAICM).

The post-Vienna Congress period can be characterised by internal policy developments that, in many cases, went beyond the usual calls for greater trade union participation and traditional worker demands. ITUC positions incorporated environmental questions, such as calls for specific government commitments on climate change.

The statement adopted for the UNFCCC COP14 in Poznan, Poland, for example, clearly shows how the ITUC was committed to positioning itself on all aspects of climate policy, including aspects where the linkages with employment and labour issues had not yet been fully explored (such as adaptation or technology transfer) (ITUC 2008). The Confederation's concern at the time was to show the world that the labour movement could be considered as a legitimate actor in the climate debate (even if this meant confronting those who saw the labour movement as a threat to the climate negotiations' success). It needs to be said that progressive labour approaches to climate change were not known at the UNFCCC. Environmental NGOs and key actors in the negotiations had only heard about trade unions' link to climate change through US debates on the Kyoto Protocol, where many US trade unions supported those running against it.

It is in this statement of 2008 that for the first time unions recognised the need for trade unions to fully address climate change because of its links with industrial and economic development, but first and foremost, because of its linkages to historical trade union values of solidarity and justice. As the document explains: 'climate change raises important questions about social justice, equity and human rights across countries and generations. It is now time for action. Trade unions engage in current climate negotiations with a message of commitment, solidarity and action' (ITUC 2008).

Other policies were adopted in this spirit, such as those related to green and decent jobs, which, while related to the climate debate, go beyond it to incorporate it as an emblem of the policies trade unions wanted to see when sustainable development policies were to be implemented.

The period that stretched from the ITUC's Foundational Congress to the ITUC's 2nd Congress (in Vancouver, 2010) was also marked by an ambitious training and capacity building programme (organised by the Sustainlabour Foundation). In less than three years, the programme involved 202 trade union organisations from 90 countries. Among the projects that were included in the programme we find the organisation of training sessions and manuals (comprising conferences, technical seminars, on-demand training events developed in consultations with trade unions and in response to specific capacity building/training needs expressed by trade union bodies), strengthening of local trade unions that deal with environmental protection, and the provision of technical assistance to trade unions in Latin America and the Caribbean, Asia Pacific, Africa and Central Europe as well as additional sessions at the sub-regional or national level.

The most significant ITUC contribution to the sustainable development debate was the development and promotion of the concept of 'just transition'.

Just transition[1]

'Just transition' was first mentioned at the end of the 1990s in Canadian union articles as 'an attempt to reconcile the union movement's efforts to provide workers with decent jobs and the need to protect the environment' (Rosemberg 2010, 141). The concept marked a considerable step towards greater recognition of the links between the defence of workers' interest and the needs of the community to protect the environment.

In the space of ten years, the union movement's approach towards environmental issues has evolved and with it the definition, boundaries and scope of the 'just transition' that is needed.[2] The ITUC defined the concept as the 'tool the trade union movement shares with the international community, aimed at smoothing the shift towards a more sustainable society and providing hope for the capacity of a "green economy" to sustain decent jobs and livelihoods for all' (ITUC 2009a, 2009b).

It is important to note that 'just transition' is not a replacement of but rather an addition to existing environmental policies. One of its purposes is precisely to strengthen the idea that environmental and social policies are not contradictory but, on the contrary, can reinforce each other. This is of particular importance when we take into account the fact that just transition has become one of the international trade union's *leitmotivs*. Would it have been possible to imagine such a trade union slogan, anchored on social justice, but also on environmental protection, only a few decades ago? Without a doubt, the impacts of environmental degradation, accompanied with massive public campaigns, but also an active promotion of trade unions' role on this topic, contributed to this shift.

This approach to the 'just transition' concept was unanimously adopted at the 2nd ITUC Congress, in 2010, when the Congress declared 'just transition' to be 'the' approach to fight climate change:

> Congress is committed to promoting an integrated approach to sustainable development through a just transition where social progress, environmental protection and economic needs are brought into a framework of democratic governance, where labour and other human rights are respected and gender equality achieved.
>
> (ITUC 2010, 1)

Other Global Union Federations, representing workers in specific economic sectors, joined this policy approach (Rosemberg 2010, 142).

In brief, 'just transition' refers to the need for long-term sustainable investments that create decent jobs, offer pro-active training and skills development policies; ensure social dialogue with unions, employers and other stakeholders; favour research and early assessment of social and employment impacts of climate policies, the development of social protection schemes and create the conditions for local economic diversification plans. It is a package of policy proposals that addresses different aspects of the vulnerability of workers and their communities: uncertainties regarding job impacts, risks of job losses, risks of undemocratic decision-making processes, risks of regional or local economic downturns, among others.

From a concept that was known to just a handful of activists, the 'just transition' concept slowly took root at the international level. The latest achievement to date was the recognition of the concept by the UN Framework Convention on Climate Change. Following an intense campaign organised by the ITUC, in 2010, during the 16th Conference of the Parties, all governments agreed to incorporate the concept into its decisions.

The UNFCCC agreed to include the concept in the following paragraph of the agreement:

> Realizes that addressing climate change requires a paradigm shift towards building a low carbon society that offers substantial opportunities and ensures continued high growth and sustainable development, based on innovative technologies and more sustainable production and consumption and lifestyles, while ensuring a just transition of the workforce that creates decent work and quality jobs.
>
> (UNFCCC 2011, 4)

Several years have passed since the labour movement started working on environmental issues. The movement's growing recognition as a serious partner in the international sustainable development debate is a result of its continuing efforts to build a coherent agenda that strikes a balance between the different challenges that are faced by our contemporary societies, in particular the need for ensuring social justice, rights and a more equal world, within the boundaries defined by the limited natural resource endowment of our planet.

From Vienna to Vancouver

In the context of 2011, the programme that was adopted by the ITUC Founding Congress might appear a rather timid statement of intent. It nevertheless provided the essential foundations for building ITUC environmental policies in the years that followed. If the process cannot be separated from the policy discussions, it was important to open new grounds and give legitimacy to the group of trade unionists that was active on environmental issues. This exercise led to a significant improvement in the ITUC's and its affiliates' positions on environmental issues, which in turn was reflected in 2010, the year in which the ITUC adopted its first resolution on the need to combat climate change through sustainable development and just transition measures.

The resolution offers the ITUC's position and policy recommendations to international institutions and national governments. The linkages between environmental degradation and the economic and social crises are now clear: '[the current economic model is] socially unjust, environmentally unsustainable and economically inefficient, incapable of providing decent work and decent lives to millions of people' (ITUC 2010, 1). For the first time in its history, the ITUC adopted a climate policy that goes beyond the immediate, job-related aspects of environmental policies.[3]

Although this first section gives a sense of accomplishment and progress, it is important not to forget that important debates are currently underway within the trade union movement. These debates are related to ongoing discussions about the movement's belief in the need for and ability to develop an alternative economic model, and the extent to which a new model should incorporate environmental issues.

Will a union-based paradigm shift solve environmental issues? Tensions and challenges for the international labour movement

In the current context of crises, the trade union movement has recognised the limits of our current economic model. In most of its international activities, the connections between the international economic crisis and the environmental crisis (particularly climate change) have been made. The idea that technological progress will not be sufficient to reach the necessary changes in our production and consumption models is gradually spreading. So there is a belief that we must collectively undertake a 'paradigm shift', even if the boundaries of this shift still have to be defined.

Despite these changes, controversies relating to the extent of the transformation that is needed still need to be addressed. While most trade unions accept that some changes are necessary and possible within the boundaries of the current economic system if we are to adequately address its intrinsically socially and environmentally destructive characteristics, the degree to which changes are necessary remains an open question.

Trade unions will have to engage in this debate and find a common political ground to build global environmental union policies. Two schools of thought are emerging within the research community, and both have had a significant impact on the labour movement.

Green growth versus no growth, is this the debate?

On the one hand, there is the so-called 'ecological modernisation' school, whose core assumption is that modernisation and growth should not have a detrimental effect on the environment. According to this theory, the current environmental crisis should be interpreted as a direct consequence of institutional and market failures. Reforming institutions and markets are the keys to environmental improvement as 'existing political, economic and social institutions can internalize the care for the environment' (Hajer 1995, 25). Markets can be greened if the externalities of economic production and processes on the environment are priced.

This theory has a few advantages. A green growth is a better alternative than a business-as-usual growth. It can revitalise the economy in periods of economic decline (jobs, investments, innovation). Green growth can also have a positive effect on markets and investments in the field of adaptation. Ecological modernists believe that resource efficiency can drive cheaper production and economic growth through reduced natural resource consumption, and from a labour perspective, it might imply less pressures over labour costs' reductions. However, resource efficiency is not sufficient to reduce the carbon intensity of our economies (Jackson 2010, 64).

This theory (which could also be called 'green growth theory') has numerous drawbacks from a trade union perspective. It excessively relies on markets: 'The market is a more efficient and effective mechanism for coordinating the tackling of environmental problems than the state' (Mol 1995, 46–47); it also tends to downplay 'issues of social justice and the processes of social inclusion and exclusion' (Swyngedouw and Cook 2009, 12).

In some countries, mentioned below, the labour movement has transformed the ecological modernisation theory in such a manner as to adapt it to the interests of workers and to the long-term goal of transforming the current economic model. In the United States, the United Steelworkers (USW), for instance, have developed a particular approach to ecological modernisation that, in a number of ways, directly challenges neoliberalism, advocating for a strong expansion of the state through investments in green sectors and job retraining programmes. At the European level, the European Trade Union

Confederation (ETUC) developed a framework for a Green New Deal. To a large extent, the ITUC's promotion of green investment policies can be seen as part of this framework. However, the strong regulatory approach, as well as the 'decent work' imperative, is there to ensure the link with a systemic change is not lost.

Other criticisms of Green Growth draw on the inherent contradictions between the current economic model and the need to protect the environment. These approaches call for an end to the 'productivist logic' and embrace simpler and less materialistic ways of life. Some of the research in this context explores linkages with labour rights, including shorter working hours, more leisure time. However, the labour movement is generally less receptive to these approaches as these are often perceived as being 'anti-development' or 'anti-social'.

Criticisms of the Green Growth paradigm's capacity to address the question of environmental scarcity are addressed by trade unions through a different angle, one that focuses on the way in which the distribution of natural resources is organised. The priority for unions is to address the uneven distribution of these limited resources. ITUC inputs in international debates on green growth have focused on the ways to redistribute economic and environmental assets in a manner that is both fair (between and within countries) and which achieves greater social and environmental justice (ITUC 2011).

New emergent approaches are also to be acknowledged, as their ideas are at the origin of debates in the labour movement, including Tim Jackson's ideas of 'Prosperity without Growth' (2009) and of 'Greenhouse Development Rights' (Baer *et al.* 2008), which focus on the ways by which societies can better share their natural resources (in this case 'carbon space') while simultaneously enabling development. If both models introduce interesting dynamics, the extent to which they incorporate traditional trade union values and demands – new rights and decent work – still needs to be clarified. However, they enable some discussion that goes beyond the usual confrontation between pro-growth and anti-growth.

If 'green growth' advocates are not always 'socially responsive', there is still an inherent benefit in taking part in a 'green economy' debate. By doing so, we can hope to define what kind of 'green economy' we want by making sure that social justice and job potential aspects are addressed. In the first place, it gives trade unions an opportunity to act as a potential bridge between those who promote a transformational agenda and those who would rather promote policies that are in line with the dominant growth model. This is of particular importance, taking into account the potentially growing gap between trade union leaders, aware of the environmental crisis, and shop stewards, who might still perceive these issues as marginal to their 'core' responsibilities.

Second, the debate is of practical interest to the trade union movement from the moment that it helps workers to grasp the linkages between environmental sustainability and social justice. This being said, we must be able to depart from growth-centred debates. Thinking 'outside the box' is challenging but is necessary if we are to ensure that our societies will prosper and be more socially just in a resource-limited world.

One of the biggest challenges faced by trade unions is to define the expected outcomes of the just transition processes, and particularly the type of society we would like to pass down to future generations. This requires a better integration of union approaches towards the environment into the new sustainable development model.

Long-term challenges

The challenges that lie ahead for the trade union movement can seem daunting. The economic crisis is far from over, and neo-liberal and anti-union thinking is spreading once again at the national and international levels, in an attempt to use the crisis as an engine for a new round of labour market deregulation. Discussions on the inclusion of environmental issues cannot be isolated from this reality.

Having said this, a number of challenges need to be addressed, including the need to ensure coherence between ambitious international labour commitments on some topics and trade union national actions, the need to develop more and new thinking on emerging environmental topics and their linkages to trade union action, building an autonomous and coherent position when it comes to dealing with the private sector, including transnational companies, and the difficulty to engage on an international scene where multilateral governance is going through a deep crisis, and little progress can be achieved.

Building coherence between the international and national levels

As we have seen before, the ITUC and its affiliates are in agreement when it comes to promoting ambitious environmental policies. It is important to note that this was not the consequence of a 'hidden' negotiation between a handful of powerful unions. On the contrary, the level of participation was extremely high for an international trade union negotiation (around 40 per cent of the submissions from national centres to the ITUC draft statements on climate change were sent from developing countries' unions). Such a high 'degree of ambition' was also possible thanks to the abstract character and little degree of national specificity of the documents. This has certainly helped to build a united, solid position on environmental topics, in particular on climate change.

Unions were aware of the consequences of the commitments expressed on the ITUC resolution on climate change. For instance, a 25–40 per cent reduction of emissions by developed countries by 2020, based on 1990 emissions, meant that European countries would have to go beyond the 20 per cent target (if they are to share the burden of reductions in a fair manner). Equally, supporting a 2°C limit in temperature rise, or as it is mentioned in the Congress resolution, exploring trade union support for a 1.5°C limit, implies, in some emerging economies, peaking emissions within the next five years. This clearly highlights where the challenges will lie in the coming months and years: maintaining momentum within the international labour movement and ensuring that, when debates are organised at the national level, trade union centres respect their international commitments towards their fellow trade union partners and the ITUC.

This is of course not an easy task for an international organisation and the ITUC was not set up to judge the practices of its affiliates. Yet, collectively, trade unions will have to find a way of ensuring a follow-up to their own commitments. At the national level, this task is also complicated by the reactions of sectoral unions that have no or little commitment to the broader climate agenda, and can therefore put pressure on national centres or directly on governments (even if this generally is not part of their mandate). Often, this happens due to the real or perceived threat to their industries that climate policies might pose. Nonetheless, this is a reason to develop further knowledge on those impacts and promote a 'just transition' agenda, rather than the potential disengagement arising from conflicts between different union members. Building cohesion and solidarity within the country's workforce and between sectors is a crucial element for achieving coherence at the international level.

International trade union policy making on environmental policies is only starting

Trade union positions on climate change, just transition, green/decent jobs or even sustainable chemicals' management have become increasingly recognised. The ITUC has spent years developing trade union positions that respect the movement's diversity without falling in the trap of a 'lowest common denominator' approach. These policies are of particular significance if we take into account the fact that they are the product of the trade union movement – and not of external forces. They were developed by trade unionists themselves and grounded on the scarce available data. This effort was also possible because in parallel, and as we explained in the first section, important efforts were made to increase trade unions' awareness on the issues at stake, and research was starting to be organised on those topics other actors did not explore before (i.e. on the employment effects of climate change). Ensuring that trade unions had an autonomous view was not an easy task, but there is a perception that on the issues mentioned above, this objective has been fulfilled.

However, it goes without saying that the amount and diversity of the environmental challenges that surround us is far greater than the issues that have been taken up by the labour movement. The loss of biodiversity, deforestation, water scarcity or 'cross-cutting' issues such as energy, mining or sustainable consumption, still need to be addressed. There are also policy gaps in issues already discussed by trade unions. This is the case, for instance, with climate-related issues such as 'green taxation' or the different aspects of the 'just transition' framework when adapted to different national contexts. Other issues need further exploration. At the international level, for example, work will be needed in areas relating to the 'traditional' trade union agenda of collective bargaining and rights. A lot of work still remains to be done on the environmental rights that could be developed, or on the ways unions can incorporate environmental protection into their collective bargaining processes.

There is an additional aspect of this challenge, related to the risk of *appropriation and/or de-politisation* of the 'just transition' idea. Trade unions can measure the extent of their success by analysing the important amount of organisations that support the concept today. However, this success comes with the need to ensure a vibrant debate with other groups (other social movements, environmental NGOs, governments) and keeping the concept 'in movement' while still reflecting trade union concerns.

Maintain international union mobilisation when multilateral governance is at crisis

Progress by trade unions on 'old' and emerging environmental issues is also challenged today by the multilateral system, which can currently be characterised as having low ambitions and being slow in progress. International climate negotiations are a good example of this.

The process that led to COP15 in Copenhagen, Denmark in 2009 was key in consolidating the trade union position as well as the commitment of affiliates towards the issue. And it would not be surprising if in the close future, the international labour movement faced a moment of 'disengagement' from international climate politics if some momentum is not brought back to the negotiations. It also has to be noted that a lack of progress in the international climate regime will have profoundly unjust consequences for the poorest of the planet. This, in turn, can also lead to the radicalisation of certain movements in the developing world – notably those active under the Climate Justice Network – and potentially weaken the alliance between Northern and Southern trade unions.

The challenge of rethinking work under a new paradigm

Incorporating environmental concerns into an 'alternative' trade union approach constitutes an important challenge for the movement; a challenge that could imply a redefinition of certain aspects of trade union identities. Perceptions of workers, as well as the evolutions in certain traditionally unionised sectors of the economy, will have a significant impact on the path taken by international trade unions' environmental policies. A different growth paradigm, like those introduced in our second section, will imply different production models and thus a different role for workers and their representatives. Building a new vision of what a sustainable economy looks like for workers and trade unions, and doing it in such a way that fosters progress today, is possibly the biggest challenge for the international trade union confederation.

Conclusion

Giant steps have been made in building an international position for the labour movement on environmental issues. In this regard, the ITUC played a key role in bringing together a cross-sectoral, cross-regional perspective, based on solidarity between countries (which implied a concerted effort to ask developed countries to take the lead on climate change, as well as within countries, through the 'just transition' framework).

These steps can only be conceived as part of a longer process, in which the labour movement will have to strengthen its engagement with certain issues where it is already involved, incorporate more issues and develop its policies in order to address them, and most importantly, better introduce environmental concerns into the alternative economic model that it is trying to build.

Notes

1 These are excerpts from another article: 'Building a Just Transition: The linkages between climate change and employment', published in 'Climate change and Labour: the need for a Just Transition', *International Journal of Labour Research*, Geneva, International Labour Office, 2010, 125–62.
2 Early mentions of Just Transition can also be found in ICFTU, *Plough to Plate Approaches to Food and Agriculture* (2000), www.icftu.org/www/english/els/escl00 foodagr.html (accessed 24 July 2012); ICFTU, *Fashioning A New Deal – Workers and Trade Unions at the World Summit for Sustainable Development* (2002), www.unep.org/Search.asp?cx=007059379654755265211%3Ajkngxjgnyii&cof=FORID% 3A11&q=fashioning+a+new+deal&sa=Go+! (accessed 24 July 2012).
3 It 'expresses, for example, strong support for the IPCC scenario for reducing global GHG emissions to 85% by the year 2050 and emphasises the need for interim targets for this to be achieved'. It also 'insists that the US$ 85 billion per year from 2013 to 2017 that the UN considers necessary in public funding for adequate adaptation by developing countries be made available' (ITUC 2010, 2–3).

References

Baer, P., Athanasiou, T., Kartha, S. and Kemp-Benedict, E. (2008) *The Greenhouse Development Rights Framework. The right to development in a climate constrained world*. Publication Series on Ecology – Volume I. Published by the Heinrich Boll Foundation, Christian Aid, EcoEquity and the Stockholm Environment Institute. Revised Second Edition. Berlin, November.

Hajer, M. A. (1995) *The Politics of Environmental Discourse: Ecological modernization and the policy process*. Oxford: Oxford University Press.

International Labour Organisation (ILO) (2012) *Global Employment Trends 2012*. Geneva: International Labour Office.

International Trade Union Confederation (ITUC) (2006) Programme of the ITUC, Adopted by the Founding Congress of the ITUC Vienna, 1–3 November.

——(2008) 'Trade unions and climate change: Equity, justice & solidarity in the fight against climate change', www.ituc-csi.org/IMG/pdf/climat_EN_Final.pdf (accessed 24 July 2012).

——(2009a) *Green & Decent Jobs. Making the 'Green Economy' work for Social*, available from: http://actrav-courses.itcilo.org/en/a352647/copy3_of_a352647-presentations/ituc-green-jobs/at_download/file (accessed 31 May 2011).

——(2009b) *A Just Transition: A fair pathway to protect the climate*, available from: http://cc2010.mx/assets/001/5232.pdf (accessed 31 May 2011).

——(2010) *Resolution on combating climate change through sustainable development and just transition*, available from: www.ituc-csi.org/resolution-on-combating-climate.html (accessed 31 May 2011).

——(2011) 'Submission to the UN Conference on Sustainable Development (Rio+20)', available from: www.uncsd2012.org/rio20/index.php?page=view&type=510&nr=42&menu=115 (accessed 31 January 2012).

——(2012) *Oil Union Leader Assassinated in Colombia*. ITUC Online, available from: www.ituc-csi.org/oil-union-leader-assassinated-in.html?lang=en (last accessed 31 January 2012).

Jackson, T. (2010). 'Poussés au bord du gouffre écologique'. *Rue 89*, 3 October, 64.

——(2009) 'Prosperity without Growth', Sustainable Development Commission, March.

Mol, A. P. J. (1995) *The Refinement of Production*. Utrecht: Van Arkel.

Rosemberg, A. (2010). 'Building a Just Transition: The linkages between climate change and employment'. *International Journal of Labour Research*, 2 (2): 125–62.

Swyngedouw, E. and Cook, I. R. (2009) *Cities, social cohesion and the environment. Social Polis Survey Paper*, available from: www.sed.manchester.ac.uk/geography/staff/documents/Cities_social_cohesion_and_environment.pdf (accessed 4 October 2010).

United Nations (UN) (1992) *Agenda 21*, available from: www.un.org/esa/dsd/agenda21/res_agenda21_00.shtml (accessed 26 May 2010).

UNEP (2006) 'Final resolution of the Trade Union Assembly at its first meeting', Trade Union Assembly on Labour and the Environment, First meeting, Nairobi, 15–17 January.

UNFCCC (2011) 'Cancun Agreements: Outcome of the work of the Ad Hoc Working Group on Long-term Cooperative Action under the Convention', Bonn, Germany, http://unfccc.int/files/meetings/cop_16/application/pdf/cop16_lca.pdf (accessed 24 July 2012).

3 From sustainable development to a green and fair economy

Making the environment a trade union issue

Laura Martín Murillo

In recent decades, the areas of labour and environment have experienced an unprecedented coming together, where trade union organisations now discuss and propose environmental policies in a progressively more decisive manner. It seems that little by little trade unionism has overcome its historical legacy: a movement born out of the industrial revolution, of the combustion engine, a movement that was proudly started and continues to have its heart in the mines, in the major steel mills and in manufacturing. This legacy has contributed to maintaining labour and environmental movements apart, often clashing over conflicts of interests, just like on many occasions social and environmental concerns have clashed when making economic decisions.

To a certain extent, this coming together of both labour and environment is due to a current global context in which it is difficult to ignore environmental challenges when making economic proposals. As we shall see later, in this sense trade unions have been compelled to take on an agenda that used to be alien to them: current socio-economic decisions need to include environmental limits in their equations.

But it would be unfair to assume that this was only an obligation imposed by external trends. The incorporation of environmental issues by trade unions has had important and innovative results: new debates have been opened, such as a better addressing of the fairness angle in environmental agendas, the need to create jobs when transitioning to a greener economy, or the importance to decide not just the final objectives, but rather how we want to achieve these objectives, summarised by unions in the successful concept of 'just transition'.

Especially following the financial crisis that began in 2008, trade unions around the world have joined in calling for a greener, job-oriented and sustainable economy. This call was taken up in the discourses of governments and international institutions, though unfortunately it has not been carried out into practice.

Trade union proposals that integrate environmental protection are an important part of a unionism that goes beyond defending the interests of its members and aims to offer proposals for society as a whole and for the different societies that inhabit the planet and that, more and more, aims to offer comprehensive development proposals, overcoming the difficulties that globalisation has caused.

This article looks at the recent history of the evolution of trade union action on environmental issues, especially at an international level but also at national and local levels; a history set in the 20 years since the Rio Summit (1992). Now, in reviewing the commitments of this historic summit, the specifics of trade union proposals can offer interesting insights.

Sustainable development: our common future, our common framework

The term sustainable development was formally used in the document known as the Brundtland Report (United Nations 1987), the result of work by the World Commission on Environment and Development, and was defined as a development that seeks to satisfy the needs of present generations without compromising the ability of future generations to meet their own needs (United Nations 1987; Smith and Rees 1998). In this report sustainable development was defined as a development made up of three pillars: economic, social and environmental development. This definition has remained more or less valid to this day (WHO 2005).

The inclusion of trade union organisations into this framework was facilitated right from the beginning by the recognition of trade union organisations as one of the nine main groups necessary for the implementation plan of the Rio summit, known as Agenda 21 (UNDESA 1992). Agenda 21 recognised the need for a participative approach to sustainable development (Allen 2001) and the need for the most important social groups to be involved in decision making and the execution of agreements, including trade union organisations. Agenda 21 also included a chapter on the need to increase trade union participation, a rare thing in United Nations agreements.

For the world of work the action undertaken in this new field of sustainable development included the following fundamental areas:

Reinforcing the social dimension of the agenda (ILO 2003).

- Incorporating employment rights and decent work as a fundamental part of the sustainable development agenda. Trade union organisations participated in both the international field and in the national sustainable development commissions set up by governments in order to monitor the Sustainable Development Commission, bringing the principles of decent work to these forums and pushing for an increase in the profile of the social pillar.
- Incorporating sustainable development into trade union action at all levels. In both the national headquarters and sector federations, the occupational health and environmental departments became the recipients of this area of work and were responsible for disseminating it within the organisations.

The Johannesburg Summit (2002) ten years later was intended to monitor and renew the commitments, helping to ensure that they were met. This summit was used to consolidate the theoretical framework, but also attempted to specifically make it operational. As part of the effort to implement the framework, the objectives of the Johannesburg Plan of Implementation were agreed. Many trade unionists participated at this summit; around 300 attended and some labour issues were included in the final text, above all those relating to the fundamental principles of the ILO, occupational health issues and the need for a closer relationship between jobs and changes in production and consumption (ICFTU/TUAC/ITS 2002).

Perhaps the most positive development during all these years of work on sustainable development has been the recognition of the need for coherent and integrated approaches to the issues. The European Trade Union Confederation (ETUC) and the International Confederation of Free Trade Unions (ICFTU) made a great deal of use of the sustainable development model, both creating extremely dynamic working groups on sustainable development. Since its establishment in November 2006, the International Trade Union Confederation – ITUC – has taken sustainable development on board as a fundamental paradigm of its global proposal:

> In order to achieve the permanent aspirations of the Confederation, it is essential for neoliberal free market policies and the incoherence of the manifest failures of the international community with regard to the current globalisation process, to give way to appropriate governance of the global economy which:
>
> • Combines the three pillars of sustainable development: economic, social and environmental;
> • Guarantees universal respect of workers' fundamental rights;
> • Creates decent work for everyone …
>
> (ITUC 2006)

However, the most negative development could be the fact that sustainable development has remained a 'theoretical approach to reality' and has resulted in only a low number of concrete union policies. The integration of the three variables has led to significant methodological difficulties. Recognising the interaction of the different facets and the appropriateness of an integrated approach does not mean that we are capable of establishing priorities, for example. Although everything is necessary, where should we start? When there is a conflict between social and environmental needs, where should we set the priorities? On occasion, these difficulties have unfortunately led to sustainable development becoming a battlefield among those aiming to promote social, environmental or economic improvements, rather than it being used as a space from which it is possible to produce balanced specific proposals. Regrettably at the Rio + 20 negotiations many NGOs and governments still started their statements reminding us that sustainable development is fundamentally about development, while some environmental NGOs emphasised that Rio was the

Earth Summit and that sustainable development is only possible if we focus on the environment.

Not just promoting sustainable development, taking the environment on board

As part of the trade union action on sustainable development, two areas of activity have been fundamental for it to be translated into specific actions: the first is the participation of trade union organisations in the protection of the environment; the second is the inclusion of labour interests in environmental debates.

Climate change in particular has since 2007 symbolised the scale of the challenge facing us and the continuity of our societies as we know them. It has probably been the only one of the global multilateral negotiations where there was the possibility of an ambitious agreement and far-reaching paradigm change, although in the end these expectations were frustrated in Copenhagen. Both factors – the seriousness of the problem and the expectations of a multi-lateral agreement – have acted as catalysts for many social players outside the field of environmental movements (e.g., faith groups, development organisations), to unite in an unprecedented mobilisation.

One of the most fundamental events that influenced the inclusion of environmental issues into the agenda of the international labour movement, and into the ITUC founding programme, was the First Trade Union Assembly on Labour and Environment organised by the United Nations Environment Programme (UNEP) and Sustainlabour (UNEP 2006). This meeting was attended by 104 representatives of trade union organisations at the highest level who agreed by means of a resolution to strengthen the links between the reduction of poverty, protection of the environment and decent work. The meeting focused specifically on the environment and addressed concrete areas: climate change, chemical risk, water management and corporate social responsibility, and was organised in a context of the unification of the international labour movement into the future ITUC. It was not only a question of moving towards a new international trade union structure but of configuring a new trade unionism in which environmental protection and sustainable development would play a substantial role (Nieto 2007).

Climate change: a global threat and a concrete example for union action

In December 2007, the ITUC decided to prioritise climate change as its important line of action in the overall union agenda. The meeting in Nairobi and the increasing effect of climate change marked a radical change in the ITUC's agenda. It is testament to the way in which scientific evidence and personal experience regarding the reality of climate change, as well as the recognition of the dramatic and potentially catastrophic consequences resulting from measures not being taken, have radically transformed the political agenda, so that climate change now appears among the main priorities of the ITUC (see ITUC 2007).

Trade union mobilisation for an international climate change agenda increased significantly at the Bali summit (December 2007), and it was at this meeting where trade unionists 'earned' their status as an observer organisation at the United Nations Convention. Seventy-five trade unionists attended this meeting, representing 60 world organisations from 22 countries. It was the last successful meeting of the convention, at which it was believed that the groundwork for the future Copenhagen Agreement had been laid down (Rosemberg 2010).

This meeting also saw the presentation for the first time of an important trade union declaration with an agreement on ambitious emission reduction targets, which was negotiated for months and received numerous contributions from national trade unions. The final version of the declaration was approved by the ITUC General Council in 2007. Beyond recognising that development must be sustainable, the ITUC also had a clear policy on climate change, with specific proposals to comply with the environmental and social integrity of the process (ITUC 2007).

From that year onwards it could be said that the trade union organisations became increasingly important among the observers of the climate convention, eventually becoming major players at the last summit in Copenhagen. On this occasion more than 400 trade unionists gathered in Denmark to support an ambitious agreement and ensure that labour issues were included in the new text, particularly in relation to just transition (ITUC 2009). This mass presence had its results; despite the fact that no official text was approved, the text negotiated by the governments at the convention, supported by each and all of the country groups and still discussed at the 2010 meetings, includes the main trade union demand at the climate summit: a reference to the need for a just transition for the workforce. This was an impressive result of the efforts of the ITUC and many national and international trade unionists. Part of this success was due to the trade union position adopted for the negotiations that addressed the different economic and social aspects of the climate crisis.

Addressing climate change has entailed a significant advance in the trade union movement's contribution to sustainable development. Its specificity and immediacy has offered an opportunity to propose and develop concrete policies (such as concrete targets for GHG emission reduction), to seek integrating solutions, resolving conflicts and reconciling interests (through mitigation-related just transition measures). Sustainable development established the framework; the focus on climate change represented a real exercise in how to move towards it. Working on a specific issue also necessarily meant facing up to its difficulties and contradictions, looking honestly at tensions, rather than hiding behind an integrated approach, which, if it does not face up to conflicts, will be devoid of meaning.

Beyond climate change: towards a fair, green economy

Trade union action on climate change opened up another new line of research: the so-called green jobs investigation. In fact, it was largely thanks to the promotion of the ITUC that UNEP and the ILO commissioned the first study on green jobs, which found an important space in the discussions of the latest economic crisis and strategies towards recovery (UNEP 2008).

The context of multiple climate, food, financial and employment crises seen since 2007 means that new ideas are being sought to help tackle the various challenges faced. The banking crisis created a further opportunity to make a reality of sustainability by rethinking the fundamentals of our economic system (Rosemberg and Verheecke 2011). Specific practices for recovery measures had to be proposed and a call for investment in green and decent jobs was required. There was a need to get out of the crisis by means of a cleaner, greener economy that created decent quality jobs in order to eradicate poverty.

In this context, a broad group of economists, researchers, trade unions and politicians called for a Green New Deal (Lovell 2008; Friedman 2007a, 2007b). The Green New Deal and the transition towards a green economy were widely promoted by unions from different countries and sectors (ITUC 2009; FNV and Natuur und Milieu 2009; AFL-CIO 2008; CCOO 2009; ACTU 2008).

One of the most important results of this union strategy calling for a green economy is that it has brought the decent employment agenda to international spheres where it had not previously been addressed. As unions were part of the proponents in the definition of the green new economy to save the planet, the need to respect labour rights has been included *from the start of the discussions.*

It should also be taken into account that the green economy has been chosen as a fundamental issue in the review of the Rio agreements to take place in Brazil in 2012, the so-called Rio + 20 summit. This will provide the issue with important visibility in the coming years.

As we have already seen, the ITUC has made a determined effort to incorporate the issue. At its last conference in Vancouver (ITUC 2010), the Resolution on Combating Climate Change through Sustainable Development and Just Transition was approved, as was a framework resolution on a fair and sustainable development model for the twenty-first century.

Moving the national agenda forward

In order to transform this theory into practice for union work, environmental or sustainable development structures were created in numerous trade union organisations. Initially, at the beginning of the 1990s, they were set up as part of occupational health departments, for various reasons. First, because there are obvious links between occupational health, community health and environmental conditions (Foster 2010); and second, because the occupational health departments were those responsible for taking care of the internal environment and it is relatively easy to transfer concerns for the internal environment to the external environment. Lastly, these occupational health departments in principle also had the technical knowledge necessary to introduce often complex environmental issues (Nieto 2007).

Through these structures, and for most OECD countries, fundamentally in Europe, but also in Canada, the United States, Japan or Australia, those in charge of the environment and sustainable development were essentially responsible for making their members aware of the problem, offering basic training and beginning to define the implications of environmental policies for trade union action. As time went on, developing countries also joined up, such as Brazil, Argentina and Uruguay: now an increasingly large number of trade union organisations have a department or at least a person responsible for the environment or sustainable development.

These structures were used to attempt to make trade unionists aware of the need to go beyond the traditional opposition between work and the environment, which was a consequence of the weight of major polluting industries in the trade union fabric.

When making environment a trade union issue, the approach taken has varied from sector to sector; the chemical industry paved the way for combined occupational health and environmental committees and workers' participation in environmental issues, and has thus been the first to recognise workers' environmental rights. Strong actions have been undertaken by the unions representing workers in the dirtiest and most dangerous industries, including steel, aluminium, copper and lead smelting, chemicals and mining, all industries well known for occupational diseases (Foster 2010). However, others such as the services or banking sectors have paid less attention to the issue, as their work has a less significant impact on the environment (Sustainlabour 2010).

Different regions have also taken different approaches, particularly in relation to the issues included in the work of these departments: in industrialised countries, action has been based on reducing the environmental impact of production activities and on the combination of the protection of industrial jobs with environmental legislation. In developing countries, however, activities are more focused on defining a development model, protecting communities, negotiating the sovereignty of natural resources or fighting against the double standards of multinationals (Martín Murillo 2011).

Beyond awareness raising: restructuring, green industrialisation and a just transition

Another important problem with the relationship between trade union action and environmental degradation is due precisely to the ever-greater importance of environmental legislation in production activities. The need to move towards cleaner production involves changes in industrial forms of production that may be undertaken by workers: for example, new skills could be required or we might see industrial dislocations, etc. Trade union organisations concerned about the long-term sustainability of their jobs must be able to understand what the expected changes are, increase their ability to influence the production system from within in order to guarantee the jobs of the future and ensure that these jobs are environmentally and socially sustainable.

For many years the environmental information to which workers' representatives had access was exclusively that provided to them by companies. A lack of technical skills and lack of interest in addressing the issues have made workers easy prey for company alarmism claiming that jobs would be threatened, which has on numerous occasions been used to fight improvements in environmental legislation. However, a better understanding of the reality enables workers to participate in the necessary changes, for example, by demanding the investment or workforce training necessary, the instruments with which the transition will be managed, or demanding democracy and transparency in decision making.

Today trade unions have significantly developed their agenda in this regard. In some industrialised countries the industry unions have seen the requirement to change production systems to ones that are cleaner and lower in carbon emissions as an opportunity for reindustrialisation. As explained for many years, manufactory unions have observed with great concern the moving of some companies and along with them their jobs, to the developing world where the salaries were lower and labour and environmental regulations were weaker. The most important negotiation tactic of the employers has been based on the threat to move production somewhere else.

The measures to combat climate change, however, impel the development of new technologies and new manufacturing, and several trade union organisations began to see an opportunity in this, for the creation of new industrial employment in their countries. This opportunity was consolidated under the term green jobs. As the leader of Steelworkers stated in 2009: 'Labor and environmental activists are pressing for the creation of green jobs as the way to re-industrialize the US' (Steelworkers 2009).

Steelworkers in the US, the TUC in the United Kingdom, the ACTU in Australia and RENGO in Japan, among others, have all launched pressure campaigns for direct investments towards the environmentally friendly sectors, mainly clean energy projects. But the aim of union participation in green jobs campaigns was also to be in a good starting position in the new sectors. As unions were lobbying for their creation, they were present from the beginning and could ensure that the new sectors were unionised.

As previously mentioned, the management of the transition is crucial. In recent years the ILO has carried out studies on social dialogue for managing transitions to low carbon economies. One of these is a case study on social negotiation tables in Spain (ILO 2010).

In this aspect, the concept of a just transition is crucial. If the production method has to be changed, trade unions demand participation in the decision making, justice in the decisions made, protection from the changes made and adaptation to local needs. The just transition, as mentioned, has even been recognised at the climate convention, but has increasingly become an extremely important theoretical concept for considering a change in the existing development model. This concept is possibly one of the most important trade union contributions to the debate on a new development model in recent years.

Meanwhile many trade unions in developing countries are undertaking major campaigns to introduce the recovery of natural resources as a public heritage. They demand to make the management of 'common' resources more transparent and participative, and fight for a more equitable distribution of such resources. Climate justice and environmental justice campaigns offer a response to these key areas. In Latin America and Africa a great number of organisations are working in this direction (Martín Murillo 2011).

Pushing for workplace tools for action: workers' environmental rights

One of the possible instruments to facilitate this work would be the recognition of environmental rights (ISTAS/CCOO 2006). In some parts of the world (some sectors in Spain, the United Kingdom, Argentina and Brazil), workers have earned the right to participate in environmental issues. In some companies, above all in the chemical sector and to a certain degree also in the metal industry, agreements have introduced clauses relating to the environment (Fiteqa 2004). Even in the international framework agreements signed by International Federations and multinationals there is a large proportion of clauses on sustainable development and the environment (for example, 30.5 per cent of international framework agreements include specific clauses on the environment). These clauses are intended to homogenise standards in the different countries, but also to recognise workers' participation in the monitoring of targets (ILO 2010).

Many national headquarters and federations also offer advice and disseminate good practices on how to introduce environmental clauses in collective agreements. In Spain, the United Kingdom, United States or Canada, for example, trade unions use action on the environment as a way of gaining new members; workers who had not before approached the union, but for whom the work being carried out offers renewed reasons for joining up (ISTAS/CCOO 2006; TUC 2008; SEIU 2008; CUPE 2007).

For example the CUPE green bargaining guide gives examples of green language and shows CUPE locals key areas to consider for bargaining on environmental provisions into their collective agreements.

Greening the workplace makes sense because:

- Cutting back on greenhouse gas emissions helps fight climate change and improves the quality of the air we breathe. It also helps preserve a future for coming generations.
- A green union and workplace will appeal to young workers, who tend to be more environmentally aware and active.

- A green workplace saves money and resources that can be reinvested back into the workplace to improve working conditions.

Bargaining green provisions is a new direction for CUPE. Traditionally, bargaining focuses on wages, hours of work, job security, grievance procedures, workplace democracy and other issues. All of these add value to workers' lives. Green language will do the same. It will also help protect workers from the changes that are coming as Canada shifts away from an intense carbon-based economy.

(CUPE 2007)

Towards Rio + 20: unions renewing the sustainable development agenda

Twenty years after the exciting and historic United Nations Conference on Environment and Development (1992), Rio + 20 aimed to take stock of all that has been achieved and establishing an agenda to move forward. The principles of the original Rio Summit – the precautionary principle, the 'polluter pays' principle, that of common but differentiated responsibilities, the necessary participation of civil society in decision making – all represent a very important legacy as well as framework for the progress of our societies.

The advances made by unions, in suggesting original contributions to environmental problems, are now more relevant than ever. Labour and environmental movements will have to come together even more if they wish to propose integrated solutions within the framework of sustainable development. The debate on the green economy will have to combine solutions for the employment crisis and propose not only a greener economy, but also a fairer and more egalitarian one.

The labour movement is in this context advocating on the one hand an integrated approach to the problem, and, on the other, a need to propose specific policies to address the crisis in a coordinated manner. In preparation for Rio + 20, trade union organisations are proposing specific measures to meet social, economic and environmental objectives, such as promoting targets for creating green and decent jobs, strengthening and integrating environmental and fair fiscal policies and reinforcing social protection systems.

References

ACTU (2008) *Towards a Green New Deal: Economic stimulus and policy action for the double crunch*, Melbourne: Australian Council of Trade Unions, www.actu.org.au/Images/Dynamic/attachments/6252/Green%20New%20Deal%20statement%20-%20081202.pdf (accessed 26 February 2012).

AFL-CIO (2008) *AFL-CIO Executive Council Statement on Greening the Economy*, American Federation of Labor and Congress of Industrial Organizations, www.aflcio.org/aboutus/thisistheaflcio/ecouncil/ec03042008m.cfm (accessed 26 February 2012).

Allen, W. J. (2001) *Working together for environmental management: the role of information sharing and collaborative learning*. PhD thesis (Development Studies), Massey University, http://learningforsustainability.net/research/thesis/thesis_ch2.html#lin (accessed 27 February 2012).

CUPE (2007) *Green bargaining guide.* Ottawa: Canadian Union of Public Employees, http://cupe.ca/updir/ONLINE_Green_Bargaining_Guide-0.pdf (accessed 26 February 2012).

Fiteqa, CCOO (2004) La nueva política de productos Quimicos y el Sistema Reach. Una Cuestion estrategica para el Sindicalismo Europeo. Departamento de Medio Ambiente. Fiteqa, CCOO.

FNV and Natuur und Milieu (2009) *An agenda for green investments.* Utrecht: Natuur und Milieu, www.natuurenmilieu.nl/pdf/140.202.01_sociale_en_groene_investeringsagenda. pdf (accessed 27 February 2012).

Foster, D. (2010) 'Blue Green alliance: building a coalition for a green future in the United States'. *International Journal of Labour Research,* 2 (2): 233–44.

Friedman, T. L. (2007a) 'A Warning From The Garden', *New York Times,* 19 January, http://query.nytimes.com/gst/fullpage.html?res=9B06E5DD1E30F93AA25752-C0A9619C8B63 (accessed 27 February 2012).

Friedman, T. L. (2007b) 'The Power of Green', *The New York Times Magazine,* April 15, www.nytimes.com/2007/04/15/magazine/15green.t.html?_r=1&pagewanted=11&ex=1176868800&ei=5087&em&en=6d53d735b961773d&oref=slogin (accessed 27 February 2012).

ICFTU/TUAC/ITS (2002) *Framework for Action, Trade Union Priorities for the WSSD,* paper presented to the Commission on Sustainable Development, World Summit on Sustainable Development (Fourth Preparatory Session) 27 May–7 June, www.earthsummit2002.org/es/preparations/global/prep-comm4/Microsoft%20Word%20-%20PaperTUdraft2.pdf (accessed 27 February 2012).

ILO (2003) *Outcome of United Nations conferences: World Summit on Sustainable Development,* Committee on Employment and Social Policy, International Labour Office, Geneva, www.ilo.org/public/english/standards/relm/gb/docs/gb286/pdf/esp-4. pdf (accessed 27 February 2012).

——(2010) *The impact of climate change on employment, Management of transition through social dialogue.* Geneva: International Labor Organisation, www.ilo.org/wcmsp5/groups/public/@ed_emp/@emp_ent/documents/publication/wcms_158730. pdf (accessed 27 February 2012).

ISTAS/CCOO (2006) *La participación de los trabajadores y sus representantes en la protección del medio ambiente en el centro de trabajo,* Madrid: ISTAS www.istas. ccoo.es/descargas/Guia%20EGP01%20Participacion%20de%20los%20trabajadores. pdf (accessed 27 February 2012).

ITUC (2009) 'Trade Unions and Climate Change. Equity, justice and solidarity in the fight against climate change'. ITUC Statement, www.ituc-csi.org/convention-on-climate-change-cop15.html (accessed 27 February 2012).

——(2007) 'Declaración sindical a la COP13', www.ituc-csi.org/IMG/pdf/COP13_Statement-FLT455-PdC-ES.pdf (accessed 27 February 2012).

——(2010) *Now the people: from the crisis to social justice,* Second World Congress of the ITUC, Vancouver, 21–25 June, www.ituc-csi.org/IMG/pdf/Congress_theme_EN_FINAL.pdf (accessed 27 February 2012).

——(2006) 'Programme of the ITUC: Adopted by the Founding Congress of the ITUC Vienna', 1–3 November, www.ituc-csi.org/IMG/pdf/Programme_of_the_ITUC.pdf (accessed 27 February 2012).

Lovell, J. (2008) 'Climate report calls for green "New Deal"', July 21, *Reuters,* www.reuters. com/article/2008/07/21/us-climate-deal-idUSL204610020080721 (accessed 2 July 2012).

Martín Murillo, L. (2011) *Observatorio Regional de Centroamérica y República Dominicana (OLACD)*, www.empleo-foil.oit.or.cr/olacd/images/stories/publicaciones/ApuntesII_2011_5.pdf (accessed 27 February 2012).

Nieto, J. (2007) 'The trade union movement and environmental participation: shaping the change, renewing trade unionism.' *Labour and the environment: A natural synergy*, Nairobi: UNEP, pp. 24–40.

Rosemberg, A. (2010) 'Building a Just Transition. The linkages between climate change and employment'. *International Journal of Labour Research*, 2 (2): 125–161.

Rosemberg, A. and Verheecke, L. (2011) 'Green growth and the need for a paradigm shift: challenges for achieving social justice in a resource-limited world'. In D. Coats (ed.) *Exiting from the crisis: towards a model of more equitable and sustainable growth*, ETUI, pp. 235–42, www.tuac.org/en/public/e-docs/00/00/09/A2/document_doc.phtml (accessed 24 July 2012).

SEIU (2008) *Environmental Labor Management Committee Collective Bargaining Agreement Language.* Washington, DC: Service Employees International Union, www.seiu.org/a/ourunion/environmental-labor-management-committee-collective-bargaining-agreement-language.php (accessed 27 February 2012).

Smith, C. and Rees, G. (1998) *Economic Development.* Basingstoke: Macmillan.

Steelworkers (2009) Radio interview, www.radio4all.net/index.php/program/46466 (accessed 24 July 2012).

Sustainlabour (2010) *Occupational Health and Safety and Environmental Clauses in International Framework Agreements.* Madrid: Sustainlabour, www.sustainlabour.org/IMG/pdf/ifas_study_report – eng.pdf (accessed 27 February 2012).

TUC (2008) *Go Green at Work: A Handbook for Union Green Representatives.* London: Trade Union Confederation, www.tuc.org.uk/extras/gogreenatwork.pdf (accessed 2 July 2012).

UNDESA (1992) *Agenda 21.* New York: UN Department of Economic and Social Affairs, www.un.org/esa/dsd/agenda21/res_agenda21_29.shtml (accessed 27 February 2012).

UNEP (2008) *Green jobs, towards decent work in a sustainable low carbon world.* www.unep.org/labour_environment/PDFs/Greenjobs/UNEP-Green-Jobs-Report.pdf (accessed 27 February 2012).

——(2006) *Final Resolution of the Trade Union Assembly on Labour and the Environment*, Nairobi, Kenya, 15–17 January, www.unep.org/labour_environment/publications/index.asp (accessed 27 February 2012).

United Nations (1987) 'Report of the World Commission on Environment and Development'. General Assembly Resolution 42/187, 11 December, www.un.org/documents/ga/res/42/ares42-187.htm/ (accessed 24 July 2012).

WHO (2005) *World Summit Outcome*, World Health Organization, 15 September, www.who.int/hiv/universalaccess2010/worldsummit.pdf (accessed 27 February 2012).

4 The International Labour Organization and the environment

The way to a socially just transition for workers

Lene Olsen and Dorit Kemter

Introduction

Since its creation in 1919 the International Labour Organization (ILO) has been at the forefront of the struggle for social justice, promoting internationally recognised human and labour rights. The ILO's role is to advance the creation of decent work and the economic and working conditions that give its constituents – governments, workers and employers – a stake in lasting peace, prosperity and progress. Its main aims are to promote rights at work, encourage decent employment opportunities, enhance social protection and strengthen dialogue on work-related issues (ILO 2011a). To do this, its tripartite structure provides a unique platform for promoting decent work for all women and men.

This mandate is all-important today, taking into account the deep economic, financial, social and environmental challenges the world is facing. ILO's work in the field of social justice is well known by many. Its role in environmental issues might be less recognised. Since 2008 the ILO has developed a wide-ranging programme dealing with green jobs – the Green Jobs Programme. However, a lot has also been done in the past, laying the ground for the work that is carried out today.

The ILO has actively participated in the long chain of environment and sustainable development activities within the UN system from the Stockholm UN Conference on the Human Environment (1972) to the upcoming Rio + 20 and the ongoing negotiations in advancing the implementation of the United Nations Framework Convention on Climate Change (UNFCCC) and the Kyoto Protocol.

This article will present ILO's involvement in environmental issues by linking its work to the major UN conferences since Stockholm. ILO discussions and resolutions have not only provided input to these meetings, but have also ensured its efficient participation in relevant meeting and its support to follow-up actions including specific programmes, projects and activities. Three main clusters of work can be recognised throughout the years. These are cooperation and collaboration within the UN system and other international and regional institutions; capacity building of the constituents; and linking the working conditions to the external environment – all this within the framework of the mandate of the ILO.

The significant work on International Labour Standards will not be included in this article, but a selection of standards particularly relevant for the environment have been included in Annex 1.

The UN Conference on the Human Environment, Stockholm, 1972

The first major international meeting on environment, held by the United Nations in Stockholm in 1972, was an event whose repercussions were felt in the ILO (Ghebali 1989).

In the same year and based on the initiative of the workers' group, the International Labour Conference (ILC)[1] adopted the *Resolution Concerning the Contribution of the International Labour Organization to the Protection and Enhancement of the Environment Related to Work* (ILO 1972) to define a possible ILO contribution to the international discussion on the working environment. The resolution emphasised that the working environment is an important and integral part of the human environment as a whole, since those factors that harm the working environment are also among the major pollutants of nature and of people's living environment. The resolution called for an extension of ILO research to such new areas as protection and improvement of the working environment in the various economic sectors and consideration of these problems by the ILO's industrial committees. It also invited the Governing Body of the ILO to place on the agenda of an early conference session the question of occupational safety and prevention on industrial accidents with a view to the adoption of new standards.[2]

Linking the working environment and the general environment

The ILO's early focus in this process was thus on the linkage between the ILO's activities related to the working environment and the general environment. The ILO's submission to the Conference (ILO 1971) had a special section *V. Development and Environment* focusing on participation of employers' and workers' organisations and other social institutions in activities for the protection of the human environment. It stressed the participation of constituents in the development of plans and policies; legislative actions; public information; education; research and training; and monitoring. Examples were also given on activities carried out by several trade union organisations worldwide.

For instance, a Department of Conservation and Resource Development was created within the United Automobile Workers' Union of the United States. The UAW has made a common cause with other organisations in efforts to improve American natural as well as human surroundings and to mobilise a national and world movement to stem the tide of pollution. The 22nd Constitutional Convention of the UAW, held in April 1970, emphasised the immediate need to force industry 'to accept responsibility for cleaning up the pollution and wastes its processes and products have created'. The UAW also co-sponsored, in June 1970 with the United Nations, a preparatory conference to the 1972 UN Conference on Man and His Environment in Stockholm. This marked the first time that a labour union had hosted an official UN activity.

Following the ILC and the Stockholm Conference in 1972, the ILO directed its attention towards the working environment and included the issue in the forthcoming ILCs.

The International Labour Conference in 1974 adopted for instance a resolution that affirmed the need for the ILO to '*work out a comprehensive and intensive approach to the problems of the working environment*'. In view of the global nature of the question, it called for the preparation, as a matter of urgency, of a '*coherent and integrated programme of ILO action*' (Ghebali 1989, 97f).

The year after, in 1975, the Director-General's concern to stimulate renewed ILO action in this field was reflected in his report published under the title *Making work more human*. Demonstrating that the scanty progress achieved in working conditions was due primarily to the absence of a strategy. The conference solemnly reaffirmed '*that the improvement of working conditions and environment and the wellbeing of workers remains the first and permanent mission of the ILO*' and endorses the DG's plan to launch a new international programme to promote or assist action to that end by member states. This resulted in the establishment of the *International Programme for the Improvement of Workers' Conditions and Environment* (referred to by its French acronym, PIACT) and further cooperation with UNEP.

At the ILO's Governing Body session in November 1975, the workers' representatives stressed the importance of standards for the protection of the environment. According to the workers' spokesperson, those standards have to be taken into account and applied particularly at the time of the establishment of a new industry. The employers' delegates, who shared that view, declared that they accepted their obligations relating to the environment in respect of new industries. Both trade unions and employers' organisations considered that an understanding of ecological factors could contribute to development and industrialisation not only because those factors are related to humanitarian considerations but also because they constitute an economic necessity (see ILO 1979).

Cooperation with UNEP and sustainable development

The Memorandum of Understanding (ILO 1977) signed in 1977 between the ILO and the United Nations Environment Programme (UNEP) recognised two important issues. The first was the need to promote the sustainable satisfaction of basic human needs everywhere and especially for those of the poorest categories of the population, thus giving attention to poverty and development. This issue was only given limited attention in Stockholm in 1972. It was not before the Brundtland Report, *Our Common Future*, was published (UNWCED 1987) that more prominent focus was given to the essential linkages between the three pillars: environment, economic and social development, through the concept of 'sustainable development' (Kohler 2010). The second issue was the need to promote awareness of environmental considerations in the ILO's ongoing education and training programmes and among workers' organisations. This was followed up in 1979 by a joint ILO/ UNEP workers' education manual entitled *Man and his working environment*, which was intended to *'help the trade union world and especially those engaged in workers' education to pass on to trade unionists a body of knowledge that will enable them to grasp environmental problems in their entirety'* (ILO 1979, V).

In 1980 the ILO in cooperation with UNEP convened a *Meeting of Workers' Organizations on the Environment* (ILO 1980a, 1980b).[3] It was attended by 21 participants. The World Health Organization (WHO), the International Confederation of Free Trade Unions (ICFTU), the World Confederation of Labour (WCL), the World Federation of Trade Unions (WFTU) and the International Confederation of Arab Trade Unions (ICATU) were represented observers.

The meeting gave the opportunity to trade union representatives – for the first time within an ILO/UNEP context – to state their view on a range of questions that directly affected the working environment; workers' living environment and natural environment. The meeting stressed the linkage between working conditions and the environment as a whole, but also the environmental problems requiring urgent action, such as toxic chemicals, uranium tailings, nuclear wastes, acid rain, atmospheric carbon dioxide, the pollution of oceans and the mismanagement of marine resources. Issues that still preoccupy workers' organisations and the ILO today.

The report to the meeting noted the growing concern about *'the steady rise of carbon dioxide in the atmosphere, which may rise the average temperature if it continues unchecked, with a possible major change of the world's climate'*. Even though the concept of just transition was not yet mentioned as such, the need for transition measures was highlighted. It was said that an essential element of an environmental policy must include arrangements for workers adversely affected, either by financial compensation, a contribution to the cost of moving to another home, retraining with pay in order to qualify for another job, early retirement without loss of benefits or other adjustment measures. Together with the importance of consultation these elements were also included in the meeting's recommendations.

Extract of Recommendations from the Meeting of Workers' Organizations on the Environment

3. In the development planning process and decisions related to location and design of industrial plants, there should be **full and continuous consultation** with representative organisations of workers; this consultation

should include the **right to information and to participation** in the decisions in the field of working and general environment.

4. Governments should adopt and implement positive environmental policies, where appropriate **in consultation with workers, employers** and should allocate sufficient resources to ensure adequate supervision, inspection and enforcement.

5. In the implementation of environmental standards, due consideration should be given to economic effects on certain branches and enterprises and the appropriate way to avoid disruption by proper management of necessary change. Workers rendered unemployed by pollution control measures should receive adequate adjustment assistance, including income maintenance, retraining and help in securing alternative employment. In 1980 the ILO in cooperation with UNEP convened a *Meeting of Workers' Organizations on the Environment* (ILO 1980a, 1980b, 39)

The meeting also highlighted that poverty is both a major cause and effect of environmental degradation in developing countries. It was agreed that workers' organisations should take a view on environmental problems that was broad in scope and long term.

The United Nations World Commission on Environment and Development (UNWCED) 1983

In 1983 the United Nations convened the World Commission on Environment and Development (WCED) to address the growing concern that environmental problems were global in nature and that it was in the common interest of all nations to establish policies for sustainable development, taking into account the essential linkages between the three pillars: environment, economic and social development. The main aim was to propose long-term environmental strategies for achieving sustainable development to the year 2000 and beyond. The suggestions were based on the Commission's work *Our Common Future* (UNWCED 1987, Kohler 2010).

As a result of the growing interest and concern regarding sustainable development and the environment, the Director-General's report to the 77th Session of the International Labour Conference in June 1990 was entitled *Environment and the World of Work*.

This report led to the adoption of a resolution on environment, development, employment and the role of the ILO. Among other items, the report points out that trade unions should be encouraged and strengthened:

- to be **involved** in the design and implementation of environmental policies and programmes which might promote new employment, protect existing employment or lead to the loss of employment;
- to work for the **access to information and participation** in the establishment of company environmental strategy or policies, the introduction of new techniques monitoring chemical emissions inside and outside of the plant, inspection and reports regarding compliance with environmental regulations and standards, etc., special attention should be paid to the role that **women** play in the environment;
- to promote the setting up of special **joint committees** to deal with general environment issues of the broadening of the mandate of existing joint committees (e.g. health and safety) to encompass the general environment;
- to enable the trade unions, especially the **workers' education**, to design and develop training programmes and training materials for workers to provide environmental awareness and the skills necessary to meet environmental objectives with special efforts to be made to ensure that workers' health and safety representatives receive appropriate environmental training.

(ILO 1990, 75f)

Although the ILO had undertaken a number of environmental training activities prior to 1990, such as traditional vocational training, management development, workers' education and employers' organisations' training programmes, more focus than ever before was put on environmental activities.

In an effort to bring the issue of sustainable development to the minds of workers around the world, the ILO's Bureau for Workers' Activities (ACTRAV) launched the programme *Workers' Education and Environment* in 1989 to focus on environmental issues and workers' education. The two-year inter-regional project covered parts of the Caribbean, Africa and Asia. The objective was to provide workers' organisations in selected regions with the means to raise the awareness of workers concerning environmental protection and sustainable development issues. This project aimed to encourage trade unions' active participation in decision-making processes, and to include environment-specific and related issues in their educational programmes.

The UN Conference on Environment and Development (UNCED), Rio, 1992

The ILO was very active in the extensive preparatory process for the UN Conference on Environment and Development (UNCED) in Rio in 1992. A key component of the ILO's strategy at that time was the preparation and wide circulation of an ILO AGENDA 21 text that was used to assist in the negotiation process in order to attempt to place ILO priority issues within the final AGENDA 21 document adopted at the UNCED Summit. The ILO contributed to the preparation of many of the 40 chapters in AGENDA 21 as well as to the Rio Declaration on Environment and Development. Introducing key terms like 'employment' within the Agenda 21 and the Rio Declaration in 1992 was a particular challenge for the ILO.

After the summit, in November 1992, the ILO organised a tripartite advisory meeting on *Environment and the World of Work*. The meeting endorsed the following four priority themes for future ILO action concerning environment and the world of work in response to Agenda 21 of the UN Conference on Environment and Development:

- the ILO should *support its constituents*, including workers and their organisations, to enable them to deal effectively and directly with relevant environmental and sustainable development matters;
- the ILO should *integrate relevant environmental and sustainable development considerations within its major programmes*, such as working conditions and education and training activities;
- the ILO should include relevant environmental and sustainable development considerations in the design and implementation of its *technical cooperation activities*;
- the ILO should *collaborate with other agencies within the UN system* especially in relation to UNCED, and other international and regional institutions concerned with environment and sustainable development.

(ILO 1993a, 4)

The meeting recommended that the ILO, in implementing these four priority themes, should '*enhance its effort through training, information exchange, and policy advice to support … workers' organizations so as to enable them to promote their own environment programmes and priorities*' as well as '*help workers' organizations to improve their environmental capacities to enable them to contribute more effectively concerning environment and the world of work*' (ILO 1993a, 4).

ACTRAV followed up the Rio Conference by holding its biennial symposium on Workers' Education and Environment in 1993 (ILO 1993a). It was attended by 22 representatives of trade unions in 22 countries, together with observers from international trade union organisations. The conclusions (ILO 1993b) from the symposium highlighted that environmental concerns should encompass the broader issues of economic and social development, poverty, consumption and the quality of life. It also stressed that trade unions, as social development organisations, have an irreplaceable role to play as promoters of social change and advocates of environmental and sustainable development. This role has to be accepted and implemented by governments and employers in practice.

The conclusions of the symposium included reference to the rights of workers and their organisations in the following fields:

- to refuse to carry out environment-unfriendly acts, and to shut down polluting plants;
- the right to information on a company's environmental performance;
- the right to education;
- the right to legal protection;
- the right to information on substances at a workplace and the hazards associated with those substances;
- the right to participate in workplace environmental audits;
- the right to joint union/management environment committees or similar institutions in the workplace.

(ILO 1993b, 47)[4]

The symposium did also outline priority areas on which the ILO Workers' Education Programme should put its focus in the field of environment protection and sustainable development. Several case studies, from awareness raising to greening workplaces, were developed. These case studies showed how environmentally sustainable development issues were integrated into the trade union work (ILO 1999).

The World Summit on Sustainable Development (WSSD), Johannesburg, 2002

The ILO also actively participated in the preparations for the World Summit on Sustainable Development (WSSD) held in Johannesburg in 2002. ILO's contributions to the summit led to a significantly enhanced profile of employment and social issues within the Johannesburg Plan of Implementation and the Johannesburg Declaration. The declaration states that governments '*agree to provide assistance to increase income-generating employment opportunities, taking into account the Declaration on Fundamental Principles and Rights at Work of the International Labour Organization*' (Para 28). The role of the ILO's Decent Work Agenda and its tripartite constituency in achieving sustainable development was particularly highlighted.

The tripartite ILO delegation to the Johannesburg Summit was led by Director-General Juan Somavia and included representatives of governments, employers and workers from the ILO Governing Body.

When the outcome of the Summit was discussed during the Governing Body in March 2003 (ILO 2003) the Worker Vice-Chairperson stated:

Within the United Nations system the ILO held chief competence for a number of the social issues addressed in the outcomes, which it could approach in particular through partnerships both with its own constituents and with other international bodies, focused on the workplace. This applied to the following areas in particular: assessments of the employment impact of sustainable development; assessments of the social aspects of environment and sustainable impact assessments and workplace assessments; the WEHAB process; research into the social and employment consequences of the move to sustainable patterns of production and consumption, including industrial relations; identifying appropriate ways to enhance the social pillar of sustainable development; international cooperation on HIV/AIDS, in particular through the ILO code of practice on HIV/AIDS and the world of work; capacity building, particularly in relation to technology transfer; and training and education necessary for implementation of the outcomes.

(ILO 2003, 29)

Growing attention to climate change and just transition

In 2006 the ILO was again involved in organising an international trade union meeting together with UNEP. The Trade Union Assembly on Labour and the Environment was held at the headquarters of the United Nations Environment Programme (UNEP) in Nairobi (UNEP 2006), followed by regional meetings in South Africa and São Paulo.

The first meeting was organised by UNEP in cooperation with the International Labour Foundation for Sustainable Development (Sustainlabour), the Varda Group and the International Labour Organization (ILO), with the support of the United Nations Global Compact. It reflected a commitment made initially by UNEP, ILO, the International Confederation of Free Trade Unions (ICFTU) and the Trade Union Advisory Committee to OECD at a high-level meeting held in 2002 during the World Summit for Sustainable Development in Johannesburg to identify linkages between sustainable employment practices and environmental management.

Many of the recommendations from the ILO/UNEP trade union meeting in 1980 were reiterated, such as the integration of sustainable development principles; action on climate change; policies for transition and workers' participation. The Assembly agreed on several objectives, including:

- to integrate the environmental and social dimensions of sustainable development with a rights-based approach;
- to take urgent action on climate change in support of the United Nations Framework Convention on Climate Change and its Kyoto Protocol;
- to introduce policies for just employment transition as a central feature of environmental protection and to ensure that workers negatively affected by changes are provided with safe and decent employment alternatives; and

- to enhance the dialogue between labour and management, consultation and negotiation in the workplace on sustainable development, and social dialogue at the sectoral, national and international levels in both public and private sectors.

(UNEP 2006, 25)

Green jobs

In 2007, the Director-General decided to focus his report to the International Labour Conference (ILC) on the theme of *Decent work for sustainable development*. The report argued for the need to anchor the vision of sustainable development as the overriding policy paradigm within which the Decent Work Agenda can make its key contribution to development, because it is in workplaces that the social, economic and environmental dimensions come together inseparably. The report identified the promotion of a socially just transition to green jobs as one of the major tasks for the ILO. Two further discussions on the challenge of climate change and on the employment and labour market implications of climate change took place in the Governing Body in November 2007 and November 2008.

In light of the internal discussions in 2007 and as a follow up to the trade union assembly in 2006, the ILO engaged in a partnership with UNEP, the International Organization of Employers (IOE) and the International Trade Union Confederation (ITUC), to promote the so-called Green Jobs Initiative.

The Initiative's objective is to assess, analyse and promote the creation of decent jobs as a consequence of the needed environmental policies to address the global environmental challenges, among others, climate change. It supports a concerted effort to promote coherent policies and effective programmes leading to a green economy with green jobs and decent work for all, in a climate-challenged world.

In 2008, the Initiative released the global report *Green Jobs: Towards decent work in a sustainable, low-carbon world* (ILO 2008). The report:

- presents the characteristics of existing green jobs in renewable energy, buildings, transportation, basic industry, agriculture and forestry;
- emphasises the role of labour market policy and social protection and advances the discussion for their instrumentation;
- discusses the effects of subsidies, tax reform, carbon markets and eco-labelling among others as key instruments for green policy; and
- raises awareness on the need to pursue a just transition, intertwining equity concerns with the need to train and educate a green workforce.

The Report identifies the chronic and worsening levels of inequality both within and between countries as the major impediments for the expansion of green jobs. The efforts to advance decent work and pro-poor sustainable development would be critical for green jobs creation across the world and in particular in developing countries.

Based on the guidance of the International Labour Conference and of the Governing Body, in May 2009, the Director-General initiated the formulation of an office-wide strategy with the participation of all regions, many departments at headquarters, the International Training Centre of the ILO (ITC) and the International Institute for Labour Studies (Institute). The resulting global Green Jobs Programme of the ILO promotes the creation of green jobs worldwide. The programme pursues two objectives: to address the employment and social dimension of environmental policies and ensure decent work for the present and future generations, and to mainstream environmental concerns into the world of work and change in the long-term consumption and production patterns.

Green jobs offer a way of generating decent work whilst simultaneously achieving environmentally sustainable economic and social development. Green jobs reduce the environmental impact of enterprises and economic sectors, ultimately to levels that are sustainable. They contribute to reducing the need for energy and raw materials, to avoiding greenhouse gas emissions, to minimising waste and pollution, and to restoring ecosystems like clean water, flood protection and biodiversity. For the ILO, the notion of green jobs summarises the transformation of economies, enterprises, workplaces and labour markets into a sustainable, low-emission economy providing decent work.

The Green Jobs Programme:

- Conducts research on a global scale on the social dimension of environmental changes, including climate change.
- Develops tools to diagnose green jobs potential and labour market impacts on national level.
- Continuously broadens its knowledge base and shares it with stakeholders and partners.
- Provides capacity building for ILO constituents.
- Identifies and addresses skills needs for green jobs.
- Assists ILO member countries with policy advice and practical approaches.
- Participates actively in international policy debates.
- Analyses options for green jobs creation in waste management, renewable energies, sustainable agriculture, construction and other sectoral approaches.

(ILO 2011b, 1)

Since its inception in 2009, the programme has grown rapidly and is currently active in more than 20 countries. It supports national initiatives through advocacy workshops and capacity building, assessments on green jobs potential, policy advice and strategic planning. It also supports local initiatives by promoting green entrepreneurship, the greening of enterprises and local development for adaptation to climate change.

The topic 'Green jobs, decent work and sustainable development' has been discussed again in the Governing Body sessions in November 2011. During this session, the workers' spokesperson stated that the programme had made good progress in terms of its strategic orientations, support for constituents and capacity building. Green jobs should reflect all dimensions of decent work, including working conditions, occupational safety and health, freedom of association, collective bargaining and wages. The links should be better analysed and should underpin the work on a just transition.

The United Nations Framework Convention on Climate Change (UNFCCC)

Enhancing international policy coherence is considered essential by ILO constituents to set a path towards sustainable development. In cooperation with its constituents, the ILO has made progress in promoting policy coherence between climate and employment and labour policies in the negotiations under the UNFCCC, and in the last years the ILO has actively participated in the yearly Conferences of the Parties. With the support of developing and industrialised countries, the Cancun Agreement of 2010 recognised the social and labour market dimension of climate change. Furthermore, thanks to the common efforts of the workers' delegation and the ILO, the Agreement includes also a reference to a just transition[5] for the workforce.

The task team on the social dimensions of climate change (SDCC), created under the Working Group on Climate Change of the High Level Committee on Programme (HLCP), is an important UN-wide partnership. It aims to raise awareness among stakeholders on the importance of including the social dimension in climate change responses. The task team is co-led by the World Health Organization (WHO), the UN Department of Economic and Social Affairs (UN-DESA) and the ILO. A working paper reflecting the shared vision of the 19 UN agencies that constitute the task team was presented in the Conference of Parties (COP 17) of the Convention on Climate Change in Durban (South Africa) in December 2011.

In the last years, trade unions have increasingly stressed the need to deepen the debate on the challenges of implementing climate change action for the world of work. Ensuring a just transition that creates decent work is one of the main issues on the trade unions' agenda. In line with these demands and as a preparation to the negotiations held in Durban at the beginning of December 2011, the ITUC called for a UNFCCC decision to request ILO's assistance as the specialised UN agency on labour issues. The ILO should periodically report on countries' progress in ensuring a just transition and provide recommendations to the UNFCCC on how better to reflect just transition components in its decisions.

The United Nations Conference on Sustainable Development (UNCSD), 2012 – Rio + 20

Twenty years after the Earth Summit in Rio, governments, employers' and workers' organisations, together with civil society, will meet again in June 2012. The

Conference, called shortly Rio + 20, aimed to renew the political commitment for sustainable development, assess progress towards internationally agreed commitments and address new and emerging challenges. The two major themes discussed will be (a) a green economy in the context of sustainable development and poverty eradication and (b) the institutional framework for sustainable development. In the context of Rio + 20, the ILO seeks to raise awareness on the importance of the environmental, social and economic pillars of sustainable development.

The ILO has continued to carry out a wide range of 'follow-up' activities linked to past UN Conferences aiming at promoting the ILO's unique and complementary mandate for employment and social matters with a view to strengthening the 'social pillar' of the concept sustainable development. The ILO's mandate, tripartite structure and potential leadership role concerning the 'social pillar' within the UN system is also the focus of the ILO's contribution to Rio + 20.

In preparation for the upcoming conference, the Green Jobs Programme has contributed to various reports and papers that will be presented at the conference including the joint-UN report *Supporting the Transition to a Green Economy* and the various regional joint-UN position papers.

The ILO contribution to the Compilation document, which serves as a basis for the preparation of a zerodraft of the outcome document of the UN Conference on Sustainable Development, includes three key messages (ILO 2011c):

- Implementation gaps

Ensure policy coherence for employment generation and poverty eradication by promoting sustainable enterprises and green jobs, and extending social protection whilst engaging with workers' and employers' organisations.

- A framework of sustainable development and poverty eradication

Ensure a just transition to a green economy. Social protection, entrepreneurship and sustainable enterprise development in green sectors, and a just transition policy framework should be adopted for workers and enterprises facing restructuring or having to adapt to climate change.

- The institutional framework for a green economy and sustainable development

Ensure tripartite participation – by governments, employers and workers – in international, national, sectoral and local governance structures for sustainable development policy formulation and implementation. International labour standards provide an important normative framework and guidance.

Conclusion

As can be seen from the historic overview of ILO involvement on environmental issues, a strong focus has always been on linking work environment to the external environment, promoting workers' participation and involvement, and on developing specific measures to cope with the negative consequences of environmental policies on workers. This is as important today as it was in the early 1970s.

The search for a fairer, greener and more sustainable development model is clearly gaining momentum in most countries at national, sub-national and local levels. The shift towards a greener economy has the potential to create new green jobs and enterprises, particularly Small and Medium Enterprises (SMEs). More and more countries want to take full advantage of this but face constraints in implementation including skills shortages in industries and at the local level. Constituents are increasingly interested to know about green jobs, particularly in a context with high under- and unemployment. Their question is whether there are new opportunities for growth and job creation, and if so, how these can best be realised to increase social inclusion and poverty reduction.

The involvement of workers and their representatives is fundamental in addressing today's environmental challenges. Research shows that participation is beneficial both for social cohesion, economic performance and sustainable development.[6] The ILO, which is the lead UN agency in dealing with workers' rights and priorities, is promoting workers' participation and just transition both nationally and internationally as it has done since its creation. Looking back at UN system meetings it is clear that the ILO has been able to influence discussions and outcomes of negotiations by including references to its mandate and concerns. Future environmental summits and meetings will show whether governments are ready to commit to more binding action-related agreements rather than just a renewal of past commitments, often not acted upon nationally.

The Green Jobs Programme will step up its efforts to provide support both at international and at country level. This will combine policy advice in tandem with innovative programmes, with a view to obtain a cross-fertilising effect. At the same time, the programme will expand its knowledge base by working on indicators and measurement of green jobs and analysing issues like gender and green growth. With other departments and field offices the programme intends to explore several issues strongly related to the creation of green jobs. This includes for example exploring the leverage forces of safety and health approaches in the greening of enterprises, pilot projects focusing on the creation of green jobs in the renewable energy sector and the inclusion of green job strategies in local economic development programmes. All together, the growing knowledge and experience will be better brought together in an interactive facility or platform, which will also serve training purposes.

Annex 1 – International Labour Standards relevant to the environment

Many of the International Labour Standards that the ILO has adopted since its creation are also referring to the external environment or have an impact on the external environment. Chemical substances and pesticides can pollute air, water and land, affecting not only the working environment but also the external environment. Others, particularly the governance standards, are useful as they provide guidance for governments, workers and employers in relation to policy coherence when it comes to sustainable development.

The list below is not exhaustive, but is meant to provide some examples of the many international labour standards that are relevant to the environment.

Toxic substances/chemicals/pollution

- Convention No. 13 White Lead (Painting) (1921) (Instrument to be revised)
- Convention No. 136, Benzene (1971) (Instrument to be revised)
- Convention No. 148 Working Environment (Air Pollution, Noise and Vibration) and R 156 (1977)
- Convention No. 170 on Chemicals (1990)

Radiation

- Convention No. 115 Radiation Protection (1960)

Protection of the marine environment

- Convention No. 147 ILO Merchant Shipping (Minimum Standards) (1976)
- Convention on Standards of Training, Certification and Watch Keeping for Sea Farers (1978)
- Maritime Labour Convention (2006)

Osh

- Convention No. 155 Occupational Safety and Health (1981)
- Convention No. 184 Safety and Health in Agriculture (2001)
- Convention No. 187 Promotional Framework for Occupational Safety and Health (2006)

Prevention of accidents

- Convention No. 174 Prevention of Major Industrial Accidents (1993)
- Convention No. 148 Working Environment (Air Pollution, Noise and Vibration) and R 156 (1977)

Governance

- Convention No. 144 Tripartite Consultation (International Labour Standards) (1976)

- Convention No. 87 Freedom of Association and Protection of the Right to Organise Convention (1948)
- Convention No. 98 Right to Organise and Collective Bargaining (1949)

Notes

1 The member states of the ILO meet at the International Labour Conference, held every year in Geneva, Switzerland, in the month of June. Each member state is represented by a delegation consisting of two government delegates, an employer delegate, a worker delegate and their respective advisers.
2 Convention No. 174 on Prevention of Major Industrial Accidents was adopted at the International Labour Conference in June 1993.
3 The conference paper describes structure and objectives of the UNEP, the role of ILO and trade unions in improving human environment, with a view towards environmental policy. The conference was held in Geneva 12–16 May 1980.
4 These were conclusions of the meeting, but not Conventions. However, some of these rights are included in ILO Conventions dealing with OSH. One example is Convention No. 148 on Working Environment (Air Pollution, Noise and Vibration) Convention, 1977. Its article 13 says: '*All persons concerned shall be adequately and suitably – (a) informed of potential occupational hazards in the working environment due to air pollution, noise and vibration; and(b) instructed in the measures available for the prevention and control of, and protection against, those hazards*'.
5 ITUC defines 'just transition' as an integrated approach to sustainable development where social progress, environmental protection and economic needs are brought into a framework of democratic governance, where labour and other human rights are respected and gender equality achieved.
6 Researchers at the European Trade Union Institute (ETUI) have developed a new tool called the European Participation Index (EPI) designed to examine the relationship between worker participation and social cohesion, economic performance and sustainable development in Europe. The Index shows that companies located in countries that recognise a greater participatory role for workers operate more in coherence with social and ecological objectives and this has a beneficial effect on European society as a whole. Europe needs skilled, mobile, committed, responsible workers that are able to identify with the objective of increasing competitiveness and quality without fear of losing their job. The 'strong rights' group of countries surpassed the others in a wide variety of key indicators: GDP per capita, labour productivity, overall employment rate, employment rate of older workers, youth educational attainment, expenditures on R&D, progress on the reduction of greenhouse gas emissions and consumption of energy (ETUI 2009).

References

European Trade Union Institute (ETUI) (2009) *Benchmarking Working Europe*, Brussels: ETUI.
Ghebali, V-Y. (1989) 'The International Labour Organization. A Case Study on the Evolution of U.N. Specialized Agencies', *International Organization and the Evolution of World Society*, Volume 3, the Graduate Institute of International Studies, Geneva, http://books.google.co.uk/books?id=wVltIwsWzr4C&pg=PA97&lpg=PA97 &dq=1972+Stockholm+conference+ILO&source=bl&ots=qlyM75Ck5G&sig=pXm E3CRQB_mwr_YYPHWZFLOxx4U&hl=en#v=onepage&q=1972%20Stockholm %20conference%20ILO&f=false, (accessed 5 December 2011).

International Labour Office (ILO) (1971) *ILO Basic Paper for the United Nations Conference on the Human Environment*, Geneva: ILO.

——(1972) *Resolution concerning the Contribution of the International Labour Organization to the Protection and Enhancement of the Environment Related to Work*, Geneva, www.ilo.org/public/libdoc/ilo/P/09734/09734%281972–57%29.pdf (accessed 15 December 2011).

——(1977) 'Memorandum of Understanding Concerning Co-operation between the International Labour Organization and the United Nations Environment Programme', *Official Bulletin* of the ILO, Vol. LX, 1977, Series A, No. 4, Geneva, www.ilo.org/public/english/bureau/leg/agreements/unep.htm (accessed 5 December 2011).

——(1979) *Man and his Working Environment*, Geneva, www.ilo.org/public/libdoc/ilo/1979/79B09_750_engl.pdf (accessed 13 December 2011).

——(1980a) *Workers and the Environment*, Conference paper, Geneva, www.ilo.org/public/libdoc/ilo/1980/80B09_181_engl.pdf (accessed 5 December 2011).

——(1980b) *The ILO/UNEP Meeting of Workers' Organisations on environment (Conclusions and Recommendations)*, in Labour Education (44), Geneva, www.ilo.org/public/libdoc/ilo/P/09707/09707%281980–44%29.pdf (accessed 9 March 2012).

——(1990) 'Environment and the World of Work', Report of the Director-General to the International Labour Conference 77th Session 1990, Geneva, www.ilo.org/public/libdoc/ilo/P/09605/09605%281990–77-part-1%29.pdf (accessed 12 March 2012).

——(1993a) *The Practical Role of Trade Unions in Improving Environmental Protection and Sustainable Development*, Background Report, EDUC/SWEE/D.1, Geneva, www.ilo.org/public/libdoc/ilo/1993/93B09_183_engl.pdf (accessed 14 December 2011).

——(1993b) *Special Issue: Workers' Education and the Environment*. Labour Education 1993/4, Geneva: ILO.

——(1999) *Trade Union Actions to Promote Environmentally Sustainable Development*, Geneva, www.ilo.org/wcmsp5/groups/public/ – ed_dialogue/ – actrav/documents/publication/wcms_122116.pdf (accessed 5 December 2011).

——(2003) *Report of the Committee on Employment and Social Policy*, Geneva, www.ilo.org/public/english/standards/relm/gb/docs/gb286/pdf/gb-15.pdf (accessed 14 December 2011).

——(2008) *Green Jobs: Towards Decent Work in a Sustainable, Low-Carbon World*, Geneva, www.ilo.org/empent/units/green-jobs-programme/about-the-programme/WCMS_158727/lang–en/index.htm (accessed 24 July 2012).

——(2011a) *About the ILO. Mission and Objectives*, www.ilo.org/global/about-the-ilo/mission-and-objectives/lang – en/index.htm (accessed 5 December 2011).

——(2011b) *Green jobs becoming a reality. Progress and outlook 2012*, Geneva, www.ilo.org/empent/units/green-jobs-programme/about-the-programme/WCMS_168068/lang–en/index.htm (accessed 24 July 2012).

——(2011c) *ILO contribution to the Compilation document to serve as a basis for the preparation of zerodraft of the outcome document of the UN Conference on Sustainable Development*, Geneva, www.ilo.org/empent/units/green-jobs-programme/about-the-programme/WCMS_169000/lang–en/index.htm (accessed 24 July 2012).

Kohler, L. (2010) *Draft Strategy Note ILO and RIO + 20,* working document, not published, Geneva.

United Nations Environment Programme (UNEP) (2006) *Report of the Trade Union Assembly on Labour and the Environment on the work of its first meeting*, Nairobi, www.unep.org/labour_environment/PDFs/TUAreport.pdf (accessed 5 December 2011).

United Nations World Commission on Environment and Development (UNWCED) (1987) *Our Common Future*, New York: UNWCED.

5 Food workers' rights as a path to a low carbon agriculture

Peter Rossman

Most trade union approaches to climate change focus on the push for 'green jobs' and the need to secure rights for workers employed in industries/sectors that would necessarily be phased out as well as rights for workers in the newly created, climate-friendly jobs ('just transition').

The shortcomings of this approach are two-fold. First, it can underestimate the extent to which current technologies are embedded in power relations that require more than rational arguments to transform. Technology is never socially neutral. Casual talk of a 'Green New Deal' obscures the extent to which the Rooseveltian New Deal was a response to an unprecedented social collapse, financed through massive public investment. Market mechanisms won't deliver what we need – global warming is the definitive 'market failure' – and pressure from financial markets following the global financial meltdown has led governments to attack public expenditure, including various subsidies and supports for alternative energy. Second, the 'just transition' approach tends to overlook that rights are never granted, but always fought for.

A different approach to the global food system and its pre-eminent role in heating the planet indicates a path to a more climate-friendly system of food production through food workers' own struggle for their rights. Approaching the issues in this way establishes workers' struggles as a key vector for changing the food sector's environmental footprint, rather than seeing workers as passive suppliants at the end of a hypothetical transition in which they have played no role. From this perspective, the transition is embodied in and propelled by the struggle for trade union rights; the movement itself is a constituting element in the transition.

The global food system today is in permanent, deepening crisis, the matrix at the intersection of the global hunger, climate and water crises. Crisis is an overused word, and is employed here in the strictly medical sense, as a condition threatening the survival of the organism. An estimated 1.2 billion people are malnourished and hungry. Subsidised overproduction feeds the destruction of local and national food-producing systems. Our food system is addicted to diminishing sources of increasingly costly fossil fuels, depleting and destroying water and topsoil through production methods that contribute massively to global warming through greenhouse gas (GHG) emissions while failing its primary task, which is to satisfy the universal human right to affordable, safe and nutritious food.

While until recently much of the discussion on food and global warming focused on transport ('food miles'), the food system's largest contribution to GHG production occurs *before* food leaves the farm gate.

According to the Stern Review (2006) (and other studies report similar results), agriculture and land use (principally agriculture and forestry) jointly account for 32 per cent of GHG emissions – greater by far than any other single industry or sector (the Stern Review puts industry and transport at 14 per cent each – and products for agriculture like fertilizers and pesticides fall under industry in this report). If one includes processing, transport, packaging, waste, etc., the food system is responsible from 40 to as much as 57 per cent of all GHG.

According to the Stern Review (*Annex 7.g Emissions from the agriculture sector*):

> Fertilisers are the largest single source (38%) of emissions from agri-culture. Agricultural emissions are expected to rise almost 30% in the period to 2020 ... Around half of the projected growth in emissions is expected to come from the use of fertiliser on agricultural soils. Nitrous oxide is 296 times more potent a GHG than carbon dioxide.

Pesticide manufacture alone accounts for up to 16 per cent of the energy input into arable crops. As agrochemicals become more complex and more toxic in response to diminishing returns, the energy input in their production rises. Moreover, *a full lifecycle analysis of their total contribution to greenhouse gas emissions has never been carried out.*

Claims that genetic modification (GM) technologies will lead to reduced agrochemical use are simply false. Increased acreage for GM corn, soybean and cotton crops has increased the use of weed-killing herbicides – in the US, according to one estimate, by 383 million pounds from 1996 to 2008 (Benbrook 2009).

Not only have various formulations of the same agrochemicals (e.g. Monsanto's glysophate) become more toxic in response to diminishing returns. There has been a gradual substitution of more GHG-emitting chemicals for lesser ones. Earlier this year, Dow AgroSciences applied for a permit to release large amounts of sulfuryl fluoride onto farm fields in four US states with the goal of 'sterilising' the soil. Originally used as an anti-termite pesticide in indoor fumigation, sulfuryl fluoride came into widespread use as a food fumigant in response to the phasing out of ozone-depleting methyl bromide. According to Dr Brian Hill, a scientist with the Pesticide Action Network, *sulfuryl fluoride is 4,780 times more potent as a greenhouse gas than carbon dioxide.*

The force driving GHG emissions in agriculture is the expansion and intensification of high input, export-driven, fossil fuel-intensive monoculture production that externalises costs, including the cost of climate change. Most of the deforestation that accounts for 18 per cent of GHG emissions is linked to monoculture expansion, of which the growth of soya in the Amazon basin is but the best-known example.

In addition to high levels of greenhouse gasses, monoculture production accelerates the already rapid loss of biodiversity, which is the foundation of life and of food. It promotes the destruction of soil organic matter (sterilising soil?), leading to topsoil erosion, flooding and the exhaustion of ground water supplies. Runoff from nitrogen fertilisers is the main factor driving eutrophication; water death means still more GHGs. The more intensive monoculture expands, the greater is the food system's vulnerability to climatic and biological shocks. These shocks have their greatest impact on the poor and the hungry – over half of whom are food producers.

Because we are literally eating oil, agriculture is trapped in the rising price curve of fossil-fuel dependency. In 2007, for example, as oil went from US$50 to $140 per barrel, the price of ammonia fertiliser for US farmers increased from US$200 per tonne to over $1,300. We see analogous developments in livestock and poultry production, which have similar driving forces and social/biological consequences. The increased concentration of animal production in fewer and larger high-input intensive production centres means more fossil-fuel dependency leading to diminished biodiversity and unmanageable (in this case methane) GHG emissions.

The antidote to GHG-intensive monoculture is not an exotic or expensive technical fix or patent-protected remedy. It is well known: the proven, and necessary alternative to monoculture is polyculture.

Sharp reductions in GHG emissions are immediately achievable through multicropping, mixed livestock/cereal production and rotational systems that use catch and cover crops to control pests, reducing GHG emissions with equivalent or higher yields. Sustainable low-intensity input techniques enrich soil organic matter, preserve biodiversity, conserve top soil and water – and with proper support can generate socially and environmentally sustainable rural employment.

According to the authoritative United Nations International Assessment of Agricultural Knowledge, Science and Technology for Sustainable Development (IAASTD):

> Agroecosystems of even the poorest societies have the potential through ecological agriculture and IPM to meet or significantly exceed yields produced by conventional methods, reduce the demand for land conversion for agriculture, restore ecosystem services (particularly water), reduce the use of and need for synthetic fertilizers derived from fossil fuels, and the use of harsh insecticides and herbicides.
>
> (IAASTD 2009, 52)

Precisely because of the power relations to which I referred at the outset, at the centre of which is embedded a core group of transnational seed, agrochemical, primary processing and trading corporations, the experience and research brought together in this huge multi-year, multi-disciplinary study has been simply ignored. Its main conclusion, unsurprisingly, has likewise been ignored: '*The food security challenge is likely to worsen if markets and market-driven agricultural production systems continue to grow in a "business as usual mode."*' To this one might add that the 'climate change challenge' is also worsening as a result of business as usual.

Business as usual underpins the system of trading in 'offsets', which encourages the expansion of intensive, GHG-emitting agriculture. It underpins the World Bank's 'New Deal for Agriculture', which offers increased funding for the expansion of monocultures through 'integration' into global supply chains and the false promise of 'market access'. And it underpins the financially driven transformation of food production into a 'strategic asset' generating super returns for investors profiting from the upsurge in land acquisitions for export monocultures.

The technical basis for a transition to environmentally sustainable food production with a reduced carbon footprint has long been known. It is available, accessible and inexpensive (all factors which mitigate against its adoption in a world of patent-protected agribusiness giants!). The barriers to change are social and political, not technology based. These can be found in the power matrix I referred to at the beginning, and include: the power and reach of the global agrifood TNCs; a world trade regime that systematically reinforces their power through expanding control over global supply, processing and retail chains; an intellectual property regime that enforces dependency on high-intensity, high-carbon, high-GHG-producing inputs; unregulated global finance; the systematic destruction by the multilateral lending agencies (IFIs) of public interest research, support and extension services for sustainable food and agriculture; and unequal access to land, water and other vital resources.

These factors have been extensively analysed and highlighted by critics of the global food system. But there is an additional factor which reinforces 'business as usual', yet is rarely articulated: the systematic violation of the rights of agricultural workers.

The world food system is usually discussed as if the only actors were 'farmers' (or sometimes 'peasants'), categories that obscure more than they enlighten. Many farmers are dependent on waged labour for survival, and farmers come in all sizes. Yet of the 1.3 billion people employed in agriculture (half the global labour force), there are some 450 million waged workers, over half of whom are women. Seventy per cent of child labour globally takes place in agriculture – a sure index of endemic poverty – and agriculture produces over 170,000 work-related deaths annually. Agricultural workers are twice as likely to die at work than in any other sector. Between three to four *milllion* pesticide poisonings occur each year, some 40,000 of them fatal. Only 5 per cent of the world's agricultural workers have access to any kind of labour inspection system or legal protection of their health and safety rights. Chronically high rates of malnutrition occur among agricultural workers: those who help feed the world are among the most food insecure. The lack of workplace rights means lack of access to adequate, safe supplies of water.

The most fundamental demands of agricultural workers – for a living wage, for collective bargaining rights, for a safe living and working environment – already take us in the direction of sustainable agriculture – 'green jobs' – yet workers remain excluded from virtually all policy analysis of the crisis of the global food system. So we have World Food Summits in which workers are not represented or even invited; reports from the UN High Level Task Force on the Global Food Crisis that fail to mention low wages as a source of hunger but instead warn of the dangers of increasing wages; FAO 'briefing papers' on world hunger that fail to mention workers or corporations. Even the IAASTD contains only one furtive reference to 'agricultural labour'. The IAASTD highlights the central importance of equity and international human rights instruments, but because it overlooks the existence of 450 million workers it neglects completely the potentially transformative role of waged labour in agriculture and with it that body of international human rights law that defines the collective rights of those workers: the Conventions of the ILO.

The ILO's Core Conventions establish the right of all workers to organise and bargain collectively. They deal with forced labour, child labour, non-discrimination and equal remuneration – acute issues on farms, plantations, orchards, etc. Convention 99 on minimum wages in agriculture should serve as the basis for a living wage for agricultural workers. Convention 184 on health and safety in agriculture sets out strict procedures for the use of pesticides and hazardous chemicals. Convention 141 on Rural Workers' Organizations commits governments to promoting the 'establishment and growth of strong and independent rural workers' organisations' for economic and social development.

These conventions are all routinely breached – not only in poor countries, but in some of the richest countries of the world. Yet if they were implemented and enforced, not only would the position of agricultural workers be radically different – agriculture itself would have to be substantially transformed in ways that are socially and environmentally truly sustainable. What government has committed itself to promoting 'strong and independent rural workers' organizations' for economic and social development? Health and safety for agricultural workers – for whom the working and living environments are identical – is simply incompatible with the massive application of chemical toxins. Justice for rural workers is not compatible with the strip mining of the soil promoted by high-input, industrialised, GHG-producing monocultures. The conquest of rights is ultimately inseparable from the transformation of production.

We are not simply talking about 'green jobs'; it is also a question of defending rural employment as such, a key element in the conservation of water and soil resources. Our affiliates tell us that in Brazil, each 8 hectares cultivated by small farmers using mixed cropping generates one job. Large-scale mechanised monocultures generate one job per 67 hectares. As agriculture steps up its reliance on fossil fuels to produce growing quantities of greenhouse gases, the countryside is being emptied, its residents thrust into urban hyper-slums where work is scarce or non-existent.

Halting and reversing global warming is about rights. Food rights are not only about the right to food, but about rights for those who produce the world's food. This implies an organising agenda to achieve greater organising and bargaining power for agricultural workers at all levels through full implementation of ILO Conventions, including those specific to agriculture. It also means a struggle to secure equal access to land, water and biological resources.

From this perspective, building trade union power for agricultural workers, and allying that power with the struggles of small rural producers, is an indispensable condition for transforming agriculture from a major source of GHG emissions to a carbon-neutral, even carbon-positive source of nutrition and resource conservation. Rights – and bargaining power through union organising – for agricultural workers are crucial to this transition.

Notes (and an afterword)

This text is essentially the transcription of a presentation made at a panel discussion in Copenhagen, Denmark on 14 December 2009 in connection with trade union meetings around COP 15. The discussion was organised by the IUF, and titled 'Low Carbon Diet: The trade union vision of sustainable food production and the right to food'. This accounts for its condensed, schematic presentation and the absence of the usual scholarly apparatus of footnotes. The 'Copenhagen Protocol' and subsequent events, in particular the renewed food price inflation of 2010–11 and associated spike in global hunger, as well as the acceleration of 'land grabbing' farmland for monoculture production and speculation, confirm the analysis. Readers interested in following up the references can consult:

The Stern Review (2006) Available at: http://webarchive.nationalarchives.gov.uk/+/http://www.hm-treasury.gov.uk/stern_review_report.htm (accessed 3 March 2012).
IAASTD (2009) Agriculture at the Crossroads. Synthesis Report. Available at: www.agassessment.org/ (accessed 3 March 2012).
Benbrook, C. (2009) Impacts of Genetically Engineered Crops on Pesticide Use: the First Thirteen Years. The Organic Centre. Available at: www.organic-center.org/science.tocreports.html (accessed 3 March 2012).
The companies dispute the figures; their own sales figures, often buried in shareholder reports and regulatory filings, tell a different story.
Many of the issues discussed here are elaborated in the IUF's 2002 publication:
IUF (2002) The WTO and the World Food System: A Trade Union Approach. Available at: www.iuf.org/cgibin/dbman/db.cgi?db=default&uid=default&id= 307&view_records=1&ww=1&en=1 (accessed 3 March 2012), and related articles on the IUF website: www.iuf.org.
While it doesn't address climate change, there is an excellent discussion of food security and the rights of agricultural workers, in which ILO Conventions are viewed as a lever for transforming the food system, in the 2010 Report of the UN Special Rapporteur on the Right to Food, Olivier De Schutter, on agribusiness and the right to food, presented to the UN Human Rights Council on 22 December 2009. Available at: www.srfood.org/images/stories/pdf/officialreports/20100305_a-hrc-13-33_agribusiness_en.pdf (accessed 3 March 2012).

6 Moving towards eco-unionism

Reflecting the Spanish experience

Begoña María-Tomé Gil
Translated by Agustín González

Opportunities for trade union environmental practices

Today more than ever before there are a number of factors that create the conditions for the birth, growth and consolidation of a trade union philosophy and practice based on the peaceful balance between human beings and nature.

First, there is the environmental, social and financial crisis, which forces us to reflect on the model of development that has caused these systemic crises.

The reduction of global fishing catches, deforestation, the irreversible loss of biodiversity, the overexploitation of aquifers, air, soil and water pollution, the decline of the era of oil production, climate change and the food crisis are clear signs of a serious environmental crisis caused by the depletion of natural resources and the overload of the planet's capacity to assimilate damage (Nieto 1998).

This environmental crisis is accompanied by unprecedented economic and social crises. Capitalism has survived previous crises by pursuing accumulation through the occupation of new territories. But that model is not viable for the emerging economies, because the natural physical basis for new appropriations simply does not exist. The scarcity of resources will create new forms of social exclusion and inequality if we fail to implement a just and organised transition to a different mode of production and consumption.

Second, the context of this crisis has revealed the vulnerability and weaknesses of our productive model, unveiling an unsustainable system based on the untenable idea of permanent economic growth. The magnitude and intensity of this crisis can be measured by its massive impact on employment (INE 2011). For instance in Spain the unemployment rate in the last quarter of 2011 was 22.8 per cent. This has serious repercussions on social security and welfare systems.

The politics of precariousness in the last decade have increased job insecurity through flexibilisation. These policies increased employment rapidly in a phase of expansion, but it also destroyed it at the same pace during recession. The suggestions of governments and employers as to how to solve the crisis have focused on labour reforms, and the well-known recipes of labour-market intervention and the reduction of social protection to ensure competitiveness

(Gorriz 2010). This has led to massive layoffs, extension of working hours, the reduction of pensions and to precarious working conditions.

Given this situation environmental trade unionism faces the challenge of situating the origin of this crisis in the usage and distribution of the planet's resources, that is, to define it as an environmental and social crisis. To accomplish this important task we need not start from zero. The higher level of environmental awareness in society in general has had a positive impact on workers' ideas and perceptions. Workers have become environmentally more responsive and even more proactive in terms of integrating environmental issues into the area of work and production.

Besides, the evolution from environmental conservationism to social environmentalism and the gradual incorporation of the labour movement into the environmental debate are favouring a progressive development transforming socioeconomic and environmental issues into the formulation of alternatives to capitalism, thereby enabling environmental and labour movements to influence each other.

Contradictions and solutions

Before assessing the challenges faced by environmental trade unionism, we must identify the different interpretations of the official concepts of sustainable growth and sustainable development.

We must first become aware of these contradictions. Unclear and ambiguous goals hinder effective action. Only a clear definition of goals will allow us to choose the appropriate indicators, determine if we are moving towards or away from them, and assess the policies and means needed to achieve them (Naredo 1996).

In the following we want to re-examine the use of concepts like sustainability, growth and development. That will lead us to question the current economic model and concepts like progress, as well as goals like competitiveness and productivity. This will eventually lead us to recognise that nature has physical boundaries. The same holds true for technology in spite of our myopic attempts to ignore such facts.

Putting the economy at the service of nature and people

The trade union movement born with the industrial revolution has traditionally been *productivist*, but natural limits to growth and the environmental impacts of industrial societies have brought the conventional model of development into question (Nieto 1998).

Market economy's constant search for profits has led us to an excessive *productivism* with no space to reflect upon what we actually need to produce. Current market dynamics favour the imposition of a minority's (capital holders') choices disregarding social needs. In market-driven societies profits define production goals, costs determine the production model and income (salaries and benefits) regulates our ability to consume. In a market economy we are no longer citizens but consumers, passive subjects whose connection to the world around is determined by monetary transactions. Indiscriminate consumption of resources and unrestricted generation of waste and pollutants are the cause of environmental degradation, unsustainable practices and the alienation of people as well as the creation of unjust and unsupportive relations between countries and between people.

Environmental unionism must locate itself within new forms of economic relations that reconnect the physical world with the monetary world and the economy with the knowledge developed in natural sciences (Naredo 1996).

Recognising the unviability of continuous growth

Contemporary union statements often use the term 'sustainable growth' derived from the notion of 'sustainable development', a term already used to defend developments opposed to sustainability and incompatible with life.

While the term 'growth' is associated with increase in purely numerical terms, 'development' is synonymous with transition, transformation and self-organisation. That is why development is more appropriate to define processes that involve the improvement of the quality of life and collective wellbeing (González *et al.* 2008).

Besides, economic growth or continuous productive growth is unviable on a planet with limited resources. Nowadays, the demand for resources exceeds the capability of ecosystems to provide them without being depleted. The biosphere cannot sustain the demand of industrialised countries and for the last decades we have been spending the earth's *capital*. The economics of growth is seriously interfering with life cycles and the pace of physical and environmental transformation caused by human activity has such acute effects on natural processes that many assure we have entered in a new geo-logical epoch: the *Anthropocene*, a term used to highlight the extent of human activity and its impact on ecosystems (Herrero *et al.* 2011).

Environmental unionism must focus on the qualitative improvement of living conditions instead of supporting quantitative economic and productive growth. Unionists must bear in mind that humans are part of natural eco-systems, depend directly on them, and therefore must adapt production to the space of natural cycles.

Correct our excessive reliance on technology

Technology, though necessary, is not sufficient to solve the environmental crisis. In many cases it proves inefficient or becomes an impediment to sus-tainability. We must observe the precautionary principle and test technology's potential hazards and disadvantages prior to their use. Such measures require technology to be controlled by society, not by the market. Technology is not good *per se* and can have negative consequences (Herrero *et al.* 2011). A good example of blind faith in technology can be found in the results in CO_2 capture and storage (CCS) results registered by the Eurobarometer (European Commission 2011). In the survey 43 per cent of the interviewed regarded CCS as an effective measure to combat climate change and even speculated about the ideal location for future CO_2 storage. However, 79 per cent of the interviewed had previously admitted they had never heard about this technology and did not know how it worked.

There is no possible financial compensation for environmental damage. Global production and consumption patterns must change

We should reject ideas that promote growth as a way to fund environmental protection measures and notions expressing that only industrialised countries are able to defend their environment and repair environmental damage.

Although certain decline in the quality of environmental protection is observed at lower economic levels, it is also a fact that unrestricted economic growth leads to progressive and irreversible environmental harm (e.g. extinction of certain species). The notion that environmental improvement can only occur once certain levels of production and economic standards have been reached, which allow for investments in environmental improvements, is not acceptable on a global scale.

What many countries have achieved so far are certain local or regional environmental improvements, based on a global model of increased imports of raw material and energy from other nations, and exports of waste, pollution and gruelling jobs to poorer countries.

Rejecting competitiveness as an end in itself and committing to a different set of values

In future scenarios continuous growth will not be unbounded. Nature's physical limitations will force us to reduce our ecological footprint one way or another. Environmental unionists should cooperate to reduce material and energy consumption by promoting a just transition (organised, coordinated, supportive and equitable) and avoiding uncontrolled, abrupt and competitive adjustments.

Unions' alternatives should build upon a new set of values that include austerity as opposed to squandering, cooperation as opposed to competitiveness, pacifism as opposed to violence, sustainability as opposed to growth, redistribution as opposed to accumulation, slowness as opposed to speed, joint responsibility as opposed to individualism and victimisation, horizontal relations as opposed to vertical hierarchies.

Basic principles of an environmental unionism

In spite of a growing environmental awareness among workers and unionists, trade unions in general are still largely invisible in environmental debates in

Spain. This is partly due to political and economic power barriers and partly to the historical indifference of unions towards the environment. Many people are still surprised when they see that unions are represented in international climate change negotiations, that they put forward proposals for sustainable mobility and that workers want to actively participate in their companies' environmental management.

Unions need to have their own view on issues regarding the protection of the environment and their own notion of sustainable development independent from the views of employers. We need a perspective that is different from the official green slogans and allows us to make further progress towards the full recognition of labour's participation in environmental protection.

Labour's response to the environmental, social and economic crisis needs to develop according to the following strategic lines (Garí 2008):

- *Recovering ethical values* in human relations, demanding solutions to unequal and unsustainable relations between the *rich North* and the *impoverished South*, and between present and future generations. At the same time relations between humans and nature need to be balanced without focusing primarily on human interests.
- *Concerning the environment* labour needs to focus on the protection of the biosphere, which is the physical and biochemical basis of human existence. This strategy requires expertise and respect for natural boundaries. Nature is the basis of life and of labour.
- *Concerning the social* labour should strive to achieve wellbeing and promote social justice and equality.
- *Politically*, environmental unionism opens new possibilities for a social, anti-capitalist alliance with new goals and demands.
- *Concerning labour* the development of environmental practices will help to prevent occupational risks and protect workers' health. Appropriate environmental regulation and practices favour the development of stronger and more sustainable forms of production and working conditions. Employers' obligations to comply with such regulation will avoid the risks of sanctions and job losses.

Environmental unionism will have to redefine what labour should be in order for it to meet true human needs. Labour should not be reduced to a mere process of earning a living, in the same way as modern unionism should not be limited to bargaining for better salaries for the labour force in the capitalist market. Unions should not simply respond with the traditional corporate approach without considering workers' triple dimension as producers, consumers and citizens (Serrano 2005).

What are the true needs of contemporary society? What societies really need is progress and well-being based on education, health, democratisation and the humanisation of working conditions. What societies need is a fair distribution of wealth, the end of unequal gender and ethnic relations and an environment that is agreeable and unpolluted. Societies need cultural and scientific as well as artistic development together with the possibility for recreation and leisure.

Therefore, trade unions should become active players in increasing the effect of labour that transforms the environment of industrial societies by organising it within more localised economies. This is important especially in respect of paid work, which has an exchange value in market economies. But it is no less important in terms of valuing and redistributing reproductive care work, which today is performed predominantly by women (Riechmann 1998). Trade unions also need to define the basic requirements for a transition to a more sustainable production and consumption system. This would involve:

- *Changing the model of energy* to allow for the development of a non-carbon economy. This might be achieved by reducing the energy demand in industrialised countries, implementing energy saving and efficiency measures, substituting fossil fuel and nuclear energy sources with a decentralised production of renewable energies.
- *Reorientation towards a new mobility model*: cities and economical activities should be redesigned in order to reduce the need for transport and make it possible to give up cars in favour of more sustainable means of transport. Transport needs to be electrified by using renewable sources to gradually decrease oil dependency.
- *Clean production* in order to allow a closed cycle of materials through:
  - Sustainable use of natural resources (water, raw material, soil) by minimising their use and promoting their renewability through rational management.
  - Efficient production processes, clean technologies and work organisation to optimise resources.
  - Optimised use of goods and services and the elimination or reduction of waste and emissions, and avoiding production inefficiencies.

A renewed trade union movement: new forms of organisation and social interaction

The policies of an environmental unionism must comprise environmental, economic, energy and industry proposals on sector and nationwide scales, as well as specific measures to address the situation in the workplace. These are essential preconditions for interventions in society at large.

We face a challenge of the large-scale greening of society, company by company, without losing sight of the fact that environmental problems often extend beyond the boundaries of the workplace. Consequently, it is necessary to revive traditional social trade unionism that was connected to the community and created connections between the factory and the neighbourhood, while keeping the systemic perspective, which enables us to tackle the environmental questions on a global level.

Environmental unionism will have to intervene into the social–labour process at different levels. This requires new and more participative forms of internal organisation, less bureaucratic practices and a wider range of consultation with the union social base to ensure legitimacy.

This new form of unionism will also need more interaction with other social groups. It needs to seek alliances with other social and anti-capitalist movements across the world. This implies a dialogue with socio-political movements: political and environmental feminism to mention a few. Several cooperation and exchange initiatives have been initiated between trade unions and environmental and social movements in Spain. These contacts are the cornerstones of a common project to achieve sustainability. Some recent examples of such collaboration include:

The founding of the *Climate Movement* (*Movimiento Clima*) by trade unions (Comisiones Obreras), WWF Spain, Intermon Oxfam (Spanish branch of Oxfam International) and consumer groups to promote civil initiatives to combat climate change. The movement later became the 'Climate Coalition', a nation-wide platform that includes 30 environmental NGOs, trade unions, researchers, consumer organisations and cooperation and development NGOs. The founding of the *Climate Coalition* (*Coalición Clima*) encouraged deep reflection by member organisations as to their most immediate common goals, while at the same time initiating a process in which they could listen to and understand the concerns of the other organisations in the coalition. This led to the development of collective proposals reached through consensus. These proposals benefitted from the input of environmental organisations, which emphasised environmental aspects, the trade unions, which sought to promote the interests of social protection (e.g., just transition), and other social movements who represented issues of cooperation, development and consumption.

The development and presentation of legislative initiatives for the rationalisation of energy consumption in Spain was another significant activity. It was drafted and submitted in 2007 by the Spanish trade union (Comisiones Obreras; CCOO), environmental groups (including Greenpeace and WWF Spain) and the left-wing political coalition (including the Green Party). It consisted of three draft bills: one on sustainable mobility submitted 2007, another on energy saving and efficiency submitted 2008, and one on environmental tax policies submitted 2009. Although the three draft bills were rejected by the socialist government as well as several right-wing opposition parties, the experience proved valuable because it allowed the different groups to find common points of interest and to specify their mutual goals.

Finally, it is worth mentioning the participation of a large group of social, trade union and environmental organisations to promote a sustainable FSC (Forest Stewardship Council) certificate for wood and paper biomass in Spain and to develop sustainable forest management standards. This was a significant challenge for the development of transparent, participative and democratic processes in respect of forest management policies in Spain. It enabled the creation of a consensus concerning sustainable forest management standards that should be applied in Spain. The different social actors were able to define common goals and to reconcile economic goals with employment and sustainability goals.

New responsibilities, forms of participation and trade union rights in the workplace

Workers' participation in environmental debates is an essential element in preventing and minimising environmental impacts in companies and implementing the best technical measures available to meet legal and social standards. It is also a key element preserving the number and quality of jobs and improving working conditions. The introduction of new production technologies and procedures in companies will imply in many cases changes in work organisation, new training needs and a shift in day-to-day practices. These actions for environmental improvements will require the participation of workers and their representatives to ensure that they are accepted and implemented efficiently. The concept of environmental participation raises questions concerning basic democratic issues for the labour movement. It will require the monitoring of company information, specific training, new trade union rights and the further empowerment of union representatives to enable unions to intervene in environmental management.

For 15 years European and Spanish legislation has granted citizens the right to access environmental information from public authorities. However, the last decade has seen significant advances in terms of citizens' rights largely due to the framework set by the Aarhus Convention.[1] The three pillars of the convention are: access to environmental information, citizens' participation in decision making[2] and access to legal procedures to revise decisions that might represent a violation of participation rights.

Although the importance of citizens' rights is widely recognised by multiple authorities and in official documents, this idea has not been fully conveyed to companies in terms of labour and union rights. Labour will have to fight for the full recognition and exercise of new rights and powers for trade union intervention in the workplace. These will include:

- *Right to participate in decision making* related to environmental conditions in the workplace. This can be exercised through new environmental councils or representatives of health and safety in the workplace. This right is not included in national legislative systems to date, although it is being gradually recognised by some large companies, in some voluntary regional agreements and in collective bargain agreements in some sectors (e.g. the chemical industry's agreement in Spain).
- *Right to environmental information* such as emissions, technology options or environmental risks in the workplace. Those risks must be identified and assessed, and relevant information must be forwarded to workers through product labels, chemical safety data sheets and training courses.

- *Protection of plaintiffs*: workers shall not be held liable or punished for reporting on practices that might involve an environmental hazard.
- *Right to refuse to perform dangerous or environmentally hazardous tasks*: workers shall not be held liable or punished for refusing to perform tasks that might entail immediate or serious harm to their health or to the environment.

(Olano *et al.* 2010)

The EU has taken important steps to grant workers and unions full participation rights in environmental issues in a relatively short period of time. A good example of this is the European Parliament's resolution on developing the job potential of a new sustainable economy, adopted in September 2010 (European Parliament 2010), which among other things calls:

- for the involvement of employees' representatives in greening the workplace, as defined by the ILO, according to national practices in order to make workplaces, companies and industries more sustainable;
- on the social partners to organise themselves and invite the Commission to promote an EU-wide exchange of best practice examples, in particular strengthen the provision of information to and consultation of workers, and the establishment of European Works Councils;
- on the Commission, the EU member states and the social partners to include essential environmental issues in the social dialogue,[3] at all levels of consultation. There should be an emphasis on sectoral negotiations; in order for transition to be socially just, workers should have a participative partnership role to play in the process;
- on creating the necessary conditions for workers to undertake further training and adapt to new technologies in order to prevent job losses; promoting and supporting for collective agreements to anticipate change and avoid unemployment; the strengthening of social security, income support systems.

Is the struggle for better jobs compatible with environmental unionism?

Is a more sustainable society compatible with job security? Will the 'greening' of production lead to inevitable job losses? Or on the contrary, might the transition to a sustainable economy and society create new jobs?

The only possible way to avoid negative labour, social and environmental consequences of globalized production and consumption is to address the issue with an international union strategy based on the struggle against the exploitation of human beings and the depletion of nature.

Nowadays Spanish unionists believe that although the substitution of polluting sectors by cleaner and more sustainable activities will lead to job losses in the polluting sectors, it will also create jobs in renewable and sustainable industries. The dilemma resides in the fact that job losses and job generation will affect sectors and locations differently and over time. This represents a challenge for unions and governments in terms of creating just social conditions during the transition from the polluting production model to a sustainable economy. This process is called 'just transition' by the international union movement (ITUC 2009).

Aware of these facts, CCOO committed themselves in their 6th Congress to 'promote [as a top priority] the integration of environmental protection into industrial policies and the orientation towards clean production'. The union also highlighted that '[a]lthough it might imply certain limitations and an end to some industrial activities, the shift to a sustainable economy will generate a new, larger, more sustainable industrial network which will provide more job security and stability' (Olano *et al.* 2010, 15).

New sectors and activities based on clean production are not only intensive but also represent a window of opportunity for the protection of jobs, especially for young people. New green jobs require a highly qualified labour force and represent new scientific, organisational and technical challenges. For example, 55 per cent of workers in the renewable energy sector are either engineers or higher education graduates. Qualified workers represent almost one-fourth of the labour force in this new green sector (Arregui 2010).

ISTAS (Trade Union Institute of Work, Environment and Health) has conducted a number of research projects in Spain to determine the job potential of new economic sectors (renewable energies, waste recycling) and of the transformation of traditional, oversized and unsustainable sectors (construction, car industry). The potential employment impact of green jobs in Spain is significant. For example, it has been calculated that the volume of jobs associated with renewable energy in Spain for 2010 was around 115,493, of which 70,152 were direct and 45,341 were indirect jobs. ISTAS estimates that achieving 30 per cent renewable energy demand will increase jobs in the renewable energy sector to 119,678 in 2015 and 204,200 by 2020 (Arregui 2010).

Energy refurbishment of houses and buildings (e.g. home energy retrofit) as a solution to unemployment in the construction sector provides another opportunity. With over 25 million houses, one-third of which are second residences or empty properties built without any consideration for sustainability, Spain has an oversized, relatively new, inefficient building stock. ISTAS estimates show that the development of an energy refurbishment plan to improve insulation (through renewable energies/equipment) for 565,000 houses a year might generate 105,000 stable jobs by 2020. This would save 20 million barrels of oil and reduce 10 million tonnes of CO_2 a year, a significant reduction of energy demand and *greenhouse gases* emissions (Dalle 2011).

There are also significant potential job gains in public transport within the framework of sustainable mobility. Modal shift from road transport to railways, electric vehicles, the development of public and collective transport services, the promotion of car sharing and bicycles are non-relocatable job niches that may prove far more fruitful than the construction of infrastructures, and might allow a compensation for gradual job losses in the car industry. Over 297,109 workers were employed in sustainable mobility jobs in transport: railways, underground rail, tramways, buses, taxis, car sharing, car rentals, bicycles, regulated parking lots and mobility management. Jobs could double by 2020 if public authorities promote this sustainable mobility model through new management tools, adequate transport/territorial planning, information, fiscal measures and funding. The number of jobs could rise to 443,870; 120,000 additional jobs in comparison with a business-as-usual scenario (Ferri 2011).

Finally, waste management is considered a 'green' sector due to its environmental impact associated with waste treatment, such as reducing the consumption of resources and energy, and polluting and toxic emissions generated by inadequate management. Furthermore, the transport of wastes increases environmental impact. A study conducted by ISTAS shows that the implementation and development of manual and automatic deposit-refund systems for retail stores increases the quality and quantity of recovered material and the value of containers. It also promotes the creation of new jobs in all the phases of the waste disposal cycle. ISTAS studies show that the implementation and development of such systems would create 14,200 new direct and indirect jobs in Spain during the first stage of development, due to the positive drag effect on related sectors as transport, logistics, construction and recycling (Pérez 2011).

The greening of the production system will imply sectoral adjustments between emerging and traditional activities but it will also require a different form of production, particularly in terms of resource and energy efficiency, work organisation, industrial relations, union participation and the distribution of wealth.

However, the transition to a sustainable economy faces difficulties. The economic crisis and the policy response of the European institutions and the International Monetary Fund are deteriorating the social situation with disastrous consequences for workers. On the social side, austerity, general cutbacks on public services (education, social services, healthcare, to name a few), the dismantling of the social protection systems and the increase of the retirement age are among the most common measures.

From the environmental point of view, several measures have also been implemented during the crisis to introduce deregulation and the 'simplification' of the administrative procedures in Europe. The prior authorisation by public administrations is progressively being replaced by declarations of 'social responsibility' and communications by companies. The European 'Directive on Industrial Emissions' reduces the control of air and water emissions for certain facilities in a context where environmental inspections are disproportionately managed by the private sector.

The apparent goal of these global strategies is to reduce costs and transform Europe into a competitive economy to create and project jobs. But these erroneous and ineffective reforms imply losses and restrictions for workers, unions, communities and affect our territory and biodiversity negatively. The main beneficiaries of these policies will be capital, financial markets and banks.

Spain, ruled by a conservative government since last November, follows the guidelines set by the EU leadership and the German government. Political decisions and government policies are increasingly being displaced by decisions made on the basis of economic results. Financial power has seized democratic institutions and policies imposing changes in the Constitution without previous consultation with citizens who will suffer the consequences. They constitute the most profound labour reform in Spain to date (Real Decreto-ley 2012). It represents an unprecedented backslide of labour rights, undermines collective bargaining and instead of creating new jobs promotes further unemployment. Some of the most serious consequences of the labour reform include:

- *Easier layoffs and cheaper redundancy.* Official authorisation for collective dismissals is no longer required.
- *The right to collective bargaining is seriously degraded.* Employers are allowed not to comply with collective bargaining agreements regarding salaries, working hours and working conditions.
- *Employment contracts become more precarious*: for example, new SME contracts introduce free dismissal.
- *Serious limitations to workers' health rights*: employees with sick leave can be dismissed for being absent from work 20 per cent of their working time within a period of two months.

While governments assume the debt of the private sector, workers and citizens suffer wage cuts, privatisation of public services and cutbacks in social expenses.

Regarding environmental policies, one of the first decisions taken by the new Minister of Energy was to cancel the public subsidies to renewable energies (while maintaining aids to fossil energies). Further actions have been already announced by the Minister of Environment. A worst-case scenario will imply:

- The *simplification of environmental regulations* by reducing the protection levels instead of ensuring effective enforcement.
- Expediting *administrative environmental procedures* by reducing a broad social participation and information in decision making.
- *Voluntary agreements* with industry and business organisations will be further reinforced, thereby postponing compliance with legal requirements.
- *Economic activity* and mass tourism will be promoted in protected natural reserves, endangering vulnerable ecosystems.
- *Damaged coast areas* (for example, by the effect of the housing bubble) will no longer be a public property and will lose their protected area status, which will allow uncontrolled private investment and economic activity. It will represent a clear incentive to destroy these natural habitats in order to turn them into private lands. This is the recipe of the Spanish government to stimulate the economy.
- *Emissions reduction targets* will be the last item on the government agenda.

To confront these developments, the union movement has now a unique opportunity to promote a new social model and resist the backlash of capital and government. This is the time for unions to renovate themselves and to actively participate in the struggle for a new sustainable society as a way to guarantee peace, justice, equity and human existence. It is necessary, it is possible and unions are not alone in this struggle.

Notes

1 The Aarhus Convention is the UNECE Convention on Access to Information, Public Participation in Decision-making and Access to Justice in Environmental Matters. It was adopted on 25 June 1998 in the Danish city of Aarhus at the Fourth Ministerial Conference in the 'Environment for Europe' process.
2 In three spheres of public activity: approval of actions, approval of plans, drafting of bills and regulation.
3 Social dialogue refers to the round tables created in Spain in 2005. The tripartite social dialogue aims to guarantee the participation of social partners (government, trade unions and employers' organisations) in the design and monitoring of the Emissions Rights Assignment National Plan (NAP).

References

Arregui, G. (2010) 'Estudio sobre el empleo asociado al impulso de las energías renovables en España'. Instituto Sindical de Trabajo, Ambiente y Salud. Madrid. www.istas. net/web/abreenlace.asp?idenlace=8317 (accessed 25 March 2012).

Dalle, M. (2011) 'La generación de empleo en la rehabilitación y modernización energética de edificios y viviendas'. Instituto Sindical de Trabajo, Ambiente y Salud. Madrid. www.istas.net/web/abreenlace.asp?idenlace=8723 (accessed 25 March 2012).

European Commission (2011) 'Eurobarometer sobre el conocimiento de la tecnología de captura y almacenaje de CO_2'. http://ec.europa.eu/public_opinion/archives/ebs/ebs_364_en.pdf (accessed 25 March 2012).

European Parliament (2010) 'Resolution on Developing the Job Potential of a New Sustainable Economy'. 7 September. www.europarl.europa.eu/sides/getDoc.do?type=TA&reference=P7-TA-2010-0299&language=EN (accessed 25 March 2012).

Ferri, M. (2011) 'La generación de empleo en el transporte colective en marco de una movilidad sostenible'. Instituto Sindical de Trabajo, Ambiente y Salud. Madrid. www.istas.net/web/abreenlace.asp?idenlace=8778 (accessed 25 March 2012).

Garí, M. (2008) 'Opiniones, actitudes y contradicciones de los trabajadores en materia ambiental', recopilado en Riechmann, Jorge (coord.) '¿En qué estamos fallando? Cambio social para ecologizar el mundo'.

González, L, Ferriz, A. and Bárcena, I. (2008) 'El ecologismo y el sindicalismo como luchas integradas'. Curso de formación Secretaría de la formación de CGT y Ecologistas en Acción'. Madrid. www.ecologistasenaccion.org/IMG/pdf_ecologismo_y_sindicalismo.pdf (accessed 25 March 2012).

Gorriz, R. (2010) 'Las relaciones laborales en el desarrollo sostenible', pp. 67–77; incluido en la obra Gaceta Sindical 'Reflexión y Debate' n° 14. 'Desarrollo sostenible y políticas públicas en España'. Madrid. www.ccoo.es/comunes/temp/recursos/1/504199.pdf (accessed 25 March 2012).

Herrero, Y., Cembranos, F. and Pascual, M. (2011) 'Cambiar las gafas para mirar el mundo. Una nueva cultura de la sosteniblidad'. Libros en Acción. Madrid.

Instituo Nacional de Estadística (INE) (2011) 'Encuesta de población activa'. Tercer trimestre de. www.ine.es/daco/daco42/daco4211/epa0311.pdf (accessed 25 March 2012).

ITUC (2009) 'Trade unions and climate change: equity, justice & solidarity in the fight against climate change'. Trade Union Statement to COP15, United Nations Framework Convention on Climate Change, UNFCCC, Copenhagen, Denmark (7–18 December).

Naredo, J. M. (1996) 'Sobre el origen, el uso y el contenido del término sostenible'. Re-edited by Gaceta Sindical, 'Reflexión y Debate'.

Nieto, J. (1998) 'Ecosindicalimo', included in Riechmann, Jorge and Fernández Buey, Francisco. 'Trabajar sin destruir. Trabajadores, sindicatos y ecologismo'. Ediciones HOAC. Madrid.

Olano, I.; Ferrer, A.; Pérez, J. (2010) 'Actuación ambiental en la empresa. Guía para la intervención de los trabajadores'. Informa Ambiental. Instituto Sindical de Trabajo, Ambiente y Salud. Madrid.

Pérez, J. (2011) 'Estimación del empleo potencial en la implantación y desarrollo de la primera fase del SDDR en España'. Instituto Sindical de Trabajo, Ambiente y Salud. Madrid. www.retorna.org/mm/file/Documentacion/ResumenEjecutivoEmpleo.pdf (accessed 25 March 2012).

Real Decreto-ley (2012) 3/2012, de 10 de febrero, 'de medidas urgentes para la reforma del mercado laboral'. www.boe.es/boe/dias/2012/02/11/pdfs/BOE-A-2012-2076.pdf (accessed 25 March 2012).

Riechmann, J. (1998) 'Trabajar sin destruir. Trabajadores, sindicatos y ecologismo'. Ediciones HOAC. Madrid.

Serrano, L. (2005) 'Sindicalismo y medio ambiente'. pp. 161–76, included in Gaceta Sindical de la Confederación Sindical de Comisiones Obreras 'Reflexión y Debate'. no. 6. Desarrollo sostenible, medio ambiente y sindicato. ISSN 1133-035X, Madrid.

7 Cars, crisis, climate change and class struggle[1]

Lars Henriksson

When the financial shit hit the fan in 2008, overproduction in the auto industry immediately became visible. In the Swedish auto industry the size of both fan and shit were especially problematic: two of the world's smallest mass producers, both at the time owned by huge, troubled US corporations, producing large, fuel-consuming, semi-luxury cars. In a country of nine million people this of course made the auto crisis a big political issue and, as I write this, more than three years later, this still remains so for one of the companies.

In Sweden, as elsewhere, the mainstream discussion on how to react to the crisis followed two lines:

1. The market liberal approach of "creative destruction".
   In short this said: the market has reached its verdict and some of the corporations have been sentenced to death. Don't fiddle with the market! That will only make things worse.[2] I have also come across a green variety of this: cars are damaging the climate. We don't need them or the companies that make them. It's good if the auto industry goes away.
2. Support the industry.
   Another position was that the government must subsidise the companies to help them through these troubled times so that they can be ready to grow again when things get back to normal. The means of this was loans, scrapping incentives, tax breaks and so on. This has been the line of the Social Democratic Party, the industry itself, many of the analysts and the unions. My union also contributed to this process, or rather made the members support it by signing a contract that temporarily reduced salaries and working time.

My answer was that both these lines of argumentation were false and, in the long term, disastrous. The "support the industry" line is based on an untenable assumption. There will not be any "back to normal", at least not if by "normal" one means an endlessly expanding production of cars. There are several reasons for this.

Road transport is responsible for about 20 per cent of greenhouse gas emissions in the EU-15 and the transport sector is the sector where emissions are increasing fastest. Even if we do not want to stop climate change, the day of the auto is over: the production of oil, the Siamese twin to the car, is going to peak in the near future and this cheap energy will not be available as it has been until now. In fact, a transport system based on the automobile is no longer an option at all. The industry's answer is the "green car", fuel efficient, running on renewable fuels. However, this is an illusion.

The average CO_2 emissions per kilometre from new cars are going down. The period between 1995–2002 saw a 13 per cent average decrease in fuel consumption for new cars in the EU. Yet, the same period saw an increase of the total fuel consumption by 7 per cent. The reason for this is that traffic has increased (Holden 2007, 107). The agrofuel "solution" is no solution at all. A few figures demonstrate the scale of the problem. In forest-rich Sweden, a few years ago politicians said that the future lay in DME, a synthetic diesel made from forest products (basically wood). Just to replace the traffic's present consumption of oil would take the total yearly yield of six billion hectares of forest worldwide. In this scenario, it would be impossible to use one single log of wood for furniture, construction, paper, heating or anything else and we would still be stuck with the fact that the Earth's forests cover an area of four billion hectares (and shrinking).

In 2005, agrofuels represented 1 per cent of the fuel consumption in road traffic. Optimistic calculations suggest a possible 13 per cent by 2050 (Dornboech and Steenblik 2007). Already this modest contribution led FAO to describe its consequences for the forests in these words: "Given the export-driven industrialization policies, continued global demand for agriculture, livestock, forest products and, increasingly, biofuel will intensify the pressure on forests" (FAO 2009, 46).

Other types of alternative fuels, like ethanol, face the same problem: there simply isn't enough arable land and water to replace the oil we burn. And, when it comes to ethanol from corn or diesel from soy, these fuels come in direct conflict with the food production for the world's people (Cotula *et al.* 2009; Dornboech and Steenblik 2007).

What about the electric car, then? Or the hydrogen engine? Although there are great gains in efficiency if the internal combustion engine (a device whose effect is mainly to heat the surrounding air) is replaced by electrical motors, this is not a solution either. Neither hydrogen nor electricity are sources of energy. They are bearers of energy that has to be produced somewhere else. Today two-thirds of the world's electricity is produced in fossil fuel power plants, a production that is in dire need of replacing with sustainable sources (IEA 2009, 24).

"We cannot innovate our way out of the emissions problem from transport", as Jacqueline McGlade, Executive Director of the EU's Environmental Agency, sharply summarised the whole issue (European Environment Agency 2007). The role of all the "green", "eco", "bio" etc. badges that are slapped on trunks in car plants all over the world today is not to save the environment. It's about selling cars by lulling us into the feeling that the environmental problems of road transport are taken care of. Everything will be fine if we just sit back and continue business as usual, building roads, driving and buying cars. This is perhaps most obvious with the electric car. While enormous sums of money, public and private, are put into developing this elusive hope for the future, the share of transport carried by well functioning, energy efficient, and electrically propelled means (train, light rail, etc.) is shrinking worldwide.

As far as I can see there is no future for a transport system that is based on the private car. This is not to say that all cars must be eliminated. There is a place for the car in a sustainable transportation system, but not as the main supporting beam of the transport system. It can at best only "seal the cracks" in a system built on more sustainable modes of transportation. The volume of transport, and especially road transport, needs to be adapted to a level that is sustainable in the long term. And this will mean the end of the auto industry, as we know it.

On top of this, the economic crisis and changing international relations are reshaping the auto industry dramatically. So, the faster we forget "as usual" the better. However, letting the industry die is even worse than keeping it alive through subsidies for three reasons: social, practical and political.

First, there are the social effects. At least in Sweden the "creative destruction" will only work half way; it will only be destructive. Industries have come and gone. In the 1960s, Sweden's textile industry moved out, and in the 1970s and 1980s the same thing happened to the shipyards. Other sectors grew including, amongst others, the auto industry and especially the public service sector. Promoting this "structural change" became the official policy of the unions and the Social Democratic Party. Today no other industries are on the rise and the public sector is facing cutbacks. In an auto-dependent economy such as Sweden's, destroying the auto industry will mean disaster. Second, an industry like the auto industry is not just a bunch of machines and buildings. Above all, it is an organisation of people. If you dissolve the organisation it's like taking a car apart and throwing the wheels, the crank shaft, the wiring and the axles on different heaps in a scrap yard. The parts and the people would be the same, but it would no longer be a machine, the industry ceases to be an industry.

So, as humanity faces its toughest challenge so far – to change an economy and production that has been built around fossil energy for 250 years – we need to use all the resources we can. It would be an irresponsible waste of resources to destroy an industrial complex that has been built and developed over nearly a century. Instead, I want to suggest a "third road" for the auto industry.

My technical starting point for this is that the auto industry is not coal mining, in other words, an industry limited to the production of only one thing. It is a sophisticated, flexible machine, a system for mass production of advanced, high-quality technical goods. It may not be your first choice if you want to produce supertankers or cellphones, but it can produce pretty much anything in between. It has been a long time since the car was just an engine and four wheels on a frame. Today, cars consist of many complex systems each of which is the result of advanced research and production processes.

Their production and development demand expertise not only in all fields of mechanics and metallurgy but also in areas as diverse as acoustics and behavioural science.

Even more important than these scientific skills is the auto industry's most significant trait: its mastery of efficient mass production. Often driven to the extreme, and at the expense of those of us who work in it, the industry has expertise in logistics, production engineering, designing for production, quality control and so on. This could be applied to many kinds of production. Of course, efficient mass production is exactly what we need if we want to replace the fossil fuel economy. Mass production is what makes complicated technical devices cheap and should be applied to the production of wind turbines and other equipment for renewable energy production, including trams, trains and other vehicles and systems for a sustainable transport system.

Even at the lowest levels, where I and my co-workers dwell, there is a deep, but often tacit knowledge of the art of mass production and the methods that are used. And, of no less importance, we are used to change and conversion. The tendency in the auto industry in recent decades has been to introduce new models at an absurdly increasing speed. Retooling, rebuilding and retraining are all part of everyday life.

This ability of conversion is not a dreamed up vision, it has actually already occurred historically. In the months after Pearl Harbor, the US government prohibited the production of private cars and gave the auto industry the order to change over to war production. Obviously, it was an industry that was easy to convert and it produced a product from which it was easy to abstain. Ford and the other producers obeyed (and earned many a good dollar) by applying their knowledge of mass production to building tanks and bombers. The US auto industry was the only branch that was entirely converted to war production. And it was specifically its flexibility and knowledge about mass production that was behind this. As legendary Ford production engineer Charles Sorensen put it:

> To compare a Ford V-8 with a four-engine Liberator bomber was like matching a garage with a skyscraper, but beside their great differences I knew that the same fundamentals applied to high-volume production of both, the same as they would do to an electric egg beater or to a wrist watch.
>
> (Sorensen 2006, 281)

To sum up: the auto industry is a fantastic and versatile organisation that is not technically tied to making cars. It could play an important role in converting our societies into sustainable, carbon dioxide neutral, societies.

But if the two reasons mentioned above – social and technical/practical – are good enough reasons in their own right not to let the auto industry die, they are not even the most important reasons for why I'm opposing the twin capitalist suggestions for the auto industry.

The climate question is not about technology. It is about politics, in other words, the class struggle.

There seems to be a common understanding (except for some "flat earth" types) that humanity must reduce its emissions of greenhouse gases, and quickly. Yet, as we all know, this is not happening. From 1992 when 192 governments signed the UN Framework Convention on Climate Change until today there has been a 40 per cent increase in greenhouse gases, instead of the necessary decline that was the aim of the convention and that has been demanded by an increasingly worried and united scientific community. This is not because the people in charge are not enlightened or because they are evil persons who want to eradicate humanity, but because the measures that have to be taken would question the fundamental mechanisms of capitalism and the power of the corporations that rule our societies and our world. When it comes to the climate issue, as in so many other issues, reason stands against the power of mighty material interests. In a struggle between reason and material interest, the material interest wins 100 times out of 100. This is nothing new to the labour movement. Not many, if any, of the improvements we have experienced have occurred by themselves. The eight-hour day, vacations, health care, universal suffrage, the right to organise unions, etc., were not the results of polite reasoning but of hard and extended struggles.

So, if we want reason to prevail, we have to arm it, equipping it with enough social muscle so that it can challenge the powers that be. This is the moment where we, the workers of the threatened auto industry, come in. To fight for our jobs is a healthy reflex, as opposed to giving in and passively hoping for the market to solve our problems.

If we are going to be able to fight for anything at all we must keep the collective together. This is another reason why the "let-the-industry-die" strategy is an even worse choice than asking for support of the industry. The starting point must be class solidarity, that is, uniting and fighting for our jobs. But it's a very hard fight and it's almost impossible to win if you keep it within one company or sector. What we must do is to turn to society at large for support and intervention.

However, if we just say: pour tax payers' money into multinational corporations so that they can keep on producing machines that destroy the earth, most people would regard us as a special interest group that is hardly worth supporting, and rightfully so. A road to success would instead be to say: the corporate leaders who now are begging the state for help have forfeited their right to run the auto industry. The state should not subsidise their power and continued destructive production. Instead, society must step in and take control of the industry and use it to solve the challenges that society is facing. Nationalise the industry and convert it to create safe jobs and a production that can help us move away from the fossil fuel economy. This is the "third road" for the auto industry I have been advocating. To connect the climate issue to the immediate need to save jobs could be a platform for a broad social alliance. And this would be a tremendous weapon in the hands of reason.

The big question though is, how can we turn these ideas into reality? One important way to do this is to make conversion credible. At the plant where I work, there is an almost total lack of collective self-confidence. This is nothing special for my plant; it is the biggest obstacle for the Swedish working class in general and, to varying degrees, for workers globally. At our plant, management has used this weakness to the maximum in recent years, in a factory regime that is increasingly authoritarian and controlling. So the idea that we – the lowest of the low, we who are controlled down to the last step and fraction of a second, who are not even allowed to decide in which order we pick the nuts and bolts that we assemble the cars with, who do not even have control over our own union – would be able not only to run the plant but the whole company and even change the direction of production sounds like science fiction to most of my co-workers. A nice idea but out of touch with reality. We wouldn't even know where or how to start.

The first step is to start talking and writing about it, to introduce the idea in as many ways as possible. It might still be science fiction to most but when you sooner or later face a plant closure or worse, it might help if at least some people have read the science fiction. That's the stage I'm still at. That's why I wrote a book about the issue in order to create a platform in the public debate (Henriksson 2011).

Actually, this is really not the first step at all. The first step is learning to fight as a collective for whatever is necessary. If we just talk about these grand schemes without engaging in the daily petty fights, we are seen as windbags, building castles in the air. Therefore, in my daily life I engage in those "small" struggles.

A second step could be to produce concrete plans as to how to convert different sectors. In 1980 we had a referendum over nuclear power in Sweden. One of the most important things the environmental movement did was to put forward a plan, the Environmental Movement's Alternative Energy Plan (Miljöverbundet 1978). The plan showed in detail how nuclear power could be abolished and replaced with renewable energy. This was a very important tool in the campaign, educating activists and giving people in the movement self-confidence.

In May 2009, environmentalists, citizen groups, researchers and union representatives from various European countries met in Cologne, Germany, to discuss a sustainable transportation system. They issued the Cologne Declaration against rail privatisation and for sustainable transport. At the conference the "RailEurope2025" was put forward, a concrete plan to transform European transport systems in 15 years in order to cut their CO_2-emissions by 75 per cent. These kinds of plans could be used by unions and other movements to build up political pressure.

In Britain, the trade union network Campaign Against Climate Change has launched a campaign with the self-explanatory name One Million Climate Jobs and published a pamphlet detailing how these jobs could come into existence and what they would achieve in reducing green house gas emissions

(Neale 2010). A similar campaign has also been launched in South Africa (One Million Climate Jobs 2012).

The third, and, as I see it, most important step, would be to develop and connect these plans and ideas to the concrete work places, to production at the grassroot level. The only example of any significance that I'm aware of took place in Great Britain in the 1970s, at the Lucas Aerospace Company, which mainly produced arms. Faced with cutbacks in military spending and encouraged by a new Labour government that set out to nationalise parts of the air industry, unions at Lucas broke with their earlier habit of demanding more money for armaments in order to save jobs. Instead, they involved the membership at the various plants into developing a plan for a large number of socially useful products that the company would be able to produce. Even if their struggle eventually was defeated the plan was used as a means to mobilise support and it had repercussions throughout the world (Wainwright and Elliot 1981; Räthzel, Uzzell and Elliot 2010).

Not that the concept of "alternative production", as the idea was called, is uncomplicated; on the contrary. In the late 1970s several different industrial sectors in Sweden were in crisis: ship building, steel and the last remnants of the textile industry. For a period, "alternative production" became a hopeful buzzword, with inspiration from Lucas. But almost all attempts to save jobs under this banner failed. This was because for most people "alternative production" meant "other profitable products". You can say a lot about capitalists, but one thing you can't accuse them of is being bad at being capitalists, that is maximising profits. We can't beat them at their own game! The way we can use the idea of "alternative production" is to point out that we want to use our skills and can use them to produce socially useful and necessary products, regardless of whether they are profitable in the capitalist sense or not. This was the strength of the Lucas Plan, talking of social usefulness and not of private profit.

To me there has also always been another appealing aspect in the Lucas experience: what happens when we step outside submission of the daily treadmill. In the late eighteenth century, Thomas Paine captured this in just a few words:

> Revolutions create genius and talent; but these events do no more than bring them forward. There is existing in man, a mass of sense lying in a dormant state, and which, unless something excites it to action, will descend with him, in that condition, to the grave.
>
> (Paine [1795] 2008, 201)

Having spent decades doing mindless jobs on the assembly line, I think that there is a great power in this perspective.

In my opinion, the most important reason to raise the issue of conversion as a response to the double crisis of the economy and of the environment is its collective nature, at the social level and in the work place. When faced with plant closures or layoffs unions often respond with demands for replacement jobs, severance packages or retraining. There is nothing wrong with these but they are individual solutions that more or less accept the dissolution of the workers' collective. All union strength comes from keeping the collective united. The idea of converting industry is based on maintaining the collective. It is a concrete demand that we can fight for together instead of one by one in the context of an insecure future.

In the spring of 2008, as the crisis was gaining steam, I took part in a debate on national Swedish radio, with, amongst others, the Minister for Enterprise and Energy Maud Olofsson. When I criticised the auto industry and its products and spoke in favour of conversion, the journalist asked me if I wasn't cutting off the branch I was sitting on. This is one of the most common questions I've met when discussing the future of the auto industry. An all too common reaction of unions in industries that have met with environmental criticism is to hold the membership hostage to the companies. The threat to our jobs has been used as an argument not to interfere with environmentally harmful production. The question that can be asked is whether it does not mean to place too big a burden on auto workers (or any other workers in polluting industries) to save the world when their jobs are in immediate danger? My answer to this is the same as the one I gave the radio journalist: I don't think that we who work in the auto industry are more environmentally conscious than the rest of the world, nor are we more responsible for the destructive effects of mass auto transport than anyone else. A conversion strategy does not demand sacrifices from us, it's the other way round: if we who work in the auto industry keep clinging to the idea that our future lies with the car, then we're lost, both as workers and as human beings. Demanding that the industry should be converted and drawing up conversion plans is a possible way of defending not only our jobs, but the world as well.

Notes

1 This article is an extract from a speech at the Climate and Capitalism conference organised by Green Left and Socialist Resistance in London on 12 September 2009.
2 For example Stefan Fölster, Chief Economist at the employers' organisation Confederation of Swedish Enterprise: "Only sound that a number of car companies are closed down" (Fölster 2008).

References

Cotula, L., Vermeulen, S., Leonard, R. and Keeley, J. (2009) "Land grab or development opportunity? Agricultural investment and international land deals in Africa". IIED (International Institute for Environment and Development) http://pubs.iied.org/12561IIED.html (accessed 5 March 2012).
Dornboech, R. and Steenblik, R. (2007) "Biofuels: is the cure worse than the disease?" Paper from the Round table on sustainable development, OECD, Paris, September, www.oecd.org/dataoecd/15/46/39348696.pdf (accessed 5 March 2012).

European Environment Agency (2007) *Transport – bottom of the Kyoto class again.* Copenhagen: European Environment Agency. www.eea.europa.eu/pressroom/news releases/transport-bottom-of-the-kyoto-class-again (accessed 5 March 2012).

FAO (Food and Agriculture Organization of the United Nations) (2009) "State of the World's Forests". www.fao.org/docrep/011/i0350e/i0350e00.htm (accessed 5 March 2012).

Fölster, S. (2008) "Bara sunt att ett antal bilföretag läggs ner", Newsmill 2008-12-04. www.newsmill.se/node/2389%23comment-8095 (accessed 5 March 2012).

Henriksson, L. (2011) *Slutkört.* Stockholm: Ordfront förlag.

Holden, E. (2007) *Achieving Sustainable Mobility: Everyday and Leisure-time Travel in the EU.* London: Ashgate Publishing Ltd.

IEA (International Energy Agency) (2009) "Key World Energy Statistics 2009". www. iea.org/publications/free_new_desc.asp?pubs_ID=1199 (accessed 5 March 2012).

Miljöverbundet (1978) *Malte 1990: förslag till miljörörelsens alternativa energiplan.* Huvudrapport. Industridepartementet, Energikommissionen.

Neale, J. (2010) "One million Climate Jobs. Solving the economic and environmental crisis". Campaign against Climate Change. www.climate-change-jobs.org/sites/ default/files/1MillionClimateJobs_2010.PDF (accessed 5 March 2012).

One Million Climate Jobs (2012) www.climatejobs.org.za/ (accessed 5 March 2012).

Paine, T. ([1795]2008) *The Rights of Man.* ReadHowYouWant. www.readhowyouwant.com.

Räthzel, N., Uzzell, D. and Elliot, D. (2010) "The Lucas Aerospace experience: Can Unions become environmental Innovators?" *Soundings,* Vol. 46, 76–87.

Sorensen, C. E. (2006) *My forty years with Ford.* Detroit, MI: Wayne State University Press.

Wainwright, H. and Elliot, D. (1981) *The Lucas Plan: a new trade unionism in the making?* London: Allison & Busby.

Analyses of trade union environmental policies across the globe

8 The neo-liberal global economy and nature

Redefining the trade union role

Jacklyn Cock and Rob Lambert

Introduction

This chapter argues for building transnational solidarity networks involving labour and environmental activists to address the current economic and ecological crises. The implication is that labour needs to move away from both the traditional, national-level organisational form as well as broadening the conventional focus on jobs and workplace issues to embrace environmental issues.

We suggest two features of the current moment of neo-liberal globalisation – the ecological crisis, particularly climate change, and the globalisation of production – make this change urgent. The chapter illustrates how both features provide new political spaces and an impetus to globalise local resistance. This is evident first in the instance of the climate justice movement's mobilisation against a World Bank loan and second in the formation of a transnational coalition, 'Global Action on Arcelor Mittal'. An analysis of two labour federations in the Global South, the Congress of South African Trade Unions (COSATU) and the Australian Council of Trade Unions (ACTU), suggests that a new kind of transnational solidarity, larger, deeper and more powerful than hitherto, could be emerging. However, we also highlight the constraints and obstacles in redefining and widening the union role to include the defence of nature.

Climate change could trigger new forms of global solidarity. Moving beyond solidarities based on interests or identities, Hyman emphasises solidarity as involving 'mutuality despite difference', based on a sense of interdependence (Hyman 2011, 26). He concludes:

> [T]he challenge is to reconceptualise solidarity in ways which encompass the local, the national, the European and the global. For unions to survive and thrive, the principle of solidarity must not only be redefined and reinvented: workers on the ground must be active participants in this redefinition and reinvention.
>
> (Hyman 2011, 27)

Most clearly in its warnings of the threat to human survival, the discourse of climate change could be contributing to such a process.

Capital's response to the ecological crisis

Capital's response to the climate crisis is that the system can continue to expand by creating a new 'sustainable' or 'green capitalism', bringing the efficiency of the market to bear on nature and its reproduction. The two pillars on which green capitalism rests are technological innovation and expanding markets while keeping the existing institutions of capitalism intact.

More specifically green capitalism involves:

• profiting from carbon offsetting as part of the carbon trading regime enshrined in the Kyoto Protocol;
• appeals to nature (and even the crisis) as a marketing tool to promote consumption;
• developing largely untested clean coal technology through carbon capture and storage, which involves installing equipment that captures carbon dioxide and other greenhouse gases and then pumping the gas underground;
• the development of new sources of energy such as solar, nuclear and wind hereby creating new markets that emphasise energy efficiency;
• the massive development of biofuels, which diverts land from food production;
• moving production to sites of weak environmental regulation.

Underlying all these strategies is the broad process of commodification: the transformation of nature and all social relations into economic relations, subordinated to the logic of the market and the imperatives of profit. However, the notion of 'green' or 'sustainable capitalism' is being subjected to growing criticism (Harris-White in Panitch and Leys 2006; Kovel 2007; Foster 2009). These critiques are rooted in the understanding that *capital's logic of accumulation* is destroying all the ecological conditions that sustain life. As Wallis writes: 'No serious observer now denies the severity of the environmental crisis, but it is still not widely recognised as a capitalist crisis, that is a crisis arising from and perpetuated by the rule of capital, and hence incapable of resolution within the capitalist framework' (Wallis 2010, 32). This is a key insight of an emerging climate justice movement.

Labour's response to the ecological crisis

This critical approach situating relations with nature within the contradictory dynamic of capital accumulation is a political choice. Such a critique of a green capitalism is not part of the discourse in Australia, a country that illustrates a social democratic approach to environmental issues, reflecting compromises between corporations (business perspective) and labour (needs of society perspective) forged in internal party battlegrounds. The *Australian Labor Party's* (ALP) election victory in 1983 ushered in an era of uncompromising endorsement of Neo-liberal restructuring, hence its commitment to a market-based solution to carbon pollution through a system of carbon trading. The Australian Council of Trade Unions (ACTU) endorses ALP government policy on climate change and is focused on the promotion of green jobs through an alliance (not movement) with the Australian Conservation Foundation (ACF), the Australian Council of Social Service (ACOSS) and the Climate Institute through the formation of the Southern Cross Climate Coalition. The actions of this coalition are based on lobbying. Amidst growing opposition to the federal ALP coalition government's proposed carbon tax, the ACTU launched an initiative in February 2011, which led to the 'Say Yes' campaign in May 2011. The ACTU and environmental groups launched a 'National YES Week' on 30 May, culminating in rallies round the country on 5 June, World Environment Day. Saying 'Yes' was narrowly focused on a carbon tax, proposed by the ALP–Green coalition.

The ACTU and ACF promoted a joint report in 2010, which argues that there is potential for the creation of 770,000 'green collar' jobs by 2030 (ACTU 2010). The 'Say Yes' campaign, which included advertising, petitioning and rallies in major cities, was framed broadly within a 'green capitalism' perspective.

> Unions welcome the agreed process … to develop an effective pricing mechanism, beginning with a fixed price in 2012 and moving to a full-scale emissions trading scheme within three to five years. A price on pollution will help change the economic behavior of Australia, which is the highest per capita producer of pollution in the world. The revenue will go towards supporting jobs and communities into the future.
>
> (ACTU 2011)

Understandably, the question of the impact of such an intervention is at the forefront of the debate. Blue-collar unions in mining, manufacturing, construction and transport sectors are concerned about the job impact of a transition to a low carbon economy. These include the AWU (Australian Workers Union), AMWU (Australian Manufacturing Workers Union), MUA (Maritime Union of Australia), ETU (Electrical Workers Union) and CFMEU (Construction, Forestry, Manufacturing and Energy Union). Within this grouping the right-wing AWU is a vociferous opponent of any action in this sphere, lobbying instead for corporate subsidies to introduce clean technology (Snell and Fairbrother 2010, 87). The AWU supported steel company opposition by contending: 'The AWU will not support a carbon tax that costs even one steel job' (AWU 2011).

The politically progressive Mining and Energy Division of the CFMEU has engaged in the climate debate from a technical and political perspective. With most of its members among coal miners, the union is one of the most active unions in the climate policy debate. The union is pursuing a 'just transition' approach. This involves efforts to protect vulnerable workers. In the Australian case it means a market solution is complemented by green industry policy plans aimed at direct public and private investment in affected regions to promote economic diversity and resilience (Maher 2011). In sup-porting the ALP policy on carbon capture and storage (CCS), the union has joined forces with the Coal Association, WWF-Australia and Climate Institute, which is seen by some climate justice groups as another front for the 'coal lobby' (Snell and Fairbrother 2010, 89).

The AMWU and the ETU are unions that look beyond the market for solutions to the climate crisis, stressing state intervention in fostering a green economy and sustainable industry. The West Australian branch of the AMWU adopted a policy in May 2010 that calls for 100 per cent renewable energy by 2020 (AMWU 2010). This position is one that is supported by the climate justice groups, which illustrates AMWU engagement with environmental civil society groups. The ETU, which represents electrical, communications and power industry workers, has maintained an active campaign against the expansion of uranium mining. The ETU has built alliances with a range of anti-nuclear groups, which includes environmental (Climate Action Network Australia) and indigenous groups. The CFMEU (E&md), with its coal mining membership, leans towards a market solution. The AWU's business unionism is consistent with their stress on the market with zero job loss. What is shared among unions, and articulated by the ACTU, is that there is likely to be a net gain of jobs with a 'just transition' to a more energy-efficient, renewable-based, low carbon economy (Snell and Fairbrother 2010, 90).

Overall, no Australian union envisages a social movement strategy to impose radical measures that the looming catastrophe demands. The ACTU and its affiliated unions are committed to supporting the ALP government's carbon tax in a politically hostile environment where the Conservative opposition as the voice of corporations is effectively articulating a no-action strategy.

The situation in South Africa is very different. The Congress of South African Trade Unions (COSATU), a trade union federation with two million members and 20 affiliate unions, is starting to recognise climate change as a developmental and social issue and promote radical solutions. At its 2009 Congress COSATU decided to increase its research capacity on climate change. At the tenth national congress the federation observed: 'climate change is one of the greatest threats to our planet and our people'. According to trade unionist Fundi Nzimande: 'We want to review climate change through the lens of working class perspectives. We want to counter the big business point of view'. This was endorsed by COSATU and two other federations, NACTU and FEDUSA:

> [W]e are convinced that any efforts to address the problems of Climate Change that does not fundamentally challenge the system of global capitalism is bound not only to fail, but to generate new, larger and more dangerous threats to human beings and our planet. Climate Change is caused by the global private profit system of capitalism. Tackling Greenhouse gas emissions is not just a technical or technological problem. It requires a fundamental economic and social transformation to substantially change current patterns of production and consumption.
>
> (*Labours' Initial Response to the National Climate Change*, Green Paper 2010, unpublished)

Such a position is consistent with the approach of the climate justice movement, which challenges the false dichotomy portraying labour–environmental relations as a trade-off between jobs and the environment. This movement argues environmental protection not only creates jobs, it also saves jobs. Forestry, tourism, agriculture and the growing leisure and outdoor recreation industries are all important sources of jobs that depend directly upon clear water, clean air and wilderness for their continuation and growth.

In South Africa the climate justice movement is organising around the notion of 'climate jobs'. This 'million climate jobs' campaign is modelled on a British trade union campaign and is taking hold in the local labour movement. It is structured on the argument that if we are to move in a 'just transition' to a low carbon economy using renewable energy instead of coal, it will be workers who will have to build wind, wave, tide and solar power capacities. It is workers who will have to renovate and insulate our homes and buildings and build new forms of public transport. The campaign stresses that the lives of working people could improve in the process.

These initiatives emphasise that climate jobs must be economically secure jobs that promote equality and justice. Progressive union federations such as COSATU contend that capital accumulation breeds inequalities – even if those forms of capital accumulation are green. Support for this notion is increasing. A meeting in Madrid in 2011 discussed a new development paradigm on the way to the Rio + 20 summit and beyond. The Spanish minister of the environment stressed that 'the social and environmental agenda should be indissolubly joined in order for a just transition to be produced towards a new model of growth'. Support for green jobs and a green economy was expressed. This is captured in the statement of Ambet Yuson, the General Secretary of Building and Woodworkers International (BWI): 'a green economy based on rights, sustainability principles and decent work can meet the challenge of our societies. … A just transition, such as the one unions are calling for, needs to be based on the transformation of all jobs into sustainable ones' (Sustainlabour 2011).

The question is, are green jobs one component of a new green capitalism that is trying to avoid fundamental change through an emphasis on expanding markets and new technologies? Or, are green jobs part of a green economy, which – based on rights, sustainability principles and decent work – can meet the challenge of a just transition? Overall the Madrid Dialogue emphasised that the contribution of trade unions is necessary to build a sustainable world, thus unions should participate in broad coalitions with other social movements. This is beginning to happen under the framework of an emerging global climate justice movement.

The climate justice movement

Such a movement has been steadily growing globally (albeit unevenly). In 1991 people in 70 countries in 500 places participated in international climate action days. In 2009 there were actions in 5,000 places and in 2010 in 7,000 places in almost every country (Bjork 2011). Some 100,000 people marched for climate justice during COP15 at Copenhagen, many calling for 'System change, not climate change'. The demands of this nascent movement are not narrowly limited to action on climate change but to resistance that seeks to confront the root causes of the ecological crisis, namely, the contradictory and expansionist logic of capital accumulation. Consequently climate justice is a frequent theme in the growing 'Occupy Wall Street' movement that has now involved actions in 900 cities throughout the world.

The acid test of further empowering this embryonic formation is the choice to directly draw trade unions into the climate justice movement. However, it takes two to tango: union leaderships need to embrace this development and redefine their role in relation to the need for a strong movement defence of nature. Clearly workers and their organisations are an indispensable force for a just transition to a low carbon economy. As Jakopovich (2009) writes: 'Environmentalists are workers and obviously potential allies in their efforts to advance workplace health and safety, and also to tackle environmental concerns of working-class communities: for workers bear the brunt of environmental degradation and destruction, both in terms of health and quality of life issues' (Jakopovich 2009, 75).

The efficacy of an integrated movement also depends on unions going global in new, action-oriented ways. To the degree that the emerging climate justice movement brings pressure to bear for such change, the process may strengthen global unionism and revitalise trade unions both globally and locally. This is possible because 'climate justice' is stressed in both global and local terms. Globally, justice is a powerful theme among climate change activists, who claim that a wide range of activities contribute to an ecological debt owed to countries in the Global South: the extraction of natural resources, unequal terms of trade, degradation of land and soil for export crops and the loss of biodiversity. Locally, there is mounting evidence that it is the poor and the powerless who are most negatively affected by pollution and resource depletion and will bear the brunt of climate change.

The network *Climate Justice Now* was formed in 2007 from different strands in the women's, environmental and democratic popular movements from the Global South such as *Via Campesina*. These Southern initiatives represent an alternative to the global coalition of well-funded environmental foundations and NGOs who often lack democratic accountability. These movements are committed to amplifying the voices of those most directly affected, particularly working people in the Global South, who are the least responsible for the carbon emissions that cause climate change.

The climate justice movement is demonstrating an extraordinary reach linking grassroots communities to global campaigns. For example in 2009 in South Africa Earthlife Africa (Johannesburg) and Groundwork mobilised opposition to the World Bank's $3.75 billion loan to Eskom to build more coal-fired power stations. They made connections between organisations and grassroots communities in the Global North and South to mobilise opposition to the loan. Within three months more than 200 organisations around the world (including some trade unions) were mobilised to endorse a critique of the loan. They pointed out that this will increase the price of electricity for poor people and increase South Africa's contribution to carbon emissions and climate change. While opposition to the loan was not ultimately successful, this action points to the kind of transnational solidarity that is emerging.

The movement also spotlights the failure of global elites to solve the ecological crisis. Despite Copenhagen, Cancún and Durban there is no global binding agreement on limiting carbon emissions. The intention of the United Nations Framework Convention on Climate Change (UNFCCC) is to protect the capitalist economy, not the climate. Recognition of these failures certainly highlights the need for an alternative, societal-based, movement approach to the defence of nature. The task is to construct, with a great sense of urgency, a powerful global social force to attain this goal. Unions need to become equal partners in this endeavour so that the movement is grounded both in society and the economy (workplaces), deploying new forms of radical action (Webster *et al.* 2008, 13). Given the dramatic impacts of global restructuring on workers, unions have – in principle – an interest in joining forces with the climate justice movement, for to evolve into a movement defending not only nature, but societies across the globe ravaged by the continuous restructuring imposed by global corporations and driven by finance capital, principally private equity.

However, as yet unions still have to translate a dawning consciousness of the planet's predicament into a *new kind of movement*, which is global in scope, yet deeply embedded in local places where the meaning of the global is a networked connectivity between these places. Harvey makes a salient point in *The Enigma of Capital*, when he argues that such a movement could be energised and mobilised if it became 'constituted out of a broad alliance of the discontented, the alienated, the deprived and the dispossessed' (Harvey 2010, 240). It is beyond the scope of this short chapter to explore this conception and the union role in such a movement, except to say that unless a new integrative movement can emerge from a multiplicity of initiatives across the globe hopes of stabilising climate appear doomed. The character of such a movement will also emerge through rigorous critiques of failed initiatives. In the next section we briefly analyse one such initiative to capture the gap between the new green discourse and the organisational reality on the ground.

Capital accumulation and nature: the case of Arcelor Mittal

In a brief timespan of 60 years, Arcelor Mittal evolved from being a relatively small local steel producer in Bengal to the world's largest steel producer by 2010. The narrative of this expansion reveals both the necessary character of Harvey's movement of the dispossessed and the extraordinary challenge that this represents. For as Doreen Massey highlights in her book *For Space* (2005, 85) such corporate expansion reflects 'the new power geometry' of neo-liberal globalisation. Freedom of trade, investment and finance created the opportunities for rapid accumulation through bargain basement buyouts of privatised steel corporations and mergers and acquisitions all over the world by Mittal. This accumulation of capital was marked by a high degree of labour exploitation, the destruction of local communities as the company instigated closures and the destruction of nature. The pollution of air and groundwater was a feature of their operations across the world. Mittal's operations in Vanderbijlpark in South Africa illustrate the human social and ecological cost of this destruction.

The destruction involved the pollution of the groundwater with toxic substances from an unlined dam that led to a high incidence of various forms of cancers and skin ailments in the community adjoining the steel mill. The local community mobilised against the corporation's environmental vandalism forming first the Steel Valley Crisis Committee and then the Vaal Environmental Justice Alliance (VEJA), which also attempted to establish connections with other workforces similarly affected by Mittal's impacts. However, these initiatives were weakened because of a lack of trade union engagement *with* the community. COSATU's union, *The National Union of Metal Workers* (NUMSA), was essentially preoccupied with job loss associated with Mittal's work-restructuring programme, which had created deep insecurity within the workforce. In South Africa the state-owned steel mill had employed 80,000 workers. However, after privatisation thousands of jobs were cut.

In 2008 a new coalition of activists formed Global Action on Arcelor Mittal, which brought together activists from Ohio, Luxembourg, the Czech Republic, Kazakhstan, Bosnia and Herzegovina, the Ukraine, India and Liberia. This is a growing network that has organised simultaneous protests in eight countries to mark Arcelor Mittal's annual general meeting and has produced two well-researched reports describing its worldwide environmental abuse. The globalised protests and the organisational upscaling from the Steel Valley Crisis Committee to VEJA and then to the Global Action on Arcelor Mittal could suggest that initiatives that are locally rooted but globally connected have potential. But the Mittal story is also illustrative of current weaknesses in going global. In June 2006, *The International Metal Workers Federation* (IMF), a global union federation headquartered in Geneva, organised a global meeting of 52 union participants representing 17 unions. However, following a European model, the emphasis was on building a partnership with management. The opening paragraph of an agreement stated:

At the conclusion of the meeting, delegates resolved to work together with their trade union brothers and sisters at Arcelor to create a culture of respect for workers' rights in the new steel giant, setting the standard for all other steel companies to follow.

(IMF 2006)

This meeting never addressed the critical issue of Mittal's impact on nature.

Herein lies the essential challenge of building a new kind of movement that aims at transcending the notion of a conflict of interests between jobs and nature. The logic of capital accumulation is a singular process, which destroys jobs *and* nature, requiring a movement in defence of both, founded on a political rejection of uncontrolled, financially driven, private equity accumulation. In this conception the fight for nature is simultaneously a battle alongside workers whose lives have been shattered by work restructuring. A struggle on this scale needs to be politically framed as a *liberation* struggle, alongside the historic movements of liberation such as Gandhi's independence movement, the fight for civil rights in the United States, the anti-apartheid struggle and battles against military regimes in the global South (Lambert forthcoming). Of course these historical movements had national goals, but the connected global threats of both neo-liberal capitalism and planetary climate catastrophe means that these visions and imaginaries of freedom and struggle have to be translated onto a global scale. A liberation movement of the dispossessed will need to be a *global* movement, coordinating and synchronising global scale action for nature and for work security.

The emergence of the movement we envisage will need to be advanced by a choice for *a new labour internationalism* (NLI), which has evolved in the Global South (Latin America, Africa, Asia and Australia) over the past 20 years in the form of the Southern Initiative on Globalization and Trade Union Rights (SIGTUR). Such an orientation is experimenting with the deployment of new forms of power, particularly symbolic and logistical (Webster *et al.* 2008, 12f). There are also debates within SIGTUR on redefining trade union identity and to embrace a more wide-ranging resistance against neo-liberalism, which simultaneously advances a new vision of an alternative, founded on a new status of and rights for nature linked to the social and democratic control of production and finance.

Conclusion

This chapter suggests that the globalisation of production and the planetary climate crisis define a new '*moment*' in neo-liberal globalisation. In response, the fundamental question is, can the climate justice movement create a new political space triggering the construction of a global social movement? Such a movement would be based on grounded networking fighting both for society (attacking work restructuring and insecurity) *and* a new commitment to nature (the fragile ecology and climate of the planet). It would be a movement of the dispossessed in which the labour movement would play an indispensable role. Could such a movement link the crisis of work security and climate change to the logic of capital accumulation?

This will not be easy: the globalisation of production has led to an extraordinary concentration of corporate power. Key questions concerning corporate power in relation to their environmental impact are: 'How can the physical environment be protected from the actions of huge multinational corporations whose activities have, until recently, gone virtually unchallenged and unregulated? How can people separated by language, politics, nationality and culture come together to challenge corporations whose power transcends national boundaries? How can the poor and disenfranchised have their voices heard?' (Markowitz and Rosner 2002, 2).

We contend the answer surely lies in strengthening social power 'rooted in the capacity to mobilise people for cooperative, voluntary actions of various sorts in civil society' (Wright 2006, 106). Whether under the rubric of a liberation or an anti-capitalist movement, a global alliance of labour and environmental activists such as those committed to challenging the abuses of corporations like Arcelor Mittal and institutions such as the World Bank could become a significant source of counter power. Harvey recognises that we could be in a new moment: 'While nothing is certain, it could be that where we are now is only the beginning of a prolonged shake-out in which the question of grand and far-reaching alternatives will gradually bubble up to the surface in one part of the world or another' (Harvey 2010, 225).

Harvey insists on the 'absolute necessity for a coherent, anti-capitalist revolutionary movement' (Harvey 2010, 228).

> The central problem is that in aggregate there is no resolute and sufficiently unified anti-capitalist movement that can adequately challenge the reproduction of the capitalist class and the perpetuation of its power on the world stage. Neither is there any obvious way to attack the bastions of privilege for capitalist elites or to curb their inordinate money power and military might. ... While openings exist towards some alternative social order, no one really knows where or what it is ... a global anti-capitalist movement is unlikely to emerge without some animating vision of what is to be done and why. A double blockage exists: the lack of an alternative vision prevents the formation of an oppositional movement, while the absence of such a movement precludes the articulation of an alternative.
>
> (Harvey 2010, 227)

This 'double blockage' is illustrated by Sweeney when he describes that

> In recent years global labour has worked on the premise that the 'real-world' historical options are essentially twofold. Either humanity will transition to some form of 'green capitalism' where economic growth is de-linked from emissions and environmental destruction generally, or we face a 'suicide capitalism' scenario where fossil-fuel corporations and major industrial, agriculture, transport, and retail interests are successful in maintaining business as usual.
>
> (Sweeney 2011)

Debating alternatives to both 'green' or 'suicide' capitalism means that trade unions have to go beyond the nation and beyond the workplace. The immediate tasks are: first to re-emphasize and redefine the core value of the labour movement – solidarity – which involves struggling against the individualism and what Leibowitz calls 'the infection of self-interest' promoted by marketised social relations (Leibowitz 2010, 144). It is also necessary to challenge the notion that trade unions have become largely obsolete in a globalising world. This argument surfaces in different forms such as the 'uncompromising pessimism' of Burawoy (2010) or the cynicism of Standing (2009), who sees a class fragmentation involving a new elite and a growing 'precariat' as displacing organised labour.

Second, we need to promote a vision of an alternative social order. As Leibowitz writes: 'if we don't know where we want to go, no path will take us there' (Leibowitz 2010, 7). 'The deepest shadow that hangs over us is neither terror, nor environmental collapse, nor global recession. It is the internalized fatalism that holds there is no possible alternative to capital's world order' (Kelly and Malone 2006, 116).

Fortunately, in South Africa a third alternative – ecosocialism – is being debated. Driven by a small grouping, the Democratic Left Forum, this embryonic eco-socialist movement is involved in the climate jobs campaign and is mobilising grassroot communities around food sovereignty, participatory democracy and the climate crisis. In the process it is becoming clear to increasing numbers that many governments are driven by vested interests and that therefore neither they nor capitalism will solve the crisis of climate change. As David Harvey writes: 'an ethical, non-exploitative and socially just capitalism that redounds to the benefit of all is impossible. It contradicts the very nature of what capital is' (Harvey 2010, 239). The only rational response to the reality of climate change is transformative change to a new kind of ethical, democratic and ecological socialism.

References

ACTU Australian Council of Trade Unions (ACTU) (2010) 'Creating Jobs – Cutting Pollution: The Roadmap for a cleaner, stronger economy'. www.actu.org.au/Media/Mediareleases/ActiononpollutionleadstomorejobsacrossAustralia.aspx (accessed 20 March 2012).

——(2011) 'Climate Change and Jobs'. www.actu.org.au/Campaigns/ClimateChangeJobs/default.aspx (accessed 20 March 2012).

Australian Manufacturing Workers Union (AMWU) (2010) 'A plan for low emissions industries and technological development'. www.amwu.asn.au/campaigns/46/CT/ (accessed 20 March 2012).

Australian Workers Union (AWU) (2011) 'Carbon Pricing: keeping workers' jobs'. *The Australian Worker.* http://www.awu.net.au/543925_5.html (accessed 20 March 2012).

Bieler, A. and Lindberg, I. (eds) (2011) *Global Restructuring. Labour and the Challenges for Transnational Solidarity.* London: Routledge.

Bjork, T. (2011) 'Social Forum Journey'. http://aktivism.info/socialforumjourney/ (accessed 11 March 2010).

Burawoy, M. (2010) 'From Polanyi to Pollyanna: The False Optimism of Global Labour Studies', *Global Labour Journal*. Vol. 1, No. 2, pp. 301–13. http://digitalcommons. mcmaster.ca/globallabour/vol1/iss2/7 (accessed 11 March 2012).

Foster, J. B. (2009) *The Ecological Revolution*. New York: Monthly Review Press.

Harvey, D. (2010) *The Enigma of Capital and the Crises of Capitalism*. New York: Oxford University Press.

Hyman, R. (2011) 'Trade unions, global competition and options for solidarity', in Bieler, A. and Lindberg, I. (eds) *Global Restructuring. Labour and the Challenges for Transnational Solidarity*. London: Routledge, pp. 16–27.

International Metalworkers Federation (IMF) (2006) 'Arcelormittal agreement on Health & Safety'. www.imfmetal.org/index.cfm?c=14251 (accessed 20 March 2012).

Jakopovich, D. (2009) 'Uniting to win: labour environmental alliances', *Capitalism, Nature, Socialism*. Vol. 20, No. 2, pp. 74–96.

Kelly, J. and Malone, S. (2006) *Ecosocialism or Barbarism*. London: Socialist Resistance.

Kovel, J. (2007) *The Enemy of Nature. The end of Capitalism or the end of the world*. London: Zed Books.

Lambert, R. (forthcoming) 'Agents of the Market or Instruments of Justice: trade union identity in the era of market driven politics', *Labor History*.

Leibowitz, M. (2010) *The Socialist Alternative*. New York: Monthly Review Press.

Maher, T. (2011) 'Why Abbott's jobs scare campaign is a sham', *Common Cause* 77 (2): 3, http://cfmeu.com.au/Common%20Cause%20April%20-%20May%202011 (accessed 16 April 2012).

Markowitz, M. and Rosner, S. (2002) *Deceit and Denial. The deadly politics of industrial pollution*. New York: Basic Books.

Massey, D. (2005) *For Space*. London: Palgrave.

Panitch L. and Leys, C. (2006) *Coming to Terms with Nature. Socialist Register*. Toronto: Palgrave.

Snell, D. and Fairbrother, P. (2010) 'Unions as environmental actors', *European Review of Labour and Research*. Vol. 16, No. 3, pp. 411–24.

Standing, G. (2009) *Work After Globalisation. Building Occupational Citizenship*. Cheltenham: Edward Elgar.

Sustainlabour (2011) 'The Madrid Dialogue took off', www.sustainlabour.org/noticia. php?lang=EN&idnoticia=132 (accessed 20 March 2012).

Sweeney, S. (2011) 'How unions can help secure a binding global climate agreement in 2011.' www.labor4sustainability.org/post/the-durban-challenge/ (accessed 11 March 2012).

Wallis, V. (2010) 'Beyond green capitalism', *Monthly Review*. February, pp. 32–47.

Webster, E., Lambert, R. and Bezuidenhout, A. (2008) *Grounding Globalization: Labour in the Age of Insecurity*. Oxford: Blackwell.

9 Questions for trade unions on land, livelihoods and jobs[1]

Andrew Bennie

Introduction

The nascent field of environmental labour studies provides a major opportunity for investigating and suggesting the ways in which, in the context of the environmental crisis, labour as a social movement can become a leading social actor in a transition to a more just and sustainable world. This chapter suggests that trade unions could explore possible links between labour movements and rural land-based livelihoods. This implies a reconsideration of the concept of 'development'.[2]

This chapter will make use of a case study of a proposed mining project in South Africa to argue that while it is critical for labour movements to take account of the current climate change crisis and focus on the creation of sustainable jobs, it needs to broaden its focus to the protection of environments and natural resources that form the basis of local livelihoods and are threatened by dispossession. The chapter will explore this link through the paradigm of development. The societal changes that are required for dealing with the climate and environmental crises require that labour movements reorient their notions of development beyond that of capitalist accumulation, economic growth.

Labour, environment and rural land-based livelihoods

The current global environmental predicament faced by the planet, characterised by climate change and environmental degradation, can be attributed to a model of development that emphasises intense resource use with little regard for the ecological base on which development depends (Sachs 1999). Trade unions have the potential to be a key social force in effecting ecological change. They have, however, traditionally participated in and supported models of development that emphasised intensive resource use as routes to expand the possibilities of social reproduction for workers. They therefore tended to promote jobs at all costs, and often environmentally destructive jobs, perpetuating a false opposition between workers and the environment (Foster 2002; Uaid 2009). Today there is a growing awareness in the trade union movement around the world about the class dimensions of environmental degradation and climate change. It is acknowledged that the dualism between jobs and the environment is not sustainable and that unions have an important role to play in transitioning to a more sustainable world.

However, the labour movement in South Africa has traditionally been absent in local environmental struggles (Cock 2007, 2008), reflecting its failure to comprehensively acknowledge the implications of the global environmental crisis and the resource constraints it places on economic growth and development (Cock 2007). It is only recently that large parts of the South African labour movement have begun to realise these dimensions. For example, at its 2011 Central Executive Committee meeting, the largest labour federation, the Congress of South African Trade Unions (COSATU), recognised that 'capitalist accumulation has been the underlying cause of excessive greenhouse gas emissions, and therefore global warming and climate change' and that a 'new low carbon development path is needed which addresses the need for decent jobs and the elimination of unemployment' (COSATU 2011). The National Union of Mineworkers (NUM), an affiliate of COSATU, has also recognised the need to respond to the global environmental situation. It has adopted the notions of 'sustainable development' and 'just transition', arguing that it is necessary to avoid framing 'sustainability questions in terms of jobs versus the environment rather than jobs and the environment' (NUM no date a). However, it still remains the case that trade unions in South Africa remain largely absent in local environmental struggles and there is little in terms of concrete policy generated as yet, apart from signing on to important instruments like the government's 'Green Accord', which aims for the creation of 300,000 'green jobs' by 2020, and the endorsement of the green economy in the government's New Growth Path policy.

At the same time, rural indigenous people and small-scale peasant farmers are engaged in struggles against the effects of climate change and dispossession and enclosure of land and natural resources by expansive development and efforts to ameliorate its ecological effects through biofuels and carbon-offset mechanisms (Joubert 2008; Daniel and Mittal 2009; McMichael 2010; Levidow and Paul 2010; Friends of the Earth 2010; Lohmann 2006).

The challenge, therefore, is to recognise the long-term implications of the global ecological predicament and to forge links between indigenous peoples and peasant farmers of the South and the organised working class around the world (Socialist Resistance 2009). David Harvey argues that it is an urgent task to unite the two key resistance movements of our time: the largely peasant-based movements mobilised against 'accumulation by dispossession' on the one hand, and on the other hand, those contesting 'expanded social reproduction', where the 'exploitation of wage labour and conditions defining the social wage are central issues' (Harvey 2005, 48–49). An urgent task, Harvey therefore argues, is to think about how such labour movement struggles and largely rural livelihood struggles could relate to each other. This implies political and research tasks. As Hart and Sitas have contended:

[M]ost researchers have pursued each of these elements in isolation: 'the land question', 'the labour question', or 'the question of livelihoods' (usually meaning non-formal employment). With a few key exceptions, such research has also been sharply divided across rural and urban lines. We argue that these themes constituted, constitute, and will continue to constitute in their social and spatial *interconnections*, a central challenge to research, policy, and social action for decades to come.

(Hart and Sitas 2004, 32, original emphasis)

The case study below will show that the communities' focus has been on the protection of natural resources from mining and how industrial expansion that might create jobs can at the same time cause ecological destruction and dispossession of land and natural resources from small-scale and subsistence farming communities. This has implications for the labour movement's conceptions of national economic development as a pathway to expanding social reproduction of the working class. This can involve a consideration for the protection of natural resources that form a basis of rural livelihoods.

Case study: Xolobeni Mineral Sands Project, Wild Coast, South Africa[3]

The site of the proposed Xolobeni Mineral Sands Project is situated in Pondoland on the Wild Coast of the Eastern Cape Province, about 250 km south of the port city of Durban. It falls within the Amadiba Tribal Area, which is divided into two zones: the coastal zone (Section 24), also known as Mgungundlovu, and the inland zone (Section 21). The Amadiba area is home to about 28,000 people, while Mgungundlovu has a population of about 5,000 people. The Amadiba area falls within the Pondoland Centre of Endemism (PCE) and is an area of high biodiversity, regarded as the second most species-rich floristic region in South Africa. The scenery of Mgungundlovu is punctuated by the homesteads (from one to six huts) that comprise the five coastal villages, bound by a river gorge in the north and the south and the coastline on the east.

Transworld Energy and Minerals Resources (TEM), the South African subsidiary of the Australian Mineral Resource Commodities (MRC), applied for a right to mine about 360 million tons worth of sand dunes along Mgungundlovu, referred to by the mining company as the Xolobeni mining tenement area, for titanium-related minerals. The tenement area begins at the Mzamba River in the north and extends south for about 21 km to the southern boundary of Mgungundlovu at Mtentu River; 5 per cent of the sand contains heavy minerals, of which about 65 per cent are commercially viable (GCS 2007a). The predominant mineral contained in the sand dunes is ilmenite, together with rutile, zircon and leuxocene.

However, the proposal to mine has created a highly contested process that has bred conflict and division within the affected communities, with the majority of them opposed to the proposal.[4] The dynamics surrounding the proposed mining were characterised by the pursuit of narrow interests, unequal power relations, and a lack of participation by the affected communities. For example, the mining company established a local 'empowerment partner', Xolco, without any consultation with the communities. It has only served as a vehicle for its members to seek personal returns.

The company's ambitions have been framed within the discourse of development. Those in favour of the mine argue that it will bring development to the Pondoland region and will contribute to sustainable development. Key actors opposed to it argue that it will destroy local ecosystems and the livelihoods of the affected population, and is therefore the 'wrong kind' of development.

In July 2008 the rights to mine were awarded without the knowledge of the communities and organisations involved. Only after realising the level of objection on the part of the communities and the fact that they had not been consulted, the Minister of Minerals and Energy withheld the licence. In June 2011, the new minister announced the withdrawal of the mining right on the grounds of severe environmental issues.[5]

An environmental impact assessment (EIA) for the mining was conducted, but it was widely criticised for omissions on some issues and lack of comprehensiveness in others. Many of the negative impacts that it did include were not acknowledged in the company's and local government's public promotion of the proposed mining. The environmental impacts would have involved digging up about 885 hectares of land, the majority of which is used for grazing. It would have displaced many households[6] and used large amounts of groundwater on which the communities are dependent, and affect wetlands and estuaries. The ability of the mining company to rehabilitate the sand dunes to pre-mining conditions and restore the floral character of the area was contested. As a botanist from a nearby area stated: 'You can re-vegetate, but you can't rehabilitate' (Abbott interview).

The positive social impacts of the proposed mining conveyed by mining supporters and the Environmental Management Plan (EMP) for the project in terms of direct job creation are highly questionable. Despite public rhetoric on the part of the mining company and those in government that supported the mine, the EMP admits that 'the community who will be most severely impacted by the proposed development are unlikely to benefit significantly from the permanent employment opportunities associated with the mine' (GCS 2007b, 3–52). The EIA confirms this: 'the potential direct employment opportunities for the local community are likely to be limited' (GCS 2007a, 7–52).

The need for development has been justified by those in favour of it by painting a picture of poverty and deprivation of the area. However, this denies local perceptions of poverty and its experience, as well as the central role that the land plays in sustaining the potentially affected communities. The following section will present the views of these communities and show how they constitute a local concept of development. This has important implications for how the labour movement relates to broader questions around environment, economic growth and development.

Environmental/land-based sources of livelihood

The state of the former South African homelands is in many respects characterised by poverty, environmental degradation and declining prospects of survival from land-based livelihoods such as farming (Bank and Minkley 2005; Ngonini 2007). However, Mgungundlovu and the coastal areas of the Wild Coast provide a slightly different case with regard to local livelihoods. One important reason for this is that betterment planning under apartheid, the aim of which was to 'modernize' African agriculture in the homelands but which predominantly led to agricultural decline and negative environmental impacts, was strongly resisted in the coastal zones of the Transkei. Therefore, about 45 per cent of the Transkei was not subject to betterment (McAllister 2003). While various means, including wage work and government grants, exist for achieving security in Mgungundlovu, local agriculture and natural resource harvesting continue to provide an important basis of income security, which Hadju (2005, 236–38) terms 'environmental security'. This is the case for much of the Wild Coast (see Shackleton *et al.* 2007; Palmer *et al.* 2002; Kepe 1997, 2001).

Virtually all households grow their own maize, and most households have a vegetable patch in which they grow a range of foods including bananas, yams (a root vegetable, locally known as *amadumbe*), sweet potatoes, onions, tomatoes, cabbage, carrots, beans and pumpkin. As one resident said, 'We have our own "gold" in the area' (quoted in *Farmers Weekly* 2010). The only food that households indicated they buy is that which they cannot produce such as rice, salt, cooking oil, tea and sugar. All homesteads have a number of various types of animals and livestock, which include chickens, cattle and goats.

Households collect firewood in nearby forests for cooking and heating and water from streams and springs. Access to the ocean also provides an important extractive source of sustenance to many households. The dependence on land-based livelihoods is in turn linked to various conceptions of the land, and the relation between humans and the local environment.

The importance of land

It is important to note that the defence of communal access to natural resources has been a central feature throughout Pondoland's incorporation into colonial and apartheid South Africa and provided important means of defence against broader social forces over which they had little control (Beinart 1982). This protection of natural resources was demonstrated in the Pondo Revolt of the 1960s, which involved wide-scale protest and violence against the implications of the 1951 Bantu Authorities Act for access to land and Pondo's relation to it (Mbeki 1964; Southall 1983, 109–14; Turok 1960).

An old man who had fought in the Pondo Revolt described the importance of the land in a way that expressed a connection to the land as well as rewards for caring for it:

> It's because we don't want to squash ourselves and we want our livestock to get enough land, and to make sure our children, they have land to build their own houses. Because there is no inheritance other than land for them, it is the only thing for them to inherit. The land is forever, but the money will disappear. After you sold out your land, what are you going to eat?
>
> (Anon. 9 interview)

Many expressed a similar sentiment: 'The mining will go, but the land is here forever. What happens after the mining is gone?' (Anon. 3 interview).

For some the land forms part of a self-understanding linked to an awareness of their survival based on the land. As one respondent said: 'I am a farmer, it is what I do' (Anon. 1 interview). For another respondent:

> The land is part of me. Everything I am using is from the land. ... My parents are also buried on this land and my livestock feed on the grass from this land. Everything is from this land. If you destroy the land, you destroy your life.
>
> (Anon. 10 interview)

The land provides a central pillar of survival for the populations of Mgungundlovu and people's connection to it constitutes an important source of identity, strongly linked to a sense of place.

The question of poverty and development

During the research on this case study, the question of poverty emerged as an important theme in understanding the local social context. All those interviewed illustrated a conventional understanding of development conveyed by government policy and municipality mandates that centred on the desire for jobs and improved basic services such as roads, clinics and schools. However, their understandings of development were largely informed by their understandings of, and relations to, the land and their ecological and social conditions of existence. All those interviewed were adamant that the improvements they desire should not threaten their existing livelihoods and way of life, nor threaten their access to natural resources, most importantly that of the land. As one respondent stated: 'We want development that doesn't remove us, to develop between us, not remove us' (Anon. 2 interview). Respondents indicated a desire for jobs, such as those in tourism, that did not destroy their local environment or negatively affect their ability to access natural resources and land.

Those interviewed and surveyed were largely opposed to the mining because they felt that it would affect their ability to secure their livelihoods through agriculture, livestock keeping and access to other natural resources. Local discourses around conceptions of nature and development therefore cohere around a sense of place. Many respondents therefore highlighted the importance of participation in the 'development' process. As the secretary of the Amadiba Tribal Authority, Mandla Ndovela, stated:

> Rich does not mean to change our lives, but improve with what our ancestors left us with instead of just jumping to something which we cannot control or we cannot guide.

> (50/50 2008)

The above quotation highlights the question of poverty. Many of those in favour of the proposed mining argued it was a way to address poverty, as well as environmental degradation apparently associated with this poverty. Contrary to these declarations, all those interviewed insisted they were not poor. This was explained to the then Minister of Minerals and Energy, who visited the area twice: first to announce the awarding of the mining licence, apparently believing pro-mining propaganda of wide-scale support for the mining, thus expecting a warm reception. The second visit, in August 2008, was a response to the local anger that the proposed mining was causing. Nonhle Mbhutuma, a key local anti-mining activist, described the visit:

> And the minister, after the people they speak, she stood up and respond on what they saying. She said, 'Ok, I heard all of you. And some of the thing it's new for me. As a person I'm working on papers, I never heard all of these things you mentioned today. But development is very important for you, because you are poor … ' Jo! She didn't finish. The people shouted at her. They ask 'Who are the poor? Are you coming with that bullshit you doing at the crèche there? You shoving us with the guns. You call all the police to kick us on our land. Are you calling us poor? Who told you that?' And the minister said, 'No, no, no, I'm sorry, I didn't mean to say that. *Some* of you are poor but *some* are not poor, I know that.' And the people said, 'Who told you that – some are poor and some are not poor?' And she said, 'Ok, you are not poor. I apologise about that. I never say it again.' Ja. And she just sit down and listen to the other people, because they just give the people chance to speak.

> (Mbhutuma interview)

As this same activist stated: 'Being rich does not mean having the big car or having the big house' (Mbhutuma interview).

Poverty in this context is understood in ways that transcend traditional indicators. To interpret the above assertions requires an analysis of the social, cultural and ecological relations that motivate such denials of poverty. This situation reflects McIntosh's description of his life growing up in the Scottish Hebrides: 'Our "poverty", if it is that, is a dignified *frugality*, not the degrading destitution of economies where an elite harbours all the resources to profit from artificially maintained scarcities' (McIntosh 2004, 29; original emphasis).

The notion of poverty depends largely on the discourse through which it is being interpreted. Conventional indicators tend to mystify the causes and nature of poverty, failing to engage with the complexities of social relations and subjectivity. Within the dominant discourse of sustainable development and ecological modernisation, poverty is constructed as being without 'development' within a development discourse in which forms of accumulation are naturalised as progress (Hallowes and Butler 2002, 58). As Ferguson (1994) has shown, the discourse of development can act to depoliticise poverty, constructing it as a lack of development rather than as a result of social and political processes that create the powerlessness that underpins poverty.

In presenting the views of the interviewees I do not intend to produce romantic images of rural life in South Africa; the difficulties of rural life have been widely documented. As Ferguson (2006) argues, the tendency for analysts of Africa to focus on the question of cultural difference and the virtues of African cultures risks precluding an analysis of material inequality. Although the people of Mgungundlovu reflect a desire for development that is rooted in the local context and will not induce drastic social alterations, one should not lose sight of the fact that the social conditions of the Transkei and the Wild Coast are also a reflection of historical political and economic inequalities. However, the answer to this is not to impose a process of 'development' that reproduces inequalities of power and resources. A participatory approach to development should account for the social, cultural and ecological factors that allow the people of Mgungundlovu to affirm that they are not poor and lay the basis for 'a powerful claim to a chance for transformed conditions of life – a place-in-the-world, a standard of living, a "direction we would like to move in"' (Ferguson 2006, 19).

What role for labour?

The mining rights were eventually declined by the Department of Minerals in August 2011 for environmental reasons, due also to the effective resistance by the community through the Amadiba Crisis Committee (ACC) and from sections of the South African environmental movement Sustaining the Wild Coast (SWC).

In its *A Growth Path Towards Full Employment*, COSATU (2010) calls for important rural development measures such as the provision of affordable inputs to agriculture, strengthening links between agriculture and agro-processing, and social and economic infrastructure in rural areas, within a 'growth and development path'. They demand 'the maintenance of adequate balance between industrialisation on the one hand and agriculture and rural development on the other' (COSATU 2010, no page number). In this vein, COSATU and NUM have called for measures to ensure communities benefit from mining activities, such as ring-fencing state royalties from mining for rural community development and increased community participation in mining operations (COSATU/NUM 2008; NUM n.d. a).

The NUM calls for the intensified exploitation of mineral resources as the centre of economic growth and development, proposing a '[r]esource-based South African Democratic Developmental State', a 'strategy that uses natural resources to catalyse growth and development' (NUM n.d. b, 24). The state is seen as the key driver and coordinator of this development and thus NUM supports the nationalisation of the South African mining industry as part of a policy of '[n]ationalisation as an ideological and economic policy for laying the building blocks for Socialism' (NUM n.d. b, 6). However, the environmental impacts of such a resource-based development path are not fully considered, and, as NUM itself concedes, state ownership of productive forces does not guarantee democratic and egalitarian outcomes, rather, this depends on 'the class character of the democratic state' (ibid.). In our case, various levels of the state, local government and the Department of Mineral Resources, were key actors in encouraging the mining, against the clear protest of the Amadiba communities.[7] NUM's largely growth centred and productivist paradigm of development, echoing old-style 'socialist modernisation' paradigms, conflicts with the communities' conceptions of development and how natural resources should be used.

Labour has yet to elaborate a transformative paradigm from below in the context of existing struggles.[8] Existing community struggles around mining and the question of how rural communities can be protected from dispossession are not dealt with. As in the case presented here, the labour movement has played little role in rural community struggles around mining South Africa. The case study allows us to draw some potential lessons for trade unions from the extractive industries that are at the heart of 'accumulation by dispossession'. We will present three central themes that can link labour with rural livelihoods allowing them to play a role in a transformation to a sustainable society: reorienting notions of 'development'; broader social movement alliances; and 'just transition'.

Reorienting ideas and practice of 'development'

The NUM's 2011 *Secretariat Report* does not deal comprehensively with issues of rural poverty and development, apart from including the rural into the union's broader societal role of ensuring 'a better life for all' (NUM 2011, 169). As I have shown, thinking about rural poverty and development is a complex issue that requires integrating the relationships between a range of factors including climate change, livelihoods, use of natural resources and participation. Specifically, it requires paying attention to power relations that underlie the reproduction of poverty and the current development practices. The mining project, if realised, would have created poverty, which according to the local inhabitants, does not exist now. It would have undermined the residents' access to natural resources and the land without providing a compensatory source of livelihoods through jobs.

Because mineral exploitation is seen as important to economic growth and job creation, the destruction of land-based livelihoods that resource extraction creates is not dealt with. Across South Africa, the trajectory of mining continues to be characterised by a concentration of ownership and wealth, and the enclosure of community lands as mining operations expand (ActionAid 2008; Benchmarks Foundation 2007). This mirrors the global trend caused by the extractive industries (Kennedy 1998).

If we are to avoid environmental degradation and dispossession the process and drivers of development need to be reconfigured: the process needs to be democratic and situated in an understanding of the needs of the communities in question as well as the social, political and economic forces driving development (Chodorkoff 2005; Payne and King 2008).

Reorienting development practice that wrests dominant control away from the market and state and towards communities poses a challenge to existing power relations. If labour movements are to take on the question of developing community–labour alliances they need to reorient their visions of development and ask: in whose interest is the project? Who is in control of the project? What kind of relationships would such a project create between trade unions, workers and communities? Are the quantitative outcomes of the project in terms of GDP and economic growth? What are the qualitative issues in terms of process? How does the project relate to the quality of life, the social relations between people, the sense of community and maintenance of cultural cohesion (Chodorkoff 2005)?

Extending labour–community alliances

In South Africa, rural populations were the key source of cheap labour integral to the development of the mining industry. Simultaneously, the rural space continued to serve as a critical site of social reproduction for the inhabitants left behind and for the immigrant workers. It also served as an important source of security for workers returning from urban employment. This is still the case in the context of widespread deindustrialisation and unemployment (Bank and Minkley 2005) especially in the mining sector where employment has been declining (NUM 2011). This is also becoming a noticeable trend in other parts of the world, as workers return to the land in the context of rising unemployment (Bello 2009). Extending alliances to rural communities would therefore mean to engage with the same communities from which mineworkers originate.

Attempting to build sustainable societies means that movements engaged in environmental, labour, urban and struggles of rural communities could find points of convergence concerning the sustainable social reproduction of disenfranchised groups and strategies of how to achieve such a reproduction.

This would imply overcoming dualisms created by traditional paradigms of development, i.e. tradition versus modernity, people versus nature, rural versus urban, etc. In the context of continued rural underdevelopment and high urban unemployment in South Africa, and much of the Global South, sustainable job creation and rural development with environmental integrity are priorities. This requires societal alliances across labour and community organisations based on mutual understanding and respect for each other's needs (see Cock and Lambert in this volume).

Just transition

The above two factors relate to social change and have implications for a just transition. Cock (2011) makes an important conceptual contribution to understanding the notion of just transition. She argues that it can either fall into the category of making 'demands for shallow change focused on protecting vulnerable workers' or into a 'deep change rooted in a vision of dramatically different forms of production and consumption' (Cock 2011, no page number). In NUM's submission on the South African government's *National Climate Change Response Green Paper*, the overall thrust is that of a just transition rooted in the notion of a green economy. It represents a just transition in the shallower sense, since the main driver of a transition to a green economy is capital controlled by government regulation and policy. The notion of bottom-up change based on alternative relations of production and consumption is not present.

The NUM has contradictory positions about the perspective of the mining industry in the context of just transition and climate change. For example, its economic report in the 2011 *Secretariat Report* documents the declining employment in the mining industry over the last two decades and its declining future prospects (NUM 2011). However, it fails to lay out what actions NUM may therefore take to attempt to deal with such declining prospects for its members. It does not take up the notion of just transition and the opportunities this may open up for new sustainable livelihood activities.

Another contradiction linked to this is the future role of the mining industry. Abramsky (2010) argues that a just transition to a sustainable society would need to place energy and energy-intensive industries under collective control, in order to ensure they are phased out or significantly reduced to the level of securing social priorities. This would involve two interconnected steps: first, their reduction for environmental reasons, and second, their subordination to social priorities rather than to profit. NUM instead argues for greater degrees of social control through state-based nationalisation, but in the interests of expanding rather than contracting the industry, arguing for it to be turned from a 'sunset' to a 'sunrise' industry (NUM n.d. b, 5, 16). This raises the question of the impacts on rural livelihoods that may result from such expansion.

While it is impractical to call for a halt to all mining activities, it is necessary to question the long-term viability of energy intensive and environmentally destructive extractive industries as key drivers of economic growth and job creation. Industries need to be guided by social goals and by ecological requirements as opposed to profit interests. A just transition to a sustainable society would be just under specific conditions: first, if it ensures that workers do not bear the brunt of the transition; and second, if it can open up the possibility of situating production in a social context that seeks also to end processes of accumulation by dispossession, thereby linking the labour movement with rural inhabitants defending their land and access to natural resources.

Conclusion

This chapter has argued that while trade unions and workers may see benefits in the jobs provided by energy-intensive and environmentally destructive extractive industries such as mining, a different understanding of development is required that sees the short- and long-term effects of this path on people and ecologies. From an environmental justice perspective, this means placing the desires and rights of the people most affected by processes of development and ecological harm at the centre of decision making. An emphasis on the ecological bases of rural social reproduction can be linked to the needs of urban reproduction by envisioning and mobilising upon a new path of development that transcends dispossession and overcomes the ecological contradictions that currently characterise modern capitalist development.

Labour movements such as COSATU have indicted capitalist accumulation as the cause of the environmental crisis. This insight would require, first, a critique of the expansion of the capitalist economy as the route to securing the wellbeing of the working class. Second, it would require seeing the link between industrial capitalist expansion and rural dispossession and third, acknowledging that greening capitalism without dealing with its expansionary tendencies is not enough. Instead, economic development needs to be reformulated to envisage how it can provide workers with sustainable jobs and rural inhabitants with an improvement of their living conditions without the threat of dispossession.

This in turn requires broader societal alliances mobilising against environmental destruction and accumulation by dispossession. As Kearns (2009, 200–201) asserts, what is required is

> ... collective action producing collective results ... collective action across a broad spectrum of direct action groups, political groups, campaign groups and trade unions coming together to say that 'this is our planet we live on and have to make a living on. It's worth fighting for.'

Notes

1 This chapter draws from arguments and empirical research that also appear in Bennie (2010) and Bennie (2011).

2 The author acknowledges the highly contentious nature of the term 'development'. For a discussion of the term see Bennie (2010, 14–28). Here, development is understood as grounded in participation, democracy and social justice, and in an appreciation of its ecological limits.
3 The methodology for this research involved extensive interviews with community members, community activists, key informants, a small-scale survey and participant observation.
4 The term 'community' is descriptive and is not intended to imply harmonious homogeneity. I recognise that the very nature of community is characterised by internal divisions and contestation (Bozzoli 1987).
5 The minister rightly noted that environmental concerns had not been sufficiently addressed, but added that the level of consultation was adequate, which was far from reality.
6 The Environmental Impact Assessment (EIA) conducted for the proposed mining predicts that of the 335 huts located in the first block to be mined, Kwanyana, about 62 are likely to be affected and 43 are located directly within the demarcated mining area. Their inhabitants will thus have to be removed and relocated, which TEM claims will be based on negotiation and compensation.
7 See Bennie (2010, 114–31) for a detailed study of the roles played by the various state actors.
8 Thank you to Vishwas Satgar for pointing this out.

Interviews

Abbott, T. His residence, Port Edward, 15 November 2009.
Anonymous 1, Xolobeni Village, Mgungundlovu, Eastern Cape, 1 July 2009, translated from Mpondo by Nonhle Mbhutuma.
Anonymous 2, Xolobeni Village, Mgungundlovu, Eastern Cape, 25 June 2009, translated from Mpondo by Nonhle Mbhutuma.
Anonymous 3, Xolobeni Village, Mgungundlovu, Eastern Cape, 26 June 2009, translated from Mpondo by Nonhle Mbhutuma.
Anonymous 9, Sigidi Village, Mgungundlovu, Eastern Cape, 21 November 2009, translated from Mpondo by Nonhle Mbhutuma.
Anonymous 10, Interview, Sigidi Village, Mgungundlovu, Eastern Cape, 23 November 2009, translated from Mpondo by Nonhle Mbhutuma.
Mbhutuma, N. Her residence, Sigidi Village, Mgungundlovu, Eastern Cape, 30 June 2009.

References

50/50 (2008) Episode on proposed mining at Mgungundlovu, broadcast on SABC 2, 19h30, 1 December.
Abramsky, K. (2010) 'Sparking an Energy Revolution: Building New Relations of Production, Exchange and Livelihood', in K. Abramsky (ed.) *Sparking a Worldwide Energy Revolution: Social Struggles in the Transition to a Post-Petrol World*. Oakland, CA and Edinburgh: AK Press.
ActionAid (2008) *Precious Metal: The Impact of Anglo Platinum on Poor Communities in Limpopo, South Africa*. Johannesburg: ActionAid.
Bank, L. and Minkley, G. (2005) 'Going Nowhere Slowly? Land, Livelihoods and Rural Development in the Eastern Cape', *Social Dynamics* 31: 1, pp. 1–38.
Beinart, W. (1982) *The Political Economy of Pondoland, 1860–1930*. Cambridge: Cambridge University Press.

Bello, W. (2009) *The Food Wars.* London: Verso.

Benchmarks Foundation (2007) *The Policy Gap: A Review of the Corporate Social Responsibility Programmes of the Platinum Mining Industry in the North West Province.* Benchmarks Foundation, www.sarpn.org/documents/d0002632/Platinum_research_summary_Bench_marks.pdf (accessed 17 October 2009).

Bennie, A. (2010) 'The relation between environmental protection and "development": a case study of the proposed dynamics involved in the proposed mining at Xolobeni, Wild Coast', unpublished research report, University of the Witwatersrand.

——(2011) 'Questions for labour on land, livelihoods and jobs: a case study of the proposed mining at Xolobeni, Wild Coast', *South African Review of Sociology* 42: 3, pp. 41–59.

Bozzoli, B. (1987) 'Class, community and ideology in the evolution of South African society', in B. Bozzoli (ed.) *Class, Community and Conflict*, Johannesburg: Ravan Press.

Chodorkoff, D. (2005) 'Redefining Development', *Journal of Inclusive Democracy* 3, pp. 117–28.

Cock, J. (2007) 'Sustainable development or environmental justice: questions for the South African labour movement from the steel valley struggle', *LABOUR, Capital and Society*, 40: 1&2, pp. 36–55.

——(2008) 'Connecting Nature, Power and Justice'. Paper presented at the South African Sociological Association (SASA) Conference, Stellenbosch University, July.

——(2011) 'Contesting a "just transition to a low carbon economy"'. http://rio20.net/en/documentos/contesting-ajust-transition-to-a-low-carbon-economy (accessed 20 December 2011).

COSATU (2010) 'A Growth Path Towards Full Employment Policy Perspectives of the Congress of South African Trade Unions', draft discussion document, 11 September, www.cosatu.org.za/docs/discussion/2010/cosatubooklet.pdf (15 December 2011).

——(2011) 'Press Statement: COSATU CEC, 22–24 August 2011'. http://www.cosatu.org.za/show.php?ID=5358 (accessed 15 November 2011).

COSATU/NUM (2008) 'Draft Submission on the Draft Mineral and Petroleum Royalty Bill 3rd Draft of 2007'. Submitted to Portfolio Committee on Finance on 12 March.

Daniel, S. and Mittal, A. (2009) *The Great Land Grab: Rush for World's Farmland Threatens Food Security for the Poor.* Oakland, CA: The Oakland Institute.

Farmers Weekly (2010) 'Protecting a meaningful way of life', 25 June.

Ferguson, J. (1994) *The Anti-Politics Machine: 'Development', Depoliticisation, and Bureaucratic Power in Lesotho*, Minneapolis: University of Minnesota Press.

——(2006) *Global Shadows: Africa in the Neoliberal World Order*, Durham, NC and London: Duke University Press.

Foster, J. B. (2002) *Ecology Against Capitalism.* New York: Monthly Review Press.

Friends of the Earth (Europe and Africa) (2010) *Africa: Up for Grabs: The Scale and Impact of Land Grabbing for Agrofuels.* Brussels: Friends of the Earth Europe.

Groundwater Consulting Services (GCS) (2007a) *Mineral Sands Resources (Pty) Ltd., Xolobeni Heavy Mineral Sands Project, Environmental Impact Assessment Report*, December, Johannesburg: Groundwater Consulting Services (GCS) (Pty) Ltd.

——(2007b) *Mineral Sands Resources (Pty) Ltd., Xolobeni Heavy Mineral Sands Project, Environmental Management Programme (EMP)*, December, Johannesburg: Groundwater Consulting Services (GCS) (Pty) Ltd.

Hadju, F. (2005) 'Relying on jobs instead of the environment? Patterns of local securities in rural Eastern Cape, South Africa', *Social Dynamics* 31, pp. 235–60.

Hallowes, D. and Butler, M. (2002) 'Power, Poverty, and Marginalised Environments: A Conceptual Framework', in D. MacDonald (ed.) *Environmental Justice in South Africa*. Cape Town: University of Cape Town Press.

Hart, G. and Sitas, A. (2004) 'Beyond the Urban–Rural Divide: Linking Land, Labour and Livelihoods', *Transformation* 56: 31–38.

Harvey, D. (2005) *Spaces of Neoliberalization: Towards a Theory of Uneven Geographical Development*. Hettner-Lecture 2004 with David Harvey. Stuttgart: Hettner-Lectures, Vol. 8.

Joubert, L. (2008) *Boiling Point: People in a Changing Climate*. Johannesburg: Wits University Press.

Kearns, T. (2009) 'Climate Change is a Trade Union Issue', in I. Angus (ed.) *The Global Fight for Climate Justice*. London: Resistance Books.

Kennedy, D. (1998) 'Mining, murder and mayhem: The impact of the mining industry in the South', *Third World Resurgence*, 93, May: www.twnside.org.sg/title/mine-cn.htm (accessed 5 August 2009).

Kepe, T. (1997) 'Communities, Entitlements and Nature Reserves: The case of the Wild Coast, South Africa', *IDS Bulletin* 28: 4, October, pp. 47–58.

——(2001) 'Waking up from the dream: The pitfalls of "fast-track" development on the Wild Coast', *Research Report No. 8*, Programme for Land and Agrarian Studies (PLAAS), Cape Town.

Levidow, L. and Paul, H. (2010) 'Global Agrofuel Crops as Dispossession', in K. Abramsky (ed.) *Sparking a Worldwide Energy Revolution: Social Struggles in the Transition to a Post-Petrol World*. Oakland, CA and Edinburgh: AK Press.

Lohmann, L. (2006) *Carbon Trading: A Critical Conversation on Climate Change, Privatisation and Power*. Development Dialogue No. 48, September. Uppsala: The Dag Hammarskjöld Foundation.

Mbeki, G. (1964) *South Africa: The Peasant's Revolt*. London: Peter Smith.

McAllister, P. (2003) 'Xhosa Agricultural Work Groups – Economic Hindrance or Development Opportunity?' Fort Hare Institute of Social and Economic Research, Working Paper No. 12.

McIntosh, A. (2004) *Soil and Soul: People versus Corporate Power*. London: Aurum Press.

McMichael, P. (2010) 'Food sovereignty in movement: addressing the triple crisis', in H. Wittman, A. A. Desmarais and N. Wiebe (eds.) *Food Sovereignty: Reconnecting Food, Nature and Community*. Halifax and Winnipeg: Fernwood Publishing.

Ngonini, X. A. (2007) 'Anxious Communities: The Decline of Mine Migration in the Eastern Cape', *Development Southern Africa* 24: 1, pp. 173–85.

NUM (National Union of Mineworkers) (n.d. a) 'The National Union of Mineworkers' Response to Sustainable Development'. www.num.org.za/Speeches/the%20national%20union%20of%20mineworkers%20response%20to%20sustainable%20development.html (accessed 27 November 2011).

——(n.d. b) *Nationalisation Discussion Papers*. Johannesburg: National Union of Mineworkers.

——(2011) *Secretariat Report 2011*. Johannesburg: National Union of Mineworkers.

Palmer, R., Timmermans, H. G. and Fay, D. (eds.) (2002) *From Conflict to Negotiation: Nature-based development on the South African Wild Coast*. Pretoria: Human Sciences Research Council.

Payne, V. and King, N. (2008) 'The Wild Coast Mining Debate – A Broader Perspective', *Vision* 10, October/November.

Sachs, W. (1999) *Planet Dialectics: Explorations in Environment and Development*. London: Zed Books.

Shackleton, C. M., Timmermans, H.G., Nongwe, N., Hamer, N. and Palmer, R. (2007) 'Direct-use values of non-timber forest products from two areas on the Transkei Wild Coast', *Agrekon* 46: 1, pp. 135–56.

Socialist Resistance (2009) 'The Three Decisive Forces that Can Stop Climate Change', in I. Angus (ed.) *The Global Fight for Climate Justice*. London: Resistance Books.

Southall, R. (1983) *South Africa's Transkei: The Political Economy of an 'Independent' Bantustan*. London: Heinemann Educational Books.

Turok, B. (1960) *The Pondo Revolt*. Johannesburg: South African Congress of Democrats.

Uaid, L. M. (2009) 'Class Struggle and Ecology', in I. Angus (ed.) *The Global Fight for Climate Justice*, London: Resistance Books.

10 Climate change, trade unions and rural workers in labour–environmental alliances in the Amazon Rainforest

João Paulo Cândia Veiga and Scott B. Martin

Introduction

In September 2010, an on-site evaluation was conducted of a five-year project to develop training and assistance for collective settlements and civil associations in the area around the Arapiuns River in western Pará. The Trade Union Solidarity Centre of Finland provided funding with support of the Finnish Trade Union Confederation (SASK). The Finnish involvement was a result of solidarity partnerships with social movements in the developing world focusing on environment issues. In 2005, when the project was set up, avoiding deforestation and strengthening local communities were its main objectives. The Rural Workers Trade Union (Sindicato dos Trabalhadores e Trabalhadoras Rurais, STTR), based in the municipality of Santarém, acted as the project manager. The evaluation took place during one week, in which the researchers travelled on the Arapiuns, Maró, and Aruã rivers to visit the communities taking part in the project. The aim was to evaluate the project's effectiveness since 2005. It was based on group interviews with local communities, union leaders in Santarém city and site visits.

The local evaluation involved the development of an analytical framework to assess how the communities perceive themselves as actors dealing with a critical set of issues: land conflicts, the timber trade, climate change and the complex local impacts of federal public policies on forestry management. One of the topics highlighted in the interviews was global warming and the structural set of changes it implied for the livelihood and working conditions of the families in the region under investigation. A huge challenge mentioned by all communities was their anxiety concerning climate change and the implied 'forced' adaptation to new living conditions that would ensure the social sustainability of forest dwellers in terms of employment and income through traditional activities like the tapioca production, fishing and collecting fruit (extractive activities). Climate change is affecting the living conditions of the families in this area and any REDD (Reducing Emissions from Deforestation and Forest Degradation) local governance system, public or private, must make sure that it creates sustainable labour and environmental conditions for the communities.

Social conflicts developed over the changing labour and environmental conditions of the families in the area of the Arapiuns River between timber traders and landowners on the one hand and communities living on small-scale activities on the other. Rural workers who are self-employed labourers in small-scale subsistence activities and their families live around the 'glebas' (large land tracts) of 'Lago Grande' and 'Nova Olinda'. One such conflict occurred in 2009 when heavy rafts carrying lumber were purposely set on fire as a result of increased tensions between timber traders and the communities of the gleba 'Nova Olinda', who resisted the extraction of timber by landowners and traders (SASK 2010).

The STTR, with support of SASK, has developed a crucial role in organising most of the communities of the gleba 'Nova Olinda' with the result that they resist the timber traders and reject the 'offers' of landowners, who want to buy their land. However, some of them, the communities of 'Novo Lugar', 'Prainha', 'Fé em Deus', 'Sociedade dos Parentes', 'Sempre Serve' have sold logging rights to the timber companies. Other communities were also under strong pressure from the timber companies who practiced illegal logging (SASK 2010).

This chapter begins by addressing the role of the Rural Workers Trade Union of Santarém (STTR) in initiating a discussion on the impact of climate change among the families and local communities from the point of view of labour. This is a central issue of the project's evaluation (section 2). The assumption is that the local communities are key players in the forest governance system and they must be part of the future local–global public–private multilevel partnerships of forest management. Local governance can improve the effectiveness of forest management and increase the legitimacy of institutional arrangements. In order for this to happen local communities need to be included in the forest management system, taking over specific tasks. For instance, communities can monitor indicators of climate change, participate in vigilance schemes and provide information about the effects of forest management (Ostrom and Moran 2009).

In section 3 we analyse labour and environmental topics in the context of different theoretical approaches to labour and the trade union movement. We argue that the relationship between labour and environmental issues is under-theorised. The literature on labour derives from interest-based approaches, which analyse labour actions in terms of agenda setting, objectives and bargaining arenas, investigating the strategic and tactical capabilities of unions and NGOs. In contrast to this we outline a new framework that seeks to understand labour–environmental alliances based on a cognitive approach where 'sharing understandings', that is, taking the ways in which local communities interpret the impacts of climate change on the forest as a point of departure, is seen as the way to enhance the social and environmental sustainability of governance systems (which will be described in section 5). We use discourse analysis as the methodology to capture these understandings (section 4). Our main conclusion is that the labour movement is developing new values and identities when it becomes aware of environmental issues such as climate change.

The pivotal role of the Rural Workers Trade Union of Santarém (STTR)

The Rural Workers Trade Union of Santarém is one of the more successful and well-established rural trade unions in the Amazon region. Since its foundation in 1973, during the military regime, and after 'authentic' leaders took the union back from government control in 1980, the union organised the rural workers along the rivers and 'igarapés'. It encompasses an extensive region of rivers and native forests that are being progressively devastated by timber companies.

The trade union was at the forefront of the landless workers' movement in the 1980s. Avelino Ganzer, the former president of the trade union as well as a former leader of the landless movement, played a fundamental role when the Central Única dos Trabalhadores (CUT) was founded in August of 1983. Later, Ganzer became the first leader of rural workers at CUT. Most of the leaders of the STTR come from the traditional communities scattered throughout the municipality of Santarém. Most of these communities comprise families who have inhabited the margins of rivers and 'igarapés' for many decades. Many of the families have indigenous as well as white Portuguese ancestors. Some of the communities we visited have existed for more than a century and undertake subsistence activities such as cassava flour production, small animal husbandry, hunting, fishing and craft production, while some have begun to receive tourists.

To cover such a large area, the basic work in the communities, and to overcome the distance between the union leaders based in Santarém, the STTR has regional leaders. Each of whom is responsible for at least one of the communities of rural workers representing a complex set of local leaders within a centralised command structure. This system enhances the information network necessary to keep the communities engaged. The Arapiuns River and its communities have eight regional leaders who live in the communities and conduct union organisational work at the local level. These leaders occupy a strategic role for the union because they participate often in union activities in Santarém. They give direction to another set of local rural workers who work directly with the community of families, responding to their needs and expectations about living conditions and labour rights. These include issues such as retirement benefits and access to federal public policies such as 'Bolsa Família' (conditional cash transfers to poor families), and public loans to buy machinery and devices for productive activities. Transportation is another strategic topic for rural workers. Everything is transported by boats, as there are no highways or railroads in the vicinity. In the 'dry' season (summer), the rivers and igarapés serve this purpose, and in the 'wet' season (winter) parts of the rainforest are underwater. Those attending any meeting or assembly in the remote areas must come by boat, and the fares are expensive.

This is how meetings were organised when communities had to decide whether to constitute legally a collective settlement and then found a civil association to apply for public loans.

The SASK project facilitated the pivotal role of STTR in getting closer to distant communities, conducting assemblies, and providing services such as assisting with the documentation of rural workers for their retirement. The SASK project assisted the travel of these leaders between communities in the period of organisation of the assemblies. It can be suggested that the SASK project has been decisive in enabling the STTR to act in this period of intense conflict, and above all, in the organisation of communities of rural workers and members of trade unions.

Environmental–trade union alliance: theoretical approaches

Alliances between labour and environmental organisations are an almost unknown topic in the trade union literature.

There are four main perspectives. Perspective (I) includes case studies of labour alliances with communities, NGOs and environmental movements predominantly at the local level. Perspective (II) draws attention to the system of industrial relations, employment relations and labour legislation. Perspective (III) explores the international labour movement, and its challenges, obstacles, advantages and constraints. In the final perspective (IV), we find the most interesting set of analyses because trade unions are considered in the context of the rise of other non-state actors in international relations and their cooperation with companies and NGOs is discussed. Moreover, unions are seen as part of the rule-making structure in the new set of international arrangements that assess, evaluate, monitor and enforce labour and environmental standards worldwide. This final perspective also recognises unions as important actors within a broader picture of world affairs.

In Perspective (I), there is an emergent 'geographical' literature that explores the engagement between trade unions and non-union actors within the broader community at the local level. The implications of coalition building in labour's strategy and in the renewed capacity of trade unions to contribute to wider communities of interest are highlighted (Sadler 2004). More institutionalised forms of decision making in such alliances at local level are evaluated (Bartolini *et al.* 2010) and specific cases like historical labour–consumer alliances in the United States are considered (Frank 2003).

One of the strands within the literature about cooperation and conflict within labour–environment coalitions investigates the 'jobs versus the environment' debate, where 'measures designed to protect the environment are said to threaten the livelihood of the workers'. A more optimistic approach claims that 'workers and environmentalists share common goals and find themselves united against a common enemy' (Obach 1999, 48). Environmentalists are seen to belong to the middle classes while unions represent the working class, thus the conflicts between them are seen as a result of their different class positions. Some argue that there are more converging interests between companies and NGOs, since environmental protection can be profitable and thus business friendly. Rose argues that 'the distribution of resources favours building alliances with corporations ... Unions and environmentalists cannot hope to compete with these material advantages' (Rose 2003, 58).

These analyses often take a pessimistic perspective, in the sense that the phenomenon of globalisation is seen to have 'undermined the trade union strategy of the "elimination of labour costs as a factor in competition"'. Improving union coordination across borders through 'information sharing', 'cementing relationships' and developing 'strategic knowledge for unions' is seen as a precondition for successful campaigns (Brecher *et al.* 2006, 8). Trade unions, it is argued, rely on state power. They are dependent on state policies to enforce labour standards and to develop programmes to raise those standards. As some authors conclude, when state effectiveness is eroded the labour movement declines (Boswell and Stevis 1997).

The rhetoric of 'labour internationalism' and 'labour solidarity' is seen in the context of a structural/systemic analysis of the future of capitalism. The 'old' internationalism of a 'homogeneous working class' contrasts with a set of organisations and institutions that constitute a variety of networks. Globalising labour networks within the 'new' capitalism recognise the politics of coalition and alliances as critical for the future of trade unionism and labour internationalism (Waterman and Wills 2001).

In Perspective IV, the literature can be divided into (1) international campaigns, which includes a diverse number of alliances aimed at fighting companies and 'market globalism' (Turner 2004); (2) debates focused on forms of cooperation between labour organisations – NGOs and companies, defining new tasks for trade unions (Bartley 2007; Compa 2004; Hale 2004; Leather 2004); (3) analyses of national variables to explain transnational activism (Caraway 2006). For this literature, the national forms of workers' representations explain variations in the unions' responses to globalisation (Anner *et al.* 2006); finally, (4) 'transnational advocacy networks', a successful concept developed by Keck and Sikkink (1998) to explore the role of international civil society organisations in the process of globalisation. Their tactical instruments are 'name and shame' and the 'boomerang effect'. The latter labels a strategy, where unions in developing countries, using transnational networks, campaign against a company and this then changes the policies of the company in the headquarters as well. They are used by trade unions and NGOs to access international headquarters of companies in order to put pressure on subsidiaries in the developing world to comply with international labour and environmental standards (Caraway 2006). In Brazil, the Social Observatory Institute has worked on different labour research agendas in respect of core labour standards in multinationals, where the trade unions and labour confederations based in the Global South put pressure on the companies' headquarters in the developed world. Success came when representatives of the company accepted that there had been violations and non-compliant behaviour at the host-country level. The 'boomerang effect' has increased labour compliance in Brazil and in some cases has strengthened local unions (Barbosa *et al.* 2011).

Surprisingly, the debate about the relationship between NGOs and labour finds that although there is a 'common agenda' between trade unions and NGOs and an 'enormous scope for NGOs and trade unions to support each others' aims', it appears difficult to forge a long-lasting alliance (Eade 2004, 5). Some scholars explain this paradox as a problem of competing agendas, quite aside from the fact that on some topics such as 'development', 'human rights' and 'informal economy', NGOs and unions have shared interests in principle. Evans and Anner (2004) speak of the difficulties of bridging a 'double divide', which is across the North–South as well as across different types of organisations.

Two arguments have been developed to understand the difficulties for alliances between trade unions and environmental organisations. The first is embedded in institutional theory applied to international relations. Trade unions, it is argued, have an advantage over NGOs because they are supported by an international organisation, the International Labour Office (ILO). It is one of the oldest international organisations, predating the United Nations system. However, it can also be described as a typical 'toothless' international organisation since states have never delegated any enforcement power to the ILO. Given its tripartite composition, the conventions and recommendations of the ILO function as an agenda-setting, not as an enforcement agency. Since the 1990s, with the adoption of core labour standards through the more recent 'decent work' agenda, the role of the ILO has been to influence the actions of governments, trade unions and the private sector at a national level.

NGOs and environmental issues have never received this centralised and focused attention by international organisations even though, as Olsen and Kemter show in their chapter in this volume, the ILO has also been concerned with environmental issues. Nevertheless, the environmental agenda has often been decentralised and divided into different core issues such as energy, biodiversity, ozone, climate change and forestry, to mention but a few. Environmental issues are dealt with in competing or overlapping agencies, such as the United Nations Environment Program (UNEP), the provider of technical information and the Commission for Sustainable Development (CSD), the political agenda setter subordinated to the Division of Sustainable Development of the Department of Economic and Social Affair of United Nations.

The second argument explaining the difficulties of NGO–labour alliances addresses their fundamentally different institutional and organisational logics. Trade unions have a mandate from their members. There is a political basis behind the authority of trade union leaders. Unionists cannot act as flexible as they might wish to when partnering non-union actors. Unionists are, at the end of the day, 'first-among-equals' because they are, in relation to NGOs, a more universal organisation, representing their membership (Compa 2004, 212).

As opposed to this NGOs have more operational flexibility because (1) they do not represent any particular constituency and (2) the complexity of the global economic integration offers them more opportunities to take on new environmental and labour issues that are distinct from traditional campaigns, advocacy or mobilisation. In this sense, NGOs work horizontally as 'one among equals', they act within an international civil society that gives them equal status with the trade union movement. NGOs see the informal sector, women workers and labour rights violations in labour-intensive export-led sectors mostly based in developing countries as the Achilles heel of trade unions (Compa 2004, 212).

Alliances between environmental groups and labour organisations have not been analysed sufficiently in the area of labour studies. This is especially true when it comes to the specific conditions of developing countries. Different 'rationales' have driven the respective actions of unions and NGOs. The former emphasise the protection of livelihoods, rights and working conditions while environmental organisations give priority to the management of natural resources, two apparently irreconcilable points of departure.

Obach (1999) argues that there are 'value dispositions' that exist independent of the way in which the material world is organised. Alliances can thus be built on such values and identities where they converge. These aim to overcome traditional Marxist and Weberian explanations of the labour movement, which are based on the concept of class struggle as being embedded in social structures and in the societal position of its protagonists (Frundt 2010). Concepts like values and identities convey a greater importance to the more intangible dimensions of people's lives. In our case they allow us to ask how families in the forest understand themselves and their actions within the context of environmental problems such as global warming.

Our assumption is that within the learning processes of forging identities and values concerning climate change, labour and environmental concerns could merge into a single dimension, creating a new 'shared understanding' by local communities. Since one way to halt global warming is to keep the rainforests intact, people might start to recognise the importance of climate change for their strategies to adapt or mitigate their productive activities. Labour activities and productive solutions must incorporate the preservation of natural resources, which enables communities to increase their incomes and well-being. Communities, supported with incentives and organised by a union, can relate with each other and forge common identities 'independent of the spheres of economic accumulation' (Frundt 2010).

Methodology and background information

Our research used a qualitative case-study approach based on semi-structured interviews with open-ended questions to be discussed in collective gatherings of local communities where families, workers, children, women, elderly people and trade union leaders were part of the process. During one week of field study along the rivers (Arapiuns, Maró and Aruã) we visited 11 local communities. Approximately 400 families participated in the collective meetings we organised. We also conducted individual interviews with regional trade union leaders.

We used discourse analysis to understand how communities collectively build different frames and references for an issue area such as climate change. On this topic, a set of questions was posed to informants, consisting of three general areas: (1) in what ways do families interpret the forest as a good to be preserved? (2) How is climate change connected with their lives in the forest? (3) Exactly which natural resources are seen as most vital to preserve?

Another set of questions was aimed at the concrete living conditions and practices in the communities: (4) how do people structure and formulate their material interests associated with the changing context of climate change? (5) What are the natural resources used in their community and for what purposes? (6) How do people connect the use of natural resources at the local level with the environmental issue of global warming?

As noted above, the encounters of local social actors in the Amazon communities with new issues such as climate change are organised as part of a communication process, whereby new knowledge is developed through a gradual 'learning process'. Climate change presents a new set of issues, which local communities grasp immediately and intuitively through its tangible impacts on their living conditions. However, the explanatory frames they develop through dialogues with allies outside the communities shape their responses to these issues. Families experience the effects of temperature increases on the supply of fish as well as the shifting seasonality of extractive activities. They are forced to change their patterns of harvesting tapioca, beans and vegetables. For those living along the rivers and near the forests these are the most visible and palpable effects of climate change in the Amazon Rainforest.

Legislation concerning the environment and land use, whether issued by the regional state government and implemented by the Land Institute of Pará State (Interpa), or issued by the central federal state and implemented by the National Institute for Agrarian Settlement and Reform (Incra), requires that communities must be heard in issues that concern the occupation of the glebas and land use within them. The needs of each community must be respected when concessions for land use are given. The process of legalising land ownership by communities takes time and there are steps that have to be taken such as holding public hearings at the local level. Modes of ownership can be collective or individual and it is up to the community to make this crucial decision. The collective modality means that families commit themselves to use the natural resources in such a way that it contributes to the preservation of the forest, and the communities cannot sell or transfer the property to third parties. A civil association is created to undertake projects and establish policies for the use of resources in cooperation with state agencies and federal bodies. In the individual mode, the areas are much smaller and the owner can sell the land. Conflicts arise during the process of discussions and deliberations within the communities about the mode of land tenure (and thus the kind of settlement and economic production) to be implemented. The decision takes place at the level of each community. If the community opts for the individual route, it means each family gets an individual plot of land (SASK 2010; Milanez 2010).

Timber companies, who have ties to the political elites of the Pará State and are close to the secretariats of the current state government (e.g. Environmental Secretariat [SEMA]), authorise the legal extraction of lumber through management plans. Theoretically, the state government monitors their implementation. Thereby, the companies can purchase land and extract timber within a 'sustainable' management plan approved by SEMA. The SASK-funded project aims to support families and communities through supporting the STTR in order to facilitate the choice and implementation of the collective settlement mode. The creation of associations promotes the execution of resource management projects that should be organised in the most sustainable manner and it enables river dwellers to have access to support from federal programs (SASK 2010).

The communities, who organise themselves through the STTR as non-profit social organisations, stand in opposition to the loggers. They have decided to fight in order to guarantee land ownership of the native communities and the traditional usage of the land. The STTR and the SASK project were decisive in helping the communities to achieve these goals. The resources financed the meetings and assemblies that took place in each community, where issues of environmental preservation and the sustainable use of natural resources were addressed. What these assemblies facilitated was the integration of families into new programmes and policies provided by the federal government. These programmes were based on traditional forms of land use like the production of flour, the extraction of fruit from naturally growing shrubs in the forest and the raising of chickens. They also included new forms of activities such as the farming of fish, the development of ecotourism and the production of handicrafts made with Tucumã leaves. It was through such traditional and alternative livelihood activities that the STTR helped the communities of 'Lago Grande' to create new collective settlements and community associations through which they could take part in programmes for the sustainable management of natural resources.

Empirical results

There are two main developments that our research identified. The first one comes from second-hand empirical material, since we visited primarily those communities in which the STTR had affiliates. However, in interviews with these community members we also received information about communities not organised by the union. Some informants reported that the logging companies offer jobs and 'presents' such as electrical generators, and promise better living conditions. However, they do not keep their promises. Few jobs are created and they are hard and low-paid jobs, predominantly cutting trees. The construction of roads has increased the destruction of the forest and harmed the environment as well as the living conditions of the communities.

All of them mentioned that climate change was occurring in the region, with rising temperatures and changes in some crops such as black pepper. The heat, they said, increases pests and decreases the size and quality of yields.

The second development can be seen with those families that have been successful in creating collective settlements and forming associations that manage sustainable forms of production. In these cases, the community leaders showed environmental awareness affirming that the preservation of the forest is the best way to prevent an increase in temperature. A stable climate, they argued, maintains the fauna and flora and the conditions for subsistence hunting. The next step of their work will be to realise the management plan for sustainable production. The activities called for in the plan are the production of manioc flour with a mechanised mill, an oven, the production of natural feed for fish and improvements in the planting of black pepper. In the following we will describe the activities in these communities more in detail.

When asked why it was important to preserve the forest, the representatives of the community 'Bom Futuro' gave an interesting response: they are the communities that use the forest, whether for wood to make houses and boats, or to gather fruit (such as açaí, bacaba, patauá)[1] and exploit the fauna through small-scale hunting. In this community, no one mentioned global warming as one of the problems associated with deforestation. Nevertheless, they said that the training courses of the SASK project helped them to develop an environmental awareness that they did not have previously. In addition, it motivated them to discuss agro-extractive projects that are better adapted to the community profile. In the case of 'Bom Futuro', they discussed aquaculture, sustainable extraction of timber, raising poultry, community gardens, beekeeping and the most important product for the community, the production of manioc flour.

In respect of aquaculture, they are testing alternative feed made in the community, to avoid the purchase of industrial feed that is too expensive. They are also discussing family production centres, which could be eligible for federal financing under the Pronaf[2] programme. To undertake the projects, it was necessary to approve the creation of community associations (i.e. a community-controlled legal entity) so that they can obtain credit to purchase machinery and realise the planned projects.

The community of 'Apodi' no longer plants along the banks of the igarapé tributaries of the river, the depth and extent of which varies greatly from wet to dry season; this practice was abandoned after the environmental impact became clear. Rules were also created to prohibit the use of some fishing nets, fishing with explosives or with the poisonous Timbó vine. There were also advances on the issue of garbage collection; each family has its own hole in the ground to dispose of trash and it cares for the garbage it produces, separating recyclable materials.

The civil association of the community of 'Coroca' was created in 1996 to improve the quality of life of the residents by helping them to acquire the knowledge needed to generate jobs and income with the natural resources available to the community. In 2002, projects were included to raise turtles for tourism, to keep bees and gather forest honey. The ministry asked to expand the projects to include a water-supply system and a laboratory for producing minnows. The community received a boat as a donation from federal government. Since the waterways are the only ways of transport, boats are extremely important.

The community of 'Santa Luzia' moved from the other margin of the Praia Lake due to disagreements with indigenous groups in their vicinity. The formation of the association (in 2003–4) and of the settlement was accompanied by discussions about their identity, a discussion derived from the conflicts with indigenous groups. In this context it is important to mention that in Brazil indigenous communities are those who define themselves as such. Some communities argue that self-definitions are done purely because it gives access to more rights.The discussion of the utilisation plan raised the environmental awareness among the community members considerably. They discussed how to avoid predatory fishing, deforestation and burning of the forest, which became the three focal points of community action. They also debated farming fish and 'tracajá' (a typical turtle found in the Amazon) and questioned their neighbours' decision to raise water buffalos, an imported species that require large acres of pasture.

The community of 'Urucureá' is squeezed between the Arapiuns River, Lake Urucureá and the Amazon River. As such, there is no timber to be cut in the region and therefore no direct or potential conflicts with loggers. Individually oriented families were once concerned only with material gains, but the community has now developed greater environmental awareness. In the past, garbage was thrown anywhere; now each house has a garbage receptacle and there are others spread throughout the entire community. Recyclable materials such as PET (plastic) bottles and metal cans are returned to Santarém by boat. For fishing, the community had used the poisonous root of the Timbó plant that kills all fish in the vicinity. This practice was banned. In the past, the forests on the river banks were clear-cut; this no longer occurs.

The community also created the Association of Residents, Farmers and Extractive workers of the Community of Urucureá (ASMOPREURA)[3] for the production and sale of crafts made from 'tucumã' leaves. The association signed a contract with Imaflora (FSC) for the certification of the 'tucumãzeiro' crafts and now sells these to various outlets in Brazil and abroad. It is a successful case of employment and income creation based on natural resources native to the Amazon Rainforest.

The community of 'Cachoeira do Maró' is close to the gleba 'Nova Olinda'. The right bank of the Maró River encompasses some communities that are allied to the loggers. This community is also divided between those who define themselves as indigenous and who want their lands declared an indigenous reserve, and those who do not, who prefer the option of becoming a collective settlement. If the indigenous reserve is accepted, it would cover part of the collective settlement. This is a source of conflict. The Indians of Maró have demanded 35–80 hectares of land. Timber companies hired anthropologists to prove that there are no Indians in the region. The fact that there are community members who do not want to assume an indigenous identity divides the community and raises additional challenges to local sustainability. Moreover, people associated rising temperatures with the deforestation caused by timber companies. Temperature rises, they claimed, were responsible for greater occurrences of fevers, vomiting and flu, principally among the elderly and children.

Conclusion

In the Amazon Rainforest there are many users that deplete the natural resources. Unless institutional arrangements are set up to create incentives to preserve the good, an optimal balance will not be maintained (Keohane and Ostrom 1995; Ostrom and Moran 2009). The STTR has played a decisive role in organising families and communities, and developed forms of sustainable management of natural resources. Since the environment is essential for the living and working conditions of the communities, their organisation has enabled a synthesis between labour and environmental issues creating a new framework of understanding how to deal with the forest.

Instead of bringing in expertise and formal knowledge from international bodies and governmental agencies a bottom-up approach has been adopted. Communities were involved in discussions about their understanding of climate change and its consequences for their lives. Their understanding of climate change during this learning process can be divided into three different forms of thinking about the environment. The first form, which we called generic, is the way in which successful communities constituted them-selves as actors in the political arena, their success or failure depending on their own efforts. Climate change is seen here as an exogenous process that represents a huge challenge. Preventing deforestation is seen as a priority as it represents a real threat to the traditional livelihoods and ways of life of rural families and workers.

The second form of thinking derives from a self-interested position. In this context, people link the issue of global warming with the measures taken by local inhabitants to mitigate or adapt to climate change. The communities come to realise that subsistence activities do not threaten the forest; that some monitoring and/or surveillance activities must be developed in order to detect and denounce illegal loggers and timber traders; and that air and water temperatures increase because of deforestation.

One could argue that the successful institutional arrangements created among the communities of the Arapiuns River could be applied in other contexts and circumstances. However, our analysis revealed significant differences across communities as they face the future in a context of climate change. In order to increase the success of environmental preservation efforts and keep the communities involved in efforts to sustain the forest, programmes and policies must consider the diverse universes of thinking and acting that exist at the local levels. Although there are many similarities, each community also sees a different picture. Consequently, it is not possible to devise a 'checklist' of problems to be considered by regional, national or international agencies.

Programmes coming from outside the communities must take into account the inhabitants in the development of these programmes and must be designed to increase family income through partnerships that connect government agencies (national and sub-national), environmental NGOs and civil society movements like the STTR. In the next years, more sophisticated institutional governance arrangements (REDD) with core enforcement and monitoring mechanisms could also help to consolidate the situation and support local actors to become stewards of the rainforest preservation and practitioners of 'sustainability' following their own understanding of that term. As allies, unions and local communities could perform these new tasks to secure a sustainable usage of the Brazilian rainforest at local and global levels.

Notes

1 'Programa Nacional de Fortalecimento da Agricultura Familiar' is a federal public programme to finance individual or collective rural production, see portal.mda.gov. br/portal/saf/programas/pronaf (accessed 3 July 2011).
2 'Programa Nacional de Fortalecimento da Agricultura Familiar' is a federal public programme to finance individual or collective rural production, see portal.mda.gov. br/portal/saf/programas/pronaf (accessed 3 July 2011).
3 Auditing reports of ASMOPREURA are available on http://info.fsc.org and in www.rainforestalliance.org (accessed 3 July 2011).

References

Anner, M., Greer, I., Hauptmeier, M., Lillie, N. and Winchester, N. (2006) 'The Industrial Determinants of Transnational Solidarity: Global Interunion Politics in Three Sectors', *European Journal of Industrial Relations* 12 (1), pp. 7–27.

Barbosa, A. de F., Veiga, J. P. C. and Vilmar, M. L. (2011) 'Padrões Trabalhistas e Empresas multinacionais, Revista da Associação Brasileira de Estudos do Trabalho (ABET)', *Brazilian Journal of Labour Relations* 10 (1).

Bartley, T. (2007) 'Institutional Emergence in an Era of Globalization: The Rise of Transnational Private Regulation of Labour and Environmental Conditions', *American Journal of Sociology* 113 (3), September, pp. 297–351.

BartolinI, J., Biddle, J., Ekiyor, T., Kang, E., Oliveira, M. G. da R., Serrotta, R., Tumaleo, Brandão J., Donadelli, F. (2010) *Alcoa Brazil's New Sustainability Model for Mining – Na Independent Review*, School of International and Public Affairs (SIPA), Columbia University and Institute of International Relations (IRI), University of São Paulo, Center for International Negotiations (Caeni).

Boswell, T. and Stevis, D. (1997) 'Globalization and International Labour Organizing: A World System Perspective', *Work and Occupations* 24 (3), pp. 288–308.

Brecher, J., Costello, T. and Smith, B. (2006) 'International Labour Solidarity: The New Frontier', *New Labour Forum* 5 (1), Spring, pp. 8–18.

Caraway, T. L. (2006) 'Political Openness and Transnational Activism; Comparative Insights from Labour Activism', *Politics and Society* 34 (2), pp. 277–304.

Compa, L. (2004) 'Trade Unions, NGOs and Corporate Codes of Conduct', *Development in Practice* 14 (1–2), February, pp. 210–15.

Eade, D. (2004) 'Editorial Overview', *Development and Practice* 14 (1–2), February, pp. 5–12.

Evans, P. and Anner, M. (2004) 'Building Bridges across a Double Divide: Alliances between U.S. and Latin American Labour and NGOs', *Development in Practice* 14 (1–2), February, pp. 34–47.

Frank, D. (2003) 'Where are the Workers in Consumer–Worker Alliances? Class Dynamics and the History of Consumer–Labour Campaigns', *Politics & Society* 31 (3), pp. 363–79.

Frundt, H. J. (2010) 'Sustaining Labour–Environmental Coalitions: Banana Allies in Costa Rica', *Latin American Politics and Society* 52 (3), pp. 99–129.

Hale, A. (2004) 'Beyond the Barriers: New Forms of Labour Internationalism', *Development in Practice* 14 (1–2), February, pp. 158–62.

Keck, M. E. and Sikkink, K. (1998) *Activists Beyond Borders: Advocacy Networks in International Politics*. Ithaca, NY: Cornell University Press.

Keohane, R. O. and Ostrom, E. (1995) 'Introduction', in R. O. Keohane and E. Ostrom (eds) *Local Commons and Global Interdependence*. London: Sage Publications, pp. 1–26.

Leather, A. (2004) 'Guest Editorial: Trade Union and NGO Relations in Development and Social Justice', *Development in Practice* 14 (1–2), February, pp. 13–18.

Milanez, F. (2010) 'Medo e Tensão no Oeste', *Rolling Stone Magazine* 49, October, Brazilian edition, pp. 154–62.

Obach, B. (1999) 'The Wisconsin Labour – Environmental Network – A Case Study of Coalition Formation Among Organized Labour and the Environmental Movement', *Organization and Environment* 12 (1), pp. 45–74.

Ostrom, E. and Moran, E. F. (2009) *Ecossistemas Florestais – Interação Homem Ambiente*. São Paulo: SENAC e Edusp editora.

Rose, F. (2003) 'Labour–Environmental Coalitions', *WorkingUSA*, 6 (4), Spring, pp. 51–70.

Sadler, D. (2004) 'Trade Unions, Coalitions, and Communities, Forestry, Mining and Energy Union and the International Stakeholder Campaign Against Rio Tinto', *Geoforum* 35, pp. 35–46.

Trade Union Solidarity Centre of Finland (SASK) (2010) *Project Evaluation: Farm-workers Union of Santarém (Pará\Brasil) and SASK (Finland)* (unpublished report).

Turner, L. (2004) 'Labor and Global Justice: Emerging Reform Coalition in the World's Only Superpower', *Industrielle Beziehungen, 11. Jg., Heft 1+2*, Hainer Hampp Verlag, pp. 92–111.

11 From 'jobs versus environment' to 'green-collar jobs'

Australian trade unions and the climate change debate

Verity Burgmann

In July 2009, Labor Prime Minister Kevin Rudd criticised those who 'constantly scaremonger about the possible loss of jobs through the transition to a lower carbon economy', because 'they constantly fail to talk about the new clean energy jobs of the future, which will arise from the introduction of the carbon pollution reduction scheme, the renewable energy target and energy efficiency measures in the future'. He launched Labor's national conference with a pledge to create 50,000 green jobs or training opportunities, at a cost of $100 million (*Illawarra Mercury*, 30 July 2009). The rhetoric of 'jobs versus environment', to which Rudd objected, has been perpetuated by business interests because it distracts attention from the fact that capitalism destroys both jobs and the environment. Capitalist economies are characterised by the underuse of labour resources and overuse of environmental resources. Corporations tend both to reduce labour costs and to use the cheapest production methods possible, regardless of ecological consequence. Thus employment options are restricted at the same time as the planetary environment is degraded (Polanyi 1944; Schnaiberg 1980; O'Connor 1988; Benton 1989; O'Connor 1998).

These characteristics of capitalism generate social movements: labour movements by the propensity to reduce labour costs; and ecological movements by the predisposition to degrade the environment. James O'Connor therefore urges the essential compatibility of red and green social movement aims (O'Connor 1998, 314–19). Red and green movement relations have often been acrimonious, but in recent times the 'natural' red–green alliance of O'Connor's political imagination has started to emerge in Australia. Union and green groups are increasingly cooperating together to produce a new discourse around green-collar jobs, which has started to replace the formerly hegemonic rhetoric of 'jobs versus environment'.

What are green-collar jobs? A complicated taxonomy was developed in 2009 by the Environment Institute of Australia and New Zealand, which decided there were three factors that described a green-collar worker: the skills and responsibilities of the individual; the industry and nature of the organisation for which they work; and whether the job and the organisation tend towards the environmental or sustainable end of the green spectrum (Connection Research 2009, 23). The Australian Conservation Foundation (ACF) definition emphasises outcomes: 'Green jobs or green-collar jobs contribute to better environmental outcomes or increased sustainability. Green-collar jobs range from low-skill, entry-level positions to high-skill, higher-paid jobs, and include opportunities for advancement in both skills and wages' (Connection Research 2009, 14).

Australian unions and climate change: a pre-history

The fact that unions, unlike their employers, have an interest in increased use of labour and decreased use of resources was stressed as long ago as the 1970s by an organisation established by unionists in partnership with the ACF: Environmentalists for Full Employment. Its National Convenor in the late 1970s was Jack Mundey, secretary of the New South Wales Builders Labourers' Federation during its famous 'green bans' period 1971–75, when building workers refused to construct environmentally damaging developments (Burgmann *et al.* 2002).

Environmentalists for Full Employment campaigned for cooperation between unions, environmentalists and other people who saw the need 'for much more thought and action on the related questions of Employment, Energy use and the Environment'. Mundey argued that, although the three 'Es' did not seem compatible, it was imperative that society found the way to secure socially useful employment for all, the wisest use of appropriate energy and resources and the guarantee of a habitable environment.

> There is a growing awareness that technology used primarily for profit, erodes jobs, and even worse, denies job opportunities for future workers. Furthermore most high technology consumes enormous capital and resources. Overall the need for humankind to reject blind adherence to all economic growth, to examine in detail which economic growth is socially desirable, beneficial and necessary, is now greater than ever before. The need to harmonise with nature is essential if civilisation is to live on in the 21st century.
>
> (Mundey 1978, 1)

Mundey outlined the new, urgent task for Environmentalists for Full Employ-ment: 'The carefully orchestrated myth that the fight for a decent environment increases unemployment must be exploded'. His organisation argued that capital ear-marked for environmentally harmful projects such as increasing electricity generation or uranium mining could provide much more social benefit and many more jobs if invested in alternative environmentally sound activities (Mundey n.d.).

The tradition of manual workers campaigning on environmental issues was continued in the late 1970s in the Movement Against Uranium Mining, with transport and maritime workers refusing to handle uranium, which succeeded in restricting uranium mining and export (Nette 1989). The frontal challenge of the green bans movement and the union campaign against uranium mining prompted business organisations to commence a propaganda war designed to alienate unionists and environmentalists from each other. The theme was, predictably, that environmental protection costs jobs (Burgmann *et al.* 2002, 4–6). Dave Kerin, a Builders Labourers' Federation member and environmental activist, argues that from the mid-1970s 'employers saw an opportunity to divide workers from environmentalists, and so began an internal conflict within the workers' movement which presented the problem as "jobs versus environment"' (Kerin 1999: 19). The union movement, Mundey noted, was constantly 'caught in a false dichotomy, where they have been presented with choosing between jobs or the environment ... a contradiction that has been fostered by opportunist politicians, corporations or government bureaucracies' (*Age, Extra*, 19 August 1989, 20). To counter that impression and provide positive solutions to ecological crisis, he argued that trade unions had to engage creatively in designing socially responsible job-creation schemes. 'So much damage has been done to the planet that just to repair the damage will require millions of workers' (Mundey 1988/89, 20).

Although 'job blackmail' remained an effective tool of companies engaged in unsustainable development and determined to bend governments to their will, some progress was made during the 1990s towards contesting the 'jobs versus the environment' notion. Australian unions were amongst the first in the world to push the issue of green jobs and were instrumental in encouraging renewable energy and green business initiatives in the 1990s, in advance of 'green capitalists' (Burgmann *et al.* 2002, 23–26). In 1991 the peak union body, the Australian Council of Trade Unions (ACTU), identified green employment as a key issue for the labour movement and adopted a 'Policy on Greenhouse' that called for the immediate implementation of all available low-cost measures to reduce greenhouse emissions; supported federal government initiatives in the international negotiations on a climate change convention; called on governments to fund research into energy efficiency and renewable energy technologies; acknowledged that reduction of emissions would require a mixture of pricing, taxation and regulatory measures, and argued that price measures alone would have an adverse effect on low-income earners and that regulatory and planning measures would be the most efficient and effective means of achieving change; and called on federal and state governments to develop a national approach to encourage improved performance in all energy production, distribution and use, for example, in power stations, vehicles, buildings, plant and equipment and domestic appliances (ACTU 1992, inside back cover).

In July 1992 the ACTU published a remarkably forward-thinking booklet, *The Greenhouse Effect: employment & development issues for Australians*, which, had it been implemented, would have positioned Australia as the global leader in climate change mitigation and greatly reduced the cost of transition to a low carbon economy. *The Greenhouse Effect* was the work of the Greenhouse Group of the ACTU Environment Committee and was researched and written by Peter Colley of the Construction Forestry Mining and Energy Union

(CFMEU). In the introduction 'Greenhouse—An Incentive for Social and Economic Change' (ACTU 1992) ACTU Assistant Secretary Jennie George announced:

> The enhanced greenhouse effect is with us now. Its impacts, and measures to counteract it, will increasingly affect Australian society and the every-day lives of working people ... There are substantial costs and benefits associated with moving towards a more greenhouse-friendly economy. For Australia in particular, it means moving away, over time, from heavy reliance on our fossil fuel industries to a more diverse and less resource-intensive economy.
>
> (ACTU 1992, inside front cover)

Australian working people and their trade unions must be active in this process. It is working people who will bear many of the costs of measures to reduce greenhouse gas emissions, and who will be responsible for implementing the necessary changes in the workplace.

George strongly urged trade unions, individual unionists and the wider community to take up the challenge presented by the greenhouse effect. Pro-phetically, she observed: 'It is likely to be one of the greatest tasks facing Australian society and industry as we enter the 21st century' (ACTU 1992, inside front cover). The concluding chapter on 'Trade Unions' Vital Role' urged high-level union involvement in consultations with governments and business groups, and closer working relations for unions with academic, scientific and research organisations, as well as consumer, environment and welfare groups, to determine 'how measures can be implemented in a way which maximises benefits, minimises costs and which at least maintain social equity' (ACTU 1992, 25). Finally, it called on union members to make greenhouse issues part of regular union activities, to work with environment groups on it and, at the same time, aim to develop 'an awareness in environment groups of the importance of employment, industry development and social equity issues' (ACTU 1992, 26).

In 1993, the ACTU and the ACF joined forces to set up a 'green jobs' programme, announcing they 'recognised that they had a common interest in the creation of jobs which are environmentally beneficial'. The ACF/ ACTU Green Jobs Unit, funded by the federal Departments of Employment, Education & Training and Environment, Sport & Territories, was established in Melbourne to conduct research and training programs, organise job placements and promote green jobs throughout the country, especially for unemployed workers, young people, Aboriginal and disabled people (Burgmann *et al.* 2002, 23–24).

As these green jobs initiatives were wound down after the election of the conservative Howard government in 1996, a union/green group called Earth-worker was formed in 1997, endorsed and sponsored by the Victorian Trades Hall Council in Melbourne. By 2000, Earthworker had three environmental organisations affiliated, plus 14 unions or divisions of unions, representing workers in industries as varied as construction, manufacturing, services, tertiary education, nursing, journalism and entertainment (McNaughton 2000, 37–38; de Boehmler 2004). Earthworker argued that the question of sustainability and sustainable work had to become as basic a part of the union movement's agenda as wages and conditions. It was envisaged that this material project would encourage a discursive transformation, creating what Earthworker called 'a jobs *and* environment dialogue' (McNaughton 2000, 44). One of its success stories was its 'Solar Wind and Water Alternative Energy Plan', which brought together unions, alternative energy activists, academics, corporations and local and state governments to create a wind industry in Victoria, cheap access to householders for solar hot water units and thousands of jobs in manufacture, installation and administration (Earthworker 1999; *Age*, 15 November 1999; McNaughton 2000, 44–45). It was also involved in the ACF Green Building project and the CFMEU-Construction Division's Environmental, Occupational Health and Safety Unit efforts to create a greener construction industry, in design and products used (McNaughton 2000, 45).

Despite continuing efforts on the part of corporations and media to pit 'greenies' and workers against each other, green jobs' initiatives and links between unionists and environmentalists persisted into the new millennium. Today, green employment initiatives are flourishing. Some unions are even going it alone. The Earthworker Social Enterprise suggests organised labour itself could create green jobs and push Australia towards a sustainable future. Inspired by the 200,000 cooperatives in Venezuela run under workers' control, this initiative is backed by the Gippsland Trades and Labour Council. It has taken the best solar hot water unit, redesigned it to make an even better product, and aims to establish a factory in the vicinity to produce these units. Others in the La Trobe Valley heard climate change sounding the death knell for the local economy, heavily reliant on coal-mining and coal-fired power stations, but the Earthworker Social Enterprise created an alternative vision of 'Workers leading the way to a green economy' (Kerin 2010).

In 2007 and 2008, opinion polling indicated that most people did not believe repeated claims that addressing climate change would adversely affect the economy (Climate Institute 2007, 12–13; ARG 2007, 5, 20). The debate had shifted in ways more favourable to green employment for two obvious reasons. First, public concern about climate change increased significantly from 2006 in the wake of authoritative scientific pronouncements, popularised by Al Gore's film and sanctioned by leading economists in the Stern Review (2006). For Australians the reality of climate change was confirmed by increasing heat and water shortages, with the first decade of the twenty-first century easily Australia's hottest on record (Climate Institute 2007, 4; Garnaut 2011, 19). Second, from 2008 the global financial crisis and global recession focused attention on protecting the livelihoods of people at the bottom end of labour markets and encouraged scepticism about neo-liberal notions that free market forces can be trusted to bring prosperity and security to all classes of society. Obama's successful campaign for the US presidency in 2008 invested hopes in a 'green New Deal' in which climate change and unemployment would be tackled simultaneously by deliberate creation of green jobs. The rise of green Keynesianism as a response to both climate and economic crisis was intimated too in the British trade union movement's campaign for a million green jobs.

The context was at last providing space for argument that challenges capitalism's tendency to underuse labour and overuse resources. Class and nature as issues that used to pit labour movement activists and greenies against each other have become more reconcilable. This becomes even more evident if climate change and the global financial crisis are not seen as unrelated events, each separately providing 'political opportunity' for environmentalists and unionists. Arguably, both global warming and global financial crisis have been brought to the planet courtesy of corporate globalisation and the neo-liberal policies associated with it, which encouraged both financial and ecological irresponsibility on the part of corporations and reluctance on the part of governments to regulate corporations on either count.

At the very least it became easier to argue that neo-liberal corporate globalisation seriously delayed a solution to the global warming problem. The dangers of the greenhouse effect were well known and publicised by scientists during the 1980s. Unions, as we have seen, pushed green employment as a significant climate change mitigation policy during the 1990s. Governments might have responded more appropriately if that important moment in the history of the planet had not coincided with the onset of the neo-liberal era, whose protagonists succeeded in subduing much of the discussion of climate change until the past few years. Neo-liberalism had also encouraged people to value economic growth and personal consumption, a cultural offensive that discouraged support for climate change mitigation even when its necessity was acknowledged.

Ariel Salleh has criticised the new green Keynesianism for reinstating an overly optimistic 1990s ecological modernisation strategy, directed simply at saving capitalism. She argues the first requirement of a green new deal should be to help people understand how the dominant global capitalist system relies on the abuse of nature and the exploitation of labouring bodies (Salleh 2010, 15). Ideally, this should be so. However, the new green Keynesianism does at the very least undermine the previously hegemonic rhetoric of 'jobs versus environment', replacing it with a 'jobs and environment' emphasis on climate change mitigation through greater use of labour rather than resources. This provides the potential for transcendence of the red/green binary, a positive outcome that could overcome barriers between labour and green movements that have prevented more effective critique of capitalism's disregard for employment and the environment. Building on its foundation work during the 1990s, in the past few years the ACTU, on behalf of Australian unions, has developed clear policies about the best means to save both the planet and people's livelihoods.

The Australian Council of Trade Unions: recent initiatives

On 16 February 2007 the ACTU convened a national Union Forum on Global Warming and Sustainable Energy to develop solutions to climate change. ACTU President Sharan Burrow announced the main aim was for the union movement to take a stronger role in providing leadership on the issue:

> Climate change is one of the most urgent problems the world faces today and we must act now—not in 10 years time and this conference is another step towards securing an energy future for Australia that strikes the right balance between sustainability of industry and security of employment. Australia is indeed the lucky country when it comes to natural resources, including wind and solar and we need to be leading the world in clean and green technology by investing in renewable energy sources, creating more sustainable agricultural industries and meeting the scientific challenge of clean coal and gas power generation.

She reiterated the connection between ecological sustainability and employment protection:

> Australia's unions have a responsibility to find and implement solutions to climate change and global warming that protect jobs and do not destabilize our industries. Indeed, the development of renewable energy sources and cleaner technologies offer the prospect of new growth areas for jobs and the Australian economy that need to be urgently explored.
>
> (ACTU 2007a)

The following day the ACTU published online its 'Principles and Policy on Global Warming'. It argued that global warming was 'the pre-eminent policy challenge of our time'. The scientific evidence was overwhelming, it maintained, that human activity was causing global warming: 'Unless decisive action is taken now to reduce greenhouse gas emissions, the planet we bequeath to future generations will be harsher and more hostile to the human condition than that which we have inherited'. This position paper carefully linked environmental and social justice issues. It reiterated the ACTU's commitment to 'reduce poverty, raise living standards, create decent jobs, provide opportunity to all' and noted that the 'environmental consequences of our production and consumption must be reckoned alongside the efficiency of its generation and the fairness of its distribution'. It noted that the cost of reducing global emissions would be high, but that the Stern Review (2006) had established that the cost of not reducing emissions was far higher. Its solutions were framed within a paradigm identifiable as ecologically modernist. 'Decisive action to reduce global emissions is necessary for continuing sustained economic growth.' Concerted national and international effort and investment targeting reduced emissions carried greater potential for better jobs and higher incomes:

Sustainable growth and quality jobs will be delivered by investment in new technologies, energy efficiency, and demand management ... Industry must face up to global warming and be accountable for investing in sustainable jobs rather than raising the fear of job losses and expecting government handouts.

Global warming presented a social and economic imperative to act, now. 'Australian unions are committed to playing a constructive role in meeting the challenge' (ACTU 2007b).

In July 2008, the ACTU, along with the Climate Institute, ACF and Australian Council of Social Service, set up as the Southern Cross Climate Coalition (SCCC) to lead debate on a fair response to climate change. The SCCC publicly argues the benefits of green jobs and lobbies governments to do more to create them, in the interests of both the environment and the economy (*Australian*, 14 September 2009). As a coalition of social, union, environmental and independent research organisations, it was well placed to stress that collaboration across all sectors of Australian society was critical to achieving an effective, fair and lasting response to climate change.

We understand that effective action on climate change means much more than reducing greenhouse emissions. It means grabbing hold of new economic and job creation opportunities at the same time as improving the living standards of all Australians fairly and sustainably.

(*Sydney Morning Herald*, 6 July 2008)

As the global financial crisis struck late in 2008, the ACTU also collaborated with the ACF to release *Green Gold Rush: How An Ambitious Environmental Policy Can Make Australia a Leader in the Global Race for Green Jobs*. With an obvious eye to job-creating opportunities as well as meaningful action on climate change, this booklet identified six industries that could result in new 'green jobs': renewable energy, energy efficiency, sustainable water systems, biomaterials, green buildings and waste and recycling. The report calculated that strong action on climate and industry policy could trigger the creation of an additional 500,000 jobs in these six sectors by 2030. It argued:

In this time of economic uncertainty, one of the few good news stories is the continued prospects for the growth of green industries. Strong action on climate change will promote green jobs and green businesses and help secure Australia's economic prosperity.

With the right policies, 'we have an opportunity to turn action to combat our environmental challenges into growth of the green economy, securing jobs and industry well into the future' (ACTU/ACF 2008, 2).

The ACTU supported the Rudd Labor government's commitment to achieve 60 per cent reduction in greenhouse gas emissions below the 2000 level by 2050 but urged a more ambitious medium-term reduction target than did the government, maintaining 30 per cent reduction below the 2000 level by 2020 was possible 'without major technological breakthroughs or lifestyle changes and at minimal cost to working people'. It also argued that any compensation to companies must be conditional and tied to investments in renewable and low carbon technologies (ACTU 2010). Burrow elaborated upon this in March 2009 in an article entitled 'Combating global warming is a shared task' in which she took issue with industry voices 'dominated by those peddling fear in order to maximise compensation'. She asked:

> [S]urely they must now be prepared to face up to the reality of global warming and be accountable for investing in more efficient practices … how about some maturity from the business community and some shared responsibility for creating a smarter economy that builds a sustainable future for all?

She claimed that by 2030 there could be 850,000 jobs in green industries and policy settings ought to ensure the investment necessary to win a big share of what would be a $US3 trillion global green market by 2020. 'The global financial crisis and the potential impact on employment show another way that we can make green investment work for the economy, the environment and jobs' (Burrow 2009, 8).

The seven-page policy document on 'A Fair Society: Environment and Climate Change Policy' endorsed at the ACTU Congress in June 2009 reiterated the ACTU's commitment to 'urgent and decisive action to transition Australia to a low carbon economy' and rejected the notion that such action would damage the economy. Rather, it drew strong connections between climate change mitigation and job creation:

> We accept that as the global economy switches to a low carbon future, the result will create multi-trillion dollar markets for low carbon and clean energy technologies, infrastructure and consequently production pro-cesses. Australia needs to ensure that its current and future industries are competitive in this global low carbon economy.
>
> (ACTU 2009, 1–2)

However, there was some backtracking on climate change policy. In addition to the usual commitment to 'promote growth in green jobs in associated/new industries and services', this document also inserted an express commitment to 'ensuring that the transition process protects jobs in carbon intensive industries' and to 'support those industries to achieve best of sector standards to remain competitive' (ACTU 2009, 1–2).

One might perceive here the hand of the Mining and Energy Division of the CFMEU, which represents workers in the hugely significant coal-mining and coal-power electricity generation sectors. Yet this union, especially under the leadership of Tony Maher, has never denied the science of global warming and the need to move to a low carbon economy (Maher 2007). A more likely regressive influence is the Australian Workers' Union, which represents workers in aluminium smelters and other carbon-intensive industries, and whose officials manoeuvred in 2010 to replace Kevin Rudd as Labor prime minister with Julia Gillard, who subsequently reduced the proposed additional taxation on mining industry super-profits.

Previous ACTU policy statements had emphasised the need to 'protect jobs', with the strong implication that job protection would be ensured overall by increased employment opportunities in green jobs. This 2009 document supported the ITUC's 'just transition' policy statement, yet its own position of protecting jobs in carbon-intensive industries was now out of line with the ITUC emphasis on transition away from such forms of employment. Also of interest is that, although it urged 'a strong emissions reduction cap' in the projected emissions trading scheme, it also stated that consequent auctioning of permits

> must be just, support vulnerable Emissions-Intensive Trade-Exposed industries during transition but be designed to ensure all industries are required to make the changes necessary to get to best practice standards to ensure global competitiveness and survival of Australia's traditional industries.

Also, where the ACTU had previously urged a steeper emissions-reduction target and regardless of the actions of other countries, this document supported the government's announced amendments to the scheme, including 'a carbon emissions reduction target of 25 per cent by 2020 in the event of a comprehensive global agreement to stabilise emissions at 450 ppm or better' (ACTU 2009, 3). On the other hand, this document did state that market measures alone would be insufficient to achieve the necessary environmental, social and economic changes required; that support for research and development and industry policy must be significant and complemented by direct government regulation where necessary; and incentives for investment in new green jobs and training programmes should include targeting areas from which carbon-intensive jobs are at risk (ACTU 2009, 5). So the ACTU and its affiliates committed to 'co-ordinate industry-wide campaigns for industry policy, investment and/or regulation necessary for making the transition to a low carbon economy' (ACTU 2009, 7).

Another joint initiative with the ACF was Union Climate Connectors, launched in August 2009 to provide an accessible forum for union members to participate in climate change action and to provide the training and resources for this purpose (Reale 2009, 9). Climate Connectors aims: to empower union members to take action to mitigate climate change in homes, workplaces and communities around Australia; and to support solutions to the climate crisis that are good for both the environment and jobs (Climate Connectors 2010). Burrow's email to Australian unionists inviting them to sign up as a Climate Connector emphasised the role of unions:

> Unions have a proud history of campaigning on environmental issues. But rarely has the stakes been as high as they are now. That is why unions around the country are joining together to encourage members to be part of the climate solution.

It explained that the Climate Connectors' campaign was developed by Australian Unions and the ACF

> to give workers an opportunity to get involved and make a lasting difference to the planet ... Through connecting together as workers we can build a low emissions future and protect ourselves, and generations to come from the terrible consequences of dangerous climate change. Australian unions are committed to being part of the solution to the climate crisis, and to building a clean economy that will provide prosperity to future generations.
>
> (Sharan Burrow and the Union Climate Connector team, 2 September 2009)

Under the heading 'The Power of Unions', the Climate Connectors' website affirms the centrality of unions in meeting the challenge of climate change: 'Union members have a vision for a clean energy future, with clean, green workplaces; and have a leadership role to play in developing and demanding the action we need to get there'. It emphasises the positive outcomes for workers: 'We know that those solutions have the power to create millions of jobs in a clean energy economy—jobs for us, and jobs for future generations' (Climate Connectors 2010). The campaign's activities include learning, communicating, implementing changes and lobbying. The ACF provides kits, web tools, phone advice and training in how to campaign for climate change mitigation in both the workplace and larger society (Reale 2009, 9). There were four Action Kits (Energy, Food, Jobs and Water) and also a special Copenhagen Action Kit. The Jobs Action Kit gave details of the potential for green jobs in particular industries and occupations and started with the observation:

> We have to stop polluting Australia and damaging our planet. By being smart we can take action on climate change to cut pollution and create new, and better jobs. It takes 49 tradies and apprentices to build 1000 solar panels—and we need millions! Wind turbines have over 10,000 parts. Who's going to make and install them? ... Clean energy technology ... is an exploding field that will touch every industry. The good news is, it's not 'jobs or the environment'. Cutting pollution creates jobs.
>
> (Climate Connectors 2010)

Late in 2009 Burrow led representatives of Australian unions at the Copenhagen Climate Summit. Admitting this did not deliver the anticipated binding global treaty to combat global warming, the ACTU stated it would continue to lobby governments worldwide for strong climate action, including 'a just transition' for workers, 'which means embedding decent labour standards and good quality jobs as the new clean energy economy emerges at home and around the world' (ACTU 2010). The ACTU, in conjunction with the ACF, released a report in 2010 on 'Creating Jobs. Cutting Pollution', which pointed out: 'Action to reduce pollution can go hand-in-hand with job creation and a prosperous and environmentally healthy Australia. ... Australia could create more than 770,000 extra jobs by 2030 by taking strong action now to reduce pollution' (ACTU/ACF 2009).

It appears that the fiasco of Copenhagen might have strengthened those voices within the ACTU that had caused the 'watering down' of the ACTU's position on climate change evident in the 2009 policy document. The ACTU website for several years until mid-2010 had announced that:

> Climate change is the most pressing social and economic challenge we face, and Australians will be hit hard if we do not respond urgently to climate change. Unions have been working hard at both national and international levels to accelerate real, workable and equitable solutions to this major problem.
>
> (ACTU 2010)

It called upon the government 'to develop policy and drive investment towards new and cleaner technologies, and new industries—to establish Australia as a global leader and to take advantage of economic opportunities'. It claimed that Australia's natural competitive advantage combined with our globally recognised skills and expertise can be harnessed to create real industry development and export opportunities. It referred to its own commissioned economic research 'which demonstrates that Australia still has an unparalleled opportunity to create hundreds of thousands of "green collar" jobs' (ACTU 2010).

However, currently the ACTU website section 'Climate Change and Jobs' states that: 'Climate change is one of the most pressing economic, social and environmental challenges we face'. The significant alteration here is that climate change is now only one of the most pressing challenges. Again, the current website incorporates the additions in the 2009 policy document, shying away from acknowledging the need for transition away from coal mining and coal-fired power generation:

> Unions are determined that adjusting to a low pollution economy must focus on support for emission-intensive and trade-exposed industries, measures to protect existing jobs, programs to attract investment in clean energy and production, and assistance to low income households. Some industries and regional economies will be impacted more acutely than

others. It is imperative that these communities are assisted to successfully adapt their industries and build new ones to ensure decent living standards, job opportunities and services continue to thrive in these areas.

(ACTU 2011a)

Otherwise, the strong message from the current website reiterates the ACTU position that has emerged strongly over the past few decades: that climate change mitigation offers employment opportunities.

It is simply not true that the shift to a low pollution economy will result in job losses. Research commissioned by the ACTU and ACF demonstrates that Australia still has an unparalleled opportunity to create hundreds of thousands of 'green collar' jobs.

(ACTU 2011a)

In the 'Your Rights at Work—February Newsletter' emailed to Australian unionists on 4 March 2011, the ACTU reassured members that workers' interests were being represented as the government prepared its carbon tax legislation. ACTU reiterated its position that a price on carbon was 'a vital step forward in taking action on climate change' and stated:

Unions representing workers in all sectors and industries are more than willing to make a strong start on the transition to a low pollution economy as long as the requirements for a 'just transition' are identified, examined in detail and properly addressed.

In April 2011 the ACTU published a colourful pamphlet entitled *Climate Change is Union Business*, which argued: 'Job creation and action on climate change are closely connected' (ACTU 2011b).

Conclusion

The current climate and economic crises offer considerable scope for transcendence of the red/green binary. Fred Rose's study of labour and environmental movements in the US examined the 'politics of division that confronts the public with tragic choices between protecting economic well-being and preserving the environment'. Powerful interests are served, he argued, by pitting citizens and their legitimate issues against each other. 'Dividing movements and social groups is a well-established strategy for undermining opposition and distracting public attention from issues of power and common interests' (Rose 2000, 5, 8).

Australian unions have a long history of action on environmental issues, including green jobs initiatives, and have campaigned alongside green organisations to overcome the false dichotomy of the 'jobs versus environment' discourse. Recently, under the leadership of the ACTU, this project has been pursued with renewed energy, aiming to position the union movement as central to the creation of a low carbon economy. The rhetoric of 'green jobs' has broad acceptance amongst unionists, because it does not require a shift away from the traditional union emphasis on employment security. Not only are there no jobs on a dead planet, it is now increasingly acknowledged there are more jobs in a sustainable green economy than a 'brown' one. Targeting the 'twin crises of economy and ecology' is both necessary and possible (Butcher and Stilwell 2009, 121). By prioritising the use of labour rather than resources, a sustainable green economy could guarantee stable and high levels of employment without the need for the harmful overall economic growth and expansion that underpins employment security in a brown economy. These 'jobs and environment' initiatives have on occasions faltered and always fall short of offering any fundamental challenge to capitalism, but they certainly assist to break down the division between unionists and environmentalists that have for so long strengthened those who profit from the exploitation of both labour and nature.

References

ACTU (1992) *The Greenhouse Effect: employment & development issues for Australians*, ACTU, Melbourne.

——(2007a) 'Unions to pursue climate change solutions including carbon trading scheme, renewable energy sources and green building codes', 16 February, www.actu.asn.au/ Media/Mediareleases/Unionstopursueclimatechangesolutionsincludingcarbontrading schemereneableenergysourcesandgreenbuildingcodes.aspx, accessed 19 May 2009.

——(2007b) 'ACTU's Principles and Policy on Global Warming', 17 February, www. actu.asn.au/AboutACTU/ACTUPubllications/ACTUsPrinciplesandPolicyonGlobal Warming.aspx (accessed 19 May 2009).

——(2009) 'ACTU Congress 2009. A Fair Society. Environment and Climate Change Policy', 2–4 June, www.actu.asn.au/Tools/print.aspx (accessed 10 May 2011).

——(2010) 'Campaign: Clean Energy Jobs', www.actu.org.au/Campaigns/CleanEnergy Jobs/default.aspx accessed 8 July 2010.

——(2011a) 'Campaign: Climate Change and Jobs', www.actu.org.au/Campaigns/Climate ChangeJobs/default.asp, accessed 12 May 2011.

——(2011b) *Climate Change is Union Business*, ACTU, Melbourne.

ACTU/ACF (2008) *Green Gold Rush*, ACTU/ACF, Melbourne.

——(2009) 'Creating Jobs—Cutting Pollution', www.actu.org.au/Images/Dynamic/ attachments/6971/ACF_Jobs_reporrt_190510.pdf (accessed 8 July 2010).

ARG (Australian Research Group) (2007) *Climate Institute Marginal Electorates Election Campaign Poll*, November, ARG, Melbourne and ARG, Sydney.

Benton, T. (1989) 'Marxism and Natural Limits', *New Left Review*, no. 178, pp. 51–86.

Burgmann, V. *et al.* (2002) *Unions and the Environment*, ACF/ACTU, Melbourne.

Burrow, S. (2009) 'Combating global warming is a shared task', *Australian Options*, no. 56, pp. 8–9.

Butcher, B. and Stilwell, F. (2009) 'Climate Change Policy and Economic Recession', *Journal of Australian Political Economy*, no. 63, Winter, pp. 108–25.

Climate Connectors (2010) www.climateconnectors.org, accessed 3 March 2012.

Climate Institute (2007) *Climate of the Nation. Australians' Attitudes to Climate Change and its Solutions*, Climate Institute, Sydney.

Connection Research (2009) *Who Are the Green Collar Workers?* Environment Institute Australia and New Zealand, Sydney.

De Boehmler, T. (2004) 'Beyond the Wedge', *Workers Online*, 19 November, http://workers.labor.net.au/247/news9_dosh.html (accessed 3 August 2012).

Earthworker (1999) 'From Fossil Fuels to Renewables: A solar, wind & water industry plan', 15 November.

Garnaut, R. (2011) *The Garnaut Review 2011: Australia in the global response to climate change*, Cambridge University Press, Melbourne.

Kerin, D. (1999) 'Challenging the Myth of Jobs vs Environment', *Chain Reaction*, no. 80, pp. 19–20, 42.

——(2010) 'Workers creating green jobs', lecture, Melbourne Trades Hall, 7 July.

Maher, T. (2007) 'Crib Rooms and Climate Change. Empowering Mine Workers', 16 August, http://cfmeumin.pwsites.com.au/downloads/crib-rooms-and-climate-change-empowering-mine-workers (accessed 5 March 2012).

McNaughton, C. (2000) 'From Little Things Big Things Grow: The Greening of the Labour Movement in Australia?', BA Hons thesis, Politics Department, Monash University.

Mundey, J. (1978) 'Compatibility of the 3 'E's' Vital to Survival', *Environmentalists for Full Employment, Newsletter*, no. 1, December.

——(n.d.) [c.1978] 'Covering letter for sending to prospective member-sponsor groups', *Environmentalists for Full Employment*, leaflet.

——(1988/89) 'From grey to green', *Australian Left Review*, no. 108, p. 19.

Nette, A. (1989) 'Digging uranium: the movement and the unions', *Arena*, no. 89, pp. 103–15.

O'Connor, J. (1988) 'Capitalism, Nature, Socialism', *Capitalism, Nature and Socialism*, vol. 1, no. 1, pp. 11–38.

——(1998) *Natural Causes: Essays in Ecological Marxism*, Guildford Press, New York.

Polanyi, K. (1944) *The Great Transformation*, Farrar & Rinehart, New York.

Reale, E. (2009) 'ANF joins climate change campaign', *Australian Nursing Journal*, vol. 17, no. 4, p. 9.

Rose, F. (2000) *Coalitions across the Class Divide*, Cornell University Press, Ithaca, NY and London.

Salleh, A. (2010) 'Green New Deal—or Globalisation Lite?', *Arena Magazine*, no. 105, pp. 15–19.

Schnaiberg, A. (1980) *The Environment, From Surplus to Scarcity*, Oxford University Press, New York.

Stern, N. (2006) *Stern Review on the Economics of Climate Change*, Cabinte Office/HM Treasury, London, http://webarchive.nationalarchives.gov.uk/+/http://www.hm-treasury.gov.uk/stern_review_report.htm (accessed 30 March 2012).

12 Just transition and labour environmentalism in Australia

Darryn Snell and Peter Fairbrother

Introduction

'Just transition' has become the new mantra for labour and environmental organisations seeking to balance the needs of workers with the need to protect the environment. As the urgency for action on climate change becomes more acute there are increasing signs that the tensions between organised labour and environmental organisations over environmental regulation are beginning to subside. Environmentalists and unions are beginning to work more closely together to campaign for a more balanced and sustainable approach to economic and industrial activity. This chapter considers the theoretical and practical implications of 'just transition'. The chapter begins by considering the philosophical and theoretical underpinnings of the notion of 'just transition' and its relationship to policy approaches and practical outcomes for workers and the environment. The idea of a 'just transition' is situated against and compared with the more dominant neo-liberal discourse and policy approaches to industrial and environmental matters. The second half of the chapter opens up these issues, both theoretically and empirically, by considering the emergence of labour environmentalism in Australia.

'Just transition': theory and practice

The inequities associated with climate change have been well documented (Page 2006; Vanderheiden 2008; Roberts and Parks 2007). While wealthy industrialised societies are responsible for the vast majority of accumulated greenhouse gas (GHG) emissions that cause climate-related harms, the impacts fall disproportionately upon poor people living in developing countries (IPCC 2007). Moreover, future generations will pay the price for 'the affluence of the world's most advantaged nations and persons' (Vanderheiden 2008, 121). Environmental action aimed at mitigating climate change seeks to address environmental destruction and the social inequities associated with maintaining the status quo.

Policy approaches to mitigating climate change, however, raise their own equity concerns for industries, organisations, workers and communities who may be affected by these policies. Unequal outcomes and perceived vulnerabilities from climate change mitigation policies have proven to be a major barrier to achieving meaningful outcomes in national and international environmental politics (Roberts and Parks 2007). Attempts to regulate and reduce emissions from GHG-intensive industries, for example, have raised concerns about the treatment of workers associated with these traditional industries. As the United Nations Environment Programme (UNEP) has recognised, climate change mitigation policies will have uneven impacts, with carbon-exposed regions potentially suffering disproportionate hardships that necessitate particular government interventions.

> [W]here industries are highly concentrated in one or a handful of regions, these impacts can have serious consequences for the local economy and the viability of communities. These regions will need pro-active assistance in creating alternative jobs and livelihoods, acquiring new skills, and weathering the transition to new industries.
>
> (UNEP 2007)

Effectively addressing the problems of anthropogenic climate change thus requires a commitment to fairness; both in terms of addressing the inequities associated with the differential impacts of climate change but also the inequities associated with the social and geographical impacts of climate change policies focused on mitigation. As Vanderheiden (2008) has pointed out, allocating the costs and burdens of GHG abatement and climate change adaptation fairly involves due consideration to the basic principles of distributive justice. 'Just transition', as advocated by trade unions, is an attempt to articulate such principles by linking the dimensions of climate action with principles of fairness.

A 'just transition' is a process of change where the move to a more sustainable society, based on a low carbon economy, is both desirable and necessary, which in turn requires an equitable distribution of costs, achieved via planning and proactive policy making and implementation (TUC 2008a, 2008b). As indicated, achieving a 'just transition' involves both an ethical and moral dimension, as well as a planned and calculated set of policies and practices. In this regard, the ideals expressed by 'just transition' seek to establish guiding norms towards which policy development should aspire.

These ideals have their origin in the trade union movements of the world, and particularly the US trade union movement. The idea of a 'just transition' has its origins in the 1970s when Leonard Woodcock of the United Automobile Workers

> proposed that workers who lost their jobs because of employer pollution abuses should have the right to bring a class action suit against their employers and to recover lost wages and benefits, lost seniority, the cost of retraining, and moving expenses.
>
> (Kazis and Grossman 1982, 226)

Slowly and in rather attenuated ways, these ideas were taken up by other unions in North America as well as in Argentina, Spain, Germany and Denmark, and less so in the United Kingdom and Australia (TUC 2008a).

'Just transition' is now used by trade unions to articulate their multiple concerns about moves to a low carbon economy. According to the Canadian Labour Congress:

> Just Transition is about many things. It is about fairness and environmental justice. It is about quality employment in an economy based on sustainable production and infrastructure. It is about communities as the focus of Just Transition programs – communities as centres of diverse, labour-intensive industries, with a strong public sector to support them. It is, above all, about *alternative employment* in a sustainable economy.
>
> (CLC 2000, 2)

At a very basic level just transition thus relates to notions of social justice in liberal democratic societies when changes are introduced that have ramifications for individuals and groups of people who are not directly in control of these changes. In the context of work, just transition can apply to principles of consultation with affected workers before major organisational and work tasks are introduced. It can also apply to much broader organisational environment changes, such as those emerging from public policy initiatives.

'Just transition' advocates a position of procedural fairness whereby justice must not only be achieved as an outcome but it must also be reflected in the means used to realise these outcomes. In its application, 'just transition' seeks to extend worker, community and union roles in the change process. Rather than focusing on the necessary steps needed when change has already occurred, just transition advocates for involvement of those affected prior to change events. In the context of the economic and industrial change from a high carbon to low carbon economy the discussion often shifts into a debate about the green economy and green jobs. In many countries it has been argued that the adjustment to the green economy, if handled appropriately, can open up opportunities for workers who have suffered disadvantages in the labour market (TUAC Secretariat 2008; ACTU and ACF 2008). In the US, the Apollo Alliance and the BlueGreen Alliance, for example, argue for a green new deal with the combined goals of stimulating the economy through job creation programmes that create a cleaner more sustainable economy and provide jobs for disadvantaged and unemployed inner city workers (Apollo Alliance 2009; BlueGreen Alliance 2007; Gould *et al.* 2004). More recently a similar stance has been taken by the Trades Union Congress (TUC) in Britain:

> Just Transition must not just be about creating 'green jobs' to meet the direct material needs of those workers affected by the shift to a low carbon economy, but must also be about ensuring those jobs are decent jobs. Environmental transition could not be described meaningfully as

'just' if the new jobs it provided could not ensure that work was productive and safe, delivered a fair income, provided security and equal opportunity in the workplace, provided social protection for families, and better prospects for personal development.

(TUC 2008a, 27)

A 'just transition' is distinct from other more prevalent approaches to addressing industrial and regional hardship. Structural adjustment, for example, which is widely used by governments and international lending agencies, should not be confused with 'just transition'. Such programs emerged out of the neo-liberal policies that brought about widespread destruction to communities and workers' lives who were exposed to the full force of global market fundamentalism (Harvey 2005; Frank 2000). Worker and community opposition to these policies forced governments and international lenders to provide improved assistance for workers and regions suffering from major economic restructuring (ILO 2009; World Bank 2002, 2000).

Unlike structural adjustment, 'just transition' advocates and necessitates an alternative development model. Such an alternative model calls into question the legitimacy of the neo-liberal paradigm in a number of ways. First, 'just transition' implies a return to industrial planning, an approach that has been undermined by those who advocate for structural adjustment. Second, 'just transition' rests on an assumption that unions, workers and local communities will contribute to industrial planning, historically seen as the domain of governments working in association with private interests. Unions and workers in these local communities may seek to ensure appropriate and decent jobs are created. Similarly unions and workers may argue for training for displaced workers. Third, 'just transition' challenges the notion that a market-based solution involving private enterprise is the only solution to regional and industrial revitalisation.

Such arguments have come to underpin trade union notions of 'just transition' and labour environmentalism more generally. Successfully and equitably moving workers and communities away from 'climate threatening' industries to 'climate friendly' industries is the challenge for unions, governments and other social actors. The realisation of a 'just transition' raises two significant questions. First, what are the conditions for a 'just transition'? Second, what capacities do unions have to influence economic and political conditions in such a way that 'just transition' can be actualised? To answer these questions we focus on climate change politics and labour environmentalism in Australia.

Labour environmentalism and climate change politics in Australia

The exploitation of Australia's rich natural resources and their associated job creation, tax revenue and infrastructure development have played a major role in the nation's remarkable social and economic achievements (Australia ranks second on the UN's Human Development Index – UNDP 2010, 144). Coal is at the heart of this advance. It is the country's most lucrative export commodity, representing 30 per cent of Australia's global trade (McNeil 2009). Moreover, coal serves as the principal fuel for the country's cheap and reliable electricity industry, a major motivating factor for the attraction and expansion of heavy energy users in the metallurgical and manufacturing sectors. It is becoming increasingly recognised that these developments have come with an environmental cost. Australia's overreliance on coal combustion for its energy needs has contributed to the country having one of the highest carbon emissions per capita in the world (Garnaut 2008). Access to cheap energy, the capacity to pollute without responsibility and generous government subsidies to the coal and heavy emitting industries has contributed to a lack of innovation among energy producers and major energy users, with, for example, some of the most energy-intensive aluminium plants in the world (*The Age*, 17 April 2011).

Australia is under mounting national and international pressures to curb its GHG emissions and to benefit from international moves towards a clean technology economy. Like many countries, climate change mitigation in Australia has been marred by deep political divisions that are played out at both the federal and state levels of government. The Australian Greens have led on the climate change mitigation policy front but as a minority party it has never had the opportunity to play a lead role in government policy making. In contrast, the conservative National and Liberal Parties, historically aligned with one another to form coalition governments, have tended to take a very cautious approach to climate change mitigation, preferring to act only when the international community does so. Although not without internal debate, the Australian Labor Party (ALP) has become the dominant mainstream political party seeking a middle ground that preserves Australian economic interests while taking steps towards addressing climate change concerns.

The first significant change in Australia's treatment of carbon emissions was signalled during the 2007 Federal election when the opposition Labor Party made climate change policy a central part of their campaign platform. The Labor Party's support for the Kyoto Protocol and Renewable Energy Targets contributed to the defeat of the conservative Howard government, in office for 12 years. The Rudd-led Labor government soon ratified the Kyoto Protocol, introduced renewable energy targets and set out to introduce an emissions trading scheme (ETS), known as the Carbon Pollution Reduction Scheme, using a cap and trade mechanism with an upper limit on the country's carbon pollution (Commonwealth of Australia 2008). Corporations, particularly the energy-intensive industries, launched a very public and hostile campaign against the legislation where the threat of job losses and future investment were centre stage (Snell and Schmitt 2011). Despite efforts to overcome the corporate sector's hostile opposition and repeated attempts to get the ETS legislation through a Parliament where they only controlled the lower house, the Rudd government made the political decision in 2010 to abandon the legislation and revoke its election promise to introduce an ETS (Snell and Fairbrother 2010).

Various state governments have also sought to regulate GHG emissions and improve energy efficiency. The Victorian government, for example, introduced its own Climate Change Action Plan in part to counter support for a Green vote, which seemed to be increasing. Under this plan, the Victorian government committed itself to a 20 per cent reduction in CO_2 emission by 2020 and to meet this by using direct funds to close down a portion of the state's lignite-fired power generation industry (Victorian Government 2010). Not long after these policies were introduced, the Victorian Labor government was defeated in 2011 by an electoral shift that favoured conservative parties. The incoming conservative coalition government distanced itself from the previous government's carbon-reduction targets and proposals to close power-generation units.

While many carbon-exposed industries welcomed the defeat of federal and state government carbon reduction policies, the political uncertainty surrounding the treatment of carbon emissions has made it increasingly difficult for business planning, with industrial giants like BHP Plc calling for policy clarity (*Age*, 14 October 2010, p. 11). Soon after the 2010 Federal election, the government, a minority Labour government (now led by Julia Gillard), supported by independents and a Green Member of Parliament, announced a commitment to introduce a new carbon-reduction scheme comprised of a transitional fixed price on carbon by July 2012 with plans to move to a full market-based ETS in three to five years. The goals are relatively clear: to better monitor, manage and reduce carbon emissions by making high-emission energy generation and usage less attractive and opening up improved market opportunities for cleaner fuels including renewables; stimulate innovation in the area of energy and energy efficiency; generate a new revenue stream for government; and demonstrate that Australia is taking steps to address climate change concerns.

Unions as environmental actors

Australian trade unions have played a lead role in defining the country's climate change mitigation policies. These unions represent one of the dominant social forces that seek to challenge not only corporate opposition to mitigation policies but also the government's handling of corporate actors and mitigation policy more generally. The Australian labour movement, through the Australian Confederation of Trade Unions (ACTU), has made it clear to government and business leaders that 'climate change is union business' (ACTU 2011, 1). While individual unions maintain different positions, which reflect the specificities of industry, political persuasion and membership interests, in general Australian unions are working to find ways to assist workers, organisations and communities to realise a transition to a low carbon economy (Snell and Fairbrother 2010). The following three cases highlight how the ideals of 'just transition' have framed these efforts.

The AMWU and the transitioning of the auto industry

> Climate Change is a problem that we can no longer avoid. We are already living with the effects of it. That's why we must act together to find solutions that will minimise the effects of climate change without disadvantaging working families and the economy.
>
> (AMWU 2008a, 2)

These bold statements introduce the Australian Manufacturing Workers' Union's (AMWU) policy position on 'Just Transitions for climate change mitigation' (AMWU 2008b, 1). The AMWU, which represents workers in all areas of manufacturing including food and confectionery, metal and engineering, paper, printing and packaging and vehicle building, has taken a lead role in articulating a practical approach to 'just transition'. The union supports placing a price on carbon as a mechanism to reduce GHG emissions and establishing a more sustainable energy base. These environmental policy positions have been praised by environmental organisations. Further, this stance separates the union from the Australian Workers' Union, the other major union representing manufacturing workers, whose position is that they 'will not support a carbon tax that costs even one steel job' (AWU 2011).

The AMWU recognises that job losses may occur as a consequence of environmental legislation, as industries are restructured and jobs and new skills are required for a new clean technology economy. It has sought to educate and explain to their members that the risks for maintaining the status quo is far greater for workers and their families than taking environmental action. Revenue generated through carbon pricing, the union maintains, provides an important opportunity for the Federal government to reinvest and redirect the country's struggling manufacturing sector and for retraining and re-skilling workers into clean technology jobs. Market intervention, industrial planning involving unions, employers and government, and dedicated industry and technology development schemes are the hallmarks of the AMWU's approach to managing a 'just transition' (AMWU 2011).

The AMWU's approach to 'just transition' is best highlighted in the auto assembly industry. Like other Western countries, tariff reductions and increased automobile imports into the Australian market have presented major challenges for the Australian auto assembly industry (Lansbury *et al.* 2008). Dominated by Toyota, General Motors and Ford, the Australian industry was predicted to collapse with the onset of the 2008 financial crisis (*The Sydney Morning Herald* 2009). The AMWU has long campaigned for an auto industry plan for the auto and auto components sector. With the election of the Rudd Labor government in 2007 and the looming concerns about the impacts of the financial crisis these ideas began to receive a more favourable reception. On 10 November 2008, Australia became one of the first countries to announce a bailout of automakers and autoparts suppliers of $A3.4 billion through to 2020. The bailout included a 'Green Car Innovation Fund' designed to assist the industry transition to more fuel-efficient automobiles (Brunel and Hufbauer 2009). In 2009, the Rudd government announced a commitment of $A35 million from the 'Green Car Innovation Fund' to help Toyota upgrade their Altona, Victoria plant to produce Hybrid automobiles (AMWU 2009a). The AMWU leadership praised these strategic initiatives as helping to 'reposition the industry's investments for the lower emission vehicles of the future' (AMWU 2009a). AMWU National Secretary Dave Oliver stated:

> The Rudd Government funding ... has given Holden [General Motors] the confidence to gear up to produce a small car. Ford has also committed to building a four-cylinder car in Victoria and Toyota will begin building an Australian-hybrid Camry from next year ... At a time when unemployment is rising and the preservation of Australian jobs is of the utmost importance, we should recognise that government investment can help secure industries that provide good jobs for Australians for generations to come.
>
> (AMWU 2009b)

The AMWU hopes this approach will be emulated in other industries and sectors. In 2011, the union released a detailed plan for 'low-emissions industry and technology development', which outlined specific proposals for transitioning other Australian industries (AMWU 2011). However, now that the threats to industries posed by the financial crisis have subsided, federal and state governments, who are ideologically committed to market fundamentals, have begun to step back from such interventionist approaches in other sectors of the economy.

The CFMEU and the clean energy transition

The Construction, Forestry, Mining and Energy Union (CFMEU), the principal union representing coal miners and those directly employed by power stations, has been one of the most active unions involved in climate change politics in Australia. The national leadership of the Mining and Energy Division (M&E) of the CFMEU has made climate change a priority concern since the early 1990s. Tony Maher, National President of M&E, has become one of Australia's leading trade union spokespersons on climate change policies. He represented the International Trade Union Confederation at the UNFCCC meetings in Bali (2007), Poznan (2008) and Copenhagen (2009). At the UNFCCC Bali conference, he served as the trade union advisor to the Australian government delegation. He also currently serves as the Chairman of the ACTU Climate Change Group and represents the CFMEU on the Non-Government Organisation Roundtable on Climate Change Department of Climate Change and Energy Efficiency (Department of Climate Change and Energy Efficiency 2011).

The M&E has argued for a state-supported market approach. On the one hand, the union proposes market-based solutions for achieving reductions in the nation's carbon emissions. On the other hand, the union berates corporations for failing to invest in research and development and argues for increased innovation in this industry. Complementing this position, the union has lobbied strongly for government and industry funding for carbon capture storage pilot projects and has also supported the building of new more efficient black coal-fired power generation plants in New South Wales. Thus carbon pricing, in their view, is needed to stimulate innovation in the electricity generation industry and provide a revenue stream to government for the funding of 'clean coal' research. However, the union has also developed a range of position papers related to climate change, mitigation policy approaches and technological innovation needed to tackle climate change (CFMEU 2008). Like many environmental organisations, the union does not support direct compensation for the mining and energy sector, labelled as a 'grab for cash' by the corporations (Maher 2011). Rather, the union has been a strong advocate of research into 'clean coal' technologies such as carbon capture and storage, which it views as important for the long-term viability of coal as an energy source.

The union has worked hard to educate its membership about climate change and 'why a price on carbon is essential' (CFMEU 2011) through member meetings and union publications. It counters public corporate driven campaigns against carbon pricing, drawing attention to the profit being generated by companies who claim they will be driven out of business or forced to go offshore as a consequence of carbon pricing. The prospect of job losses has been the touchstone reference for union campaigns. Countering corporate rhetoric about the threat to jobs has been one of the union's biggest challenges, particularly in the coal-fired energy generation sector. In the Latrobe Valley, Victoria, for example, coal-fired generators source coal from vast open-cut lignite mines. This region suffered significant economic hardship and major job loss when the industry was privatised in the 1990s, with a lasting impact on the region's communities and workers (Victorian Government 2000). Recently, there has been considerable public debate and direct action by environmental protestors about the need to close these inefficient and technologically dated 'dirty' power stations (ABC Gippsland 2010). But the corporate owners of these generators have been outspoken about their opposition to the carbon pricing policies, raising the prospects of major job losses and threats to energy security (Snell and Schmitt 2011). Unlike other states, the M&E workers in the Latrobe Valley are tied to the vulnerable domestic electricity generation industry. If these workers are displaced, for example, by the closure of a power station, comparable jobs, both in terms of skill and salary, are not currently available (Latrobe City Council 2009; Victorian Government 2010). In this environment, the stance by the national union leadership has often been rejected by local members, concerned about job security and a view that the union's position is putting their jobs at risk. Some members have sent letters to local newspapers announcing their resignation from the union for what they perceive to be an inappropriate stance. This uncertainty has also contributed to the electoral loss of this traditional ALP stronghold to the conservative National Party, which promised local voters that they would protect power industry jobs. While other unions in the region have sought to engage the region's workers and the broader community on preparing a 'transition' plan for the region when one or more of the power stations are closed, M&E has found it difficult to engage with members on such an agenda (see Gippsland Trades and Labour Council 2011).

Regional trades and labour councils charting a low carbon future

One of the recent developments, with strong parallels in the US, is that unions have begun to work through regional labour confederations, in alliance with employers, municipal bodies, higher education institutions and others to develop transition plans (see Whalen 2007). In 2009, one region on the south coast of the state of New South Wales (NSW), known as the Illawarra, drew together a coalition to develop such a plan under the auspices of the South Coast Labour Council, the regional union confederation (see, South Coast Labour Council 2009). Illawarra is a traditional industrial community south of Sydney, where job loss continues and where the industries have been the focus of much debate about the transition to low carbon economies. In an attempt to address this history and thereby shape and influence state government policy, the confederation commissioned a study of transition. This state government-financed project, the Illawarra Green Jobs Project (Donaldson *et al.* 2009), was initiated in 2009. It brought together the South Coast Labour Council, the University of Wollongong, TAFE NSW–Illawarra Institute, the Illawarra Business Chamber, Australian Industry Group, local municipal and NSW government representatives. This project sought to demonstrate to investors and various levels of government that the Illawarra could lead the nation as a 'sustainable region' through 'greener residential and commercial buildings, alternative power generation, manufacturing alternative energy equipment components as well as future training and research pathways' (South Coast Labour Council 2009, 1). The report identified existing enterprises that had a sustainability focus (e.g. water recycling), assessed industry capacity to make a transition and developed skilled labour profiles for attracting new 'green' industries. It specified the policy measures needed to advance Illawarra's position in the green economy.

The centrepiece of the transition plan was a co-generation plant at BlueScope Steel's Port Kembla Steelworks near the industrial city of Wollongong, which, since 2002, had been proposed by the company. This proposed investment was the foundation of the 2009 report:

> The construction of a cogeneration power plant at the Port Kembla Steelworks, with an investment of an estimated $1billion, would create an estimated two thousand jobs over a three year construction. It would abate up to one million tonnes of greenhouse gas emissions a year that

would otherwise have resulted from coal fired power generation. This would make it the largest carbon abatement project in the nation.

(South Coast Labour Council 2009, 8)

The driving thesis for the unions and the South Coast Labour Council was that by developing constructive approaches to community transition and productive approaches to partnership and cooperative relationships may emerge (Rorris 2009). The labour confederation's ability to identify and promote steps towards a transition trajectory were important developments; however, there are limitations to the Confederation's ability to influence change. First, 'transition' built upon and relied on ongoing corporate commitment to transition, in a climate where transition has become fiercely contested, where corporations seek transition aid, and where government support and resources are essential. By 2011, the steel company announced that it would delay building the cogeneration plant for at least a decade because of financial constraints (*Illawarra Mercury* 2011a, 2011b; Langford 2011). Second, such programmes rest on government support, to initiate the study in the first place and to implement it once agreed. This latter point is especially important in relation to the development of skills and associated education strategies. Without such support unions face difficulties in promoting these broad-brush transition plans.

Discussion

Australian unions, as elsewhere, are seeking to combine a vision of 'just transition' with a practical approach to social and environmental change. 'Just transition' has become an opportunity for unions to renew their sense of purpose in times of change and environmental challenges (Snell and Fairbrother 2011). These histories draw attention to the way some unions are opening up questions about the possibility of a 'just transition' to a low carbon economy. Often the approaches by unions to such questions are caught in a tension between the transformational and the pragmatic day-to-day concerns of employment and work. One resolution of this dilemma is to emphasise a reformist form of labour environmentalism rather than a transformational one.

One feature of this history is that unions did learn lessons from privatisation and industrial restructuring in the 1980s. In the main, unions performed a reactive role with regards to industrial and workplace changes, and demonstrated that while unions could often secure enhanced adjustment packages for workers who lost their jobs, they could do little to secure a viable future for workers and communities (Fairbrother *et al.* 2002). In light of these outcomes, 'just transition' was redefined by many union activists and union leaders. It is now perceived as grasping an understanding of change, planning for change and putting mechanisms in place to ensure transition occurs to something more long-term than redundancy and unemployment benefits. Rather than resist change unions have become advocates of change to a more sustainable economy that occurs through an informed, considered and fair process that does not unduly disadvantage workers, workforces and communities.

Most unions thus have become advocates of the case for a 'just transition'. There are three dimensions to this advocacy, which also reflect the tensions unions face between defending jobs *in situ* and social transformation. Some unions have taken steps to promote a more active and widespread union engagement in advocating a 'just transition' through membership education and policy initiatives aimed at mitigating climate change. These seemingly small steps are in fact major accomplishments, often in coalition with other environmental actors and activists who have come to realise the practical and urgent significance of 'just transition'. The challenges of developing and realising a fair outcome for workers are immense; calming the fears of workers who are told by their employers that their future is at stake if environmental regulation is tightened; developing the research capacities to understand the real impacts of government policies on their industries and identifying the way that individual organisations can contribute to and realise economic development initiatives towards a 'just transition'.

In taking steps towards a 'just transition' unions are drawing on social democratic traditions in relation to state intervention in market relations. For most unions, it is clear some level of direct action by the state will be required. As the AMWU states:

> We have learnt from the mistake of letting the market forces determine industry and the results have been massive off-shoring and downsizing of jobs. We can't let the same mistakes occur whilst managing climate change. Protecting industry, protecting workers and supporting communities must be our primary objective.
>
> (AMWU 2008a)

Convincing governments to fulfil such roles will not be easy when confronted with the conviction of neo-liberal policy makers and matched with the fact that 'just transition' 'may cut deeply into ... taxpayers' pocketbooks' (Roberts and Parks 2007, 241).

Of equal importance, unions and some of their regional confederations have taken steps to begin to play a lead role in industry transition and economic revitalisation and diversification. So, while some unions have engaged in exercises aimed at transitioning carbon-exposed regions, the Illawarra case being one example, these exercises, while important, have highlighted the weaknesses of labour as a regional development actor in an environment where more powerful corporate actors operate and governments are loath to intervene in industrial and regional planning, beyond the provision of assistance and subsidies to private sector actors aimed at preserving their investment. These transition plans have also been aligned with and supported by Labor governments and susceptible to falling victim to electoral politics once removed from office. Unions are not unfamiliar with any of these challenges and drawing upon earlier experiences they are attempting to find ways to address the unfairness of expecting working people to bear the brunt of the adjustment that result from the disappearance of unsustainable jobs.

Australia's labour environmentalism is defined by a reformist agenda embracing ecological modernist notions that an ecologically sustainable world can be built through the 'greening' of capitalist enterprises. They advocate the ecological modernisation of 'polluting' sectors through technological innovation (e.g. hybrid automobiles, 'clean coal', etc.) as opposed to the reduction or even phasing out of an environmentally harmful industry (e.g. coal mining). Unions are defined by their role in ensuring members' jobs, wages and social gains are protected, which relies heavily upon the expansion of capital accumulation. Labour environmentalism occurs within and against these structural constraints. Unions representing workers in 'polluting' sectors find it difficult to support a position that would bring about rapid and deep cuts in emissions from their industries. Unlike environmental Non-Governmental Organisations (NGOs) who try to press governments into rapid action on the climate, unions advocate a gradual and managed approach that provides time for 'clean' technological innovation to occur and/or workers and communities to adjust to changing industrial circumstances. Unions, however, are conscious of 'polluting', industries' failure to innovate and are challenging the notion that the corporations that dominate these sectors should be allowed to dictate both public discourse and policy related to climate action. A revitalisation of state institutions (through industrial planning, environmental regulation, clean technology research and development, and 'just transition' for affected workers and communities) are necessary to create more ecologically sustainable and socially responsible organisations. To what degree this reformist labour environmentalism will ensure long-term environmental stabilisation is an open and contested question where unions and environmentalists may never agree (see Angus 2010).

Conclusions

'Just transition' is a concept defined in multiple and contested ways by individuals and groups for often different and competing political purposes. Inclusive of most notions of 'just transition', however, is a basic principle of fairness advocating that the cost of policies that aim to benefit society should not be disproportionately borne by those who are hurt by them. Governments, unfortunately, have not always lived up to this principle. The restructuring and privatisation of state assets that have occurred throughout the world have typically resulted in widespread hardship for workers and communities dependent on these industries. Environmental regulations to mitigate against climate change have the potential to deliver an unjust outcome for workers and communities who are dependent on 'polluting' industries. Nonetheless, organised labour demonstrated a commitment to climate action and is seeking to mitigate the worst outcomes of these policies. Unions are redefining their purpose and moving beyond positions of job protection at any social and environmental cost.

For trade unions, climate change mitigation opens up the possibility to reclaim a new development model in which the harshest of unregulated markets are tempered by government intervention and industrial and regional planning with ideals of fairness and equity underpinning economic development agendas. Through their educational activities they aim to develop a workforce with the sophistication, skills and knowledge to deal with issues that climate change, climate change policies and new technologies are going to present to local industry. Unions, as advocates of 'just transition', are seeking to formulate a grassroots approach to climate change mitigation that transitions industries, workforces and regional economies without compromising the job futures for its members. In this quest, unions have renewed their promotion of industrial planning. While not always explicit in their rhetoric, unions are challenging the neo-liberal policy frameworks of the past that have contributed to economic and environmental destruction. They are calling on governments to work with them, local government and employers in developing both short-term and long-term strategies for a smooth transition to a low carbon economy. If not successful in convincing governments, corporate leaders and their members of the necessity of returning to a more interventionist state, the danger is that unions will once again be forced into uncomfortable positions of defending jobs over the environment.

References

ABC Gippsland (2010) 'Tight security at Hazelwood protest', 10 October, www.abc.net.au/local/photos/2010/10/10/3034179.htm, accessed 16 January 2011.

ACTU (2011) *Climate Change is Union Business*, ACTU, Melbourne.

ACTU and ACF (2008) *Green Gold Rush: How Ambitious Environmental Policy can make Australia a Leader in the Global Race for Green Jobs*, ACTU, Melbourne.

AMWU (2008a) 'We need Just Transitions to ensure climate change does not disadvantage workers', www.amwu.org.au/read-article/media-detail/12/We-need-Just-Transitions-to-ensure-climate-change-does-not-disadvantage-workers/, accessed 3 March 2012.

——(2008b) *Making our Future: Just Transitions for climate change mitigation*. AMWU National Office, Granville, www.amwu.org.au/news/37/research%20reports%20submissions/, accessed 3 March 2012.

——(2009a) 'Toyota commences production of hybrid Camry', www.amwu.org.au/read-article/news-detail/353/Toyota-commences-production-of-hybrid Camry/, accessed 3 March 2012.

——(2009b) 'Auto Industry Plan Saves Jobs', 2 June, www.amwu.org.au/read-article/news-detail/302/Auto-Industry-plan-saves-jobs/, accessed 3 March 2010.

——(2011) *A Plan for Low-Emissions Industry and Technology Development in Australia*, AMWU National Office, Granville, www.amwu.org.au/campaigns/46/CT/, accessed 23 June 2011.

Angus, I. (2010) *The Global Fight for Climate Justice*, Fernwood Publishing, Black Point, Nova Scotia.

Apollo Alliance (2009) 'Homepage', http://apolloalliance.org/, accessed 14 May 2009.

AWU (2011) 'The AWU will not support a carbon tax that costs even one steel job', www.awu.net.au/search.html?cx=018268310074248265473%3A_lkk2sarnfc&cof=FORID%3A11&ie=UTF-8&q=carbon+tax&sa=, accessed 3 March 2012.

BlueGreen Alliance (2007) 'Homepage', www.bluegreenalliance.org/home, accessed 14 May 2009.

Brunel, C. and Hufbauer, G. (2009) 'Money for the Auto Industry: Consistent with WTO Rules?', *Peterson Institute for International Economics Policy Brief 9–4*, Peterson Institute for International Economics, Washington, DC.

Canadian Labour Congress (CLC) (2000) *Just Transition for Workers During Environmental Change*, Canadian Labour Congress, Ottawa, www.canadianlabour.ca/sites/default/files/pdfs/justransen.pdf, accessed 3 March 2012.

Commonwealth of Australia (2008) *Carbon Pollution Reduction Scheme Green Paper*, Department of Climate Change, Commonwealth of Australia, Canberra.

Construction, Forestry, Mining and Energy Union (CFMEU) (2008) 'Response to the Carbon Pollution Reduction Scheme Green Paper', 10 September, http://cfmeu.com.au/downloads/cfmeu-response-to-crps-green-paper, accessed 16 April 2012.

——(2011) 'Why a Price of Carbon is Essential for our Future', http://cfmeu.com.au/why-a-price-on-carbon-is-essential, accessed 16 April 2012.

Department of Climate Change and Energy Efficiency (2011) 'Non-governmental roundtable on climate change', www.climatechange.gov.au, accessed 15 May 2011.

Donaldson, M., Burrows, S., Hodgkinson, A., Neri, F., Kell, P., Gibson, C., Wait, G. and Stillwell, F. (2009) *Power to the People: Building Sustainable Jobs in the Illawarra, A Report for the South Coast Labour Council*, University of Wollongong, www.sclc.com.au/pdf/People%20Building%20Jobs.pdf, accessed 28 January 2010.

Fairbrother, P., Paddon, M. and Teicher, J. (2002) *Privatisation, Globalisation and Labour: Studies from Australia*, The Federation Press, Annandale.

Frank, T. (2000) *One Market Under God: Extreme Capitalism, Market Populism and the End of Economic Democracy*, MIT Press, Cambridge, MA.

Garnaut, R. (2008) *Climate Change Review: Final Report*, Cambridge University Press, Cambridge, www.garnautreview.org.au/index.htm, accessed 25 January 2010.

Gippsland Trades and Labour Council (2011) 'Homepage', http://gippslandtlc.com.au/, accessed 12 June 2011.

Gould, K., Lewis, T. and Roberts, J. T. (2004) 'Blue-Green Coalitions: Constraints and Possibilites in the Post 9–11 Political Environment', *Journal of World-Systems Research*, 10(1): 91–116.

Harvey, D. (2005) *A Brief History of Neo-liberalism*, Oxford University Press, Oxford.

Illawarra Mercury (2011a) 'Plant delay kills off carbon agreement between BlueScope and Govt', 1 March, p. 1.

——(2011b) 'BlueScope says carbon price could sound manufacturing's death knell', 25 February, p. 1.

ILO (2009) *Guide to Worker Displacement: Some tools for reducing the impact on workers, communities and enterprises*, 2nd edition, ILO, Geneva.

IPCC (2007) *Climate Change 2007 Synthesis Report*, Intergovernmental Panel on Climate Change, Geneva.

Kazis, R. and Grossman, R. (1982) *Fear at Work: Job Blackmail, Labor, and the Environment*, Pilgrim Press, New York.

Langford, B. (2011) 'BlueScope puts $1 billion project on back burner', *Illawarra Mercury,* 26 February.

Lansbury, R., Saulwick, J. and Wright, C. (2008) 'Globalisation and Employment Relations in the Australian Auto Assembly Industry', in R. Blanpain (ed.) *Globalisation and Employment Relations in the Auto Assembly Industry: a Study of Seven Countries*, Kluwer Law International, Alphen aan den Rijn, pp. 13–34.

Latrobe City Council (2009) *Latrobe City Council CPRS Policy Position Consultation Draft Report*, Latrobe City Council, Morwell.

Maher, T. (2011) 'Why Abbott's jobs scare campaign is a sham', *Common Cause* 77: 2, 3. http://cfmeu.com.au/Common%20%Cause%20April%20-%20May%202011, accessed 16 April 2012.

McNeil, B. (2009) *The Clean Industrial Revolution*, Allen and Unwin, Sydney.

Page, E. (2006) *Climate Change, Justice and Future Generations*, Edward Elgar, Cheltenham.

Roberts, J. T. and Parks, B. (2007) *A Climate of Injustice*, Cambridge University Press, Cambridge.

Rorris, A. (2009) 'It's Survival of the Greenest', *Illawarra Mercury*, 8 April.

Snell, D. and Fairbrother, P. (2010) 'Unions as Environmental Actors', *Transfer*, 16 (4): 411–24.

——(2011) 'Towards a theory of union environmental politics', *Labor Studies Journal*, 36 (1), pp. 83–103.

Snell, D. and Schmitt, D. (2011) '"It's not easy being green": Stationary Energy Corporations and the Transition to a Low Carbon Economy', *Competition and Change Journal* 16 (1): 1–19.

South Coast Labour Council (2009) *The Green Jobs Illawarra Project*, www.sclc.com.au/content/greenjobs.php, accessed 26 October 2010.

The Sydney Morning Herald (2009) 'Crisis means curtains for Holden: Expert', 14 April, http://news.smh.com.au/breaking-news-business/crisis-means-curtains-forholden-expert-20090414-a50b.html, accessed 12 April 2011.

Trades Union Congress (TUC) (2008a) *A Green and Fair Future For a Just Transition to a Low Carbon Economy*, Touch Stone pamphlet 3, Trades Union Congress, London, www.tuc.org.uk/social/tuc-14922-f0.cfm. accessed 3 March 2012.

——(2008b) *Trade Unions and Climate Change: A Just Transition*, TUC Climate Change Conference, 16 June, Congress House, London, www.tuc.org.uk/extras/climatechange08.pdf, accessed 16 April 2010.

TUAC Secretariat (2008) *Green Jobs and Climate Change*, Meeting of Trade Union Experts on Green Jobs and Climate Change, OECD, Paris, 13 March, www.youtube.com/watch?v=BYFynRRn3RA, accessed 11 February 2010.

UNDP (2010) *Human Development Report 2010*, New York, United Nations Development Programme.

UNEP (2007) *Labour and the Environment: A Natural Synergy*, United Nations Environment Programme, Nairobi.

Vanderheiden, S. (2008) *Atmospheric Justice*, Oxford University Press, Oxford.

Victorian Government (2000) *Contracting, Privatisation, Probity and Disclosure in Victoria, 1992–1999*, Victorian Government Department of Premier and Cabinet, Melbourne.

——(2010) *Taking Action for Victoria's Future: Victorian Climate Change Action Plan*, Victorian Government Department of Premier and Cabinet, Melbourne.

Whalen, C. (2007) 'Union-driven Economic Development Initiatives and Community Solidarity in Western New York', *Ephemera*, 7(3): 403–18.

World Bank (2000) *Balancing Protection and Opportunity: A Strategy for Social Protection in Transition Economies*, World Bank, Washington, DC.

——(2002) *Structural Adjustment in the Transition: Case Studies from Albania, Azerbaijan, Kyrgyz Republic and Moldova*, World Bank, Washington, DC.

13 Will they tie the knot? Labour and environmental trajectories in Taiwan and South Korea[1]

Hwa-Jen Liu

If the 1970s was an era in which feminists sought either a healthier marriage to or a divorce from Marxism (Hartmann 1981), by the 1990s a different partnership was being suggested. Given the economic and environmental devastation under neoliberal globalisation through the 1980s, the coming together of "teamsters and turtles" in Seattle as a red–green alliance offered a glimmer of hope for social movements (Mitchell 2009). As any good marriage consultant might suggest, however, it is advisable to know potential partners better to avoid a disillusioned breakup. I propose to compare two labour movements in Taiwan and South Korea against their environmental counterparts in a hope of seeing a viable red–green alliance coming into being.[2]

By comparing the four movements, the first thing we notice is two sharply distinct movement trajectories. For the labour trajectory, both labour movements began with a Satan's mill story taking place in the labour-intensive industries: low wages, hellish working conditions, long hours, pervasive respiratory diseases and protests in despair. These early spontaneous protests were quickly put down by government repression. Then both movements began to organise strategic industries such as auto, petrochemical, postal services and shipbuilding. Once this strategy bore fruits, accusations like "labour aristocracy" and "union action at the expense of public interest" began to prevail in the media. We also began to see the support base of union movements eroded under capital's counterattack. Alarmed by fits of crisis, both labour movements strove to move beyond the confine of "enterprise unionism", to procure broader social support, and to reframe their battles in light of general interests.

With regard to the environmental trajectory, both the Taiwanese and South Korean environmental movements grew in response to widespread industrial pollution in the wake of industrialisation. The early protests were buttressed by a loose coalition of pollution victims and urban intellectuals. This coalition was short-lived due to different expectations as to protest outcomes and the intervention of new and improved environmental administration. As pollution victims faded out of the coalition, both movements deployed discursive resources in policy research. Most energy was spent on mastering the art of PR campaigns and to create newsworthiness. The very success of both environmental movements to push through institutional and policy changes created new, powerful opponents. EPA and private capital fought for a commanding position to sway public opinion and environmental consciousness. Furthermore, both environmental movements in Taiwan and South Korea had a hard time defending the interest of the socially disadvantaged, as at the same time they were losing battles against corporate power. Pressured and alarmed, the two environmental movements tried to rebuild grassroots linkage and to incorporate diverse economic interests into environmental agendas.

The difference in movement trajectories, I argue, results from the fact that labour and environmental movements pursue different types of movement power vis-à-vis their opponents (Liu 2008, 2011). In the literature, many have discussed how the powerless often use protest – negative inducements or threats – to pressure the authorities to engage in a bargaining process (Lipsky 1968; Wilson 1961). Piven and Cloward (1992, 141) highlight the power of institutional disruption: "the lower-stratum protesters have some possibility of influence ... if their actions violate rules and disrupt the workings of an institution on which important groups depend". Flacks (2004, 114) says it even more explicitly: "the power of the powerless is rooted in their capacity to stop the smooth flow of social life" and "social movements ... can be most fruitfully examined as social formations that seek ... to maximize the power available to their constituencies".

I expand the previous discussions of movement power and make an ideal-typical distinction between two types of power – leverage and ideology – that labour and environmental movements respectively exercise vis-à-vis their opponents. Leverage and ideological power are both concepts rooted in rich theoretical and empirical literatures, but they have not been applied in combination to explain labour and environmental trajectories that I am trying to tackle here. Leverage is positional power, presuming that the leverage holders are positioned in an interdependent, even if asymmetrical, relationship with their target and that the former's cooperation in sustaining the relationship is indispensable. Corresponding to its positionality, leverage power is target-specific and "context-bound" (Lukes 2005, 75, 79). Industrial workers may launch strikes in the factories, college students may stage a building occupancy against university administrations (Heirich 1971), and low-ranking clerks may withhold information and sabotage the functioning of complex organisations (Mechanic 1962). Yet their positional powers do not automatically hold true if contexts and targets change. In this sense, I argue that the power of the labour movement rests on workers' indispensable role in the system of production and service delivery. By simply withholding labour power, workers prevent capitalists from realising profit. The exercise of the structural power of the working class (Silver 2003; Wright 2000) may result in economic compromises whereby the state and capital give in to the working-class demands. Experiences from the Nordic countries (Esping-Andersen 1985; Korpi 1974; Korpi and Shalev 1979) and the US New Deal programme (Brenner 2007) attest to this thesis.

Ideology is the power of ideas, or more precisely, the power of popular consent to a "concrete phantasy [sic] which acts on a dispersed and shattered people to arouse and organize its collective will" (Gramsci 1971, 126). Melucci's portrait of contemporary social movements also hints at ideological power: "What they [social movements] possess is ... the power of words. ... They speak a language that seems to be entirely their own, but they say something that transcends their particularity and speaks to us all" (Melucci 1996, 1). A movement's ideological power is located in the *persuasive work* it performs right under the nose of the dominant ideology, and is contingent upon the movement's discursive capacities to initiate a cognitive revolution in an audience previously subscribing to the dominant ideology. The effectiveness of the persuasive work depends on an appropriation of the means of communication to reach different sectors of the population. In most cases "the means of communication" refer to radio, television, newspapers and magazines with national circulation. As Therborn (1980, 80) has argued, "[ideologies] are always produced, conveyed, and received in particular, materially circumscribed social situations and through special means and practices of communication, the material specificity of which bears upon the efficacy of a given ideology". In this vein, I argue that an environmental movement builds its power by persuading its audience and even its opponents to accept a new ideology, based on the claim that it is working toward the universal and collective good. In the past 30 or 40 years the environmental movement was in fact one of the few social movements that procured broad social support and turned movement causes into the dominant ideology. As Bramwell (1994, 180) said: "We all want to save the planet. Few, faced by an opinion poll, would declare themselves to be anti-planet, or pro-planetary destruction". Even someone who had refused to endorse the Kyoto Protocol proposed Clear Skies legislation and climate-change initiatives. This ideological power based on discursive persuasion is what I consider the most distinctive feature of environmental movements.

Once it is acknowledged that labour and environmental movements rest on different types of power, once we see movement trajectory as a process of power maximisation and dealing with the consequences of this strategy, the distinct labour and environmental trajectories begin to make sense. Labour proceeds by pursuing the leverage power in economic struggles and environmental movements maximise their ideological power. Once they stepped on the path of power maximisation, the composition of the movements changed and the leadership was entrusted to those who were at the best position to exercise these two types of power: semi-skilled male workers in the strategic industries and urban intellectuals. Power-maximising strategies resulted in counterattacks from opponents and obstacles that undermine each movement's primary power base. On the side of labour, capitalists engaged in plant relocation, withdrawal of lifelong employment guarantees, new managerial strategies, and the deployment of "unorganisable" immigrant and temporary workers. All of these measures undermine labour movements' leverage power. On the environmental side, consulting firms and environmental research institutes funded by big corporations began to challenge the movement's monopoly of environmental discourses. It is at the juncture of crisis that labour and environmental movements worked toward acquiring the second source of power to compensate for the erosion of their own home advantage. Labour engages in ideological struggles to shed the bad name of sectional interest. Environmental movements seek to acquire leverage power and consolidate grassroots support in order to solve the conflict between their ecological vision and the interest of the socially disadvantaged.

The labour trajectory: from leverage to representing general social interest

Labour movements in Taiwan and South Korea began mainly in the textile industries, which had sustained export-oriented industrialisation since the 1960s (Chun 2003; Huang 1999). In the wake of working-class formation, unskilled workers who suffered from low wages and poor working conditions initiated the first wave of labour activism in both countries.[3] But mobilisation in the labour-intensive sector was quickly crushed by state repression. Union leaders and activists were fired, blacklisted, arrested and prosecuted; independent unions were disbanded (Chu 1995; Wu and Liao 1991). In the Taiwanese case, the decisive moment was the defeat of one major strike at the Far-Eastern Chemical Fiber in 1989 (Chao 1991, 1995); in the Korean case, it was the decimation of independent unions between 1980 and 1981 due to a tightened labour policy under the new military regime (Koo 2001; Ogle 1990).

Such defeats resulted in major strategic reorientations. New strategies were employed to organise workers in strategic industries such as auto, petrochemical, shipbuilding, heavy metal and telecommunications. In the Taiwanese case, these targeted industries were predominantly under the control of state enterprises. In the Korean case, they were mostly controlled by *chaebol* (gigantic private capital) such as Hyundai or Samsung. A Taiwanese labour organiser aptly summarised the rationale of this strategic move:

> The soil of Taiwan's labour movement is barren. 70 per cent or 80 per cent of business establishments belong to private, small- or medium-sized enterprises, hiring less than 30 workers. It's impossible to have private-enterprise unions lead this movement. The most effective way is to take over the state-enterprise unions under the control of the ruling party. ... Telecommunication, electricity, petroleum, postal services, major big unions were our targets.
>
> (Chen 2002)

A Korean labour leader eloquently articulates the strength differential between textile workers and *chaebol* workers by stating that:

> In the 1970s and 1980s, in the light [manufacturing] industry, medium-sized or big companies reduced [the number of] workers, [originally] four

hundred, three hundred, now becoming one hundred workers. If you had a strike, it neither had much impact nor raised the concern of [outside] activists. But for *chaebol*, four thousand, five thousand or ten thousand workers were on strike. All the activists were interested [in joining the fight].

(Choi 2003)

The point is that this new wave of labour organising targeted workers who were endowed with better bargaining power vis-à-vis the state and capital. In contrast to a strike at a textile factory, a halt of production or service delivery in any of these strategic industries would have far-reaching effects on industrial production. This was the basis of the greater leverage of state-enterprise and *chaebol* unions.

Out of this conscious decision to organise strategically, the composition of "vanguards" in both labour movements changed. In Taiwan, state-enterprise unions replaced the private-sector unions, and in Korea *chaebol* unions occupied centre stage. Over time, the leadership of both labour movements was entrusted to those who were in the best position to exercise economic leverage. Along with the leadership shift, movement agendas changed to align with the concerns of the new vanguard groups. The new agenda of Taiwan's labour movement was to fend off the project to privatize state enterprises. On the Korean side, capitalists deployed a series of managerial strategies to counter labour militancy, such as subcontracting and using temporary workers to elude high wages and pensions. The Korean labour movement fought back to defend regular employment in heavy industry, the stronghold of the movement. In short, labour's agenda shifted from wages and working conditions, which concerned workers in the labour-intensive sector most, to campaigns against privatisation and a business offensive that directly undermined the privileged position of workers at state enterprises and large private corporations.

Very soon after both labour movements started down the path of maximising their economic leverage, they were forced to confront the consequences of this strategy. The good news was that, due to their greater leverage, the new leading groups of both labour movements secured certain economic compromises. Taiwan's state-enterprise workers, though unable to stop the privatisation plan, secured better retirement plans and improved severance packages. On the Korean side, workers from the *chaebol* unions secured wage increases and benefits through annual national wage struggles.

But good news for the workers with more bargaining power was at the same time bad news for both movements. Capital struck back by relocating production units, increasing the use of irregular and immigrant workers, withdrawing lifetime employment guarantees and introducing new managerial techniques to control the shop floor (Jung 2000; Yu 1995). In the long run, all of these counteractions undercut labour's leverage. Furthermore, the state and capital collaborated with media outlets and engaged in aggressive ideological campaigns to paint labour struggles as pursuits of sectional interest at the expense of the public interest. In the case of Taiwan, the anti-privatisation drive suffered from the stereotypical impression that state-enterprise workers were inefficient bureaucrats holding "iron rice bowls" and enjoying excellent pension/retirement plans picked out of taxpayers' pockets, an image that undercut the popularity of the anti-privatisation cause among the general public. The Taiwan government and private capital, interested in taking over state assets, exploited this anti-labour public perception to successfully defame the anti-privatisation drive. Political elites justified the liquidation of state assets on the grounds of fixing the endemic problems that plagued state enterprises: inefficiency and budget deficits. Labour's anti-privatisation campaign was portrayed as the desperate effort of a group of well-paid workers who resisted fair market competition. As a result, state-enterprise unions lost the backing of unions from the private sector as well as broad social support (Chang 2001, 215f).

On the Korean side, during each year's "Spring Struggle" for wage negotiation, the media consistently portrayed labour struggles as senseless actions initiated by a group of greedy, militant labour aristocrats who were gainfully employed but kept demanding more at the expense of national competitiveness. A glimpse at Korean newspapers captures the hostile attitude toward the labour movement:

> How powerful would the confederation [Korean Confederation of Trade Unions] have to be for even the foreign press to note how the Korean government and business are at the mercy of hard-line unions and how the unions are the greatest source of instability for the Korean economy? ... No foreign capital will be so blind as to want to invest in this country when they see a union that turns the street into a sea of fire.
>
> (*Chosun Ilbo* 2003)

Headlines like "Koreans less tolerant of union actions" (*Korea Herald* 2003) and reports of skyrocketing wages putting firms out of business constantly occupied the news pages. "The 'British disease' was frequently quoted to highlight negative consequence of the militant labour movement. Also Thatcherism was mentioned as a cure for the British disease" (Shin 2003, 161).

If an ideological backlash and a lack of public support were new obstacles originating from outside, the power-maximising strategy also created problems from within. It increased the level of difficulty in coordinating diverse interests among the working class and led to endless internal strife. Both labour movements acted and were portrayed as if they were mainly defending the interest of workers in state enterprises and *chaebol* unions. Struggles for wage increases and job security in the "privileged" sector were often construed as self-interested actions, and both labour movements were accused by radical labour organizers of neglecting the interests of downtrodden female, immigrant, unemployed and temporary workers.

In the case of Taiwan, the rights of immigrant workers and the unemployment problem of the native working population had loomed large since the 1990s. Both issues signified a diverse and stratified labouring population whose respective interests did not easily coincide. Yet the labour movement did not effectively tackle these issues, and this glaring negligence provoked many criticisms from within. On the Korean side, the Korean Confederation of Trade Unions (KCTU) – the umbrella organisation of democratic trade unions – was charged with neglecting the interest of female and temporary workers. Some argued that although female labour activists raised the issue of irregular employment in the 1980s, the mainline unions brushed aside their concern. While the state, capital and labour unions negotiated the terms to legalise the employment of temporary workers in selected occupations during the IMF restructuring, the mainline unions fought fiercely for those occupations in which their own members were dominant, but did not object to the transformation of other occupations that were not their support bases. The end result was that the occupations in which temporary employment was "legalised" were principally female-dominant and non-unionised ones. By the time the KCTU finally began to address the issue, the problem was exacerbated to the point that more than 50 per cent of the labour force and 75 per cent of the female labour force in Korea fell into the category of irregular employment.

To sum up, the power-maximising strategy firmly established both labour movements as legitimate players in national politics, yet their reputations were severely tainted. Pressured and alarmed by all of the external and internal challenges, both movements pursued various strategies to shed the interest-group image and to build broader social support.

In the case of Taiwan, mainline unions pressured the government to revise immigration policies that forfeited immigrant workers' rights in favour of satisfying business interests. Labour organisations also engaged unemployed workers in high-risk protests such as occupying railroad tracks and blocking major expressways (*The United Daily* 1996). Union leaders further demanded policy revisions to alleviate the unemployment of domestic workers. Regarding anti-privatisation campaigns, state-enterprise unions reframed their struggles not merely in terms of their own job security, but also in terms of "safeguarding state assets". It was argued that the profit from state enterprises contributed to government revenue that would be used for redistributive purposes, such as education, welfare expenditures and basic infrastructure. The current privatisation policy was a *de facto* state–capital collusion in which the government cheaply sold out state assets due to pressure from private capital and the need for short-term cash to deliver on policy promises made during various elections. In the long run, privatising basic industries like water, electricity and telecommunications only benefited private capital, everyone else lost (Wei 2003). The labour movement also reached out to various issues that concerned general interests, and union members were encouraged to participate in reform efforts in education, environment, medical care, community empowerment and the welfare system (Chuang 2003).

On the Korean side, the KCTU was pressured to address the issues of irregular and female workers. It is also reported that, during wage negotiation, *chaebol* unions included a clause demanding that corporations donated 5 per cent of net profits as a special fund to help irregular workers (*Hankyoreh 21* 2004). Major unions like the Teachers' Union passed resolutions to allocate 30 per cent of leadership positions to women. Under the KCTU, a confederation of women's trade unions was organised. Furthermore, the KCTU began to tackle a variety of "social issues". The KCTU's former policy chief argued that, to effectively deal with the growing inequality between workers' working conditions and to build greater solidarity, the KCTU should protect the rights and living conditions of weak social classes, workers at small- and medium-sized enterprises and irregular workers. Furthermore, labour unions pursued not only short-term goals such as higher wages or the improvement of working conditions, but also pushed to expand safety nets and social welfare, reform the tax system, improve the education system, solve the housing and environmental problem and other issues related to general interests (Kim 1998). With the founding of the movement's political wing, the Korean Democratic Labour Party, labour's ambition to organise and lead public opinion in a broader political arena became even more pronounced. This can be attested by the public relevance of the six main themes of the 2004 Mayday rally: (1) opposition to the WTO and Free Trade; (2) work, with health; (3) public participation; (4) withdrawal of the troops from Iraq; (5) eradicating differential treatment of regular and irregular workers; (6) labour's three rights: rights to unionise, bargain and take industrial action.

Here we witness a convergence of the two labour movements. In the face of weakened economic leverage, they sought to acquire ideological power to fend off the stigma of "sectional interests" imposed by their opponents, and to build greater solidarity among workers and forge broader alliances with other social groups. This was a difficult task to coordinate the diverse interests within the labour movement; it was even more taxing to establish a productive relationship with a broader public sphere. This self-transformation project entailed a series of ongoing negotiations to lessen resistance and suspicion from all sides. Many, however, have criticised mainline unions for only paying lip service to their purported constituency. A KCTU policy advisor summarised the situation aptly:

> Now the KCTU tried to show its "social-movement unionism," as many foreign observers explained. It showed very strong solidarity with social movements, like the peace movement, the anti-Iraq War movement. But, it's at the confederation level. At the enterprise level, workers were not interested in these issues. That's the problem. ... At the enterprise level, there were conflicts between social-movement organizations and labour unions.
>
> (Kang 2003)

The difficulty of transcending economic–corporate interests is well recognised. As another member of KCTU staff acknowledges the difficulty of bridging the gap between *chaebol* unions and small-enterprise unions, "it is a big problem, an important problem we have to overcome. We couldn't organise and coordinate them on many occasions. We haven't succeeded but we are trying" (Oh 2003). Even if the tasks ahead for the two labour movements have no end in sight, "but we are trying" is a powerful statement that signifies a clear understanding of the difficult situation and a fierce refusal to surrender.

The environmental trajectory: from ideology to reconstituting the grassroots

The Korean and Taiwanese environmental movements both grew as a result of widespread industrial pollution in the 1970s. From the outset they were supported by a loose coalition of pollution victims and urban intellectuals. But the intellectual side quickly came to the ascendancy. Two factors contributed to the dissolution of this coalition. First, it was the disparate expectations of different parties in the coalition. Urban intellectuals wanted to clear up the pollution mess in its entirety, yet pollution victims asked for financial compensations that contradicted the social expectation for a movement claiming to defend universal interests. This fragile coalition was destabilised by pollution compensation and relocation subsidies from the outset. In various writings and personal interviews on pollution protest in the 1970s and early 1980s, pollution victims' "material concerns" were often blamed for breaking the urban–rural coalition.

Besides the conflict over financial compensation, the newly installed environmental administrative systems also contributed to the dissolution of the coalition. Once Environmental Impact Assessment, monitoring programmes, due process in pollution disputes and the compensation mechanism came into being, pollution victims went directly to official channels to address their grievances. "There is no need for pollution victims to solve their problems through extra-institutional means like social movements anymore", remarked a Taiwanese activist (Lu 2003).

After the dissociation, the movement agenda took an "ecological turn". Among major movement campaigns, the significance of anti-pollution issues decreased as ecological issues and conservationism rose in importance. One telling indication is that the flagship NGO of Korea's environmental movement changed its name from the Korean Anti-Pollution Movement Association to the Korean Federation of Environmental Movements in 1993. The fact that "anti-pollution" was dropped signified a new era in which the movement dwelled on discussions of forest, reservoir, wildlife habitats, wetlands and issues with which it was "much easier to reach consensus" (Kwang 2003). In both Taiwan and Korea, environmental campaigns began to bank heavily on conservationism and other ecological visions to counter major development projects in the 1990s. When fighting against the project of an industrial complex, environmentalists called for public support to protect endangered species and coastal wetlands and to maintain eco-diversity.

Once urban intellectuals dominated the environmental movements, discursive capacities were put to use on all fronts. Big environmental NGOs set up their research centres to cover a variety of environmental policies; smaller NGOs began to specialise in specific policy areas. In addition, the movements' news releases and policy reports relied heavily on the use of scientific language to establish credentials. More and more energy and human resources were put into mastering the art of public-relations campaigns, writing catchy news releases and creating newsworthiness.

Like their labour counterparts, South Korean and Taiwanese environmental movements were forced to confront the consequences of their power-maximising strategy. On the positive side, both enjoyed overwhelming social support, and certainly did not suffer from ideological defamation the way organised labour did. But once the environmental movements proved to everyone the importance of environmental protection, and even private capital began to appropriate environmental symbols to advance its own agendas, problems arose. The difficulty that both environmental movements confronted was twofold: first, the rise of new institutional competitors for discursive power over environmental issues; second, the environmental movements were unable to organise public consent on issues involving acute conflicts of economic interest. In terms of new institutional competitors, *chaebol* began to set up their own environmental research centres (Korea) and invest in public-relations campaigns (in both Taiwan and South Korea). Environmental consulting firms were paid by corporations to prepare Environmental Impact Assessment reports for development projects (Taiwan). The state began to set up advisory committees comprising experts with varying degrees of commitment to environmental causes. The key point is that government and business wanted to take back the power to define pollution, natural conservation and environmental management. Although the building of a comprehensive environmental administrative system was at first a response to the demand from the environmental movements, in the long run it became a powerful tool to gain the upper hand in ideological warfare with both environmental movements.

Furthermore, both the Taiwanese and Korean governments actively recruited movement activists to sit on the advisory boards and consultation bodies on environmental policies, and incorporated the idea of "public participation" in due process. The impact on the environmental movements was "a shift of focus".

> [Working inside the government agencies] reduces the "movement character" of environmental NGOs. Right now these groups focus on technical problems, like how to implement certain policies ... At this stage, movement organizations paid less attention to running a movement, but focused more on policy implementation.
>
> (Chang 2002)

With the rise of new institutional competitors, the task of organising public consent became increasingly difficult. For environmental issues with a high level of consensus, such as Environmental Impact Assessment and tougher pollution regulations, the government set up new administrative bodies to take over the task. For controversial issues in which new institutional competitors mobilised social support and the environmental movements secured no overwhelming public consent, such as nuclear-energy programmes, it was a difficult fight. The movements' ideological power was not based on permanent social relations such as work or kinship but on the persuasiveness of ideas. This rendered the movement powerless when its discursive campaigns failed to sway public opinion, and the movement had no solid mass support through which to pressure its opponents. At the moment of movement downturn we hear laments like this:

> [Taiwan's environmental movement] did not have power. … [W]hen you look at labour and peasant movements, the government made concessions to … a specific group of people. This is why Taiwan's environmental movement was going downhill these years: [it] didn't have a specific group of supporters, [it] had issues and an amorphous social base. So you are not going to exert much pressure on the government.
>
> (Lu 2003)

Another Korean activist also remarks: "In reality, if an environmental organization fails to organize people's worry and consciousness, it's a paper tiger. In some issues, we are near to changing the world, but in many other issues, we are just a paper tiger" (Kwang 2003).

After the "ecological turn", the movements in both countries faced the problem of being divorced from the grassroots, a trade-off resulting from the need to increase ideological power by parting company with "sectional interests" represented by pollution victims. A Korean activist says:

> Between the 1980s and the middle of the 1990s, over half of the staff [in my organization] were organizing. But now, most people stick to their desks, writing statements, talking over the phone. This tells us what has changed … we are becoming much more like office workers, not field organizers.
>
> (Kwang 2003)

This dissociation from the grassroots created headaches for environmental NGOs as they handled the conflict between their ecological vision and the interest of disadvantaged groups. The exemplary cases are Taiwan's *Magaw* Cypress National Park and Korea's *Saemangeum* wetland conservation. In the national-park case, Taiwan's environmental groups sought to preserve a forest of 46,000 hectares of cypress trees, "the only homogenous forest of red and yellow cypress trees of its kind in the world … [meeting] standards set by UNESCO to be classed as a world heritage site" (*Taipei Times* 2000). But the creation of a national park infringed on the aborigines' rights to live off the land and continue their traditional hunting practices. In the *Saemangeum* wetland case, Korea's environmental NGOs opposed the reclamation project for a new industrial complex, whereas local residents, long suffering from Korea's uneven development, welcomed the project.

In addition to their inability to address the interest of the economically weak, both environmental movements repeatedly lost battles against corporate interests. As focus shifted to ecological issues, corporate practices generally disappeared from their radar screen. Even if environmental NGOs occasionally took on the battle against big corporations, they usually lost due to either a lack of media backing or smear campaigns waged by the corporation-backed media. It is ironic that the environmental movements were often in a position to force feed the economically weak an ecological vision that threatened the latter's livelihood, but they were not so effective in imposing the same vision on the economically powerful.

Like their labour counterparts, both movements attempted to overcome the new challenges by trying a variety of strategies that could be roughly categorised as professionalisation and rebuilding grassroots linkage. Professionalisation is very clearly directed at new institutional competitors on the terrain of environmental discourse. A Taiwanese environmental activist contends:

> An environmental group has to confront the government, academia, and capitalists; all of them have more access to information and better capacity to integrate data. If you don't have discursive capacities, you don't have access to good data, it is impossible to confront those techno-bureaucrats. Without these, not to mention fighting [the bureaucrats], you don't even have the ability to strike a conversation with them.
>
> (Wu 2003)

Rebuilding the grassroots connection is directed at reincorporating diverse economic interests into environmental agendas. Since the mid-1990s, the Korean environmental movement has strived to enlist a large membership pool, at the urging of activists influenced by the ways the student and labour movements were organised in the 1970s and 1980s. Furthermore, environmental groups began to build relationships with labour unions that had leverage power that the environmental movements lacked:

> There were debates about the privatization of the company [Korean Power company] ... The environmental movement was pro-privatization, but the trade union was against it ... But we understand most pollution victims are workers, and the union also understands how serious environmental issues are. There are regular meetings between trade unions and environmental groups nowadays ... in specific cases we can find common ground, we can make alliances.
>
> (Lee 2003)

In the Taiwanese case, most environmental groups did not use aggressive membership drives to expand their base. Rather, each group was comprised of a small number of committed activists rooted in one community and expanding the breadth of environmental issues at the particular locale. The best example is Meinung People's Association, which started with an anti-dam campaign and then moved to address community empowerment, organic farming and preservation of local culture. Another environmental group embedded itself in the community at the designated site of the nuclear power plant. In recent years, this group of activists tracked down temporary workers who used to work at nuclear power plants to observe any long-term health effects of radioactive exposure. In this process, the practices of big corporations were a major concern of environmental groups. In 1998, an environmental group revealed that the largest private corporation in Taiwan, Formosa Plastics, illegally exported 3,000 tonnes of mercury toxic waste to Cambodia; the revelation led to a huge wave of international protests. Environmental activists also looked into opportunities to collaborate with the labour movement. One environmental activist says:

> *As labour and environmental movements mature, their goals are eventually the same.* ... In [Taiwan's] labour movement, so far they haven't talked about workers' rights from an environmental perspective. Environmental rights [workplace safety, workers' health, occupation hazards] haven't been addressed in the labour movement. This is a point we have been trying to communicate with our friends in the labour movement.
>
> (Wu 2003, emphasis added)

At this point, we observe a convergence between the two environmental movements. Confronted with new institutional competitors and the difficulty of organising public opinion, the two movements sought to acquire leverage power through aggressive membership drives and community organising. They also took on a new round of battles against private capital, and even found their ways to work with organised labour.

Concluding remarks

The maturation of a movement is constituted by a succession of battles in the economic and ideological domains. This chapter tells the story of labour and environmental trajectories from a movement-power perspective. Some movements like organised labour start with struggles in the economic domain and then move on to the ideological one. Environmental movements fight ideological battles first and later head toward the economic domain. Labour movements were backed by their indispensability in production but were short on discursive resources to fight ideological battles, whereas the environmental movements were resourceful in ideas and discourses, but had no built-in advantage in the economic domain. The key reason that a movement will travel into a different domain of struggle is because the previous gains in its home domain are eroding and only by gaining ground in another domain can its past advantage be recovered. Among the four movements studied, the two labour movements strove to articulate "general interests" only after their leverage power had been truncated.[4] The environmental movements tried on a variety of strategies to consolidate their grassroots only after their ideological supremacy had been challenged. Putting labour and environmental trajectories side by side, we see that they constitute a mirror image of one another (see Figure 13.1).

Looking through the lens of movement power the four movements' own initiatives and their opponents' counteractions propose an alternative theory of the long-term development of labour and environmental movements. If we look at labour and environmental movements elsewhere in the world, the trajectories shared by the Taiwanese and Korean cases are not unfamiliar. The point that the development of social movements is a process of overcoming obstacles is developed in Lopez's study of the American labour movement (Lopez 2004, 218). The recent struggles of US labour to counter ideological offensives and to win public support are well documented (Chun 2005; Clawson 2003; Fantasia and Voss 2004; Voss and Sherman 2000). These efforts to transform the image and content of the US labour movement took place at a moment of crisis in which the economic leverage previously exercised by major unions was eroded. Japan's environmental activism, after its anti-pollution peak in the 1970s, dwindled throughout the 1980s and the early 1990s, suffering from declining public interest in environmental issues and "the Liberal Democratic government's rather swift and apparently thorough legislative and administrative responses to the pollution crisis" (Mason 1999, 189). This is another indication that the environmental movement created new institutional competitors and gradually lost the capacity to sway public opinion effectively. All of these provide fruitful parallels to the Taiwanese and Korean experiences.

For those interested in a red–green alliance, the lesson is that labour and environmental movements have been "travelling towards each other". I argue that the most favourable timing of alliance making between labour and environmental movements is while labour is at the stage of pursuing ideological power and the environmental movement is seeking the leverage power, i.e., when each of them travels into the home advantage of the other. By acquiring each other's home advantage and traversing the terrains of economic and

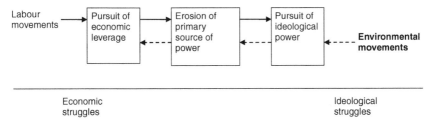

Figure 13.1 Labour and environmental trajectories juxtaposed

ideological struggles, by engaging in new battles through which their counterpart movements have secured certain victories, activists in the labour and environmental movements might begin to appreciate each other's plight and accumulated skills; the possibility of forging a genuine red–green alliance thereby increases.

Notes

1 This is an abridged version of a paper presented at XVII ISA World Congress of Sociology, Research Committee 44 Labour Movements, Gothenburg, Sweden, July 16, 2010. Sections of this chapter were drawn from Liu (2008). Used by permission of *Taiwanese Sociology*, copyright © 2008.
2 Taiwan and South Korea are what I would call 'perfect twins' in the imperfect world of cross-national comparisons. Both were former Japanese colonies the first half of the twentieth century, experienced divided statehood after the Second World War, and became the US protégés under the geopolitical framework of the Cold War. Both were under the rule of decade-long authoritarian dictatorship and joined in the 'third-wave democratization' to restructure domestic political landscapes in the late 1980s. Furthermore, both countries underwent the process of industrialisation at roughly the same time and at similar speeds. Overall national wealth of both countries was accumulated at such a rapid speed that both induced wonder from international development agencies and envy from other late industrialising countries.
3 This is a different starting point from that in France, the United States and Germany, where artisan culture and craft union traditions played critical roles in the early period of working-class formation (Katznelson 1986, 23).
4 Debates over "what's workers' general interest" are also discussed elsewhere (Räthzel and Uzzell 2011, 1220).

References

Bramwell, A. (1994) *The Fading of the Green: The Decline of Environmental Politics in the West*, New Haven, CT: Yale University Press.
Brenner, R. (2007) "Structure vs. Conjuncture: the 2006 Elections and the Rightward Shift", *New Left Review*, 43: 33–59.
Chang, C.-F. (2001) *The Privatization of State-Owned Enterprises in Taiwan: A Critique of the Economic Myth (in Chinese)*, Taipei: Institute of Sociology, Academia Sinica.
Chang, M.-S. [pseudo.] (2002) "Interview by author", tape recording, Taiepi, 4 November.
Chao, K. (1991) "Labour, Community, and Movement: A Case Study of Labour Activism in the Far Eastern Chemical Fiber Plant at Hsinpu, Taiwan, 1977–89", PhD dissertation, sociology, University of Kansas.
——(1995) "Taiwan's Unions, State, and Labour Movements in 1987: the Case of Far Eastern Chemical Fiber Union (in Chinese)", in Cheng-Kuang Hsu and Hsin-Huang Michael Hsiao (eds) *Taiwan's State and Society*, Taipei: Dong-Da Book.
Chen, H.-W. [pseudo.] (2002) "Interview by author", tape recording, Taipei, 19 November.
Choi, S.-C. [pseudo.] (2003) "Interview by author", tape recording, Seoul, 17 April.
Chosun Ilbo (2003) "Out to Ruin the Country", 11 November.
Chu, Y.-W. (1995) "The Struggle for Democracy: A Comparative Study of Taiwan and South Korea", PhD dissertation, sociology, University of California at Davis.
Chuang, Y.-C. [pseudo.] (2003) "Interview by author", tape recording, Taipei, 21 July.

Chun, J. J. (2005) "Public Drama and the Politics of Justice: Comparison of Janitors' Union Struggles in South Korea and the United States", *Work and Occupations*, 32(4): 486–503.

Chun, S. (2003) *They Are Not Machines: Korean Women Workers and Their Fight for Democratic Trade Unionism in the 1970s*, Burlington, VT: Ashgate.

Clawson, D. (2003) *The Next Upsurge: Labor and the New Social Movements*, Ithaca, NY: Cornell University Press.

Esping-Andersen, G. (1985) "Power and Distributional Regimes", *Politics & Society*, 14(2): 223–56.

Fantasia, R. and Voss, K. (2004) *Hard Work: Remaking the American Labor Movement*, Berkeley: University of California Press.

Flacks, R. (2004) "Knowledge for What? Thoughts on the State of Social Movement Studies", in Jeff Goodwin and James M. Jasper (eds) *Rethinking Social Movements: Structure, Meaning, and Emotion*, Lanham: Rowman & Littlefield Publishers, Inc.

Gramsci, A. (1971) *Selections from the Prison Notebooks*, New York: International Publishers.

Hankyoreh 21 (2004) "Imggeumtujaengeul neomeo sahoegaehyeokeuro [A Wage Struggle toward Social Reform]", 507: 32–33.

Hartmann, H. (1981) "The Unhappy Marriage of Marxism and Feminism: Toward A More Progressive Union", in Lydia Sargent (ed.) *Women and Revolution: A Discussion of the Unhappy Marriage of Marxism and Feminism*, Montreal: Black Rose Books.

Heirich, M. (1971) *The Spiral of Conflict: Berkeley, 1964*, New York: Columbia University Press.

Huang, C.-L. (1999) "Labour Militancy and the Neo-mercantilist Development Experience: South Korea and Taiwan in Comparison", PhD dissertation, political science, University of Chicago.

Jung, Y.-T. (2000) "Labour Movement and Democracy in the Age of Global Neoliberalism: The Case of Korea", *Korea Journal*, 40(2): 248–74.

Kang, Y.-S. [pseudo.] (2003) "Interview by author", tape recording, Seoul, 5 April.

Katznelson, I. (1986) "Working-Class Formation: Constructing Cases and Comparisons", in Ira Katznelson and Aristide R. Zolberg (eds) *Working-Class Formation: Nineteenth-Century Patterns in Western Europe and the United States*, Princeton, NJ: Princeton University Press.

Kim, Y.-S. (1998) "Minjunojoundong'eui hyoksin'eul wuihan jae'eon [Suggestions for A Revitalization of the Democratic Labour Movement]", *Nodongsahoe [Labour and Society]*, 25.

Koo, H. (2001) *Korean Workers: The Culture and Politics of Class Formation*, Ithaca, NY: Cornell University Press.

Korea Herald (2003) "Koreans Less Tolerant of Union Actions", 7 August.

Korpi, W. (1974) "Conflict, Power and Relative Deprivation", *American Political Science Review*, 68(4): 1569–78.

Korpi, W. and Shalev, M. (1979) "Strikes, Industrial Relations and Class Conflict in Capitalist Societies", *British Journal of Sociology*, 30(2): 164–87.

Kwang, Y.-Y. [pseudo.] (2003) "Interview by author", tape recording, Seoul, 18 April.

Lee, H.-S. [pseudo.] (2003) "Interview by author", tape recording, Seoul, 26 March.

Lipsky, M. (1968) "Protest as a Political Resource", *American Political Science Review*, 62(4): 1144–58.

Liu, H.-J. (2008) "Rethinking Movement Trajectories: Labour and Environmental Movements in Taiwan and South Korea (in Chinese)", *Taiwanese Sociology*, 16: 1–47.

——(2011) "When Labour and Nature Strike Back: A Double Movement Saga in Taiwan", *Capitalism Nature Socialism*, 22(1): 22–39.

Lopez, S. H. (2004) *Reorganizing the Rust Belt: An Inside Study of the American Labor Movement*, Berkeley: University of California Press.

Lu, C.-W. [pseudo.] (2003) "Interview by author", tape recording, Taipei, 8 January.

Lukes, S. (2005) *Power: A Radical View*, 2nd edition, New York: Palgrave Macmillan.

Mason, R. J. (1999) "Wither Japan's Environmental Movement? An Assessment of Problems and Prospects at the National Level", *Pacific Affairs*, 72(2): 187–207.

Mechanic, D. (1962) "Sources of Power of Lower Participants in Complex Organizations", *Administrative Science Quarterly*, 7(3): 349–64.

Melucci, A. (1996) *Challenging Codes: Collective Action in the Information Age*, Cambridge: Cambridge University Press.

Mitchell, D. O. (2009) "Teamsters and Turtles: the Rise of the Planetariat", *Briarpatch Magazine* November/December, http://briarpatchmagazine.com/articles/view/teamsters-and-turtles-ten-years-on (accessed 19 June 2011).

Ogle, G. (1990) *South Korea: Dissent within the Economic Miracle*, London: Zed Books.

Oh, H.-K. [pseudo.] (2003) 'Interview by author', tape recording, Seoul, 24 April.

Piven, F. F. and Cloward, R. A. (1992) "Normalizing Collective Protest", in Aldon D. Morris and Carol McClurg Mueller (eds) *Frontiers in Social Movement Theory*, New Haven, CT: Yale University Press.

Räthzel, N. and Uzzell, D. (2011) "Trade Unions and Climate Change: The Jobs versus Environmental Dilemma", *Global Environmental Change*, 21(4): 1215–23.

Shin, K.-Y. (2003) "Democratization and the Capitalist Class in South Korea", *Korean Journal of Political Economy*, 1(1): 131–75.

Silver, B. J. (2003) *Forces of Labour: Workers' Movements and Globalization since 1870*, Cambridge: Cambridge University Press.

Taipei Times (2000) "Aborigines Agree to National Park in Cypress Forest", 21 December.

Therborn, G. (1980) *The Ideology of Power and the Power of Ideology*, London: Verso.

The United Daily (1996) "Unemployed Workers Blocked Railroad Traffic", 21 December.

Voss, K. and Sherman, R. (2000) "Breaking the Iron Law of Oligarchy: Union Revitalization in the American Labor Movement", *American Journal of Sociology*, 106(2): 303–49.

Wei, H.-M. [pseudo.] (2003) "Interview by author", tape recording, Taipei, 14 January.

Wilson, J. Q. (1961) "The Strategy of Protest: Problems of Negro Civic Action", *The Journal of Conflict Resolution*, 5(3): 291–303.

Wright, E. O. (2000) "Working-Class Power, Capitalist-Class Interests, and Class Compromise", *American Sociological Review*, 105: 957–1002.

Wu, J.-S. [pseudo.] (2003) "Interview by author", tape recording, Taipei, 21 February.

Wu, N.-T. and Liao, J.-K. (1991) "Counterattacks of the Empire: Sacking Union Cadres, Labour-Capital Relations Laws, and Class Conflict (in Chinese)", paper presented at the Symposium of Labour Market and Capital-Labour Relations, Academia Sinica, Taipei.

Yu, H. (1995) "Capitalism, the New World Economy and Labour Relations: Korean Labour Politics in Comparative Perspective", PhD dissertation, political science, Northwestern University.

14 Green jobs? Good jobs? Just jobs?

US labour unions confront climate change[1]

Dimitris Stevis

During recent years US labour unions, largely in manufacturing, construction and infrastructure, have advanced 'green jobs' as an effective and equitable response to climate change (AFL-CIO 2008; Global Labor Institute 2011a; BlueGreen Alliance 2011b). The argument is that green jobs are the route to good jobs as well as the best foundation for a 'just transition' to a climate-friendly economy (AFL-CIO 2008). The US' continued rejection of binding global regulation and the failure to adopt domestic climate policy in 2009 have raised green jobs and technical innovation to the status of the most promising, albeit indirect, routes to climate policy. The primary goal of this chapter is to place the green jobs strategy of US unions within the broader political economy and to explore its implications in the absence of comprehensive climate policy. In the first and shorter part I establish the parameters of US labour environmentalism by asking whether any US labour unions have moved beyond an instrumental approach to the environment or whether their green language masks other priorities. This account will highlight the contested and often contradictory approaches to the environment and climate change within the US labour movement. In the second part I place the US unions' green jobs strategy within the broader political economy by expanding the scale and scope from which we look at it. Combined, then, this chapter serves both an empirical and a methodological purpose. On one hand it outlines, however briefly, the state of US labour environmentalism while on the other it suggests some tools that can be used to evaluate the environmentalism of any labour union.

The parameters of US labour environmentalism

US labour environmentalism has a history that goes back to the 1970s (Miller 1980; Kazis and Grossman 1991; Leopold 2007). In addition to concerns over occupational health and safety a number of labour unions, activists and leaders sought to achieve a rapprochement with environmentalists and to introduce environmentalism into their own unions. In the 1980s these efforts lost steam but did not disappear (Kazis and Grossman 1991; Obach 2004a). During the 1990s they revived, largely as a result of union and environmentalist efforts to regulate regional and global economic integration. Ever since, unions and environmentalists have been involved in a variety of collaborative initiatives, including the Apollo Alliance (2011) and the BlueGreen Alliance founded in 2006 by the United Steelworkers and the Sierra Club (who were also members of the Apollo Alliance) (Steele 2008). In 2011 the Apollo Alliance and the BlueGreen Alliance joined forces. While the Apollo Alliance emphasised energy independence as much as green industrialisation the BlueGreen Alliance has been much more explicit in its call for green/clean jobs (BlueGreen Alliance 2011b).

The strategy of 'green jobs' as a route to a green economy is not new (Renner 1991). In the years before the 2008 crisis there was a resurgence of attention to this strategy, a confluence of collaboration between labour unions, environmentalists and global organisations such as the ILO and UNEP (UNEP 2008; Renner *et al.* 2009 for a summary). In the US organisations such as the BlueGreen Alliance and the Apollo Alliance were also sensitive to the possibility of an industrial strategy that was attentive to employment. With the onslaught of the 2008 crisis and the increasing prospects of a Keynesian policy under a Democratic Administration the 'green jobs' strategy received broader attention (Pollin *et al.* 2008). In some cases the argument was that existing jobs could easily be made green by refocusing sectors, like steel production, towards renewables. Others hoped that 'green jobs' were the DNA of a green economy that required more than shifting existing industries toward renewables. Still others saw green industries and jobs as a necessity if the US was to preserve its world leadership. This variability was and remains evident amongst both environmentalists and labour unions.

It is fair to say that despite the existence of pockets of more radical environmentalists amongst unions and their allies, the range of labour environmentalism in the US ranges from reformism to a rather instrumental use of the environment. There is not yet in the US such a profound synthesis of labour and the environment evident in a few countries such as Spain or Australia (see Gil, Snell and Fairbrother, and Burgmann in this volume).

With this background in mind we can identify three general tendencies within US labour environmentalism and towards the green jobs strategy. It would be misleading to place US unions that have adopted some type of environmental programme into fixed categories. Although there are patterns, overlaps and contradictory positions are more common. This is due to a number of external and internal factors. Externally, shifting Federal priorities towards unions and the environment and an absence of a tradition of social dialogue lead unions to adjust their own strategies more tactically than strategically. Additionally, while some corporations may be willing to engage in social dialogue with unions or environmentalists these are in the minority. Internally, unions in the manufacturing sector are largely agglomerations of workers from different sectors with often-conflicting priorities about the environment. Only about 20 per cent of the United Steelworkers, for instance, are in the steel industry. Competing priorities become even more central when unions are involved in alliances. Accordingly, it is better to talk about trends or tendencies of labour environmentalism, which can often coexist uncomfortably within the same union or the same alliance. The Laborers' International Union of North America (LIUNA) and the Plumbers and Pipefitters, for instance, are both members of the BlueGreen Alliance as well as key supporters of the Keystone XL Pipeline (see Sweeney in this volume).

One trend recognises that environmental priorities are not merely instrumental to other goals. This trend, exemplified by most members of the BlueGreen Alliance and the Alliance as a whole, supports binding and global climate policy while also supporting greening the economy through clean industry and technical innovations (BlueGreen Alliance 2011a, 2011b). A second trend, exemplified by the AFL-CIO and some industrial unions, is ambivalence or opposition to binding climate policy, placing the emphasis on green industry and technical innovations (AFL-CIO 2007, 2008, 2011). A third tendency, exemplified by the United Mineworkers and the International Brotherhood of Electrical Workers (IBEW), emphasises specific technical innovations of immediate relevance to them, such as clean coal, nuclear power or green construction. Under better circumstances one would not consider this trend as part of labour environmentalism. Given the fact that some industrial unions do not have anything approximating an environmental policy, while others promote strategies that are blatantly hostile (see Sweeney in this volume), we can consider this trend as setting the boundary between labour environmentalism and its absence. The goal of this section is to map US union environmentalism within these parameters.

While ecological modernisation has not been used to frame environmental politics in the US (Cohen 2006; Schlosberg and Rinfret 2008) there are significant pockets of it in the US and within unions. Arguably President Carter's late 1970s policies would qualify as ecological modernisation strategies while Al Gore's approach is largely within ecological modernisation. Additionally, many state-level policies, such as those of California, Colorado and New Jersey, are arguably efforts at ecological modernisation. In general terms ecological modernisation is a strategy that aims at modernising the economy (which would be the case with the move from non-renewable to renewable forms of energy, for instance) by adopting socio-technical innovations that are environmentally sound (Jaenicke and Lindemann 2010). In that sense ecological modernisation accepts and encourages the need to reform current economic practices in a green direction.

Beyond that common ground, however, there is a great deal of disagreement as to how far meaningful change is possible within the existing parameters of the political economy. Some would argue that ecological modernisation can deliver results (Fisher and Freudenberg 2001) while others would argue that it does not go far enough in changing production and consumption (see Warner 2010). For the sake of convenience we can group the various modernisation views as weak ecological modernisation and strong ecological modernisation (Christoff 1996).

Weak ecological modernisation recognises that the environment ought to be protected but seeks to develop solutions that minimally perturb the existing political economy, whether capitalist or state capitalist. Strong ecological modernisation seeks to fuse recognition of inherent rights for nature with social priorities. Social choices must have an in-built concern for their environmental implications while environmental policies must do the same for society.

The organisation closest to weak ecological modernisation is the Blue-Green Alliance. In addition to supporting binding climate policy it is also a strong advocate of green industrialisation and jobs. Profound and innovative as many of its proposals may be, the BlueGreen Alliance does not propose a fundamental social and ecological challenge of the nature of the US economy. This is not simply due to lack of vision by its leaders, some of whom have fairly comprehensive views on the subject. Rather the reasons are both external and internal to the labour and environmental movements. As noted earlier neither the US state nor US capital are inclined to participate in social dialogue while the US labour and environmental movements have long conceded to capital the power to make key decisions. Stated differently, US unions and environmentalists seek to improve the impacts of capital's practices rather than challenge the social power relations that it embodies.

While ecological modernisation has its origins in Continental Europe and has focused on the whole economy, eco-efficiency and industrial ecology have emerged in the US and has focused on corporate (and individual entity) eco-efficiency and innovation (Frosch and Gallopoulos 1989; Deutz 2009). This divergence reflects to a large degree the varieties of capitalism approach (for an application on environmental policy see Mikler 2010). Accordingly, 'liberal capitalist systems', such as that of the US, are likely to be less collaborative and corporatist than coordinated capitalist systems, such as those found in Continental Europe.

The BlueGreen Alliance's programme also exhibits elements of industrial ecology. On the other hand the attitude of the AFL-CIO and the Union for Jobs and the Environment (UJAE) range between industrial ecology and a strategic focus on particular technical innovations (Gereffi *et al.* 2008 and UJAE 2011). Others in this alliance are much more focused on promoting clean forms of traditional sources of energy, such as coal and nuclear power. However, judging from their support of the Keystone XL Pipeline some of the unions in the BlueGreen Alliance (Plumbers and Pipefitters and LIUNA) and the UJAE (Plumbers and Pipefitters, the IBEW and the Teamsters) may well be considered non- or anti-environmentalist and as strong opponents to binding global climate policy. That the divisions over the XL Pipeline cut deeply is evident by the fact that the BlueGreen Alliance has not formulated a position on the matter (Higgins 2011).

While ecological modernisation and industrial ecology can be considered as types of industrial and employment strategy not every industrial or employment strategy that promotes clean forms of energy, green jobs and other practices that we associate with a green economy can be considered as an instance of ecological modernisation or industrial ecology. A number of analysts and activists have suggested that greening the economy can take place through an industrial strategy (Marszalek 2008). But, industrial strategies can very well employ green technologies in an instrumental fashion, abandoning them with ease or articulating them around patently non-ecological practices to the point of rendering them useless (see cases in Block and Keller 2011). However, in a country like the US where employment and industrial strategies are contentious terms, unions and environmentalists have sought to promote such strategies under the legitimating cover of greening the economy (Block 2011; BlueGreen Alliance 2011b; Jenkins *et al.* 2011).

Industrial and employment strategies can well converge towards labour environmentalism. This is less likely to happen when they prioritise competitiveness and military security priorities, tendencies that were central to the Apollo Alliance narrative and are also present within the BlueGreen Alliance's programme (Lombardozzi 2011). The most environmentalist amongst unions do have competitiveness in mind but their primary concern is to enhance the role of the US state (national and subnational) in steering the economy and, in fact, they would welcome more 'socialist' measures along a broad swath of the national political economy (see Apollo Alliance 2008; BlueGreen Alliance 2011b).

Those unions that prioritise competitiveness may or may not call for an industrial policy, especially a green industrial policy. Quite often they will call for a wide range of tools that protect often declining or threatened ones such as coal mining. While industrial policy provides, at least, a broad vision that may include social dialogue between labour, state, capital and environment, competitiveness is more opportunistic and often employs images of the 'other' to excite political action (see Alliance for American Manufacturing 2009). Finally, those that are concerned with military (as distinguished from human) security can very well be nationalist or even nativist in their motivation. Security policies have historically been the foundation of industrial policy in the US but with the end of the Cold War there is some distancing. However, many major companies (and thus unions) are part of the military–industrial complex. It is certainly possible to make stealth bombers that use biofuel but it would be difficult to imagine that ecological priorities will determine whether they will be built.

On balance, there is not a single or dominant US labour environmentalism. Rather, we have a number of trends or tendencies that are competing for leadership. If anything positive has happened during the last ten years it is the emergence of the BlueGreen Alliance. What remains to be seen is whether the BlueGreen Alliance will be able to enshrine environmental priorities within the labour movement and continue to develop a comprehensive green strategy or whether it will remain a promoter of industrial and employment strategies with a green hue. In either case, US labour environmentalism will have to confront the global implications of its green choices since these are as much about the political economy as they are about nature.

Putting 'green jobs' in their place

The churning of the global economy routinely visits a great deal of suffering on workers and communities. While it may be apparent even to them that major changes are necessary and inevitable it is also evident that human suffering cannot be washed away by the logic of restructuring. In the absence of a safety net, as is the case in the US, workers, unions and whole communities often join alliances with states and capital to outcompete other communities both nearby and far away. It is tempting to argue that such strategies are the only or best option given the circumstances. We know now that the picture is more complex. For instance, had capital, unions and local elites taken advantage of the opportunities presented to them in the 1970s to build more fuel-efficient cars they would have avoided the worst of the crisis that has affected the automotive sector and its communities.

One of the pressing empirical tasks of our times, therefore, is to place particular activities and strategies, in this case those of labour unions, in their transnational contexts. By doing so we accomplish two goals. First, we can identify empirically the political economy within which they occur. It is meaningless, for instance, to treat oil or natural gas production as solely a local practice when these are global commodities. Second, we can better ascertain whether a local or national strategy that seems to serve a certain purpose at that level serves the same at a different level. A desperate and necessary struggle to prevent toxics from being dumped in one's community may well displace the harm to even weaker communities in the absence of a comprehensive strategy on toxics. This chapter seeks to place the economic, environmental and social quality of the 'green jobs' strategy within their broader political economy. This is not to refute the fact that states and capitals have more power than unions, certainly in the US. It is not to blame labour unions for the predatory behaviour of business and states in a neoliberal economy like the US. However, it is to ask that unions reflect on the implications of their choices and practices, whether these are forced on them or chosen by them (Räthzel and Uzzell 2011). As the history of the US labour movement shows unions have made many choices over time ranging from choosing to adopt business unionism over social unionism, to privilege white men over others, to become more inclusive than not, to exclude radicals from their ranks, to fight the Cold War in alliance with administrations that attacked them at home and so on.

As political and economic geographers have fully recognised, deployments in space and time are integral to social organisation (Gough 2010; Castree *et al.* 2004). How particular issues are framed in terms of scale and scope is the result of political contestation. A combination of environmental and globalisation discourses, for instance, has left the impression that the only scale of major environmental issues, such as climate change, is the global scale. Without rejecting the significance of climate's globality, it is necessary to identify the actual scales of particular activities because both their production and impact are spatially uneven. Climatic change, for example, is affected by all sorts of local emissions and many of the policy proposals, such as the Clean Development Mechanism and Reducing Emissions from Deforestation and Forest Degradation, have specific local implications. Ultimately, we have to identify how specific local practices affect ecosystems that range well beyond legal boundaries and how transnational practices become localised in the process obscuring their transnationality.

Being sensitive to scale does not mean being sensitive to scope (Stevis 2002). It is possible, for instance, to adopt a global scale but limit our scope to the 'internal stakeholders' (e.g., formal workers and management) at the expense of 'external stakeholders' (e.g., suppliers and their workers or whole communities). Product cycle assessments, footprints and commodity chain analyses can be technically revealing but can also obscure uneven power relations amongst stakeholders. Production networks analysis can be more useful to the degree that it recognises the contested and shifting direction of global processes. But, even production network analysis can be partial and incomplete if it does not inform a more comprehensive view of the world political economy.

In order to more fully address the political economy of a particular ecological modernisation or green industrial strategy, therefore, we must ask how the various affected parties are (re)organised. The production of solar power, for instance, can proceed in more or less centralised fashion and can use more or less water-intensive technologies. When centralised in large 'concentrating solar thermal' (CST) plants solar power will reproduce distribution patterns similar to coal or oil energy. Since the CST plants require significant amounts of water then existing users will have to give up some of those rights. On the other hand, if buildings and cities are organised to maximise the use of in-situ photovoltaic technologies then the organisation of the industry and the broader political economy is likely to be different. Even then, however, we risk falling prey to the attractiveness of localism and overseeing the impacts of the commodity chains that are implicated in the production of distributed technology (Mulvaney 2011).

But a strategy may be fully inclusive of human stakeholders but not of 'natural' stakeholders, whether species, habitats or ecosystems. In fact, efforts to be broadly inclusive of marginalised or threatened human constituencies are often at the expense of nature. A full internalisation of the environment (or gender, race or ethnicity) must move beyond symbolism, paternalism or alliances with environmentalists. Labour environmentalism must, at a minimum, extend some standing to nature or some recognition of natural processes and limits. The environment must become part of the constitution of what unions are and do rather than an external arena that must be watched for adverse or useful developments (Sweeney 2009; Burgmann in this volume; Gil in this volume). This is not to say that nature is valued more than people anymore than it is to say that the emancipation of women meant that they were valued more than men. Rather, it requires that the labour movement internalise the environment and commit to fighting its own battles within these new parameters. Social ecology and socialist ecology suggest ways in which unions can develop a political ecology but so do stronger forms of ecological modernisation (cf. Hay 2002 and Dryzek 2005).

These concerns are not purely ecological in inspiration. They are also practical from the point of view of global labour politics. From the start of the modern labour movement there was an uneasy encounter between labour's participation in shaping national economies and the need to avoid nationalism (Stevis and Boswell 2008). This was particularly pressing since national economies were part and parcel of the world economy and their strategies had unavoidable impacts on others. Early labour and socialist internationalists recognised that in the absence of collaborative mechanisms the uneven and combined development of national capitalisms was destined to lead to predatory competition that would spread to labour unions. Climate strategy, whether direct like the Kyoto Protocol, or indirect, like green jobs, are not about a reified environment or nature. Rather they are about the reorganisation of national and local economies within an uneven world political economy. The environmental goals and strategies of national or transnational unions, therefore, can and must be evaluated in terms of the political economy or ecology that they are likely to produce, stripping away both public relations and misplaced priorities. This is all the more pressing when competitiveness and security figure so prominently on the agendas of many labour environmentalists and unions. Attention to the scale and scope of their goals and strategies must be front and centre of the analysis.

Green jobs, good jobs, just jobs?

Labour unions are not simply interested in 'green jobs'. They are fully cognizant of the fact that green jobs are not necessarily decent or 'good' jobs (Renner *et al*. 2009, 7–9; Materra 2009). I believe that they would also agree that green and decent jobs may not necessarily be just and that climate justice has to be addressed head-on (Global Labor Institute 2011b). In what follows I examine the green jobs discourses of US labour unions in terms of their economic, environmental and social dimensions. As will become apparent, this account will reinforce the earlier claim that there is a great deal of variability amongst those labour unions that have adopted some kind of strategy regarding climate change.

Green jobs?

What does it mean to say that a job is green? Does this refer to the process or the outcome? Are some 'green jobs' not green under any circumstances? Can green jobs in one particular locality depend on dirty jobs along the supply and distribution chains? Is it possible that competition for green jobs may lead to collective irrationality, rather than the greening of the economy?

There are a number of debates about green jobs. These debates reflect different priorities and they need to be separated from each other. A strong criticism of 'green jobs' comes from the libertarian right and argues that green jobs are neither well defined nor definable (Morriss *et al.* 2009). These criticisms are not really about green jobs but, rather, about any public policy on the matter. Thus, they use a well-worn technique that suggests that if something cannot be exactly defined it is neither meaningful nor useful. By that logic practically every major social concept, including the property rights so dear to them, is meaningless.

In this author's view there is enough empirical evidence to suggest that there are and can be many jobs that employ green processes and produce green products (Renner *et al.* 2009). On balance, the concept of green jobs places workers and work at the centre of greening the economy. There cannot be a green economy unless it is also greened at the point of production. There can be, however, a debate as to whether certain jobs that seem green are, in fact, green in process and product (Brookings Institution 2011).

There is an ongoing effort to balance priorities about energy sources within the US labour movement. A number of unions (particularly but not only the United Mineworkers) are in favour of clean coal (Banig and Trisko 2011), which many consider an oxymoron. The 'poster child' of this debate is nuclear power whose global resurgence promises substantial medium- and longer-term jobs (Savage and Soron 2011; Bogardus 2010). These views highlight an important challenge: are some kinds of jobs inherently not green or can almost any job be made green provided that they are undertaken in particular ways? However, there is a wide variety of less controversial jobs and whole sectors whose green potential is inherently debatable, ranging from making means of war less energy intensive to hybrid SUVs. Even within patently green sectors it is easy to raise doubts about the environmental potential of particular solar or other renewable energy technologies. It is likely that workers and unions do not have a say in the key decision-making steps that result in such green-looking activities. The 2005 Energy Act, for instance, reserved most of the subsidies for nuclear power, responding to the priorities of a strongly antiunion administration. Unions with environmental agendas cannot accept and legitimate such choices over and over again any more than they can accept discrimination in the name of jobs.

Another important question that unions must address is whether a green job is one that results in a green product or one that is characterised by a green process (Gereffi *et al.* 2008; Materra 2009). It is possible that a green product – whether a wind turbine, a solar panel or a train – may be the result of an environmentally unsound process (Mulvaney 2011). The environmental hazards involved in the production of a green product may be spread throughout its production and supply chain. For example, the production of wind turbines involves the use of chemicals and the generation of fine particles that can prove harmful. More importantly, sophisticated wind turbines involve thousands of parts and significant amounts of raw materials. These generate an economic, environmental and social footprint that is as difficult to trace as it may be destructive. While technology-intensive greener jobs are likely to be located closer to the final destination of the product, the dirty parts of the production chain will be located in places that produce the raw materials. Unions in industrial countries have to address these issues directly because they are involved in their creation. To my knowledge there has been no systematic study by labour unions on the implications of production networks that situate higher end or environmentally more sound activities in the core of the world political economy (but see Global Labor Institute 2011b).

Even when the products and processes are environmentally sound, labour environmentalists must consider the possibility of a 'rebound' effect. Green strategies that rely on technical tools rather than comprehensive environmental goals are subject to Jevons's paradox or the 'rebound' effect (Schipper 2000; Polimeni *et al.* 2008; Jenkins *et al.* 2011). The argument here is that increasing efficiencies and innovations at the corporate, local or even national economy level may lead to more production and consumption, albeit of individually more environmentally efficient products. There are those who argue that there is no evidence for the rebound effect and that it is something promoted by corporations who want to avoid efficient innovation (Goldstein *et al.* 2011). While this fear is justified, the assertion that efficient technologies ('tools') will lead to better environmental outcomes in the absence of rules that limit and redirect production and consumption is too optimistic (Lohman 2009). Energy efficiency, like other efficiencies embedded in a logic of accumulation, lowers the costs of production and leads to speeding up the treadmill of production (Obach 2004b). The absence of binding climate policy in the US makes green job proposals that emphasise efficiency particularly susceptible to this dynamic.

Good jobs?

What are the characteristics of 'good' green jobs? What broader socioeconomic goals are green jobs called upon to serve? At the micro level it is possible to provide a number of attributes that characterise a good green job. Such jobs must pay a living wage, must be long term, must be safe and must empower workers (Renner *et al.* 2009; Materra 2009). Beyond that they ought to provide for personal growth and a sense of contributing to the common good.

Labour environmentalists are also aware that good green jobs are not necessarily those that are the most capital intensive (Materra 2009). Rather, the green jobs strategy must serve a macroeconomic role that is not simply tailored to the demands of capital. If more people are working in good green jobs then the social fabric will also be positively affected. This is an important ingredient of the green jobs strategy and one that does go against the tendency of capital to replace workers with technology, as is the case with oil and coal extraction, or to engage in labour-intensive activities only when workers are abundant and disposable. Seen from a different angle, good green jobs may contribute to slowing down the treadmills of production and destruction by virtue of slowing down the pace of capitalist accumulation (Obach 2004b).

Yet, it is not clear that the advocates of 'good green jobs' in the US place them within the broader political economy. A job may be good and green (and thus pursued by the most environmentalist amongst unions) because it satisfies all of the above criteria at the place of production or within the US. It may actually depend on environmentally harmful but well-paying and unionised jobs along the same production chain.

In addition, while this more labour-intensive environmentalist approach to green jobs seeks to slow down the logic of capitalist accumulation it is limited in its broader demands about the organisation of the US economy. Retrofitting buildings can create good jobs but does not enhance the decision-making role of unions about the place and function of these buildings (and, in fact, the environmental reconfiguration of space is not central to US labour unions and beyond).

Overall, then, US unions face two important challenges. First, it is possible that a portion of US workers will enjoy the benefits of good jobs in the same way that workers in sectors of the grey industry have been enjoying them. And, as with the grey industries, workers along the supply chain may contribute surplus value, some of which goes to create good jobs at the core. These workers may be elsewhere in the world or within the same country. Second, jobs may be considered good but, as far as empowerment is concerned, workers may be limited to some protections and a 'fair share' – rather than enjoy the right to affect the organisation of the economy. In short, good green jobs may be simply jobs in the green sector rather than vehicles for more profound ecological citizenship rights.

Just jobs?

The issues raised by the discussion of the environmental and economic dimensions of green jobs also apply and illuminate the question of whether good green jobs are necessarily just. Can good green jobs be considered green if they displace grey jobs across space and time? Can the solution of an injustice in one place cause injustice elsewhere? How can the green jobs strategy be fully articulated with a comprehensive 'just transition' that addresses equity across all those affected?

The issue of environmental justice has been a central issue for US environmental politics and labour unions have contributed a great deal to making it a prominent concern. Central to this trajectory has been the work of Tony Mazzocchi who, as a leader of the Oil and Atomic Workers union, pushed his union and the broader labour movement to take a more proactive approach towards environment and to tie environmental improvements to the overall regulation of the economy and to questions of equity (Leopold 2007). The concept of a 'just transition' has its roots in the efforts of this and other US unions to navigate the environmental challenges of the 1970s. Yet, like economic and environmental practices it also looks different when viewed from various scales and scopes. There is good reason to suggest that a great deal of what falls under environmental justice in the US focuses on the distributive impacts of industrial practices, such as the dumping of toxics, and less on the overall social relations that drive these inequities. Stated differently, it remains a liberal rather than a socialist approach to justice (Gough 2010).

If the green jobs strategy is nothing more but the legitimation of industrial policy (the most benign of the challenges discussed earlier) it is likely to produce two results – both of them unjust. One result would be the concentration of jobs in particular regions, which will then turn the rest of the world into their supply chain. Such a global division of labour could be benign if not associated with national or local competitiveness strategies and narrow corporate priorities. When these are the motivating factors then we can envision the reproduction of the same kinds of historical inequalities present in grey sectors. The point here is not that every locality can or should have the same position in the global division of labour, but rather the emerging green global division of labour can take on characteristics that are no different from those associated with the existing global divisions of labour. Perhaps jobs that are more place bound, such as retrofitting buildings and infrastructure, may be the exception to some degree. Yet, even these more place-bound activities do require products and raw materials that are produced in places other than those of their final use.

References to unfair competition fuelled by inferior environmental and labour standards in the Global South are ubiquitous in discussions and debates about green jobs. As a result, one of the recurring conditions for supporting climate policy is that key Southern countries also join. Yet, the US is the largest Foreign Direct Investment (FDI) recipient in the world, second only to the EU and ahead of China (UNCTAD 2011). A lot of the new FDI is in manufacturing and much of it goes to the Southern US or, now, Northern states desperate for investment (Uchitelle 2011). US unions have sought but have not been able to unionise the Southern US because of determined corporate and local elite resistance. Consequently, unions in other industrial countries can well use the same language about the US, especially when US unions ally with anti-union forces to put the blame on foreigners when domestic politics is so much the cause of the problem.

There are important equity implications associated with the transition to a green economy in the same sense that the transition to the grey economy during the nineteenth century reorganised the world political economy. Some sectors and some jobs will have to be downsized or abandoned altogether. This realisation can produce anxiety about the future, thus hindering a transition to a green economy. As a result, unions have developed a 'just transition' strategy (TUC 2008; Global Labor Institute 2011b; Snell and Fairbrother in this volume). Tellingly, perhaps, there is no just transition programme by any US union, as far as I know. The just transition strategy recognises that there has to be a move away from environmentally damaging jobs and sectors. It also calls for a planned transition that does not victimise workers and communities. The just transition strategy raises important questions about the nature of the political economy since it requires the recognition of the interests of workers and communities and their active involvement in determining how the transition ought to take place. It also calls for a broader public role. In short, it goes to the heart of the political economy because it broadens and deepens both voice and choice.

Imagine, however, that workers, unions and communities along the supply chain also called for a just transition. For instance, if miners in raw material or oil-producing countries called for a just transition away from mono-production or if they demanded that higher end and greener parts of the production process remained local (as many unions in industrial countries are arguing). Stated differently, it is possible that calls for a 'just transition' in the Global North and, in fact, parts of the Global South, do not fully interrogate the scale and scope of power relations implicated in the solutions they envision for themselves. Thus, the just transition strategy, when limited in scale and scope, can be structurally unjust.

This kind of concern is not limited to communities, unions and workers in other places. The same kinds of issues can emerge within the same space, as precarious workers or hitherto marginalised communities feel excluded by solutions that protect skilled or otherwise protected workers. They can become even more poignant when the concerns of some historically marginalised groups are addressed but those of others are left behind. In such cases the divisions are no longer between the powerful and the weak but, also, amongst the weak.

Conclusions

US labour environmentalism has not reached the level of some other countries, such as Spain or Australia. But, it is fair to say that it has reached a higher organisational and programmatic level than at any time since the 1970s. However, there are important tensions within the broader labour movement, within the BlueGreen Alliance, and within the unions leading the charge. The BlueGreen Alliance, or the Apollo Alliance before it, were not simply a response to the crisis and the prospects of a Democratic administration (although they have close relations with the liberal wing of the Democratic Party). The roots of their Keynesianism go further back. But the prospects of influencing national policy did have an impact on labour environmentalism, bringing together both those committed to it and those attracted to the spoils of green Keynesianism. Will the move towards labour environmentalism survive the fact that climate policy is not likely at the US national level, that Keynesian programmes are being blocked by the Republicans, and that natural gas and shale oil are promising energy abundance?

I do not think that extreme energy will destroy renewables (which are becoming a major portion of energy investment worldwide) nor green innovations. However, having a vibrant green sector is not the same as having a climate strategy. This requires more than green production and consumption, both of which can very well aggravate the problem in the absence of any limits to them. And labour environmentalism is more than some unions in some sectors playing a leading role and getting good green jobs.

By placing green jobs within the broader political economy we can adduce the following profile of US union responses to climate change. Economically there is a significant tendency that promotes weak ecological modernisation but that tendency is externally and internally contested by non-environmental strategies that may promote green jobs and technologies for instrumental and non-environmental reasons. This contestation, combined with the absence of comprehensive climate policy, raises the possibility that even policies that aim at ecological modernisation may end up externalising rather than containing activities that harm the climate while also raising the spectre of a serious rebound effect that adds additional pressures. Finally, the US labour movement has not developed a 'just transition' strategy that takes into account its structural role in the world political economy. Rather, it has adopted a very particularistic approach that may well solve local problems by reproducing global inequalities.

Combined with a notoriously hostile business sector and a largely neoliberal state, the achievements of labour environmentalists are fragile. Many unionists and environmentalists recognise these tensions and are considering ways in which they can both jump-start the greening of the US economy as well as avoid green nationalism. The emergence of such a group of unionists (and environmentalists that are sensitive to union priorities) has given rise to important debates about how unions can develop imaginative programmes that minimise nationalism, maximise greenness and serve as learning grounds for practical and political collaboration between unions, environmentalists, local states and ethical capitalists (BlueGreen Alliance 2011b). The goal of such unionists is to create a 'California effect' across the national and global economies rather than serve to concentrate and keep good green jobs in particular countries or localities. Such an approach seeks to create strategic pockets of public regulation that take some of the more predatory elements out of a company's or a state's (or a union's) calculations. The point here is not that national and global policies are undesirable. In fact, they are necessary if appropriately crafted. Rather, that the wait for national and global rules should not justify inactivity and the initiatives of labour environmentalists must be acknowledged (BlueGreen Alliance 2011b; Apollo Alliance 2011). If these stronger environmental modernisers are successful in putting in place local, regional or sectoral 'best practices' then the prospects that union environmentalism will survive this conjuncture of opposition to climate legislation and unions rights will be brighter.

Note

1 Many thanks to Stratis Giannakouros, Romain Felli, Dustin Mulvaney and Pete Taylor for their comments and suggestions for additional readings.

References

AFL-CIO (2007) 'Legislative Alert! AFL-CIO Energy Task Force: Jobs and Energy for the 21st Century'. 1 July. www.workingforamerica.org/documents/PDF/1agexecutivealert. pdf (accessed 20 November 2010).

——(2008) 'Greening the Economy: A Climate Change and Jobs Strategy that Works for All'. 4 March. AFL-CIO Executive Council Statement.

——(2011) 'The AFL-CIO, ITUC and the 2010 Climate Negotiations'. http://blog. aflcio.org/2009/10/01/bad-climate-change-bill-could-cost-4-million-us-jobs/ (accessed 10 June 2011).

Alliance for American Manufacturing (2009) *An assessment of environmental regulation of the steel industry in China.* Washington, DC: Alliance for American Manufacturing.

Apollo Alliance (2008) *The new Apollo program: Clean energy, good jobs.* San Francisco, CA: Apollo Alliance.

——(2011) *Achievements.* http://apolloalliance.org/about/achievements/ (accessed 26 February 2011).

Banig, B. and Trisko, E. (2011) *Low-carbon jobs potential.* www.greenlaborjournal.org/ articles/ potential-low-carbon-jobs (accessed 26 February 2011).

Block, F. (2011) 'Crisis and renewal: the outlines of a twenty-first century new deal'. *Socio-Economic Review* 9: 31–57.

Block, F. and Keller, M. (eds) (2011) *State of Innovation: The U.S. Government's Role in Technology Development.* Boulder, CO: Paradigm Press.

BlueGgreen Alliance (2011a) 'About the BlueGreen Alliance'. www.bluegreenalliance. org/about_us? id = 0001 (accessed 26 February 2011).

——(2011b) *Jobs21! Good jobs for the 21st century.* www.bluegreenalliance.org/admin/ publications/files/Platform-vFINAL.pdf (accessed 30 December 2011).

Bogardus, K. (2010) 'Labor likes prospect of new jobs from nuclear', *The Hill.* http:// thehill.com/business-a-lobbying/94983-labor-likes-nuke-jobs-prospects (accessed 28 February 2011).

Brookings Institution (2011) *Sizing the Clean Economy: A National and Regional Green Jobs Assessment.* Washington, DC: Brookings Institution.

Castree, N., Coe, N., Ward, K. and Samers, M. (2004) *Spaces of work.* London: Sage.

Christoff, P. (1996) 'Ecological modernisation, ecological modernities'. *Environmental Politics* 5 (3): 476–500.

Cohen, M. (2006) 'Ecological modernization and its discontents: The American environmental movement's resistance to an innovation-driven future'. *Futures* 38: 528–47.

Deutz, P. (2009) 'Producer responsibility in a sustainable development context: ecological modernization or industrial ecology?' *The Geographical Journal* 175 (4): 274–85.

Dryzek, J. (2005) *The politics of the earth: Environmental discourses.* 2nd edition. Oxford: Oxford University Press.

Fisher, D. and Freudenberg, W. (2001) 'Ecological modernisation and its critics: Assessing the past and looking toward the future'. *Society and Natural Resources* 14: 701–709.

Frosch, R. and Gallopoulos, N. (1989) 'Strategies for manufacturing'. *Scientific American* 261 (3): 144–152.

Gereffi, G., Dubay, K. and Lowe, M. (2008) *Manufacturing Climate Solutions: Carbon-Reducing Technologies and U.S. Jobs.* Durham, NC: Center on Globalization, Governance & Competitiveness, Duke University.

Global Labor Institute (2011a) 'U.S. Labor and the Energy Transition'. Draft discussion paper. Provided to author by Global Labor Institute, ILR, Cornell University.

——(2011b) 'Climate Justice, Social Justice: Towards a Fair, Ambitious and Binding Global Agreement'. Provided to author by Global Labor Institute, ILR, Cornell University.

Goldstein, D., Martinez, S. and Roy, R. (2011) *Are there rebound effects from energy efficiency? – An analysis of empirical data, internal consistency, and solutions.* www.electricitypolicy.com/Rebound-5-4-2011-final2.pdf (accessed 30 December 2011).

Gough, J. (2010) 'Workers' strategies to secure jobs, their uses of scale, and competing economic moralities: Rethinking the "geography of justice"'. *Political Geography* 29: 130–39.

Hay, P. (2002) *Main currents in Western environmental thought.* Bloomington, IN: Indiana University Press.

Higgins, S. (2011) 'Dueling rallies highlight labor-green split over pipeline'. 7 October. http://blogs.investors.com/capitalhill/index.php/home/35-politicsinvesting/5350-dueling-rallies-labor-green-split-pipeline (accessed 30 December 2011).

Jaenicke, M. and Lindemann, S. (2010) 'Governing environmental innovations'. *Environmental Politics* 19 (1): 127–41.

Jenkins, J., Nordhaus, T. and Shellenberger, M. (2011) *Energy Emergence: Rebound and Backfire as Emergent Phenomena.* Oakland, CA: Breakthrough Institute.

Kazis, R. and Grossman, R. (1991) *Fear at work: Job blackmail, labor and the environment.* New edition. Philadelphia: New Society Publishers.

Leopold, L. (2007) *The Man who Hated Work but loved Labor: The life and times of Tony Mazzocchi.* White River Junction, VT: Chelsea Green Publishing Company.

Lohman, L. (2009) 'Toward a different debate in environmental accounting: The cases of carbon and cost-benefit'. *Accounting, Organizations and Society* 34 (3–4): 499–534.

Lombardozzi, B. (2011) 'Buy America: One Element to the Solution of our Job Crisis'. http://apolloalliance.org/blog/buy-america-one-element-of-the-solution-to-our-job-crisis/ (accessed 30 December 2011).

Marszalek, B. (2008) 'Green-Collar Jobs, Industrial Policy and a Society with Future'. *New Labor Forum* 17(3): 30–36.

Materra, P. (2009) *High Road Or Low Road? Job Quality In The New Green Economy.* Washington, DC: Good Jobs First.

Mikler, J. (2010) 'Apocalypse now or business as usual? Reducing the carbon emissions of the global car industry'. *Cambridge Journal of Regions, Economy and Society* 3: 407–26.

Miller, A. (1980) 'Towards an environmental/labor coalition'. *Environment* 22 (5): 32–39.

Morriss, A., Bogart, W., Dorchak, A. and Meiners, R. (2009) *7 Myths About Green Jobs.* PERC Policy Series 44. Bozeman, Montana: PERC. www.perc.org/files/ps44.pdf (accessed 30 December 2011).

Mulvaney, D. (2011) 'Are green jobs, just jobs? Innovation, environmental justice, and the political ecology of Photovoltaic (PV) life cycles'. Manuscript provided by author.

Obach, B. (2004a) *Labor and the environmental movement: The quest for common ground.* Cambridge, MA: The MIT Press.

——(2004b) 'New labor: Slowing the treadmill of production?' *Organization and Environment* 17(3): 337–54.

Polimeni, J., Mayumi, K., Giampietro, M. and Alcott, B. (2008) *The Jevons Paradox and the Myth of Resource Efficiency Improvements.* London: Earthscan.

Pollin, R., Garrett-Peltier, H., Heinz, J. and Scharber, H. (2008) *Green Recovery: A Program to Create Good Jobs and Start Building a Low-Carbon Economy.* Amherst, MA: Center for American Progress, and Washington, DC: PERI.

Räthzel, N. and Uzzell, D. (2011) 'Trade unions and climate change: The jobs vs environment dilemma'. *Global Environmental Change* 21: 1215–23.

Renner, M. (1991) *Jobs in a Sustainable Economy.* Washington, DC: Worldwatch Institute.

Renner, M., Sweeney, S. and Kubit, J. (2009) *Green Jobs.* Washington, DC: Worldwatch Institute.

Savage, L. and Soron, D. (2011) 'Organized Labor, Nuclear Power, and Environmental Justice: A Comparative Analysis of the Canadian and U.S. Labor Movements'. *Labor Studies Journal* 36(1): 37–57.

Schipper, L. (2000) 'On the rebound: On the interaction of energy efficiency, energy use and economic activity: An introduction', *Energy Policy* 28 (6–7): 351–53.

Schlosberg, D. and Rinfret, S. (2008) 'Ecological modernisation, American style'. *Environmental Politics* 17(2): 254–75.

Steele, D. F. (2008) 'Globalization and Cooperative Activity Between National Labor Unions and National Environmental Organizations in the United States'. *International Journal of Social Inquiry* 1(2): 179–200.

Stevis, D. (2002) 'Agents, subjects, objects or phantoms? Unions, the environment and liberal institutionalization'. *Annals of the American Academy of Political and Social Science* 581 (1): 91–105.

Stevis, D. and Boswell, T. (2008) *Globalization and labour: Democratising global governance.* Lanham, MD: Rowman & Littlefield.

Sweeney, S. (2009) 'More than green jobs: Time for a new climate policy for labor', *New Labor Forum* 18 (3): 53–59.

Trade Union Congress (TUC) (2008) *A Green and Fair Future: For a Just Transition to a Low Carbon Economy.* Touchstone Pamplet #3. www.tuc.org.uk/touchstone/ justtransition/greenfuture.pdf (accessed 26 February 2011).

Uchitelle, L. (2011) 'Working for less: Factory jobs gain, but wages retreat'. *New York Times* (29 December). www.nytimes.com/2011/12/30/business/us-manufacturing-gains-jobs-as-wages-retreat.html?ref=workingforless (accessed 30 December 2011).

UJAE (Unions for Jobs and the Environment) (2011) www.ujae.org/ (accessed 30 December 2011).

UNEP (2008) *Green Jobs: Towards Decent Work in a Sustainable, Low-Carbon World.* Nairobi: UNEP/ILO/IOE/ITUC.

United Nations Conference on Trade and Development (UNCTAD) (2011) *UNCTAD Global Investment Trends Monitor,* No. 5, January 17. www.unctad.org/en/docs// webdiaeia20111_en.pdf (accessed 25 January 2011).

Warner, R. (2010) 'Ecological modernisation theory: Towards a critical ecopolitics of change?' *Environmental Politics* 19 (4): 538–556.

15 US trade unions and the challenge of "extreme energy"

The case of the TransCanada Keystone XL pipeline

Sean Sweeney

This chapter draws attention to the dangers of the "extreme energy" scenario where the use of fossil fuels, rather than being phased as a result of climate policy and increasing scarcity (or some combination of the two) is actually expanded both in relative and absolute terms. It examines the case of the proposed Keystone XL pipeline that, of this writing (August 2011), is being considered by the US State Department for approval. Actively supported by four North American unions representing two million workers, TransCanada corporation is seeking to construct a 1,700-mile-long pipeline that will on a daily basis bring 900,000 barrels of tar sands oil from Alberta, Canada to heavy crude refineries in Texas – a development that will double the amount of tar sands oil exported to the US and further "lock in" the US' dependence on unconventional fuels.

The prospect of a new era of fossil-based extraction – often achieved in new and extreme forms – should be the concern of all unions. First, unless it is intercepted politically, the realisation of the extreme energy scenario will mean that the global effort to reduce emissions to the levels required to limit global warming to two degrees Celsius is probably destined to fail, a view that is today shared by the International Energy Agency (IEA 2011a). The prospects of "green growth" and green jobs will similarly be dashed. Second, extreme energy threatens to pull certain unions into an open partnership with energy corporations who, in return for jobs (in the form of Project Labor Agreements in the US), will provide active political support for controversial extreme energy projects. This is what is happening now with Keystone XL. An explicit alliance has been formed between the American Petroleum Institute (API) and certain energy and construction unions. The objective of the alliance is to build political support for policies that promote and develop domestic sources of fossil-based power (API 2009).

Union support for the approval of Keystone XL is hugely damaging to the US labour movement and to the efforts of unions everywhere – including at the global level – to promote climate protection and sustainable development and to build alliances with other social movements. However, the "jobs versus environment" formulation fails to capture the full gravity of the environmental destruction that will be unleashed if the plans of extreme energy corporations are not intercepted. The choices for unions are difficult, both within and beyond the energy sector. But there can be only one course of action – movement-wide and consistent opposition to extreme energy.

The economics of extreme energy

In recent years the idea that there need be no contradiction between job creation and environmental protection has taken hold in many unions both in the US and internationally. Such a view has been accompanied by the notion that, as UN General Secretary Ban Ki-Moon expressed it, "[a] transition to a Green Economy is in the end inevitable"(UNEP 2011) due to the fact that fossil-based sources of energy are running out and the threat of climate change would compel governments to reduce emissions. A string of studies have been released that point to the growth and future potential of green jobs and other economic and social dividends resulting from climate and environmental protection policies (UNEP 2008). In 2008, bold words by political leaders on the dangers of climate change and the potential for "green growth" seemed to set the stage for a major policy shift towards a global Green New Deal as the world slumped into a major recession. A 2011 report by the pro-union Economic Policy Institute and the BlueGreen Alliance in the US noted that the "unprecedented intersection" of high oil prices and climate change "translates into clean energy being the most significant growth opportunity of the global economy" (BlueGreen Alliance 2011).

The Keystone XL case draws attention to the very real danger of an energy system emerging that is not only far from clean, but is even dirtier and more damaging than the system based on conventional fossil fuels. As the production of high-yield, low-cost fossil fuels dwindles, corporations are planning to replace them with new sources of "extreme" fossil-based power. In North America, this entails the further exploitation of Canadian Tar Sands oil; the harvesting of natural gas stored in shale formations by a process known as hydraulic fracturing or "fracking", and the expansion of surface coal mining in states like Wyoming and Montana where the Wyodak coal bed, the US' leading source of coal, covers 10,000 square miles in the Powder River Basin. The climate and broader environmental implications of more fracking and strip mining for surface coal are also extremely serious, but cannot be dealt with here (Howarth *et al.* 2011). Suffice to say, these new sources of fossil-based energy are in the process of changing the global political economy of energy. According to the IEA, there is enough economically exploitable coal, oil and gas to meet the world's growing demand for energy for the next 150 years or so – even if these reserves are becoming increasingly more difficult to extract (IEA 2011b).

True, annual global investment in renewable energy rose almost six-fold in 12 years to 2007, dipped during the recession, but has since rebounded. In 2010 investment reached $240 billion – a 30 per cent increase on 2009 figures (WEF 2011). For some this level of increase reinforces the idea that the green economy is steadily moving forward. But most of the increase during this period can be attributed to either government stimulus funding or to China's commitment to scale up renewable sources of power (WEF 2011). In fact, China was responsible for around 45 per cent of the global investments in clean energy in 2010 (UNEP 2010). Furthermore, the growth in the demand for energy means that the rise in the level of investments in renewables, while impressive, is nowhere near enough to displace fossil fuels. According to the IEA's "Current Policies Scenario", renewables will supply just 14 per cent of the world's energy supply by 2035 (IEA 2011b). However, the IEA also estimates that $550 billion needs to be invested in renewable energy and energy efficiency each year from 2009 to 2030 to reduce CO_2 levels to somewhere close to where they need to be, more than double the present level (IEA 2011b).

The rise in the price of conventional crude oil may have made renewable energy more attractive, but it has also made tar sands oil "economical" despite the heavy labour and energy inputs needed to extract it. Plans to scale up exploitation of the tar sands also entail building the infrastructure to transport the fuel to refineries and distribution points. To deploy an old saying, news of the death of fossil fuels have been wildly exaggerated – and the investments in the tar sands merely underscore the point. In 2008 Greenpeace warned *investors not to put money into tar sands, arguing that "[a]s climate change moves ever further up the agenda of the G8 and the wider international community, it will be increasingly understood that carbon intensive tar sands production is moving counter to the international consensus"(Greenpeace 2008). Four years later, this sentence could be rewritten as follows: "As oil prices rise, and climate change moves further down the agenda of the G8 (and other elite fora), it will be increasingly understood by corporations that investing in the tar sands is a wise business move". Indeed, in 2008 and 2009, BP and Royal Dutch Shell invested a total of $81 billion in the tar sands. According to one study, an additional $379 billion could be invested between 2010 and 2025 (World Wildlife Fund 2009).

The Keystone XL project is therefore not simply about laying a pipeline, and union support for the project is therefore not simply a matter of upsetting a few farmers and environmentalists. Two pipelines (Keystone 1 and the Alberta Clipper) already bring tar sands oil to the Midwestern states. The notoriously anti-union Koch Industries has a major stake in the continued production and expansion of tar sands and the construction of the Keystone XL. Koch Industries and its subsidiaries already import and refine up to 25 per cent of all tar sands entering the US. Shell is more than doubling its refining capacity – from 275,000 to 600,000 barrels of oil a day – at a refinery in Port Arthur, Texas. The refinery is half-owned by Saudi Aramco, the state-owned oil company of Saudi Arabia.

These investments in the extraction, transportation and refining of tar sands oil can be further explained by the fact that there is an estimated 173 billion barrels of recoverable tar oil that is worth, at today's prices, at least $15.7 trillion.

And while many renewable energy companies for the most part struggle to make meager returns, the top five US oil corporations made $952 billion in profits from the year 2000 to 2010 (Committee on Natural Resources 2011). But the profit potential of the tar sands can only be realised if there are ways to get tar oil out of Alberta and into the world's energy system – and that is what makes Keystone XL such an important project.

The climate impacts of tar sands and Keystone XL

The tar sands is already the world's largest industrial project and indisputably its largest ecological disaster. Aside from the destruction of Alberta's boreal forests, the ecosystems they support and the profound impact on the (mainly indigenous) local communities, emissions generated by the project equals or exceeds the emissions from all the motor vehicles in Canada. Producing one barrel of oil from the tar sands produces three times the amount of GHGs produced from conventional oil, making the overall GHG lifecycle of a barrel of tar sands oil up to 45 per cent higher than conventional oil (*Moose Jaw Times* 2011). Canada's emissions presently stand at a level 33.8 per cent above its Kyoto commitment, which it abandoned in 2012. According to leading NASA scientist James Hansen, the uncontrolled use of tar sands oil will render futile all of the existing efforts to control global warming pollution. He estimates that the tar sands alone store enough carbon to raise the CO_2 levels in the atmosphere an additional 200 parts per million, making it (in his words) "game over" as far as climate stabilisation is concerned (Hansen 2011).

Unions internationally need to be clear that extreme energy is not a problem that can be quarantined in North America. Most obviously, the emissions generated by the extraction and use of tar sands oil are everyone's problem. Moreover, tar sands oil (along with shale gas and surface coal) is being scaled up in North America to serve the rising global demand for energy as economies like China and India continue to grow at a rapid pace. Corporations already have plans to build the Northern Gateway pipeline to carry tar sands oil across British Columbia for export – a project that has been met with fierce resistance from First Nation and coastal communities. A good portion of the oil that will gush down the Keystone XL will, according to some studies, probably end up being finally consumed in China and India (Droitsch 2011). Tar oil and shale formations are not confined to the North American continent. Energy corporations are moving at great speed to exploit those deposits in other regions of the world.

Extreme energy is changing the political discourse

The availability of extreme energy is also changing the political discourse in North America, and fossil fuel companies are reframing the debate by openly supporting climate change denial, and by citing both the need for jobs and for energy security and/or independence. The failure of COP15 in Copenhagen has often been explained in terms of a problem of "political will", but some of the reasons for the failure to reach a binding global climate agreement at COP15 can be traced directly to the political will of fossil corporations and their extreme energy agenda. In the US, big coal, oil and gas companies were the main force behind the failure of Congress to introduce an economy-wide cap and trade system in 2010, a development that has led to the US doing its best to undermine the UNFCCC process and to openly challenge the idea that a binding global climate agreement is either needed or possible (Stern 2011). Other developed countries have followed the lead of the US – in some instances pushed on by their own energy companies as part of a globally coordinated campaign designed to defeat, delay or dilute government climate protection initiatives (Greenpeace 2011). Without an ambitious and binding global climate agreement, the impetus to transition to a green low-carbon economy will be, and already is, much weaker. The political impact of extreme energy has already been felt at the global level.

"Carbon unionism" – labour support for Keystone XL and extreme energy

Unions in the US have a long history supporting coal and other fossil fuels for the simple reason that they have members who work for mining, drilling, transportation and power utilities who produce, move or use those fuels. In recent years, US unions in power generation and heavy industry have enthusiastically supported a carbon capture and sequestration (CCS) pathway for coal. But these unions have not made CCS a condition for supporting continued coal use, and the poor prospects for CCS has thus far had little noticeable impact on union support for continued coal use and industry expansion – including higher volumes of coal for exports.

Meanwhile, the AFL-CIO has never supported either the Kyoto agreement or the science-based emissions reduction targets proposed by the IPCC and supported by the International Trade Union Confederation (ITUC). It did not support the extension of the Kyoto Protocol in the lead up to the UN talks (COP17) in South Africa and has been generally supportive of the US government's insistence on a voluntary "pledge and review" approach to emissions reductions, an approach rejected by the ITUC. Overall, the US labour movement's climate and energy policy has historically been mostly shaped by a small number of unions in energy and manufacturing, and the rest of the labour movement – representing the vast majority of union members – have (with few exceptions) steered clear of what is, or could be, a divisive issue.

As long as it looked like fossil fuels would over time be replaced by renewable energy or made cleaner by CCS, "carbon unionism" could be considered a problem that would slowly disappear. In the US, the environmental movement has been successful in stopping the construction of more than 100 coal-fired power stations in the past decade, and the anticipated imposition of a price on carbon through a cap and trade system that was considered by Congress would, had it been passed into law in 2010, have put pressure on the coal companies in particular. But today the significance of union support for fossil fuels needs to be assessed differently. CCS is still in its infancy, and renewable energy is barely 2 per cent of US power generation (excluding hydro). Meanwhile extreme energy threatens a "second coming" for fossil-based power.

Four unions have signed Project Labor Agreements (PLAs) with TransCanada to complete construction work related to the pipeline and are urging the US State Department to approve the project. The four unions are the Laborers', Operating Engineers, Plumbers and Pipefitters, and Teamsters. In November 2011 the International Brotherhood of Electrical Workers also issued a statement supporting Keystone XL and announced it had signed a PLA with the company. The unions that support Keystone XL state that they do so because Keystone XL means work for their members, many of whom have been idle or left underemployed by the recession. However, it would be naive to regard union support as a simply on-off and motivated merely by feelings of desperation about the need to secure jobs by any means necessary in difficult economic times. The industry–union alliance goes much deeper. In June 2009 the American Petroleum Institute and 15 labour unions announced "the historic creation of the Oil and Natural Gas Industry Labor-Management Committee, which will work to promote job retention and growth ... by promoting innovative and affordable access to energy that is vital to the American economy" (API 2009). The committee would engage in "a communications effort to educate the public and other stakeholders about the effects of legislation that would restrict exploration or hinder processing, refining and marketing of U.S. oil and natural gas products" (API 2009).

When viewed in this context, trade unions' support for Keystone XL reflects an explicit industry–labour partnership designed to promote an extreme energy agenda with a public message built around the issue of jobs and energy independence. This is therefore more than about getting some precious jobs during hard economic times. Rather, this is a case where a few unions are consciously and actively helping to secure an energy future that most of the world's workers could well do without, one marked by much more global warming pollution and much more political and economic power for the big oil, coal and gas companies.

Tar sands and Canadian unions

The tar sands is already a major employer in Canada, providing 75,000 direct jobs in Alberta, and an additional 165,000 indirect jobs (CAPP 2011). The tar sands contributed 40 per cent to Alberta's GDP. The work mostly pays well. However, the cost of living has skyrocketed in the vicinity of the project (individual trailer homes can fetch $300,000 and simple houses $600,000 or more). Nearly 30 per cent of the people living in the tar sands area actually live below the poverty line. Tens of thousands of workers live in huge work camps, having moved into the area from Newfoundland and Labrador. Approximately 17 per cent of the population of Fort McMurray are from those two regions. Workers endure 10–12-hour shifts and sometimes work for several weeks without any days off. Not surprisingly, the area has seen unusually high rates of drug addiction, suicides and high levels of spousal abuse.

Most Canadian unions, however, oppose Keystone XL on the grounds that the upgrading of tar sands bitumen will be "offshored" to the US and perhaps even beyond the borders of the US. The value added resulting from the upgrading then is lost to the Canadian economy, and so are the jobs for workers employed in the refineries. As recently as 2008, a dozen new or expansion "upgrader" projects were planned for the Fort McMurray and Industrial Heartland areas (just outside of Edmonton) of Alberta. The Industrial Heartland Association calculated that the eight upgraders would create approximately 22,000 construction and 12,000 permanent jobs in the region (IHA 2007). If constructed, these upgraders would not only provide much-needed jobs in the region, but they would also lay the foundation for Alberta to manufacture refined petroleum products such as gasoline, diesel and petrochemicals, and thus retain much of the value added from tar sands production. While a few of these upgrader projects have gone forward, the vast majority of them were postponed or cancelled due to the global recession. The construction of pipelines like Keystone XL further reduces the likelihood that these upgraders will be built, as companies will now look to exporting tar sands oil to US upgraders and refineries. According to the Alberta Federation of Labour, "[t]he size and number of these US refineries and American-bound pipelines is significant because it means that US oil refiners will have the capacity to absorb all expected increases in Alberta's oil sands production over the next 10 years" (AFL 2009). Keystone XL will further eliminate the need for upgrading facilities in Alberta, thus ending the possibility of diversifying Alberta's energy economy and the thousands of potential construction and permanent jobs in those facilities.

The main tar sands union, the Communications, Energy and Paperworkers' (CEP) union, sees the retention of oil refinery jobs in Canada as a crucial means of developing a vibrant Canadian renewable energy sector. The CEP is not in favour of closing the tar sands, instead it opposes the presently unsustainable levels of expansion and calls for directing revenues from the refining of tar sands oil into publicly owned and administered renewable energy sources. For the CEP, this is a feasible 'just transition' approach to the tar sands that is both environmentally responsible and offers a future for Canadian energy sector workers (CEP 2009). The CEP and Alberta Federation of Labour's perspective is broadly consistent with the positions taken by the Canadian Labour Congress (CLC). The CLC's position on climate change is particularly forward looking and progressive (CLC 2008).

However, not all Canadian unions oppose Keystone XL. The construction trades unions of Canada are supportive of the project because of the work it would create constructing the section of the pipeline in Canada. In fact these unions are regional affiliates of the construction unions based in the United States. Both the Teamsters and the Laborers' have large numbers of members in Canada – 225,000 and 80,000 respectively. The public debate around Keystone XL approval in Canada in several instances pitched the pro-pipeline unions against both the Alberta Federation of Labour and Communication, Energy and Paperworkers Union of Canada who opposed the project.

Jobs in the United States

The construction of Keystone XL would also produce jobs in the United States. A US State Department study determined that the construction of the Keystone XL would create "approximately 5,000 to 6,000 working years over the 3 year construction period", or less than 2,000 jobs per year on average. Between 10–15% per cent of these jobs are expected to be filled by local residents of the six states along the route of the pipeline (US State Department 2011). However, using data provided by TransCanada, a Perryman Group study claims that 20,000 direct jobs will be created by Keystone XL, and the oil revenues will generate 465,000 jobs by 2035 (The Perryman Group 2010). Not surprisingly, the American Petroleum Institute uses the Perryman study to help make the case for the approval of the pipeline (API 2011).

The four pro-Keystone XL unions have also cited the Perryman job projections in their efforts to urge the State Department to approve Keystone XL (Teamsters 2011). In a letter to US Secretary of State Hillary Clinton, the four union presidents counterpoise jobs and the environment – choosing the former while dismissing the latter. The letter acknowledges the fact that "further development of Canada's oil sands puts in jeopardy U.S. efforts aimed at capping carbon emissions and greenhouse gases" and that "comprehensive energy and environmental policy should strive to address climate concerns while simultaneously ensuring adequate supplies of reliable energy and promoting energy independence and national security". However, the presidents of the four unions claim that the pipeline will "pave a path to better days and raise the standard of living for working men and women in the construction, manufacturing, and transportation industries". It will allow "the American worker" to "get back to the task of strengthening their families and the communities they live in" (Teamsters 2011). In July 2011, the four unions took another controversial and seemingly self-defeating step. They helped get the US House of Representatives to pass a Republican-sponsored bill to expedite the approval process of the Keystone XL pipeline, effectively overriding the official objections of the US Environment Protection Agency. The House bill's main sponsor, Nebraska Representative Lee Terry, is notoriously anti-union. According to the AFL-CIO, Terry has voted against the interests of working families more than 90 per cent of the time.

While it is important to be aware of the proactive measures being taken by the four pro-pipeline unions, the passive "none of our business" approach of the rest of the labour movement also needs to be addressed. The unions supporting the pipeline represent roughly 13 per cent of union members in the US and only a tiny fraction of that 13 per cent stand to gain anything from the project. This means that 50 or so unions (representing 13 million workers) have not taken a position on Keystone XL, either because they do not yet know about the project or because they do not wish to cross paths with the unions who support the pipeline. Moreover, the ITUC, along with many of the Global Union Federations, have taken strong positions on climate change and environmental protection, but have thus far not (to the knowledge of this writer) made any intervention to urge their US affiliates to address the issue.

Developing union approaches to extreme energy

The final section of this chapter offers a set of suggestions that might help unions in the US and internationally address Keystone XL specifically and the challenge of extreme energy more generally. There are, of course, no easy solutions. High unemployment in the US – particularly in construction – has certainly hardened the position of the pro-pipeline unions, although there is no evidence to suggest that these unions would not have supported the project had unemployment been at pre-recession levels.

Some unions have a tradition of not supporting projects that conflict with the broader interests of the working class, even if it means their own members' short-term interests will be negatively affected. Lack of space prevents a detailed review of this kind of approach. This tradition dates back to the time of the American Civil War when textile workers in Lancashire (UK), the majority of them women, continued to support the abolition of slavery even though the lack of cotton from the Southern states had inflicted mass unemployment on English working-class communities. Much more recently, the US-based Oil Chemical and Atomic Workers (OCAW) developed the idea of a "superfund" for workers to help them transition from producing nuclear weapons to the making of other products. In this volume, the Australian construction union, the CFMEU, takes a similar class approach to environmentally damaging construction work (Burgmann in this volume). The International Longshore and Warehouse Union in the US has on numerous occasions refused to load cargo – such as arms shipments to the dictatorships in Chile or El Salvador during the 1970s and 1980s – that it regarded as damaging to workers generally or in some specific context.

None of these examples are directly applicable to the Keystone XL case. However, such an approach can be modified to help unions deal with the challenge of extreme energy. The six points made below could help begin a discussion on finding ways to oppose specific extreme energy projects and build support for a renewables-based energy system.

Energy should be the concern of every union

When it comes to energy policy, unions outside of the energy sector or energy-intensive industry have almost invariably deferred to those unions who represent the workers in those sectors. However, the "we're not an energy union" response fails to grasp how important energy choices are to all workers and society as a whole.

As discussed above, four US unions support the Keystone XL pipeline, which then filters into public discourse as "unions support Keystone XL because of jobs" – when most of the labour movement has no knowledge of the project or its likely environmental impacts. No union has expressed opposition to Keystone XL. Most know nothing about this or similar projects, and the few that do are staying on the sidelines because they do not wish to publicly oppose the position of another union that has an immediate stake in the outcome. This is traditional trade union practice in the US. Unions will clash with each other over jurisdictional issues and the right to represent different groups of workers; they often side with different political candidates in both primaries and general elections – but a union without an obvious stake in an issue or project will not normally challenge a union that does – especially when jobs are involved. This has always caused problems for US unions' overall reputation, the effects of which have often been mitigated by the many other positive things unions do in the workplace and in society. But extreme energy projects are different – they "lock in" social and environmental damage for decades; they erase the possibility of good, green jobs, and threaten to turn large sections of the population against unions. In the US, polling data suggest Asians, Latinos and young people support environmental protection by large majorities – alienating these huge constituencies will damage the prospects of the entire labour movement (LCLAA 2011).

Stop defending the indefensible

Unions may feel compelled to support extreme energy projects like Keystone XL, but they really have no need to state that such projects are good for "the American worker" or the US economy. They also have no need to downplay or remain silent regarding their many negative environmental and social impacts – especially when those impacts are often extremely serious and will negatively affect the public good. If unions are not able to openly oppose projects that do harm, the least they can do is not pretend that the work being performed is making a positive contribution to society (Teamsters 2011).

Similarly, it is clear that extreme energy corporations commission studies that exaggerate the numbers of jobs their projects will bring to any given community. Or the corporations refer to indirect jobs in the same way as direct jobs – thus giving the impression that extreme energy is a major job creator when, in fact, these projects are often capital intensive, and the jobs created are relatively few, temporary and non-local. Unions therefore do not have to uncritically echo the claims of these corporate-sponsored studies, and in so doing weaken the efforts of those in the communities who are highly sceptical of such claims. Jobs lost as a result of extreme energy projects also need to be considered, as well as the health and environmental impacts on jobs and quality of life. The BP disaster in the Gulf clearly showed how reckless oil development puts many other livelihoods at risk – such as fishing, farming and tourism.

Be consistent

A growing number of unions have passed good resolutions on climate change, the environment and support for the green economy. However, sometimes these statements stand in clear contradiction to decisions taken around individual projects. Such inconsistencies could at least be acknowledged and dealt with openly. For example, in recent years the pro-pipeline Teamsters union promoted green trucking and worked with communities suffering from poor air quality as a result of deregulated trucking and unenforced environmental standards in the industry. Teamster efforts around the Clean and Healthy Ports Campaign have helped advance the needs of truckers for higher standards and better conditions, and probably saved many lives by cutting pollution in places like the Port of Los Angeles. However, by supporting the Keystone XL pipeline (which will generate only 1,500 Teamster jobs), the union is supporting a project that will generate massive amounts of additional pollution in places like Houston and Port Arthur, Texas.

Another pro-pipeline union, the Laborers', has taken a strong position on climate change and is one of just five US unions that openly support science-based emissions-reduction targets. The union has also invested considerable political and financial capital in training workers (many from economically excluded communities) for weatherproofing and building retrofit work. However, the union feels that lack of a national mitigation commitment has put it in an untenable position – and this has made it the target of criticisms about environmental and climate destruction that really should be aimed at policy makers and corporations. This is a valid point – but there are obvious drawbacks to the "if you can't beat them, join them" approach. By supporting a Republican House bill to expedite the approval of the Keystone XL project, unions have helped the Republicans present themselves as the party that is concerned about jobs. The sections of the Laborers' union that could benefit from an aggressive mitigation policy will find themselves in a far weaker position.

The need for consistency also extends to national federations and the global trade union bodies. If affiliated unions are not even alerted to the fact that they are in violation of the global trade union position, then the goal of reaching a coherent and movement-wide approach to climate protection, sustainable development and the green economy will be forever out of reach. Given what is at stake for both workers and the planet, the reluctance to take even this small step for fear of upsetting an affiliated union must be quickly overcome.

Take it to the members

Unions can take steps to put complex and challenging energy issues before their memberships for discussion and debate. This is most likely to happen in unions who have some locals or divisions that are likely to gain jobs from extreme energy projects. But it can also happen in unions that may be facing a loss in membership as a result of the actions taken by the environmental or environmental justice movements. Involving the membership opens the door to ideas and suggestions that may not have been anticipated in advance – and allows union members an opportunity to wrestle with the available options and become fully conscious of the different sides of the issue. Anecdotal evidence around the Keystone XL dispute suggests that some members of the pro-Keystone Laborers' union emerged from the public hearings, organised to discuss the pipeline, bewildered and perplexed wondering why their normally progressive union was asking them to speak up (loudly) for jobs alongside CEOs of a transnational corporation, and on opposite sides of the First Nation representatives, farmers and ranchers, and environmentalists who were testifying against the pipeline. According to *Mother Jones*, some of the union members seemed "put-off by the situation". One participant wearing a Laborers' union shirt apparently said: "I agree with the other side now ... I didn't know this was an environmental issue"(Sheppard 2011).

By opening up debate, job-related issues can also be considered alongside the union's longer-term goals and reputation; the impact on its organising campaigns, and public welfare in general. Involving the members in this way also serves an educational role.

Build alliances with friends, not enemies

It is today commonplace for unions to recognise the need to forge alliances with other movements. However, the battle over Keystone XL has seen a broad anti-pipeline coalition develop with no trade union support. The only alliance being formed by unions around this issue happens to be with Trans-Canada Corporation and the American Petroleum Institute. Labour and the corporations versus the people is not a good arrangement.

The anti-Keystone XL coalition sees the pipeline as posing a direct environmental and health threat to communities that live along the pipeline's route. Increased pressure and temperatures are needed to move the dense tar, likely increasing the number and severity of spills. The tar sands are also more corrosive than conventional oil and communities living along other tar sands pipelines have seen numerous spills over the past several years. Concerned about the potential threats to agriculture and the Midwest water supply, a growing number of community, farmers' groups, local officials, indigenous communities, land owners and others have started to resist the construction of the pipeline either through public action or by refusing to sell their land. Not surprisingly, those that have resisted giving up their land to TransCanada have been threatened by the use of eminent domain (compulsory purchase).

In the battle over collective bargaining and workers' rights in Wisconsin, unions in the US were happy to receive the solidarity of farmers, students, environmentalists and unorganised citizens that rallied to labour's cause.

Many of those same organisations oppose Keystone XL and need the support of the labour movement.

US labour cannot afford to take an instrumental approach to alliance, participating in broad coalitions in one instance and then joining with corporations in another in accordance with the unions' interest at the time.

Propose bold policy alternatives

Extreme energy must also be challenged vigorously at the level of policy. A full discussion on policy alternatives falls outside the scope of this chapter, but there has never been a better time (in the US at least) for unions to work with the environmental, environmental justice and other movements in promoting the need for a National Energy Transition Plan coupled with reform of the energy sector. The Utility Workers' support for public ownership of utilities deserves broad and active labour involvement and is a key component of a reform agenda aimed at decarbonisation, unionisation and democratisation of power generation. Signing a few Project Labor Agreements will not alter the fact that wages, conditions and levels of unionisation are falling across the fossil fuel sector. Just 8 per cent of oil, gas and coal extraction is unionised. Coal transportation is becoming increasingly non-union.

The case for a New Deal approach to job creation is strong and is attracting some attention. It is widely known that the state of the US' infrastructure is very poor and much of it is dangerous and dilapidated. The Laborers' union has shown leadership on this issue – drawing attention to the work that could be done if the US was to make infrastructure a priority. There is no shortage of water and sewage pipelines that need to be fixed or replaced, bridges and tunnels that need emergency repair, new low-carbon transportation systems that need to be developed, and clean energy infrastructure that need to be constructed. Many jobs could be created in energy conservation, upgrading the grid, maintaining and expanding public transportation – jobs that would help our communities and protect our environment.

Recent studies have urged policy makers to learn the lessons of the New Deal, when Federal and regional direct-hire programmes like the Public Works Administration and Civic Works Administration put more than 11 million unemployed people to work during the Depression era.

Some unions in the UK and South Africa have argued that the quickest and most effective way to concurrently address climate protection and the need for jobs is to generate a major public "climate jobs programme" (CJP). An ambitious emissions-reduction target would determine both the scale and character of the programme, which would, in turn, be situated within a broad spectrum of climate protection measures. Ideally, a CJP would be generated at the Federal level and be guided by a national emissions-reductions commitment. While this is unlikely to happen before 2013 in the US, states can begin to put in place hiring programmes that are designed to serve state-level emissions-reduction targets. For example, 16 states presently have an emissions-reduction target (80 per cent reduction by 2050 based on 1990 levels). What they do not yet have is a jobs programme that can help them reach their 2050 targets.

Tough decisions, but no choice

As noted at the outset, the choices for unions in this situation are difficult, both within and beyond the energy sector. But there can be only one course of action – movement-wide and consistent opposition to extreme energy.

This opposition needs to be grounded in three fundamental truths:

> Extreme energy threatens to bring with it new levels of environmental destruction and a sharp rise in global warming pollution. The "jobs versus environment" formulation fails to capture the full gravity of the environmental destruction that will be unleashed if the plans of extreme energy corporations are not intercepted. But weighing the jobs gained against the environmental havoc unleashed is ultimately a fool's equation and self-defeating. There are not enough jobs on the planet that can justify destroying the planet.

A green economy cannot be built on dirty energy. Moreover, an economy based on fossil-based energy is a job killer, even if a few jobs can be gained in the short term. The promise of green jobs in public mass transit, energy efficiency in buildings, grid modernisation, sustainable farming, pollution control technologies, wind, solar and other renewables, etc., will simply not be realised if "cheap" extreme energy drives out renewable energy, low-carbon public mass transit and fuel-efficient vehicles, and energy conservation.

Labour cannot present itself as *a progressive social movement* while at the same time siding with extreme energy corporations and against those in the communities whose lives and livelihoods are jeopardised by these dirty energy developments. Labour can also not afford to alienate its allies in the environmental and climate justice movements who share labour's broad social objectives and have been actively engaged in the battles to protect workers' rights and collective bargaining.

Update

Since this chapter was written, Keystone XL has become a national issue in the United States. In late August 2011, more than 1,200 people were arrested outside the White House in Washington, DC for engaging in non-violent civil disobedience against the pipeline. On 6 November 2011, more than 12,000 people surrounded the White House in an anti-Keystone protest.

The movement against the pipeline received an important boost when, in mid-August, the Transport Workers Union and the Amalgamated Transit Union became the first US unions to publicly oppose Keystone XL. In a joint statement, the two unions declared:

We need jobs, but not ones based on increasing our reliance on tar sands oil. There is no shortage of water and sewage pipelines that need to be fixed or replaced, bridges and tunnels that are in need of emergency repair, transportation infrastructure that needs to be renewed and developed. Many jobs could also be created in energy conservation, upgrading the grid, maintaining and expanding public transportation—jobs that can help us reduce air pollution, greenhouse gas emissions, and improve energy efficiency. We therefore call for major "New Deal" type public investments infrastructure modernization and repair, energy conservation and climate protection a means of putting people to work and laying the foundations of a green and sustainable economic future for the United States.

(ATU and TWU 2011)

In early November, the National Domestic Workers Alliance and Domestic Workers United also declared their opposition to the pipeline. These new unions represent home cleaners, childminders and other excluded workers – industries that are almost 100 per cent women and foreign born. The statement against Keystone XL noted:

Many of our members come to the U.S. from countries already severely impacted by climate change and environmental devastation. ... NDWA and DWU add our voices to the rising opposition to this dangerous project. We stand with those in the labour movement who oppose Keystone XL.

(NDWA 2011)

However, many large unions maintained an officially neutral stance, and this remains the case at the time of writing (December 2011). The majority of the mainstream media continue to report that "the unions want the pipeline" even though there is some trade union opposition and the number of unions supporting the pipeline numbers only five in total.

On 10 November 2011, the State Department announced it would delay a decision on either granting or denying a Federal permit for the project until it studies new potential routes that avoid the Sandhills areas of Nebraska and the Ogallala aquifer, a vast underground water supply. The process would take at least a year. President Obama issued a statement expressing support for the State Department's decision.

The environmental movement considered the "delay Keystone" decision to be a major victory, although the pro-pipeline unions reacted angrily and criticised Obama for turning his back on the unemployed and working families. However, in December 2011, pro-Keystone unions collaborated with Congressional Republicans in their successful effort to attach a "decide on Keystone in 60 days" directive to the president as part of a bill extending income tax cuts introduced by the administration as an economic stimulus measure. The State Department and the president had until the end of February 2012 to accept or reject TransCanada's petition to construct Keystone XL.

On 18 January 2012, the State Department denied the permit to TransCanada to build the pipeline. Three large unions (Steelworkers, CWA and SEIU) issued a statement saying the president had "acted wisely" in rejecting the pipeline. The two transport unions (ATU and TWU) also added their names. Incensed by the statement, the Laborers' withdrew from the BlueGreen Alliance on 19 January 2012.

References

AFL-CIO (2011) Congressional Voting Record.

Alberta Federation of Labour (AFL) (2009) *Lost Down the Pipeline*, March. www.afl.org, accessed 20 March 2012.

Amalgamated Transit Union and Transport Workers Union (ATU and TWU) (2011) "ATU & TWU Oppose Approval of the Keystone XL Pipeline and Call for End of Increased Use of Tar Sands Oil". August. www.atu.org/media/releases/atu-twu-oppose-approval-of-the-keystone-xl-pipeline-and-call-for-end-of-increased-use-of-tar-sands-oil, accessed 14 March 2012.

American Petroleum Institute (API) (2009) www.api.org/news-and-media/news/news items/2009/jun-2009/api-labor-sign-historic-jobs-promotion-agreement.aspx, accessed 20 March 2012.

——(2011) "API: Keystone XL Pipeline bill will create hundreds of thousands of new American jobs". Cited by Jeremy Brecher, The Keystone XL Pipeline and Labor, Labor Network for Sustainability. www.labor4sustainability.org/articles/pipeline-climate-disaster-the-keystone-xl-pipeline-and-labor/, accessed 5 July 2011.

BlueGreen Alliance, with Economic Policy Institute (2011) *Rebuilding Green: The American Recovery and Reinvestment Act and the Green Economy.* www.bluegreenalliance.org/news/publications/rebuilding-green-the-american-recovery-and-reinvestment-act-and-the-green-economy, accessed 20 March 2012.

Canadian Association of Petroleum Producers (CAPP) (2011) "Oil Sands Fact Book". http://issuu.com/capp/docs/oilsands-fact-book?mode=embed&layout=http%3A%2F%2Fskin.issuu.com%2Fv%2Flight%2Flayout.xml&showFlipBtn=true&autoFlip=true&autoFlipTime=6000, accessed 20 March 2012.

Canadian Labour Congress (CLC) (2008) "Climate Change and Green Jobs: Labour's Challenges and Opportunities", www.canadianlabour.ca/news-room/publications/climate-change-and-green-jobs-labour-s-challenges-and-opportunities, accessed 13 August 2012.

Committee on Natural Resources (2011) "One Trillion Dollars in Profit – And Still at the Trough: Oil and the Gas in the 21st Century". Democratic Staff Report, US House of Representatives, Senator E. Markey. http://democrats.naturalresources.house.gov/reports@id=0003.html, accessed 20 March 2012.

Communications, Energy and Paperworkers (CEP) (2009) "Just Transition to a Sustainable Economy in Energy" (Policy 915), www.cep.ca/docs/en/policy-915-e.pdf, accessed 13 August 2012.

Droitsch, D. (2011) "The Link between Keystone XL and Canadian Oilsands Production". Pembina Institute, April. www.pembina.org/pub/2194, accessed 20 March 2012.

Greenpeace (2008) *BP and Shell: Rising Risks in Tar Sands Investment.* www.greenpeace.org.uk/files/pdfs/climate/RisingRisks.pdf, accessed 20 March 2012.

——(2011) "Who's Holding Us Back? How carbon-intensive industry is preventing effective climate legislation". www.greenpeace.org/international/en/publications/reports/Whos-holding-us-back/, accessed 20 March 2012.

Hansen, J. (2011) 'Inside Climate News'. http://insideclimatenews.org/news/20110826/james-hansen-nasa-climate-change-scientist-keystone-xl-oil-sands-pipeline-protests-mckibben-white-house?page=2, accessed 20 March 2012.

Howarth, R. W., R. Santoro, and A. Ingraffea (2011) "Methane and the greenhouse gas footprint of natural gas from shale formations". *Climatic Change Letters*, 13 March.

Industrial Heartland Association (IHA) (2007) "Alberta Presentation: Alberta's Industrial Heartland Oilsands". 101 Update, 23 June, pp. 15–18; 31.

International Energy Agency (IEA) (2011a) *World Energy Outlook*, Chapter 6. www.worldenergyoutlook.org/, accessed 20 March 2012.

——(2011b) *World Energy Outlook*. Executive summary. www.worldenergyoutlook.org/, accessed 20 March 2012

Labor Council for Latin American Advancement (LCLAA) (2011) *Attitudes of Latino Voters on Energy Policy and Climate Change*. http://latinocoalitiononclimatechange.org/resources/, and www.youtube.com/watch?v=xyTyJb4mmYc, both accessed 20 March 2012.

Moose Jaw Times (Edmonton) (2009) 12 October. www.mjtimes.sk.ca/Canada – World/Business/2009-12-10/article-243834/Albertas-oilsands:-well-managed-necessity-or-ecological-disaster%3F/1, accessed 20 March 2012.

National Domestic Workers Alliance (NDWA) and Domestic Workers United (2011) 'Statement on Keystone XL". November. www.domesticworkers.org/by-issue/51-allies-news/303-we-need-real-jobs-solutions-not-the-keystone-xl-pipeline, accessed 20 March 2012.

Sheppard, K. (2011) 'The Final Decision on the Keystone XL Pipeline is Coming Soon', *Mother Jones*, 7 October, www.motherjones.com/blue-marble/2011/10/keystone-xl-consideration-moves-final-stages, accessed 13 August 2012.

Stern, T. (2011) "U.S. Special Envoy for Climate Change". Press conference on 11th Meeting at the Leaders. Representative level of the Major Economies Forum on Energy and Climate. Brussels, 26–27 April. www.youtube.com/watch?v=IuuHPQ3ZwT0, accessed 20 March 2012.

Teamsters (2011) "Message urging members to urge elected officials to support Keystone XL". https://secure3.convio.net/ibt/site/Advocacy?cmd=display&page=UserAction&id=531, accessed 21 July 2012.

The Perryman Group (2010) "The Impact of Developing the Keystone XL Pipeline Project on Business Activity in the US: An Analysis Including State-by-State Construction Effects and an Assessment of the Potential Benefits of a More Stable Source of Domestic Supply". June. www.transcanada.com/docs/Key_Projects/TransCanada_US_Report_06-10-10.pdf, accessed 21 July 2012.

UNEP (2008) *Green Jobs: Towards Decent Work in a Sustainable, Low Carbon World*. September. www.unep.org/labour_environment/features/greenjobs-report.asp, accessed 20 March 2012.

——(2010) *Renewables 2010: Global Status Report*. www.unep.org/sefi-ren21/, accessed 21 July 2012.

——(2011) *Green Economy: Pathways to Sustainable Development and Poverty Eradication*. Ban Ki Moon contribution. www.globalinitiatives.com/files/B4E_Seoul_2010_summary_report.pdf, accessed 12 March 2012.

US State Department (2011) 'Draft Environmental Impact Statement'. www.key stonepipeline-xl.state.gov/clientsite/keystonexl.nsf?Open, accessed 10 March 2012.

World Economic Forum (WEF) (2011) http://www.weforum.org/news/green-investing-report-examines-ways-reduce-financing-cost-clean-energy, accessed 12 March 2012.

World Wildlife Fund (2009) "Opportunity Cost of Tar Sands Development". BP Annual Review 2009 and Shell March 2008 and 2009 Strategy Update. www.wwf.org.uk/wwf_articles.cfm?unewsid=3758, accessed 10 March 2012.

16 From blue to green

A comparative study of blue-collar unions' reactions to the climate change threat in the United States and Sweden

Meg Gingrich

This chapter draws upon neo-institutional and rule systems theory to analyse how four blue-collar unions – the United Auto Workers (UAW) and United Steelworkers (USW) in the US and IF Metall and Kommunal in Sweden – have reacted and adapted to the climate change question. All four unions represent workers whose jobs may be threatened either by changing environmental conditions or through policy/changes in economic production aimed at curbing anthropogenic climate change. The focus of this chapter is not to assess the effectiveness of trade union action on climate change; rather, it explores how and why the four trade unions reacted to a similar threat in unique ways. Overall, the larger political and economic context in which the trade unions act, along with the unique organisational circumstances combined with material conditions, determine how the unions frame and express the climate change threat in relation to their own cause.

Case study selection

The selection of the US and Sweden allows for much comparing and contrasting and helps to assess the importance of such factors as political structure, trade union power, forms of organisation, and ideology in how and why trade unions have acted as they have regarding environmental issues.

I selected two Swedish and two American unions that represent workers related to the energy sector, energy-intensive industries, or workers in fields that release high amounts of greenhouse gases. While the two American unions and IF Metall in Sweden all have large portions of their membership involved in energy-intensive industries or industries whose products release large amounts of greenhouse gases (such as automobiles or iron/steel making), Kommunal represents blue-collar municipal workers and agricultural workers in Sweden. I picked the United Steelworkers and the UAW as they are two blue-collar manufacturing unions that are part of the same federation and represent similar types of workers, but who have taken different paths on climate issues. The choice of IF Metall emerged, as it is the Swedish blue-collar union that is most comparable to *both* the USW and the UAW – in terms of their members' work and their size within its federation. The choice of Kommunal is less obvious. Due to the structure of membership in the Swedish trade union federations, it was difficult to choose a union similar to IF Metall that has acted differently regarding a common issue. Based around notions of blue-collar solidarity, the Swedish trade union federation LO is set up to prevent membership competition, thus there is little overlap in the types of workers represented by each union (Kjellberg 2005). After contact with LO researchers and exploratory work, I chose Kommunal, as it is the blue-collar trade union that has been most active environmentally.

Trade union density

Current union density in the US is 12 per cent overall; the manufacturing sector also has a unionisation rate of 12 per cent (Hirsch and MacPherson 2011), down from the peak manufacturing unionisation rate of 40 per cent in 1970 (Waddington 2005). In Sweden, the overall unionisation rate was 71 per cent in 2010 for wage earners (with 90 per cent covered by collective agreements) (LO 2010). The rate for blue-collar workers was 70 per cent and 82 per cent of municipal workers (Kjellberg 2011).

The United Steelworkers (USW)

The United Steelworkers was one of the first labour organisations in the United States to acknowledge the existence of anthropogenic climate change, evidenced in their 1990 environmental policy report "Our Children's World", where they identified "global warming as the single most important environmental issue of our lifetime" (United Steelworkers 2006a, 2). In many ways emanating from historical work relating environmental and workplace issues, the Steelworkers emphasised the fundamental link between climate degradation and economic exploitation of workers. Admitting that the work of much of the membership may directly affect the climate and that attempts at combating climate change could threaten the employment of its members, the Steelworkers have continuously argued that the only way to solve the crisis is to combine the joint issues of work and climate, rather than acting defensively to protect existing members (Young 2009; United Steelworkers 2006a). Since the release of "Our Children's World", the Steelworkers have developed strategies of action based around the inextricable link between climate and work. Steelworker president Leo Gerard stated that "much of the pollution from production is born out of the same greed and need for ever-increased profits that leads to the exploitation of workers" (Grossfeld 2008).

After the USW recognised the relationship between economic and ecological exploitation, it became necessary to act on this understanding and to incorporate action on the joint issue into the union's mandate. The Steelworkers attempted to achieve this through use of their organisational structure, which

Table 16.1 Membership numbers and workers represented (2010)

Union	Founding date	Membership numbers	Workers represented
United Steelworkers (United Steel, Paper and Forestry, Rubber, Manufacturing, Energy, Allied Industrial & Service Workers International Union)	1936	850,000 active 350,000 retired	Metals (aluminium and steel); paper and forestry products; chemical industry; healthcare workers; pharmaceutical workers; public employees; mining
United Autoworkers (United Automobile, Aerospace & Agricultural Implement Workers of America International Union)	1935	Active: 390,000 Retired: 600,000	Automotive, aerospace and defence; heavy trucks; farm equipment; technical; office; professional
IF Metall (Industrifacket Metall)	Metall 1888; IF Metall 2006 (merger with industriar betaresfackfor-Bundet)	354,322	Ironworks; automobile; mechanical engineering; plastics; building components; technical
Kommunal	1910	506,878	Blue-collar municipal workers such as health care workers and bus drivers; agricultural workers

Source: www.usw.org ; www.uaw.org ; www.kommunal.se, www.ifmetall.se*;* www.lo.se

allowed for multi-level activism and experimentation, including action on climate change (Young 2009). Activism at the regional level in the 1990s, specifically by former District 11 (which encompasses the Northwest United States, extending from Minnesota to Washington, all the way to Alaska) president David Foster, allowed for the emergence of joint activism with environmental groups concerning such issues as logging in old-growth forests (Young 2009). The federal organisational structure of the union, and the ability of each district to address issues outside of the realm of those deemed to be immediately crucial at the federal levels, allowed Foster to illuminate the importance of environmental activism at the district level. Additionally, working within the district led to speaking with, learning from and working with other social groups (especially environmentalists) with the aim of creating a more comprehensive union activism aimed at addressing combined threats to workers and the sustainability of the environment that provides the jobs to workers.

Moreover, the Steelworkers frame climate change and its unequal effects (between rich and poor, North and South) to inequalities in economic distribution rather than a simple technological failure in need of a technological fix (although the promotion of greener technology is still important, according to the Steelworkers) (United Steelworkers 2006a). The Steelworkers adapted to the perceived organisational threat presented by climate change and action aimed at combating it by incorporating strategies that combine climate work into their union's mission. They defined the problem and issue in a way that leads to a central involvement of their organisation's membership in recognising the causes of and participating in solutions to climate issues. This is exemplified by Gerard's emphasis on the membership's willingness to shift to production of environmentally friendly products and to develop the use of renewable energy sources (Gerard 2009). The Steelworkers contend that their membership can play an active role in recognising the initial effects of climate change as well as use their expertise in various types of employment to lead the way towards a greener economy. Additionally, a merger with the environmentally active union PACE (which included the Oil Chemical and Atomic Workers, one of the first unions to stage an environmental strike against Shell Oil in 1973) also pressured the union to fully integrate the fight against climate change into the cause d'être of the union. The Steelworkers now have an entrenched health, safety and environment department that links the day-to-day issues of the union at various levels with larger environmental problems, including climate change.

Furthermore, the Steelworkers advocate for a solution aimed at protecting their current membership and maintaining a manufacturing sector in the United States (Gerard 2006; Greenhouse 2008). Thus, policy testimony, policy releases and interviews all demonstrate that they believe in solutions that combat clauses in trade agreements that allow for capital flight in response to one country increasing environmental standards. They also demand that there should be progressive taxation on the *consumption* (the target of American legislation is often largely on production) of products with high carbon emissions regardless of where they are made, so as to ensure companies cannot avoid abiding by emissions legislation by importing goods made in countries with lower environmental standards (Gerard 2009). Accordingly, they focus on green jobs (a term with contested definitions), which they define as jobs that aim to revitalise the American manufacturing sector through using manufacturing workers to produce environmentally friendly goods, such as wind turbines or public transit vehicles (United Steelworkers 2008b). Moreover, the Steelworkers advocate for the creation of green jobs as a means of renewing urban areas that have been hit hard by capital flight and environmental destruction (areas near chemical plants that tend to be poor, for example) and as a pathway out of poverty (Apollo Alliance 2008). In order for the USW to obtain legitimacy regarding their climate work in the American political system (for instance from the Democratic Party), they must present solutions that are not viewed as too radical. In response, they support a domestic, market-based cap-and-trade system aimed at reducing GHG emissions nationally, while maintaining an American manufacturing base. The Steelworkers often frame the climate issue as one that could lead to a loss of American industrial competitiveness (through carbon leakage, for example, in which stringent GHG reductions mechanisms could lead to capital flight to parts of the world with more lax regulations). They argue the role of the union is to ensure that any policy aimed at combating climate change protects an American-based workforce.

Also originating from their emphasis on the direct connection between work and climate, the Steelworkers believe that creating progressive alliances that include both labour and environmental organisations is essential to comprehensively solve climate issues while ensuring solutions are economically just. Thus, they have forged alliances with broad-based environmental actors such as the Sierra Club, forming the BlueGreen Alliance in 2006, which is currently active in six states and aims at creating a long-term united labour–environment force.

United Auto Workers (UAW)

The UAW was slow to recognise the existence of anthropogenic climate change and of its possible effects, siding with industry (in the 1980s, up until the Kyoto Protocol of 1997) to challenge the validity of scientific arguments that focused on the need to reduce carbon dioxide emissions to properly address climate change (Obach 2004a). Interpreting this argument (rather than the problem of climate change) as a fundamental threat to their survival, the UAW acted defensively to protect the jobs of their existing membership, emphasising scientific uncertainty surrounding climate change. Their members have declined significantly, peaking at one million in the 1970s and declining to roughly 390,000 active members today. The UAW has viewed and presented the jobs provided by the auto industry as directly related to the working class's upward mobility into the middle class and sees the car as a fundamental aspect of American life. This has fallen in line with the dominant perception of the automobile and the jobs provided through its production within American culture. The issue of climate change and arguments in favour of targeting automobile emissions are believed to pose a threat to this fundamental aspect of American class mobility.

The increasing general consensus surrounding anthropogenic climate change forced the UAW to address the issue. They have framed both the potential effects *and* proposed solutions to climate change as threats to the jobs of their membership (United Auto Workers 2009). Using a strategy to protect their current membership, the UAW has continually asserted that increased Corporate Average Fuel Economy (CAFE) legislation would disproportionately target the work of their membership. In congressional testimony, former UAW president Ron Gettelfinger discounted CAFE's effectiveness and argued it would disproportionately hurt the light truck industry, hurting American workers (Gettelfinger 2007). Even though they have reluctantly recognised the existence of climate change, the UAW still maintains a narrow focus, acting almost entirely on legislation surrounding automobile emissions standards.

Perceiving emissions legislation as unfairly targeting the American auto industry, the UAW has proposed an alternative, which would target all industries with high emissions equally. Gettelfinger stated further that the US needs "a comprehensive policy, which would include all sectors discussing ways to reduce emissions" (Gettelfinger 2007). They want to avoid auto manufacturers moving production to another state or country with lower labour and environmental standards in case of increased emissions standards. Following from their framing of the issue as one in which the American auto industry is necessary for the existence of an American middle class, the UAW argues solutions to the high emissions of automobiles should be combated through government funding of research and development of cleaner technology, in order to ensure the industry's continued existence. For this they are demanding a new "Marshall Plan" (United Auto Workers 2009). It would include government funding for new technology that would help keep the American auto industry competitive, would keep "good union jobs in America" and would help reduce overall emissions (Gettelfinger 2007; United Auto Workers 2009). Ultimately, they frame the issue as one of survival, thus their solutions are aimed at ensuring the continued place of the auto industry within the American economy and social life.

Stemming from this focus on ensuring the survival of the American automobile industry, interacting with the federal American system and realising the need to address climate change, the UAW has focused on fighting for the creation of a single national fuel efficiency standard, rather than creating variable regional/state legislations. The UAW has primarily used its influence within the Democratic Party to effect legislation regarding emissions standards. Recently, the UAW elected a new president, Bob King, who argues that climate concerns must become more integral to the union, rather than something they reluctantly deal with. While the UAW had not worked with environmental groups, arguing that their interests were too divergent, since King's election, it has joined the BlueGreen Alliance, of which the Steelworkers were already a part. This is part of a larger shift in strategy by the UAW in response to both membership declines and crises in the American automobile industry. It is difficult to assess at this point whether there will be a substantive shift in the UAW's understanding, framing of and action on climate change.

IF Metall

IF Metall, initially reluctant to acknowledge the threat of climate change and its relation to human activities, eventually did so in the mid-1990s, "when everyone else did", as one researcher stated (Bern 2009). IF Metall has strong historical ties to the Swedish Social Democrats (SAP). The union was influenced by former SAP Minister of State Goran Persson's advocacy on climate issues in the mid-1990s (Bern 2009). Despite admission of the climate change threat, IF Metall does not believe that the energy-intensive work of their members plays much of a role in climate change, arguing that Sweden has been able to combine economic growth with a reduction in carbon emissions (Bern 2009). This is in line with the social democratic ideology of the union, which has focused on the material well-being of workers in the Swedish context, achieved through an export-based economy with a strong manufacturing sector and effective wealth redistribution policies. IF Metall's activities on climate change occur largely within Sweden, rather than in an international context.

Generally, IF Metall seeks to find solutions for problems (including climate change) through consultation and compromise with well-established actors. This leads to a hesitance to accept and work with new, potentially disruptive actors (as IF Metall perceives them) within the Swedish political system, including environmental interest groups. LO, the large blue-collar federation (of which IF Metall is a part), is one of the major actors within the neo-corporatist political system. The federation actively played a role in institutionalising particular labour–capital relations, affording labour a central role in the political system. As Metall was the largest LO union for a long time, they held particular power and have had strong ties with the Social Democratic Party in power during much of the latter half of the twentieth century, participating as a board member on the previous Social Democratic government's Oljekommission (Oil Commission), which sought to develop policy and ideas concerning renewable energy use. It is through the Social Democrats and working with industrial partners that IF Metall has focused most of its climate/environmental work. The union continues to try to assert most of its influence through these historically established actors. Since 2006, the governing party in Sweden has been the centre-right Moderate Party. When asked if IF Metall planned to work with or influence the party's environmental/climate policy, one researcher succinctly stated "no, not at all" (Bern 2009).

However, as IF Metall has acknowledged climate problems, the union has begun to open up to the idea of speaking with environmental groups as they have become increasingly legitimate (Bern 2009) and the power/influence of the Social Democrats and Swedish trade unions has declined. Most of IF Metall's advocated solutions involve the central union working with industry and the state to develop technocratic solutions to environmental issues, with little consultation with and input from environmental groups (Bern 2008). IF Metall's main report on energy issues, "Industry: A part of the solution", used interviews and other data from 12 major companies for which IF Metall's members work, but did not include consultations with environmental organisations. Further, IF Metall is reluctant to relinquish power to other influences over the Social Democratic Party, criticising and being slow to accept the views and proposals of other political partners, Miljöpartiet (the Green Party) and Vänsterpartiet (the Left Party) (Johnsson and Pettersson 2009).[1] Furthermore, IF Metall supports the continued existence of nuclear power, while the major environmental groups in Sweden are staunchly opposed to it, as are elements within the Social Democrats (Friberg 2008). This is a contentious issue and has complicated partnerships between labour, environmental groups and political parties. However, one researcher at IF Metall believes this is a minor issue that has been exaggerated and overblown in the media (Bern 2009).

Kommunal

Largely influenced by the 1992 UN Conference on sustainable development in Rio de Janeiro, Kommunal (in 1994) boldly stated that they were to become the greenest union in Sweden (Berglund 2009). This represented a desire to incorporate a new area of action within their realm, as environmental issues had not been seen to be a major trade union issue. However, this case is one of institutional lag, and despite the shift in the understanding of the issue, established norms and rules of action prevented a full realisation of this ideal (Berglund 2009). Still, Kommunal is active in incorporating climate issues into their framework of action, presenting them as an essential trade union issue, as the choices and actions of the membership have direct climate impacts (Thörn 2007).

Kommunal frames the problem as one that can be addressed through the lifestyles and work of its members and they conceptualise and frame climate change as an international issue. Kommunal's rhetoric on affecting climate change focuses on the need for sustainable agricultural practices both in Sweden and abroad, as this is the area of the union where the connection between work and climate is most obvious (Kommunal 2008; Berglund 2009). In 2002, Kommunal merged with the Agricultural Workers' Union, partly because Kommunal wanted to increase the profile of its environmental work. The Agricultural Union exemplified a direct connection between work and environment and was seen as an area in which their environmental work could be of particular importance. Since the merger, agricultural issues as they relate to climate have become an integral part of Kommunal's environmental work. This can be seen with the release of the report "Vattna, gödsla och gallra" (roughly translated as "Water, Fertilize, Weed!") from their June 2010 congress that discusses the importance of and specific means to reducing climate impact of agriculture and food production; they also discuss the importance of making non-agricultural workers aware of the links between food choices and climate impact.

The trade union emphasises that the Global North is disproportionately to blame for the causes and effects of climate change, but the Global South bears the disproportionate brunt of its effects, as former chairperson Ylva Thörn stated in 2007: "we, the rich countries have been the environmental villain for years dumping our waste in developing countries; now we're asking those countries to clean up our mess?" (Thörn 2007, 3). So, the trade union believes – as a response to internal barriers to complete integration of the issue and due to a focus on international worker solidarity – that they need to incorporate climate concerns into their realm of action. Further, Kommunal frames the issue as one that is related to other forms of exploitation, such as gender (stating that women in the developing world are and will be the most affected by climate change) and class and that it is always the role of the trade union to fight beyond the workplace to combat larger social inequalities, both within and outside of Sweden. As Thörn states, it is the union's role to stand up for "rights/fairness and solidarity and to reduce economic and environmental pressures" (Thörn 2007, 3). Overall, Kommunal has incorporated issues of climate change into their framework of action. Confronting them stems from their belief that the union's role extends beyond the local workplace into the larger society and even internationally to ensure equality and social justice.

They believe the union has to play an educational role, teaching the membership about the causes and effects of climate change as well as what they as citizens can and should do about it (Kommunal 2008). Through their union newspaper, congress publications and speeches, Kommunal focuses on actions, such as conserving energy in the home or pressuring employers to change energy sources (public heat and energy consumption account for about 10 per cent of total emissions in Sweden) or use food that is produced locally and in non-energy-intensive ways. This focus is framed and interpreted as a need to create a more direct link to the action and influence of the membership over climate issues (Kommunal 2008).

Comparison and conclusions

While all four unions define the struggle against climate change in terms of protection of their membership, there are distinct differences in the ways they have reacted to and framed the climate change threat. This can be partially explained by the formal rules and informal political culture in which the unions are acting. Various authors, such as Obach and Imig, argue that the competitive, federal and plural nature of the American political system presents a paradox for organisations seeking to affect institutional and social change, as they rely on distinguishing themselves individually in order to be perceived as having a valid purpose, while simultaneously they must ally with other organisations in order to survive economically and to have a political lobbying power (Obach 2004b; Imig 1992). In contrast, the Swedish sociopolitical system is defined as neo-corporatist, in which social tensions and conflicts (both existing and potential) are regulated through institutionalised integrative strategies (Burns and Carson 2005). Not only are the strategies to resolve tensions well defined, so too are the legitimate actors in the system, including trade unions and environmental movement organisations. This difference helps to understand why there have been more alliances in the US than in Sweden *and* why the UAW has acted so narrowly in defence of its membership. Both Kommunal and IF Metall emphasise the importance of dialogue with established actors. Since they are themselves established actors in the system, they have not felt the need to ally with environmental groups *nor* did they act as narrowly as the American unions.

Organisational structure and material conditions are also important determining factors explaining the different approaches of Trade Unions in different countries. While both the USW and the UAW are federal in structure, the UAW is much more regionally concentrated than the Steelworkers and represents a much narrower membership. This condition, along with declining membership and industry crisis, helps explain why they have been so defensive of their existing members and of the continued existence of the automobile sector. Since the membership and types of employment the Steelworkers represent are much more diverse, it has enabled them the freedom and opportunity to experiment with environmental work at multiple levels. Likewise, it allows them to advocate for a shift to a greener economy, as potential targets against any particular economic sector would not have as many adverse effects as on the UAW membership. Like the American unions, the structure of the Swedish unions reflects the larger state structure. Both unions are centralised with workplace branches. Thus, most action and decision-making on climate change emanates from the centre and is disseminated to the members through education. This is in sharp contrast to the Steelworkers, where much of the climate, alliance and activism work originated at the local and regional levels. Kommunal, while still quite centralized, has used multi-level work in order to incorporate climate change as a trade union issue, though in this case at the international level. This occurred in part in reaction to internal hesitance to fully incorporate climate issues into the cause of the union, while the leadership had a strong desire to make climate change one of the central union issues.

Overall, while we can see that the setting and structure in which trade unions act affects how they react to various threats – in this case climate change – it is clearly not the only defining factor determining their actions, understanding and framing of the issue. This is evidenced by the fact that the two unions in each setting have acted quite differently from one another and in fact, one may see more similarities between the Steelworkers and Kommunal and the UAW and IF Metall than between the two unions in each country. Another useful concept for understanding the unions' differences concerns collective interpretations of an issue as it relates to an organisation's main cause. Not only are collective interpretations important, so too is ideology. These combine to influence ways of conceptualising issues, problems, interests, goals and problem solving. By focusing on these collective interpretations and understanding that they differ even among actors with similar goals, we can begin to understand some of the similarities between the active unions, the Steelworkers and Kommunal. Both work within a social unionism framework, which stipulates that the role of the union is to go beyond the workplace and to actively use their social, economic and political position to ameliorate social problems, regardless if there is any immediate trade union connection to a given issue. Thus, Kommunal, working from a social unionism perspective, has made climate change a trade union issue as they believe it to be an essential social and economic problem in need of action. This is partly based on their historical commitment to addressing international social, economic and political problems. This framework has led Kommunal to define climate change as a fundamental threat to human well-being and their focus on social unionism and internationalism has led them to characterise the issue as one related to international economic inequality and exploitation. It has also led them to view climate change as something related to the day-to-day work of the membership. Hence, they have focused on education and clarification of the relationship between individual and municipal action and effects on the climate. Similarly, the USW are working within an ideology of social unionism and have defined climate change as international in nature and as fundamentally related to the social and economic well-being of people, including their membership.

The UAW and IF Metall, partly due to their historical power, maintain a narrower ideological view, in which they are focused on maintaining a partnership with industry and of protecting their existing membership/institutional power. Consequently, they have been unwilling to integrate new ideas, in particular those regarding climate change, into their union ideology. Over time they have reluctantly accepted that climate change is a trade union issue, and the framework in which they work has largely determined how they have presented the problem. Specifically, they outline the challenge as one that can be overcome by tweaking existing industrial practices and working with actors already deemed legitimate, such as industry and particular political parties. This fact is especially apparent for IF Metall, which was once the largest trade union in Sweden, but has had a declining membership in recent years. Similar to the UAW, IF Metall has acted defensively in order to try to protect its historical institutional power. Overall, it is an interaction of many factors, including, but not limited to, the organisational structure; the types of employment represented; the political structure and the "rules of the game"; combined with the collective interpretation of climate change by each organisation and key actors that influence the way each trade union reacts in the face of a common threat like climate change. This analysis demonstrates that, depending on the relationship of influential factors and political conjunctures, unions can play an integral role in combining work and environment issues and finding solutions to climate change.

Note

1 Since the 2010 election and the re-election of the centre-right alliance, the left-green alliance has split up.

References

Apollo Alliance (2008) "The New Apollo Program: Clean Energy, Good Jobs", in *An Economic Strategy for American Prosperity*, Apollo Alliance, San Francisco.

Berglund, S. (2009) Interview with the author, 19 March.

Bern, A.-B. (2008) *Industrin-en del av lösningen*, Sandvikens Tryckeri, Stockholm.

—— (2009) Interview with the author, 26 March.

Burns, T. and Carson, M. (2005) "European Union, neo-corporatists, and pluralist governance arrangements: lobbying and policy-making patterns in a comparative perspective", *International Journal of Regulation and Governance*, vol. 2, no. 2, pp. 129–175.

Friberg, L. (2008) "Conflict and Consensus: The Swedish Model of Climate Change", in H. Compsten and I. Bailey (eds), *Turning Down the Heat*, Macmillan, New York.

Gerard, L. (2006) "United Steelworkers: Letters to Congress", www.usw.org, accessed 24 January 2009.

—— (2009) "United Steelworkers: Speeches/Interviews-Testimony of Leo W. Gerard on Aspects of Trade on Climate Change Before the Subcommittee on Trade", www.usw.org, accessed 7 April 2009.

Gettelfinger, R. (2007) "Testimony of Ron Gettelfinger before the Subcommittee on Energy and Air Quality; Committee on Energy and Commerce", Testimony of Ron Gettelfinger, President, International Union, United Automobile, Aerospace & Agricultural Implement Workers of America (UAW) on the subject of "Climate Change and Energy Security: Perspectives from the Automobile Industry", US Government Printing Office, Washington, DC.

Göteborgs-Posten (2008) "Metall ska försöka ändra mp:s politik", 17 May.

Greenhouse, S. (2008) "Millions of Jobs of a Different Collar", *The New York Times*, 26 May.

Grossfeld, J. (2008) "Leo Gerard 'Absolutely Indispensable' to Labor-Environmental Alliance", *USW News*, 16 June.

Hirsch, B. and MacPherson, D. (2011) www.unionstats.com, accessed 29 November 2011.

IF Metall (2008) "IF Metall: Industrin ska bidra till en bra miljö", 7 March, www.ifmetall.se, accessed 29 January 2009.

—— (2008) "IF Metall: Gruppvisa diskussioner om programförklaringen", IF Metall Kongress, Stockholm.

—— (2008) "Kongress Extra: IF Metalls första ordinarie, Kongress 13–16 Maj 2008", *Kongress Extra*, IF Metall, Stockholm, pp. 1–8.

Imig, D. (1992) "Resource Mobilization and Survival Tactics of Poverty Advocacy Groups", *The Western Political Quarterly*, vol. 45, no. 2, pp. 501–520.

Johnsson, G. and Pettersson, L. O. (2009) "Sahlins samarbete stort hot mot partiet", *Dagens Nyheter*, 14 February.

Kjellberg, A. (2005) "Mergers in a Class-segmented Trade Union System", in J. Waddington (ed.) *Restructuring Representation: The Merger Process and Trade Union Structural Development in Ten Countries*, P.I.E.-Peter Lang, Brussels.

—— (2011) "The Decline in Swedish Union Density Since 2007", *Nordic Journal of Working Life Studies*, vol.1, no. 1, pp. 67–93.

Kommunal (2008) "Klimatpolitik i pratiken-hur gör man", www.socialdemokraterna.se/Internationellt/Klimatkonferens-den-6-september, accessed 26 January 2009.

LO (2010) "LOs Energi Politik", Trade Union Policy Report, LO, Stockholm.

Obach, B. (2004a) *Labor and the Environmental Movement: The Quest for Common Ground*, MIT Press, Cambridge, MA.

—— (2004b) "New Labor: Slowing the Treadmill of Production?" *Organization and Environment*, vol. 17, no. 3, pp. 337–354.

Thörn, Y. (2007) "Ylva Thörn"s tal pa Kongressen", Kommunal, Stockholm.

United Auto Workers (2009) "UAW: Energy and Environment", *UAW Website,* www. uaw.org, accessed 26 January 2009.

United Steelworkers (2006a) "Securing Our Children"s World: Our Union and the Environment", United Steelworkers, Pittsburgh, PA.

—— (2006b) "USW Slams Feds for Turning Blind Eye to Public Health Threat", *USW News*, 13 November.

—— (2008a) "United Steelworkers: Health, Safety and Environment Department", www.usw.org, accessed 26 January 2009.

—— (2008b) "USW: BlueGreen Alliance", www.usw.org, accessed 26 January 2009.

Waddington, J. (2005) "United States: Merging in a Hostile Environment", in J. Waddington (ed.) *Restructuring Representation: The Merger Process and Trade Union Structural Development in Ten Countries*, P.I.E.-Peter Lang, Brussels.

Young, J. (2009) Interview with the author, 6 March 2009.

17 Trade unions and the transition away from 'actually existing unsustainability'

From economic crisis to a new political economy beyond growth

John Barry

> Every society clings to a myth by which it lives. Ours is the myth of economic growth.
>
> (Jackson 2009, 5)

Introduction: the inevitability of the transition from unsustainability and the greening of trade unionism

Trade unions have played an important role in mitigating the excesses of capitalism and other forces of non-democracy historically. It is clear that they can and must rise to the challenge of the transition away from unsustainability, the political challenge for the twenty-first century. Yet trade unions have played an often contradictory role in the struggle for a less unsustainable and unjust world.

On the one hand, if one takes a broad conception of unsustainability – one which encompasses democracy, justice, equality, quality of life as well as environmental concerns – one can present a case for trade unions as always having had a concern with the creation of a less unsustainable social order. That they have failed (and often continue to fail) to live up to this hope does not diminish their current and future importance in the political struggle for a transition away from 'actually existing unsustainability' (Barry 2012). From campaigns around public health, worker safety, job security, defending human rights, freedom of speech, democratic politics, as well as supporting struggles for access to land and other resources, to 'green bans' in the 1970s and 1980s, these and other campaigns make the trades-union movement a movement against unsustainability, injustice and inequality. Yet, on the other hand, as this chapter will argue, we have to also recognise that much like the broad 'labour movement', and the traditional political left (socialism and social democracy), trade unionism has also been a force supporting and promoting unsustainability. This is perhaps nowhere more evident than in its uncritical embracing of orthodox economic growth (and capital accumulation) and consequently an overly narrow focus on issues around formal employment, pay and conditions. For example, trade unions have supported 'coal production, nuclear power and airport expansion' (Wall 2010, 132–3) and often have explicitly mis-portrayed environmental conservation issues in terms of 'jobs versus the environment' and sided with political forces for unsustainability – such as the nation-state and corporations – against environmentalists. In this support of orthodox economic growth, the trades-union movement is in keeping with the almost full spectrum domination of the political imagination of both the advanced capitalist, industrial societies and the Global South by this imperative for undifferentiated, orthodox GDP-measured economic growth. In so supporting and having its policies largely orientated towards orthodox economic growth, formal employment, etc., this chapter suggests that significant sections of trade union movement (especially in Europe and North America) have become divorced from a vision of the purpose of the trade union movement as the fundamental transformation of social, economic and political structures of society.

This chapter suggests that in freeing itself from the stultifying grip of economic growth, and in embracing the idea that the creation of a sustainable society is about the struggle for a different type of society (as opposed to an 'environmentally friendly' version of the current one), that the emergence of a green trade unionism (one which links the struggles against unsustainability, inequality and injustice) represents the opportunity for the *repoliticisation, re-radicalisation and revitalisation* of the trade union movement. Without this fundamental repoliticisation and re-radicalisation it is difficult to see how the trade unions and broad labour movement can contribute much to our thinking and action on providing solutions to the real and present dangers (and transformative opportunities) presented by climate change, peak oil and gas, biodiversity devastation, growing national and global inequalities, the feminisation of world poverty and the ethical obscenity of the most vulnerable in the world suffering most from actually existing unsustainability. Actually existing unsustainability was not caused by the most vulnerable nor have they enjoyed its fruits. In this context of actually existing unsustainability, there is an opportunity – one is minded to say obligation – for trade unions to rethink their aims and objectives, to re-orientate themselves towards the inter-linked struggles against unsustainability and injustice.

There are good reasons for placing the question of the relationship between trade unionism and the environment within the broader context of the *politics of actually existing unsustainability* rather than a *politics for (future) sustainability*. This recasts the usual way of thinking issue, which is inevitably about the realisation or achievement of sustainability, sustainable development or environmental protection. The analysis of actually existing unsustainability should take priority over the analysis of sustainability. One gets a very different analysis when one begins from where we are in conditions of injustice, suffering and avoidable harm, rather than seeking to develop compelling and intellectually coherent – but abstract – benchmarks or criteria against which we can judge present-day, real-world conditions of injustice. *In short, in a similar way that the fight against injustice is not the same as a fight for some positive conception of justice, likewise the struggle against unsustainability is not the same as the struggle for sustainability.* According to Simon (one of the few contemporary political thinkers to develop a theory of injustice, as opposed to justice), we can identify injustice without recourse to a theory of justice (that is injustice cannot be reduced to meaning the lack or absence of justice), largely through the ideas of identifiable human suffering and harm. That is injustice can be based on an expanded notion of identifiable forms of human harm and suffering. As he puts it:

> It makes a difference whether we describe our political actions as part of a *fight against injustice, against other people's suffering*, or as a contest for justice. The two labels do not constitute different ways of talking about the same thing ... Justice beckons us to create the positive in the future whereas injustice frantically yells at us to eradicate the negative in the present.
>
> (Simon 1995, 1; emphasis added)

An interesting point Simon makes in this regard is that from an environmental perspective a critique of the current unsustainable economic system does not and should not depend for its validity on the specification of some positive sustainable alternative. While from a political point of view of persuading people of one's position, one might wish to develop a worked out alternative, this should not be a requirement for the critique to be politically considered and taken seriously in public policy debate. As he notes:

> the negative recommendation stands on its own, without the inclusion of a positive alternative ... *Requiring that negative recommendations depend upon positive alternatives has the effect of undermining the negative recommendations.* We need to listen to the negative recommendations, irrespective of whether the negative criticisms also contain positive proposals.
>
> (Simon 1995, 14; emphasis added)

The argument presented in this chapter is that the trade union and labour movement should be primarily concerned with tackling and reducing unsustainability, inequality and harm, full stop, rather than feeling forced (as much of the green movement has) to also develop a costed, evidence-based, policy-ready alternative sustainable development model. It is because we can identify harm and suffering without recourse to a theory of justice or sustainability, that we can say the experience of injustice and unsustainability cannot be reduced to the absence of being treated in accordance to some account of justice or living in some version of a 'sustainable society' (Dobson 2007, 53–103). Presenting the relationship between trade unionism and the environment in terms of reducing harm and focusing on helping the most vulnerable is, I suggest, a powerful way to address the urgency of actually existing unsustainability and its associated exploitation of people, abuse of the planet and the non-human world. This focus on unsustainability and injustice also has the advantage of allowing the possibility for political action and struggle now without the need for some shared 'blueprint' or 'green-print' for what a future sustainable and just society looks like (Barry 2012), which can take time, energy and create unproductive divisions amongst potential allies.

Beyond economic growth to economic security

A long-standing green argument is that to address unsustainability the economy needs to be reorientated towards enhancing and being judged by its capacity to promote 'quality of life', 'well-being' and 'happiness', rather than orthodox economic growth. As the new economics foundation (an organisation that perhaps more than any other has consistently lobbied and provided the evidence base for a post-growth green economic perspective within the UK) puts it:

> the purpose of economy should be to enhance the well-being of the citizens of the country, in a way that is socially just, and environmentally sustainable. That is, the level of economic growth achieved in an economy is not a sufficient measure of that economy's success or failure to deliver prosperity to society. This is because economic growth does not, in itself, tell us anything about our quality of life.
>
> (new economics foundation 2008, 1–2)

The economy and economic growth are, after all, means not ends in themselves. We live in societies with economies, not economies with societies, a view which profoundly challenges neo-classical economics and the neoliberal worldview. And it has to be said that traditional trade union thinking and politics has often focused on the uncritical acceptance of the imperative for economic growth and full employment (often male) in the formal economy. As outlined more fully below, 'economic security' could be a replacement for 'economic growth' within a more thoroughly green (and politicised) trade unionism. Such a move would enable unions and the labour movement to shape arguments and policies for a new type of economy, in which structural issues that have rather fallen off the trade-union movement (certainly in the developed world), such as redistribution and reducing socioeconomic inequality (Wilkinson and Pickett 2009), once again become central concerns of trade unionism. 'Economic security' has the advantage of presenting a positive and attractive discourse for addressing the problems of actually existing unsustainability. Using the language and analysis of economic security introduces ways of arguing and presenting the case for a less growth-orientated economy and high-consumption society, which at the same time aims to raise quality of life while lowering inequality. It is important (not least strategically) that a green critique of 'growth' should be viewed as a critique of orthodox and *undifferentiated growth* as measured by conventional economics. It is important to stress that the critique of growth is reserved for what Daly calls 'uneconomic growth' – the expansion of economic activities (production and consumption) that (after a threshold) undermine or compromise human flourishing and the ecological and resource preconditions for the human economy. It is perfectly consistent to criticise orthodox/capitalist economic growth, which creates the growth of credit-fuelled consumerism, arms and weapons, yet support growth in, for example, education, public health, public transport or subsidised organic farming. *Thus, when we talk of 'economic growth' it refers to 'undifferentiated, orthodox economic growth' as measured by conventional national accounting measurements such as GDP.*

One of the long-standing and defining features of modern green politics since its origins has been its heretical critique of economic growth, particularly consumerism. Yet, as the current economic crisis aptly demonstrates, if (too many) people save rather than consume, the capitalist system becomes unstable as economic growth fails, people lose jobs, there is widespread destruction of economic potential, disinvestment and a whole plethora of social, community, personal, psychological and political problems associated with economic recession. In short, what the current economic crisis demonstrates is that a capitalist economy becomes unstable if it cannot maintain annual growth rates of around 3 per cent. As Tim Jackson puts it: ' ... modern economies are driven towards economic growth ... in a growth-based economy, growth is functional for stability. The capitalist model has no easy route to a steady state position. *Its natural dynamics push it towards one of two states: expansion or collapse*' (Jackson 2009, 64; emphasis added). The challenge for trade unions lies here: if orthodox, capitalist-based economic growth is both bio-physically impossible (in terms of climate change, water shortages, etc.), and also politically and socially undesirable in terms (as indicated further below) of being unable to lower socioeconomic inequalities and tackle poverty, what replaces economic growth?

There are many potential contenders for what replaces economic growth that have been canvassed over the last 150 years – from John Stuart Mill's 'stationary state', to more recent work on 'quality of life', 'well-being' and 'prosperity' (Jackson 2009). All share a number of components and have a large degree of overlap. The one I wish to explore here is the notion of 'economic security' (Barry 2009). I take this term from a 2004 report by the ILO entitled *Economic Security for a Better World*, which found that 'economic security' coupled with democratic representation and equality were the main determinants of well-being, tolerance and social stability (ILO 2004). Of particular interest, given the connection between consumerism, irresponsibility and diminished human well-being, are the opening lines of the report:

> All human beings need a sense of security, to give a sense of belonging, a sense of stability and a sense of direction. *People who lack basic security in themselves, in their families, in their workplaces and in their community tend to become socially irresponsible. They tend to behave opportunistically, and they tend to lose a sense of moderation.* Moreover, periods and areas of

mass insecurity have, historically, always bred intolerance, extremism and violence.

(International Labor Organization 2004, 3; emphasis added)

The fact that this research was produced from an organisation that includes the trade union movement is significant, since it offers some grounds for a green 'step change' in the thinking, purpose and strategy of trade unions in the twenty-first century. How this has influenced trade unions 'on the ground' is less obvious. Some unions, such as the Trades Union Congress (TUC) in the UK, seem to be moving in this direction (TUC 2008). The ILO Report defines economic security as follows:

> *Economic security* is composed of *basic social security*, defined by access to basic needs, infrastructure pertaining to health, education, dwelling, information, and social protection, as well as *work-related security*. The report delineates seven components of *work-related security* ... two are essential for basic security: income security and voice representation security. Basic security means limiting the impact of uncertainties and risks people face daily while providing a social environment in which people can belong to a range of communities, have a fair opportunity to pursue a chosen occupation and develop their capacities via what the International Labor Organization calls decent work.
>
> (ILO 2004, 1)

The report found that:

> People in countries that provide citizens with a high level of economic security have a higher level of happiness on average, as measured by surveys of national levels of life-satisfaction and happiness ... *The most important determinant of national happiness is not income level – there is a positive association, but rising income seems to have little effect as wealthy countries grow more wealthier. Rather the key factor is the extent of income security, measured in terms of income protection and a low degree of income inequality.*
>
> (ILO 2004, 1; emphasis added).

Such findings, also echoed in the work of others such as Wilkinson and Pickett (2009) and Standing (2002), give some empirical support to long-standing arguments stressing the need for policies to lower socioeconomic inequality to enhance individual and collective socioeconomic security and increase well-being. The ILO report finds that 'welfare state' provision of social security for citizens is an important determinant of high economic security. The report also points out that insecurity is generated by patterns of economic globalisation, which produce endemic or structural insecurity in terms of employment, social welfare and income. The report indicates how the need to attract 'footloose' multinational capital, or the imperative of 'economic competitiveness', results in cuts to income protection or publicly provided goods and services such as education or health, all of which undermine economic security. As forms of *structural*, manufactured vulnerability, the report suggests that existing 'social insurance' approaches to cover these risks are inadequate (ILO 2004, xvii). More wide-ranging and radical structural change in how the economy operates is required to minimise these threats to economic security.

To focus on economic security as a main objective of macro-economic policy does not imply an end to entrepreneurialism or innovation. Any alternative to our current economic growth-focused model needs to take the question seriously, how to ensure that stagnation and regress will not be the outcome of a post-growth economy. We have reasons for thinking that innovation comes 'from consuming different things, rather than more of the same things' (Wilkinson and Pickett 2009, 221). Once one begins to free up key economic goals – such as 'innovation' from its technological–economic straitjacket, 'growth' from its reduction to material wealth or capital accumulation, 'work' from being identified solely with formally paid 'employment' – there is reason to suppose that *more, not less, innovation and creativity* (beyond technological or institutional spheres) will be the result of living in such a society, rather than stagnation or regress. In fact, such forms of innovation and creativity are *necessary features and therefore 'required'* for low-carbon, high well-being lives and communities, and not some 'added extra'. I suggest that this agenda of social innovation, a focus on well-being, not orthodox growth, work, not employment, the social economy, not the formal/cash economy, ought to be the agenda for a 'fit for purpose' twenty-first-century trade unionism.

The ILO report confirms the long-standing green critique that economic growth beyond a threshold need not necessarily contribute to well-being. It states that 'there is only a weak impact of economic growth on security measured over the longer-term. In other words, rapid growth does not necessarily create better economic security, although it sometimes can do if it is accompanied by appropriate social policies' (ILO 2004, 30). One of the key issues of the report is that it provides evidence of why and how the pursuit of orthodox economic growth policies can undermine economic security. It finds that

> being insecure has resonance in people's attitudes, which at times can be detrimental to their ideas of a decent society. In a recent survey taken by the Latino *barometro* in Latin America, 76% of the people surveyed were concerned about not having a job the following year, and a majority said that *they would not mind a non-democratic government if it could solve their unemployment problem.*
>
> (ILO 2004, 1–2; emphasis added)

As I have argued elsewhere (Barry 2012, 160–161) the pursuit of economic growth per se as a policy objective is largely an 'elite' phenomenon. The quote above demonstrates that most ordinary citizens are not necessarily concerned about GDP or GNP increases. What concerns them about any stalling of growth is the threat and associated negative consequences of unemployment. A key issue in the context of replacing economic growth with economic security is to find ways of safeguarding employment (and 'work' more generally) without it being connected to economic growth. The problem the ILO report indicates is the one that Booth highlights: 'Under existing macro-economic arrangements, growth is the only real answer to unemployment– society is hooked on growth' (Booth 2004, 153). In this context, to worry about unemployment can be interpreted as worrying about economic growth. If not only states (Barry 1999) but also citizens can contemplate embracing non-democratic ways in pursuit of orthodox economic growth objectives, then economic growth does not only threaten well-being but democratic values as well. Therefore, one has to seriously question the pursuit of policies aimed at promoting orthodox undifferentiated economic growth as a permanent economic objective. One could suggest that the support for non-democratic, and indeed unjust forms of orthodox economic growth, confirms its ideological character and capacity for capturing and limiting visions of what is socially and economically possible. Growth threatens economic security and in so doing causes social and geopolitical instability, deepens inequality and a potentially dangerous competition for resources (whether oil or formal employment).

The problem of economic insecurity (experienced at an individual or collective level) can also be applied at the level of the existing economic system itself. An economic system that has only two options – continual growth or collapse – cannot be stable or secure. On the one hand, this economic system is unsustainable, i.e. it is simply *biophysically impossible* to achieve continual economic growth. Although there is much hope put on the idea of 'decoupling' orthodox economic growth from energy, resource and pollution impacts, we have no evidence that this is either possible on the scale required or that there is any evidence for such 'ecological modernisation' within advanced industrial economies. For Jackson this decoupling is a 'myth' and 'assumptions that capitalism's propensity for efficiency will allow us to stabilise the climate and protect against resource scarcity are nothing short of delusional' (Jackson 2009, 7). This is the case even if growth is associated with more egalitarian and redistributive policies, that is alternative left-wing views that demonstrate or argue that less inequality does not undermine orthodox economic growth (Kirby and Murphy 2010; Putterman *et al.* 1998). So while clearly better from the point of view of equality and providing economic security, 'egalitarian growth' is, qua continuous economic growth, also biophysically impossible and therefore unsustainable.

On the other hand, capitalist stagnation brings with it its own dangers, i.e. no-growth is *not socially desirable* or politically acceptable (Jackson 2009; Barry 2009). Economic stagnation – as with the global economic crisis experienced since 2008 – is associated with high levels of unemployment, social dislocation, disinvestment and a lowering of well-being. This macro-level or system-level critique of the capitalist economy represents an updated version of Marx's analysis of the endemic 'crisis-ridden' character of capitalism. Hence, more radical conceptions of green political economy often accept significant elements of the Marxist analysis of capitalism, though without necessarily going along with its proposed solutions for or alternatives to capitalism, since most (though not all) streams of Marxism are committed to economic growth (Barry 1999, 2012). However, it is the 'myth' of exponential and economic growth as a permanent feature of an economy that is itself the problem and that needs to be abandoned. The current situation is that the majority of trade unions only go so far as advocating the 'greening of growth' and 'green capitalism' (such as can be seen in Green New Deal type policies) rather than fundamentally questioning economic growth itself. This reformist 'green growth/capitalism' strategy fits more easily with traditional trade union objectives such as securing well-paid formal employment and increasing the share of collectively produced wealth and income (i.e. orthodox economic growth) that goes to labour.

To tackle 'actually existing unsustainability' what is required is to explore ways of increasing the ecological and energy efficiency of human flourishing, not simply to focus on improving the energy and resource efficiency of economic growth (Barry 2012). Most Green New Deal type policies and strategies can be viewed as necessary but not sufficient to tackle actually existing unsustainability (Luke 2009), since they do not fundamentally challenge either economic growth or capitalism. What needs to be considered is this: what does a trade unionism that focuses on increasing the ecological efficiency of human flourishing and sees that objective as incompatible with orthodox economic growth and capitalism look like?

Economic security, equality and well-being

One of the most significant impacts of a shift away from economic growth as a central goal would be to undermine the justification of socioeconomic inequalities. The latter are usually justified or tolerated on the grounds that inequalities are necessary 'incentives' to motivate people (via the promise of differential, unequal rewards) towards entrepreneurial activity, 'hard work' and thus stimulate economic growth. As early proponents of the 'steady-state economy' pointed out, the shift from a society geared towards economic growth to a society where material growth is not a priority may lead to more extensive redistributive measures. This is a point made many years ago by forerunners of green economic thinking such as Herman Daly (Daly 1973). According to the orthodox growth view, growth is needed to eliminate poverty (by making the 'economic pie' bigger, not slicing it less unequally as it were). If, however, the option of baking a bigger pie is neither (ecologically) possible nor (socially) desirable, then poverty elimination can be solved only by more direct redistributive measures. It needs to be clarified that inequality causes poverty, not vice versa.

This focus on the 'dark side' of orthodox economic growth in terms of it managing rather than reducing socioeconomic equalities, should, on the face of it, offer a strong link to trade unionism's enduring principle of egalitarianism. It requires trade unionism to return to its explicitly political and oppositional origins by challenging capitalism's inevitable imperative for increasing inequalities and differences in life chances between classes. The link between a post-growth economic vision and a reduction of socioeconomic inequalities requires trade unionism to make redistribution and social justice more central. Since the struggle for equality must now be within a post-growth paradigm, this requires trade unionism to see its objectives in terms of transforming and challenging capitalism, rather than of seeking a greater share of the growing capitalist economic pie for workers. One of the reasons for focusing on lowering inequality is that socioeconomic inequality is both a driver and a product of orthodox economic growth. If one argues for a post-growth economy, it implies that the traditional political strategy for simply managing inequalities is no longer an option. As Seabrook puts it: 'The heroic age of consumption is surely over. Eventual curbs on consumption, the result of an omnivorous and accelerating depletion of the natural world, are inevitable. This will bring to the fore the issue of distributive justice once more' (Seabrook 2008, 6).

As Wilkinson and Pickett's research demonstrates, unequal societies almost always come out worse on a range of policy issues ranging from obesity, childhood mortality, drug use, literacy, social mobility, trust, teenage pregnancy and incidences of mental illness:

> Economic growth, for so long the great engine of progress, has, in the rich countries, largely finished its work. Not only have measures of wellbeing and happiness ceased to rise with economic growth but, as affluent societies have grown richer, there have been long-term rises in rates of anxiety, depression and numerous other social problems. *The populations of rich countries have got to the end of a long historical journey.*
> (Wilkinson and Pickett 2009, 5–6; emphasis added)

The issue for trade unions here is the misdistribution of wealth, implying that the focus of their work should be on lowering inequalities rather than focusing on increasing economic growth as a *permanent feature of an economy, and therefore as a permanent feature of the strategic objectives of the trade union movement.* Economic growth is not to be rejected 'in principle' as being 'intrinsically' bad, but is to be seen in terms of a society's evolution over time, as a policy that needs to be periodically reviewed, rather than a 'locked-in' or permanent feature of a society. One threshold (apart from obvious ecological ones) that can be identified to signal the point beyond which economic growth needs to be reconsidered, is when greater levels of inequality are required for economic growth, which reduces the range of components central for human flourishing. Other thresholds could be more directly related to human flourishing such as mental health, social trust or measurements of community and solidarity.

Another striking implication of inequality is its negative effect on social trust, social solidarity and sense of community (Lane 2000). This has significant implications for democracy, and can lead to hierarchical and paternalistic relations between supposedly equal citizens. Relations of dominations can occur, which are based on internalised senses of inequality and inferiority, where people are ashamed of their social status and believe to be a 'second-' or even 'third-class' citizen (Wolff and De-Shalit 2007). As Wilkinson and Pickett note: 'The problem is that second-class goods make us look like second-class people' (2009, 222). This is similar to the argument one often finds in the environmental justice movement, which finds that those marginalised communities who house a disproportionate amount of unwanted land uses (incinerators, waste dumps, etc.) often express the injustice and inequality of this in making the link that siting rubbish/waste easily communicates that those who live there are equated and linked with rubbish and waste (Schlosberg 1999). Such forms of social stratification (around race, class, ethnicity, sexuality or gender) are therefore incompatible with the fundamental equality required for democratic politics, and for living in a democratic society of equals. The empirical evidence is that as inequality increases in a society (as it has done over the past 30 years in most 'developed' countries), the rich become better able to shape the scope and nature of politics and determine the grammar of politics and economics, including promoting the ideology of economic growth. Work stretching from Goodin and Dryzek in the early 1980s to the more recent work of Solt (2008) finds that less well-off citizens give up on discussing political matters and effectively withdraw from politics.

Conclusion

One of the main concerns of this chapter was to embark on outlining and developing an alternative political economic vision and rationale for trade unionism able to contribute to the transition away from 'actually existing unsustainability' (Barry 2012). It suggests that trade unions outline their political project/s and strategies within a 'post-growth' context, which has until now largely been the preserve of green activists. While much of the above has been pitched at a theoretical or high strategic level, one practical implication is the need for deeper alliances and coalitions between the trade union and labour movements and the green movement. For example, the politics of a 'green new deal' (Green New Deal Group 2008; Barry 2010) and a 'just transition' have created one such opportunity in which labour and green movements can join to develop a strategy of the managed transition to a green, low-carbon and renewable-energy economy including the creation of decent, green-collar jobs. This helps to overcome some of the historical opposition between the two movements and the false view that the creation of a less unsustainable economy is incompatible with trade union objectives for economic security for workers and the creation of a less unequal society. However, the fact that this transition to a green economy is not uncontested or automatic also presents opportunities for both green and labour movements to engage in oppositional struggle. One recent example of this in the UK was the red–green coalition that formed to challenge the decision by the wind-turbine manufacturer Vestas to close its factory in the UK (Wall 2010, 132). Workers occupying the factory were supported by both green and union movements. We can distinguish between a 'greening trade unionism' that fits within a 'Green New Deal' paradigm (greening growth and capitalism) and a more radical and fully fledged 'green trade unionism', which challenges both orthodox economic growth and capitalism and like the Vestas occupation moves both green and union movements towards oppositional forms of political action. Examples of the latter might include the growing links between advocates for the 'social and solidarity economy' and the trade union movement, since the social and solidarity economy is a form of 'decoupled' economic activity that is not subject to the negative 'growth dynamic' of orthodox economic growth and contributes directly to human flourishing (Barry 2012). The social and solidarity economy stands as a sphere of activity within which economic security, equality and human flourishing can be attained and which stands in opposition to, rather than the 'greening' of, actually existing unsustainability. This is perhaps most noticeable in Latin America (Allard *et al.* 2008), but it also includes trade union support for cooperatives within the social and solidarity economy (ILO 2011).

Both reformist and more radical strategies are needed. They will differ according to countries, economic sectors, trade unions and other potential political allies (such as the green movement). There is no 'blueprint' or 'greenprint' that can dictate or predict such struggles and alliances. However, one clear implication of the argument presented in this chapter is that the reason why the 'green new deal' and arguments for the 'greening of the economy' can create such relatively easy alliances between the labour and green movements is that they remain within the paradigm of 'economic growth', formal employment. They are perhaps best seen as necessary steps, but insufficient in terms of developing a shared 'post-growth' political economic vision, which, as this chapter has suggested, is needed. This is a political debate to which the trade union and wider labour movements have yet to contribute. Whether couched in terms of 'economic security' as a possible replacement for economic growth, and/or prioritising of lowering of inequalities and the defence of democracy, what we need to see in the coming years is the transition from the 'greening' of the trade union movement to the emergence of an explicitly 'green' trade unionism. In this transition lies not only a measure of how politically relevant trade unionism will be to the challenges of life in a carbon-constrained, climate-changed world, but also how politicised it becomes as it challenges not just capitalism but also itself as part of the struggle for a 'just transition'.

References

Allard, J., Davidson, C. and Matthaei, J. (eds) (2008) *Solidarity Economy: Building Alternatives for People and Planet*, Changemaker Publications, Chicago.

Barry, J. (2012) *The Politics of Actually Existing Unsustainability: Human Flourishing in a Climate Changed, Carbon Constrained World*, Oxford University Press, Oxford.

——(2010) 'Towards a Green New Deal on the Island of Ireland: from economic crisis to a new political economy of sustainability', *Journal of Cross-Border Studies*, vol. 5, pp. 71–87.

——(2009) '"Choose Life" not Economic Growth: Critical Social Theory for People, Planet and Flourishing in an "Age of Nature"', *Current Perspectives in Social Theory*, vol. 26, no. 1, pp. 93–113.

——(1999) 'Marxism and Ecology', in A. Gamble, D. Marsh and T. Tant (eds), *Marxism and Social Science*, Macmillan, London.

Booth, D. (2004) *Hooked on Growth: Economic Addictions and the Environment*, Rowman and Littlefield, New York.

Daly, H. (ed.) (1973) *Toward a Steady State Economy*, W.H. Freeman & Co, San Francisco.

Dobson, A. (2007) *Green Political Thought*, fourth edition, Routledge, London.

Goodin, R. and Dryzek, J. (1980) 'Rational Participation: The Politics of Relative Power', *British Journal of Political Science*, vol. 10, no. 3, pp. 273–292.

Green New Deal Group (2008) *The Green New Deal*, new economics foundation, London.

International Labour Organization (ILO) (2004) *Economic Security for a Better World*, International Labour Organization, Geneva.

——(2011) 'Social and Solidarity Economy: Our Common Road towards Decent Work', www.ilo.org/empent/units/cooperatives/WCMS_166301/lang – en/index.htm (accessed 1 January 2012).

Jackson, T. (2009) *Prosperity without Growth: Economics for a Finite Planet*, Earthscan, London.

Kirby, P. and Murphy, M. (2010) 'Globalisation and Models of State: Debates and Evidence from Ireland', *New Political Economy*, vol. 16, no. 1, pp. 19–39.

Lane, R. (2000) *The Loss of Happiness in Market Democracies*, Yale University Press, New Haven, CT.

Luke, T. (2009) 'A Green New Deal: Why Green, How New, and What is the Deal?', *Critical Policy Studies*, vol. 3, no. 1, pp. 14–28.

new economics foundation (2008) *Think Piece for the Commission for Rural Communities: Economic Well-being*, new economics foundation, London.

Putterman, L., Roemer, J. and Silivestre, J. (1998) 'Does Egalitarianism Have a Future?', *Journal of Economic Literature*, vol. 36, no. 2, pp. 861–902.

Schlosberg, D. (1999) *Environmental Justice and the New Pluralism*, Oxford University Press, Oxford.

Seabrook, J. (2008) *Why do People Think Inequality is Worse than Poverty?* Joseph Rowntree Foundation, London.

Simon, T. (1995) *Democracy and Social Injustice: Law, Politics and Philosophy*, Rowman and Littlefield, Lanham, MD.

Solt, F. (2008) 'Economic Inequality and Democratic Political Engagement', *American Journal of Political Science*, vol. 52, no. 1, pp. 48–60.

Standing, G. (2002) *Beyond the New Paternalism: Basic Security as Equality*, Verso, London.

Trades Union Congress (TUC) (2008) 'A Green and Fair Future: For A Just Transition to a Low Carbon Economy', www.tuc.org.uk/social/tuc-14922-f0.cfm (accessed 1 January 2012).

Wall, D. (2010) *The Rise of the Green Left: Inside the Worldwide Ecosocialist Movement*, Pluto Press, London.

Wilkinson, R. and Pickett, K. (2009) *The Spirit Level: Why more Equal Societies Almost Always do Better*, Allen Lane, London.

Wolff, J. and De-Shalit, A. (2007) *Disadvantage*, Oxford University Press, Oxford.

18 Local place and global space

Solidarity across borders and the question of the environment

David Uzzell and Nora Räthzel

The globalising division of work

Global environmental degradation and the global division of labour are consequences of the overarching process of economically driven globalisation, one aspect of what Leichenko and O'Brien refer to as 'double exposure' (Leichenko and O'Brien 2008, 28). The focus of our analysis is on how these processes intersect with industrial relations and the formulation of trade union environmental strategies. Globalisation has heightened the 'North–South' divide where global income inequality has increased between countries (ILO 2008) as well as within individual nations (Cornia and Kiiski 2001). It has set workers of the South and the North in competition with each other. Under such conditions it is difficult for unions in the South and the North to develop common strategies that could benefit workers in all countries (Chan and Ross 2003; ILO 1998). Since economic globalisation is driven by transnational corporations (TNCs), trade unions are potentially, as the largest democratically organised institution in the world and traditionally the most powerful defenders of workers' rights, in the best position to challenge the negative effects of globalisation.

Globalisation represents a new form of dependency between the global and the local, which is why some authors talk about 'glocalisation' (Robertson 1992; Bauman 1998). Trade unions could be said to be 'glocal' organisations. On the one hand they are locally rooted in workers' everyday lives and have a deep knowledge and are part of the societal conditions in which work is embedded. At the same time, trade unions and workers worldwide are thrown together into a common global space, particularly when employed by the same TNC. The challenge for trade unions is to turn this 'throwntogetherness' (Massey 2005) into active negotiating power.

Climate change and social justice

Some of our respondents in the North expressed the view that unions in the South were more reluctant to accept climate change as a trade union issue. We found, however, that positions varied across and within unions, in the

South as well as in the North. For example, some unionists in Brazil and South Africa explained that their efforts in this area had not developed as much as they had in the North and that they had learned a lot from the North in this respect. One has to see this in the context of the economic and social conditions in these two countries, such as the unemployment rates and especially the high percentage of jobs in the informal economy; South Africa has an official unemployment rate of 23 per cent, while in Brazil it is 9 per cent (OECD 2010). Unemployment figures, however, do not distinguish between people who are experiencing short-term unemployment and the long-term unemployed. Additionally, there is in both countries a large 'informal sector' that is not uncommon in countries with large numbers of small unregistered companies, and where workers are neither covered by laws securing their working conditions nor are they members of unions. In Brazil it is estimated that 39 per cent of the workforce is in this sector, and in South Africa between 24 per cent and 32 per cent. But even in 'regulated' areas, often the most basic demands for safe and healthy working conditions are not met. One of our respondents in South Africa explained how he had to pressure to change government legislation that allowed for much higher exposure to toxins than the ILO permitted. He had to press government, business and unions to introduce a fair election of health and safety representatives instead of them being chosen by the management. Finally, he was responsible for helping workers claim their rights when they had developed work-related illnesses. These few indicators show how basic requirements of 'decent work' are still something for which workers in these two countries, even in relatively privileged working conditions, have to fight. Against this background it is difficult for progressive unionists to put climate change on their unions' agenda when workers say, '*I will die quicker from not having a job than from climate change*'. Nevertheless, together with environmental organisations, like Earthlife, the national Union COSATU and sectoral unions, among them the metalworkers Union NUMSA, have for instance started a campaign for green jobs (Alternative Information and Development Centre 2011), following the UK campaign (Campaign Against Climate Change 2010).

Interviewing trade unions

This chapter presents some of the findings of analyses of trade union policy captured through discussion papers, participant observation at conferences and in-depth interviews with senior trade union officials and senior members of national and international organisations that interact with the trade union movement. Thirty-five interviews were conducted with officials of national unions in Brazil, Malaysia, South Africa, Spain, Sweden and the UK, as well as with the international federation officers of unions in Brussels, Geneva, London, Singapore and Paris. The interviews were conducted between March 2009 and December 2010 and lasted between 1.5–2.5 hours. They were recorded with the interviewees' agreement and then transcribed. Anonymity was guaranteed, which is why we neither give the interviewees names, nor describe their place or country of work. In some cases we have changed the name of the union. This was necessary because we are discussing sensitive issues of trade union conflicts. Names are only given where we quote from publicly available documents. We have omitted redundancies in the spoken statements, but where we have added elements to create full sentences we have put these in [ ] brackets. We have sent the quotes to all the interviewees and they agreed for them to be used.

Solidarity across borders

Waterman and Timms (2004, 184) have argued that although trade unions are representative democratic organisations, largely comprising a voluntary membership who work to either defensively protect the interests of their members and workers, or proactively seek to support social and democratic movements for liberation and poverty reduction, they nevertheless often take on forms of neo-corporatism themselves:

> They tend to reproduce or at least reflect the structure and behaviour of inter-state agencies. They were and are largely Northern-based, led and staffed. They have tended to reduce the complex reality of working people worldwide to a western model of unionised (or unionisable) male worker in lifetime employment in large-scale capitalist or state enterprise.
>
> (Waterman and Timms 2004, 185)

In our research we have found support for this analysis, coming mainly from unionists in Brazil and South Africa. In the following sections we will present how these North–South relationships are experienced by unionists in Brazil and South Africa in their encounters within international unions, and in the kind of relations existing between national unions of the North and South. We will also present some of the strategies Southern unions have developed to overcome what they see as international power relations working against them. We then discuss the implications these North–South relations have for an international trade union position on the globalisation of work division and climate change policies. Finally, we conclude with a perspective of how alternative modes of development might be able to bridge the North–South divide.

Power relations within international unions

Union officials in South Africa and Brazil thought that Northern unions were sympathetic and supportive of the unions of the South, but that this did not stop them using their superiority in numbers and their financial power to dictate terms within the international unions.

So you get the North American unions, you get the Europeans, and then you get the Japanese, and then the Nordic countries. And that's – you know. They pay more, they have more members. And, you know, we have picked up a fight about even subscriptions or membership. I mean, we sometimes pay in Swiss francs, but we don't control the value of currencies! I mean, there should be solidarity there! ... our view was that we didn't create the floating exchange rates – why should we be paying in Swiss francs? It just shows the power in these organisations.

It is from a position of the increasing power of some Southern unions that existing power relations between North and South are challenged:

I don't know if you're aware of it, but in the last congress of the INTF we built an alliance to support a candidacy for a general secretary in which we united all the Southern unions. Well, in a certain sense [we succeeded]. Not totally, because we didn't elect them. But we made a good agreement on a platform in which we increased the number of Southern delegates ... And the discussion was pretty much like this, you know, like ... the balance of power and the world is changing, but the INTF remains a European organisation, not a world organisation. So we should incorporate the new experiences, the other experience, to try to build something different, something better. To learn from each other ...

Some Southern unions felt they could not participate in the initiative because they were financially supported by Northern unions and were afraid to jeopardize this support if they joined. A similar position was expressed by one of our interviewees describing international meetings: 'But look, they've got the dollars; so they hire this place, everybody's there, and all those delegates from the South probably feel, "If we're saying too much maybe they won't invite us again!" '

Having arrived at the meetings, there are still opportunities for excluding Southern unionists from determining the agenda:

Every time INTF had a meeting (...) it was like déjà vu. I go to a meeting. I go into one, I saw all of them: they've got translators there, they've all got their headphones on. There's the INTF people in the front, completely in charge of the agenda! Completely in charge of the process! And then all the others, and the delegates from the South will give their regional reports. Next year you go to exactly the same thing!

Such processes are not only typical features of a bureaucracy but more essentially one of power relations. While 'headquarters', predominantly made up of members of Northern unions, discuss the general issues, members of Southern unions are relegated to 'regional reports'. We asked one of our respondents whether he thought that changing representatives in the higher positions of international federations would change their policies:

> I don't know, it is a powerful structure, and they have a certain way of working. I'm not too convinced about their ability to transform those. I mean, this is not just dependent on the people, but the more you get away from the shop floor, the more the thing becomes procedural, and sometimes with the difficulty of people to relate to things that are far away from them.

While some unionists attempted to change the structures through changing representations, others believed that international relations should not be organised through large organisations but instead take place directly between workers, as we discuss in the next section.

International solidarity between international unions

As our respondents in South Africa and Brazil acknowledged, North–South collaboration can enable workers to perceive and understand the conditions of workers elsewhere. International solidarity is especially important when unions live under conditions of state oppression. Their possibility to survive depends to a large degree on workers from outside supporting their demands.

> I'm for sort of international worker-to-worker. I mean, take South African workers. This is now when it was illegal to work for black trade unions. The first recognition agreement in the Seventies about that [black unions] came from Kellogg's. And this was sometimes with the support of workers in other countries, who said: 'Look, from the parent home country we must recognise the unions'. And those companies were forced to – and they would break the law and recognise unions.

And from Brazil:

> Yeah, this is an important question [North–South relations]. Because, as you know, our trade union movement [Brazil] comes from the Twenties and the Thirties, but during the military dictatorship that was stopped, because you had state intervention. The unions simply did not represent workers' interests until the late Seventies, when you had all the strikes and the new trade union movement coming again. So at that time all the help possible was very, very important because the unions didn't have any funds, because the state would intervene in all of them, and they had to rely on people's solidarity … it was the support of many, many trade union movements in the world that helped the Brazilian trade union movement.

These forms of international solidarity, however, came at a price:

> ... as you know, when you have international support you have the international policies that come with that, you know. Because – don't get me wrong here, but the perspective that comes from the international cooperation from Europe is very much like that, you know. We have all the resources. We're going to help you and pay you and ... you should go in this direction and that direction.

How should unions counter this kind of pressure? Moody argues that the best terrain for mounting opposition to transnational capital and its politicians is '*in their own backyard ... Most of the struggle against the structures and effects of globalisation necessarily occurs on a national plane. That, after all, is where the workers live, work and fight*' (Moody 2005, 260). This view was also reflected in some of our respondents' accounts:

> Because up to now solidarity or internationalism in the unions is only seen as 'what you do overseas' – you know, your international policy. Now, my view of international work is also what you do in your own country. For instance, participation in shaping the policies of the South African Government on migration. Now, there's no internationalism that beats that one! And I think, I don't know, conceptually this thing of internationalism being what you do – which is necessary – in support of maybe another struggle far away, it takes away the immediacy of the issue.

The idea of local action for international effect is important and supports the concept of unions as 'glocal' organisations. Such a strategy may require policy makers persuading workers that their interests are served as much by focusing on what seems like remote but important strategic international issues as their everyday concerns at the workplace: 'the distance of the union internationals from their worker bases increases such dangers [the unions' social presence and impact] ... They are remote from the workers on the shop floor, in the office or in the community, who, with exceptions are unaware of their existence' (Waterman and Timms 2004; 184). At the same time our interviews show that it is precisely unionists 'farther away' from the everyday battles of the shopfloor who are developing more strategic long-term perspectives concerning environmental policies (Räthzel and Uzzell 2011).

A Southern Alliance

An alternative form of internationalism, advocated by some Southern union-ists, is to strengthen South–South relations. The first institutionalisation of these South–South relationships was created at the beginning of the 1990s. A succession of meetings of unionists, initially in Australia, saw the need for a '*Southern* rather than a geographically bound network of democratic unions, where a Southern identity denoted a political experience of exploitation and marginalisation that arose out of a particular position of subordination in the new global economy' (Lambert and Webster 2001, 41). SIGTUR was the outcome. Lambert and Webster argue that a Southern organisation was not in opposition to the North, but rather sought to complement the work of the ICFTU (now the ITUC) to create 'a vibrant, powerful internationalism ... ' and 'a unified struggle against globalisation' (ibid., 45).

The advantages of South–South relationships were described in the following way:

> I would say that South–South cooperation is more suitable because it's a more equal kind of relation. It's not a paternalistic kind of cooperation; we try to exchange the needs and the demands of each part. Basically we're talking about the same kind of trade union structure, the same kind of history, the same kind of development, the same kind of issues.

This positive account can best be understood in the context of the conversation where power relations between North and South within the international union movement were central. The same interviewee also pointed out that their duty now as a powerful union within the South–South context is not to repeat the errors that the Northern unions committed by trying to influence the way in which other Southern unions organised and devised their policies.

However, while power relations are seen as less problematic in South–South relations, there are political and organisational differences that make relationships difficult:

> They've [Northern Unions] got more developed international relations departments, which mainly push for relationships to take place. And the problem with the South is that the organisations are weak. Yeah, the relationships we have tend to be more with the North, although we have tried to build a South–South relationship. We had trilateral meetings. We have annual meetings. But we have never taken it further. Because politically we almost agree with the South, but organisationally we still have some little bit of differences, how to build an organisation.

It was also suggested that the structure of organised labour in the South is more varied than in the North. We were told, for example, that the relationships with Indian trade unions were difficult because the union landscape there was very fragmented. While authors like Lambert and Webster (2001) and Waterman (1998) tend to see South–South relations as a way to develop a new form of social movement unionism that will enable new forms of international solidarity, this perspective has, according to our empirical material, its own difficulties and contradictions that need to be researched further. As we see it at present, there might be a new hierarchy developing with unions from the BRIC countries (i.e., Brazil, Russia, India and China), that is, the emergent economies, forming stronger alliances and leaving behind unions from less-developed countries with far weaker trade union structures.

A view from the North

How are North–South relations seen from a Northern perspective? While all the unionists we interviewed in Brazil and South Africa were critical of existing power relations with the North, the views looking southwards were diverse. Some unionists in the North agreed with Southern views:

> We have a lot of cooperation with trade unionists in the world. We help to organise, to build the trade union house, to help with the training. But we send essentially a member to explain what a good method is, and the method is the occidental method. I am sure that is not a good thing! It is a charity attitude towards a trade union. For example, for sustainable development we prepare one document in the INTU for the trade unions worldwide—not only for the European trade unionists; it is prepared centrally. We have a discussion within a working group. But the problem is, the members of the working group are essentially members of European unions. It is a problem of means: we do not have the means to pay the travel. It is better, for example, that the national trade unions help the international trade union, to organise a meeting, than to provide money to buy a new photocopier in Africa. But it is not easy because the budgets are usually earmarked for something else.

Another unionist suggested that the problem was not only one of resources:

> I mean, bring in developing countries? There are active members in the working group from developing countries. These people are not going to make the developing countries quieter. They are active and trained people, they know what they are talking about. And they're talking. So, well! How many people are going to pay for the opposition?

The reluctance of Northern unions to fund the participation of Southern unions in central meetings can thus also be seen as the result of conflicting interests, perhaps an issue which will grow in significance as the political and numerical strength of unions in the South grows. Other respondents in the North chose to express this in the less controversial language of 'differences', for example:

> I regularly travel to the meetings at the European level, where we discuss common policies on different issues, such as the climate issue or the economic situation or competition issues. And now I'm going to South Africa. But since their situation is so completely different, it's more a matter of me

travelling to teach them about business administration, more than it is cooperation. So it's, it's more of a support, I would say.

Although this unionist is sensitive to the difference between the North and South, it is notable that he feels he is able to discuss policy with fellow unionists in the North, but can only provide support for Unionists in the South. He conceives the North–South relationship as a donor relationship rather than one of a partnership of equals or even of mutual learning. Moreover, for him, 'the South' was closer to home than is typically assumed:

> It isn't exactly easy to cooperate with, for example, the French unions when it comes to climate issues or competitive issues like innovation, either. 'Cos they're totally different from us. They don't believe in cooperating with companies. They think innovation is the enemy. And some of them even don't accept that there is such a thing as climate change. So they have quite an opposite view! The further south you go in Europe, the bigger the problems get!

These claims do contradict our fieldwork experience in South Africa. Among our respondents from across the world, trade unionists in the South African Metalworkers Union (NUMSA) were some of the most engaged in developing climate change policies and also some of the sharpest analysts of contemporary societies and processes of globalisation. What our Northern respondent is describing as differences and what makes it difficult for him to discuss trade union policies with Southern unions are political differences, and not differences in experience and qualification as he suggests in the first quote.

Unions of the North learning from unions of the South

One might infer from the above discussion that the direction of influence and learning is largely from North to South. However, we have also come across moments where unions of the North acknowledged that they had learnt from unions of the South, most notably at the *Trade Union Assembly on Labour and the Environment* (ILO 2006), organised by UNEP/Sustainlabour/Varda Group/ ILO in Nairobi in 2006. A number of our Northern respondents spontaneously mentioned this conference as an event that changed their ways of thinking about climate change. This was one of the most detailed accounts:

> When we were in Nairobi for the UN conference three years ago, the ITUC Working Group held a whole day workshop with the Kenyan TUC. We met about twenty trade union leaders from Agriculture, Forestry, Transport, Health, Industry, Public Services, and other sectors, talking about climate change and the impact of the unseasonal rains, floods on the coast, and the desert coming south. We discussed the effects on employment, notably in farming, of these trends. Reforestation programmes were a major issue,

which the unions are actively involved in. That was the first time that many of us in the ITUC group had really come up hard against the fact that we hadn't got this policy area of the impacts of climate change on the South properly mapped out. And it did have a big impact on the policy position in the ITUC, which was always quite strong on mitigation, but where we knew we had to work harder was on adaptation issues. And the ITUC policy paper for the UNFCC talks was revised over the year after that. And I think it's a better balanced policy position now, which tries to deal with those tensions around North and South.

The Northern union representatives were struck by the effects of climate change on countries in the South and the kind of programmes in which unions were involved (reforestation) which were different from the issues faced by Northern unions. A realisation of the issues Kenyan unions were confronting enabled Northern unionists to bridge political and organisational differences and change international policy in order to include Southern concerns. This account raises a number of critical questions which we discuss in the following section: how are conflicts in North–South relations connected to the question of the environment and to climate change? How does the issue of climate change shape the North–South and the South–South relations? What are the most contested issues with regards to environmental policies between unions and within unions of the North and South? And what are the issues where convergences and mutual support are more likely to happen?

A level playing field? Climate change policies and the North–South divide

To a certain degree Northern as well as Southern unions agree that technological innovation must be one of the solutions to climate change. They seem to deliver a double dividend: protecting industry and thus securing employment, and protecting the environment by reducing emissions. As one unionist argued:

> There was a report that was produced by the International Energy Agency which said that if you took the best technology there is today from steel and you replicated that through every plant in the world, you would reduce the emissions from the steel producers by over 50% just by doing that. So there's a huge potential there.

There are, however, at least two problems arising from technological innovation. One is explained by the same unionist: 'you've often seen a steel plant that would employ at one time 20,000 people would now employ 3,000 and produce the same amount of steel'. This demonstrates that technological innovation is not socially neutral. Measures would have to be taken, such as reducing working hours and creating new jobs in other areas, in order to compensate for job losses through technological innovation (Räthzel and Uzzell 2011). Second, technological innovation can accentuate the North–South divide:

> ... we'll have to deal with some of the problems about technological spheres, intellectual property rights ... basically the same multinational corporations are now positioning themselves to lead in what they call the 'Green' revolution, so BP now is Beyond Petroleum! And they are basically seeing the Green technologies as a source of new accumulation.

Therefore, a dominant demand by Southern unionists is for technological transfer and the availability of patents, a demand that has become part of ITUC policy as a means to create a 'level playing field' for economic development worldwide. In the climate change negotiations between countries of the North and the South this issue is still debated.

Other policies are more divisive among unions and the North–South. For example, the imposition of 'border adjustments' is regarded by the United Steelworkers of America as one tool amongst several (e.g., transition assistance, technological transfer) for 'encouraging' countries who are slow to take action in reducing their carbon emissions. Border adjustments mean that products from countries that do not apply similar carbon abatement measures are subject to a compensatory import tax or are prevented from importing steel altogether in order to protect national higher cost low-emission production. Environmental protection in this case is paid for with job protection, which is at the expense of North–South solidarity. The IMF/ICEM/EMF/EMCEF argue:

> We are concerned that international regulation on carbon emissions unless binding and applied evenly will lead to carbon leakage ... climate change legislation must contain strong provisions dealing with international competitiveness in order to ensure that nations that lack a strong emissions programme do not receive an unfair advantage. Such provisions should include border adjustments in energy intensive products when they are produced for export markets.
>
> (IMF/ICEM/EMF/EMCEF 2009, 4)

Such a suggestion, argued in tandem with the management concept of 'competitiveness', is not designed to dissolve the suspicion held by Southern unions that Northern unions are mainly interested in 'protecting their own jobs' instead of seeking solutions that create a 'level playing field' for all workers globally (see also Stevis in this volume, who defines this as 'green nationalism'). For some Southern unions, measures like border adjustments are only a disguise for maintaining the North–South divide: 'It will be a matter of time before regulations and green standards are introduced in the North to block entry of products from developing countries into markets in the developed world, under the guise of environmental protection' (Gina 2010).

In a talk given at an international IMF conference 2009 Irvin Jim from NUMSA stated:

> ... for us in the poor South, we fear that some of the roots of climate-change politics may be an attempt to monitor how we live our lives and to curb our consumption in the Global South. We find implicit in some of the demands made by environmentalists in the West which seek to place limits on growth in the developing world, nothing but eco-imperialism.
>
> (Jim 2009, 2)

This criticism is not only directed at environmentalists, governments and TNCs, but also at Northern unions, which are asked to support Southern unions' needs:

> We accordingly demand that European workers must simultaneously discuss with us how we are going to deal with the global system of capitalism, even as we seek technical and other solutions to the damage global capitalism is doing to our Earth and common humanity. Only through such a process can we seek to forge a common platform on the challenge of climate change. ... A good starting point here is for us in the South to call for understanding and solidarity from our richer Northern Brothers and Sisters: we cannot participate in the same way and at the same pace as they in this struggle to defend the Earth from global capitalism.
>
> (Jim 2009, 2, 4)

Both Gina and Jim understand the struggle against climate change as a struggle against capitalism and therefore reject what they see as reductionist technological solutions. Jim connects this broader analysis with a demand to engage more slowly in climate change measures. Though both acknowledge the seriousness of climate change, their statements also indicate that they see climate change and climate change policies as imposed on them by the North. This is why, as Rosemberg argues (this volume), there can only be a consensus between Northern and Southern unions concerning climate change and climate change policies as long as they are relatively abstract and demand green jobs and just transitions. Our material shows how they become more divisive when they become more concrete, creating another fault line between the North and the South. The ITUC openly recognises that '[t]here is still no consensus within the union movement on the way to address this [i.e. carbon leakage] critical challenge' (ITUC 2009).

Some concluding perspectives

We began this chapter with several axiomatic assertions. Climate change is a global threat with the potential to draw labour movements from across the world together. Second, trade unions, as the largest democratically organised institution in the world and traditionally the most powerful defenders of workers' rights, are potentially in the best position to challenge the negative effects of globalisation. Third, trade unions are 'glocal' organisations and thus well placed to counter the challenges of their 'glocal' adversaries, TNCs.

To this list one might also add that they have as a goal the desire to replace competition with solidarity. It is clear from talking to trade unions in the North and South, however, that solidarity is difficult to sustain in an unequal relationship in terms of resources, power and interests. As one respondent said:

> Unfortunately the old phrase of 'Workers of the world unite' nowadays is very difficult to put into practice. You have to find a common agenda, common demands. For me that is not ideal: all workers in the world should have the same demand.

While unions have the potential capacity to 'unite', it would be naive to think that the history of unequal power relations and exploitation of the South by the North has not influenced, and does not continue to influence, the relations between unions as well. As researchers have argued (Wallerstein 2011), workers in the North have also gained from the unequal relations of exchange between the North and the South. We have shown how these different historically developed positions have played out in North–South relationships.

One barrier to collective action is seen to be the structure and organisation of international bodies. It may be because, like most hierarchical organisations, international unions have become more remote from the everyday lives of those they represent. Additionally, Southern unions are under-represented in the leading bodies and feel they do not have a voice. Some representatives of Northern unions have recognised this and international unions have tried to bring change about, such as the environmental task force of the ITUC, which uses much of its resources to fund the participation of Southern unions in international meetings.

In some cases the barriers are seen as a consequence of a lack of support and action through the domination of international unions and federations by the North. The view of some Southern unions was that Northern climate change policies are simply protectionist smokescreens to safeguard jobs and Northern industries. The Southern (trade union) critique sees climate change as a result of capitalism and claimed that until that is addressed, along with what they called eco-imperialism, social injustice and environmental degradation would remain. While this perspective is legitimate enough, it does act as a hindrance to the development of measures against climate change that could be specifically apt for the conditions in countries like South Africa and Brazil.

At the same time, exposure to the problems of the South has had a significant impact on Northern unions, which shows that sharing experiences and listening to each other are two ways of finding common ground, though they alone will not suffice. Returning to the problem of institutionalised internationalism, one Southern trade unionist was sceptical and questioned the benefits of South–South or North–South travelling for the trade union work:

I'm not too sure how much we're investing in those relationships (South–South) and how we're nurturing them, and how we've been sucked into trade union internationalism. I sometimes say, look, this is not internationalism, this is trade union tourism! But that is me being cynical.

While one can imagine that issues of bureaucratisation and even hierarchies in organisations can be overcome through time, as Southern unions become more powerful and thus more able to put pressure on Northern unions, other discrepancies are more fundamental. There are the political differences in terms of the analysis of climate change, where some Southern unions demand a more critical and holistic strategy; some strong and corporate unions in the North prefer a closer cooperation with capital. Most importantly, there are significant material differences.

Unionists in Brazil and South Africa told us again and again: 'You have developed, now it is our turn and now you are telling us that we shouldn't'.

We have briefly described some of the economic conditions under which unions in South Africa and Brazil operate. Clearly, development is necessary. However, given the evidence of environmental destruction and the crisis of justice, there is a need to reconfigure what development means. The model of development that has created environmental degradation in general and the threat of climate change in particular cannot be continued without destroying the foundation of any kind of sustainable development. 'Strong' models would necessitate challenging the capitalist basis of development and the yardstick against which development and progress are currently measured. 'Weak' models might look to emphasise the need to transform our ways of life and strive for 'prosperity without growth' (cf. Stevis in this volume and Jackson 2009), or aim for what Schor (2010) refers to as the triple dividend: reducing unemployment, cutting carbon emissions and providing people with an enhanced quality of life by reducing working hours, i.e., getting more from less. Although some 'weak' models already transcend the capitalist model of development, they have been designed for the North, where there is overconsumption and overproduction.

In the South, group movements (e.g., indigenous, farmers, the landless) as well as national philosophies in countries like Bolivia have developed alternative modes of development both in theory and practice. They suggest a form of development that invests 'mother earth', as the Bolivians say, with rights and advocate growth that does not destroy the nature that nurtures it. The environmental movements we interviewed in Brazil and South Africa (Earthlife and FBOMS) are working with unions, with cautious optimism for successful collaboration. In his address quoted above, Gina referred to Bolivia's climate change initiatives as a perspective and stressed the needs for unions to connect their struggles with those of other movements. He criticised his union for its failure 'to link [its campaign] to massive struggles that erupted in the 2000s in black townships'. He saw the reason for this inability in the 'workplace focus [that] alienated us from non-workplace movements on energy issues'. A similar point is made by Lambert and Webster (2001) when they argue that trade unions need to ally themselves with citizens who are already interested and mobilised through membership of environmental and justice movements.

Alternative models of development being created in the North and the South by unions and by environmental movements might provide the bridge to connect the seemingly irresolvable conflicting interests of Northern and Southern unions. The task appears less impossible when we remember that historically unions were created precisely to solve a similar conflict between the individual interests of workers competing against each other and the need to organise a unified response against exploitation. This same conflict exists now at a global level and this time it is globalising environmental degradation and the globalising work division that pose the need for a unified response from workers.

This could be a critical moment in trade union history – 'a moment of danger' (Benjamin 1974) – where trade unions recognise that although addressing climate change is a non-traditional area of trade union concern, it could be decisive for their future, not only in terms of the effects it will have on jobs, but also for the impact it could have on international solidarity. The threat of climate change, in the context of 'double exposure', presents difficulties but also opportunities to work across the North–South divide.

References

Alternative Information and Development Centre (AIDC) (2011) *The Million Climate Jobs Campaign*. Cape Town. www.climatejobs.org.za/ (accessed 1 March 2012).

Bauman, Z. (1998) *Globalisation*. New York: Columbia University Press.

Benjamin, W. (1974) 'On the Concept of History', in H. Eiland and M. W. Jennings (eds) *Selected Writings, Volume 4: 1938–1940*, Cambridge, MA: Belknap Press.

Campaign Against Climate Change (2010) *One Million Climate Jobs*. www.climate-change-jobs.org/sites/default/files/1MillionClimateJobs_2010.PDF (accessed 1 March 2012).

Chan, A. and Ross, R. (2003) 'Racing to the bottom. International trade without a social clause'. *Third World Quarterly*. Vol. 24. No. 6, pp. 1011–1028.

Cornia, G. A. and Kiiski, S. (2001) *Trends in Income Distribution in the Post–World War II Period: Evidence and Interpretation*. UNU/WIDER Discussion Paper 2001/89, United Nations University, World Institute for Development Economics Research, Helsinki. www.wider.unu.edu/publications/working-papers/discussion-papers/2001/en_GB/dp2001-89/ (accessed 1 March 2012).

Gina, C. S. (2010) 'Experiences from the South', address at the International Seminar on Energy, Work, Crisis and Resistance, 22–24 January, Graz, Austria.

ILO (1998) *Declaration on Fundamental Principles and Rights at Work*. Geneva: International Labour Organisation.

——(2006) *Environmentally sustainable development: the WILL is There*. Geneva: International Labour Organisation, www.ilo.org/global/about-the-ilo/press-and-media-centre/news/WCMS_067242/lang – en/index.htm (accessed 1 March 2012).

——(2008) *World of Work Report 2008: Income inequalities in the age of financial globalization, International Institute for Labour Studies*. Geneva: International Labour Office.

IMF/ICEM/EMF/EMCEF (2009) 'Cutting emissions, transforming jobs: Working in green jobs for a secure future', paper prepared for Conference on Towards a Common Platform on Climate Change, 14–15 October, Bad Orb, Germany.

ITUC (2009) 'Trade unions and climate change: equity, justice & solidarity in the fight against climate change', Trade Union Statement to COP15, United Nations Framework Convention on Climate Change, UNFCCC, 7–18 December, Copenhagen, Denmark.

Jackson, T. (2009) *Prosperity without Growth? The transition to a Sustainable Economy*. London: Earthscan.

Jim, I. (2009) 'Global Capitalism and the Challenge of Climate Change', paper presented to Climate Change Meeting, 14–15 October, Bad Orb, Germany.

Lambert, R. and Webster, E. (2001) 'Southern Unionism and the New Labour Internationalism', *Antipode*. Vol. 33 No. 3, pp. 337–362.

Leichenko, R. M. and O'Brien, K. (2008) *Environmental Change and Globalization. Double Exposures*. Oxford/New York: Oxford University Press.

Massey, D. (2005) *For Space*. London/Thousand Oaks: Sage.

Moody, K. (2005) 'Towards an international social-movement unionism', in L. Amoore (ed.) *The Global Resistance Reader*. London: Routledge.

OECD (2010) *Tackling Inequalities in Brazil, China, India and South Africa: The Role of Labour Market and Social Policies*, OECD Publishing.

Räthzel, N. and Uzzell, D. (2011) 'Trade Unions and Climate Change: The Jobs versus Environment Dilemma', *Global Environmental Change*. Vol. 21, pp. 1215–1223.

Robertson, R. (1992) *Globalization: Social theory and global culture*. London: Sage.

Schor, J. (2010) *Plenitude: The New Economics of True Wealth*. New York: The Penguin Press.

Wallerstein, I. (2011) *The Modern World-System, IV: Centrist Liberalism Triumphant, 1789–1914*. San Francisco: University of California Press, and New York: The New Press.

Waterman, P. (1998) *Globalisation, Social Movements and the New Internationalisms*. London: Cassell.

Waterman, P. and Timms, J. (2004) 'Trade Unions Internationalism and a Global Civil Society in the Making', in H. Anheier, M. Glasius and M. Kaldor (eds) *Global Civil Society*. Cambridge: Polity Press.

Index

References in **bold** indicate tables, those followed by a letter n indicate end of chapter notes.

Printed in the United States
by Baker & Taylor Publisher Services